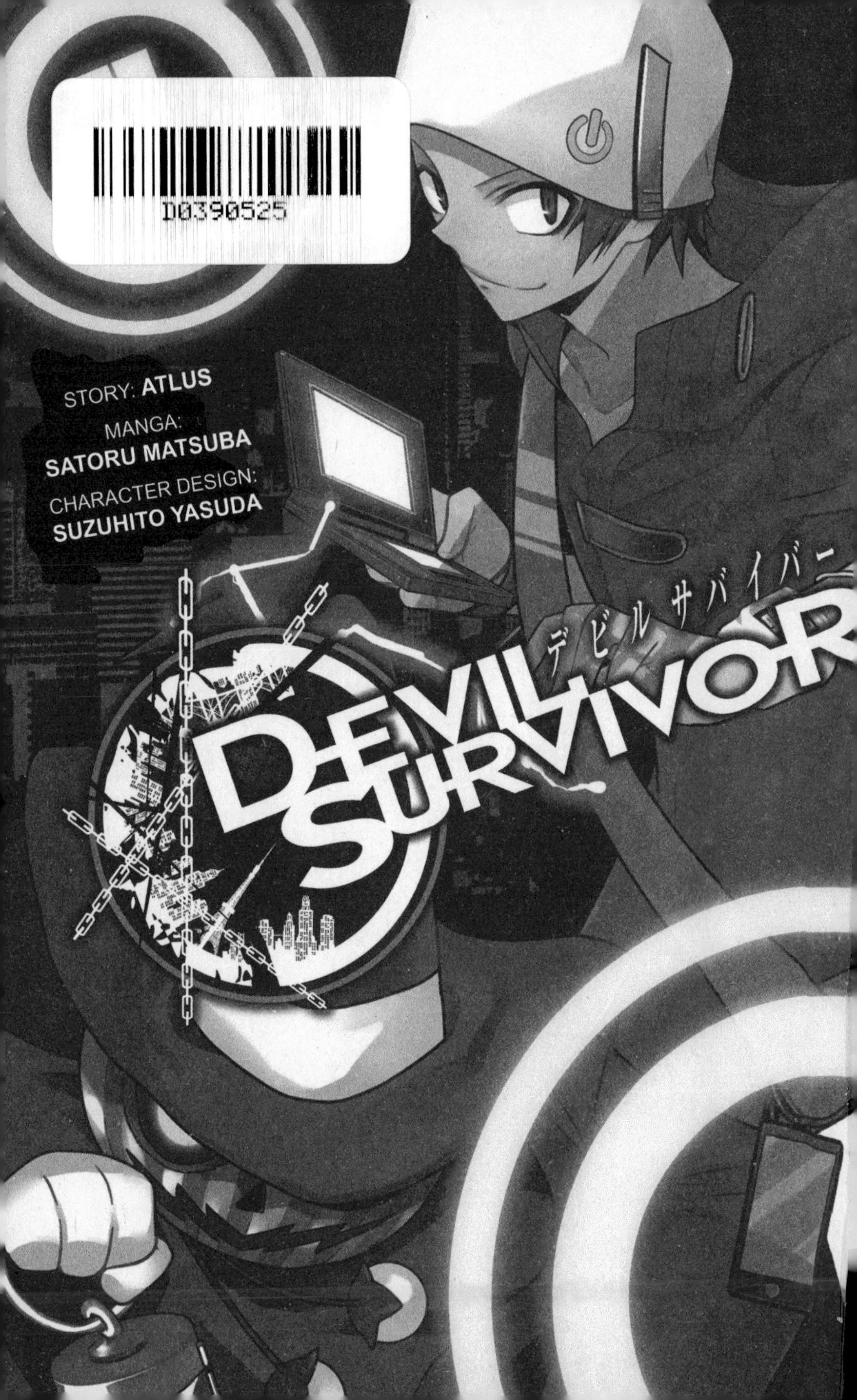
STORY: ATLUS
MANGA:
SATORU MATSUBA
CHARACTER DESIGN:
SUZUHITO YASUDA
デビルサバイバー
DEVIL SURVIVOR

MAIN CHARACTER

NAOYA
(NAOYA)
Kazuya's cousin. He lost his parents at a young age and lived with Kazuya's family until last year. He's known as a genius programmer with staggering insight.

KAZUYA MINEGISHI
(KAZUYA)
Uses a portable gaming device known as a COMP to make contracts with demons after gaining the power to command them.

YUZU TANIKAWA
(YUZ)
A friend of Kazuya's since childhood. They currently attend the same high school.

ATSURO KIHARA
(AT-LOW)
Kazuya's classmate and best friend. He's an aspiring programmer, and has been hanging with the big boys on the internet since he was in grade school.

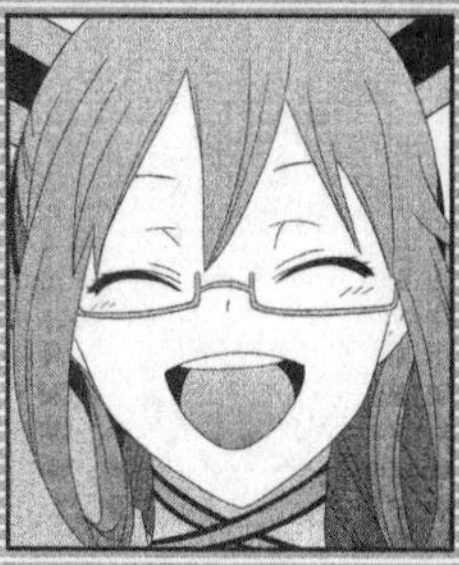

MIDORI KOMAKI (DOLLY)

An internet idol who enjoys tremendous popularity as the cosplayer Dolly. The influence of her late father, combined with her own desire to transform herself, gives her a strong yearning to be a defender of justice.

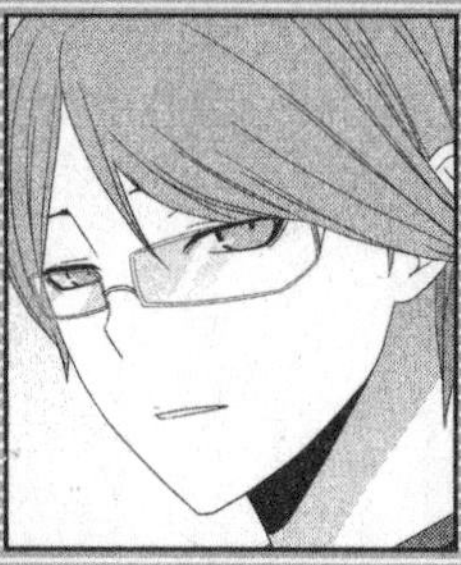

KEISUKE TAKAGI (K-T)

A middle school classmate of Atsuro's. He has a righteous streak, which led him to save Atsuro from bullying, and hates all kinds of wrongdoing.

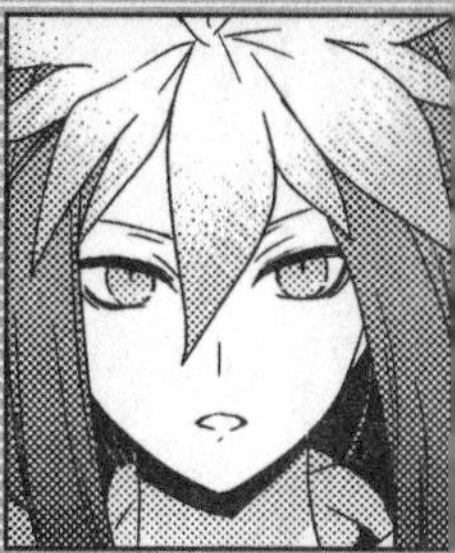

AMANE KUZURYU (AMANE)

A priestess of the Shomonkai religious organization. She can create barriers to prevent demons from approaching.

STORY

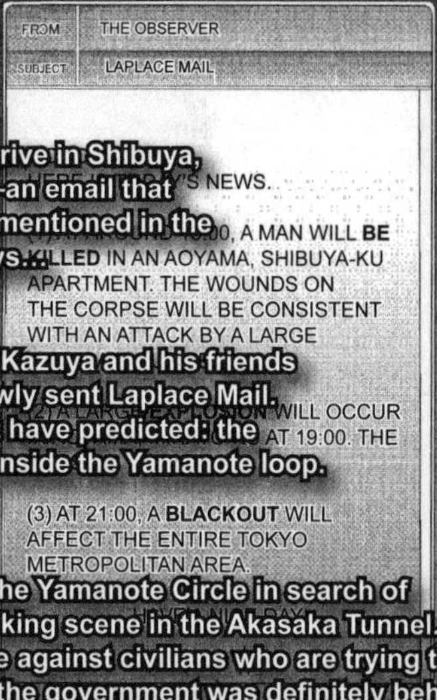

FROM THE OBSERVER
SUBJECT LAPLACE MAIL
A MAN WILL BE KILLED IN AN AOYAMA, SHIBUYA-KU APARTMENT. THE WOUNDS ON THE CORPSE WILL BE CONSISTENT WITH AN ATTACK BY A LARGE
WILL OCCUR AT 19:00. THE
(3) AT 21:00, A BLACKOUT WILL AFFECT THE ENTIRE TOKYO METROPOLITAN AREA.

DAY BEFORE (AN END TO THE ORDINARY)

At Naoya's request, Kazuya, Atsuro, and Yuzu arrive in Shibuya, where they receive the Laplace Mail newsletter—an email that predicts the future. The explosion and blackout mentioned in the email foreshadow the death of their peaceful days...

1ST DAY (TOKYO LOCKDOWN)

After spending a night in the Aoyama Cemetery, Kazuya and his friends head to Shibuya to verify the accuracy of the newly sent Laplace Mail. What awaited them was something they couldn't have predicted: the Defense Force had locked down the entire area inside the Yamanote loop. The prophetic email had come true.

2ND DAY (ANY WAY OUT)

Trapped inside the lockdown, our heroes roam the Yamanote Circle in search of an exit. In their wanderings, they witness a shocking scene in the Akasaka Tunnel. Members of a special government team open fire against civilians who are trying to escape. That was the moment they learned that the government was definitely behi the lockdown.

To make matters worse, the immortal Beldr has been revived. Defeated by Beldr, Kazuya is separated from his friends. What does fate have in store for them...?!

Our story begins on the **3rd Day (Beldr)**!!

C O N T E N T S

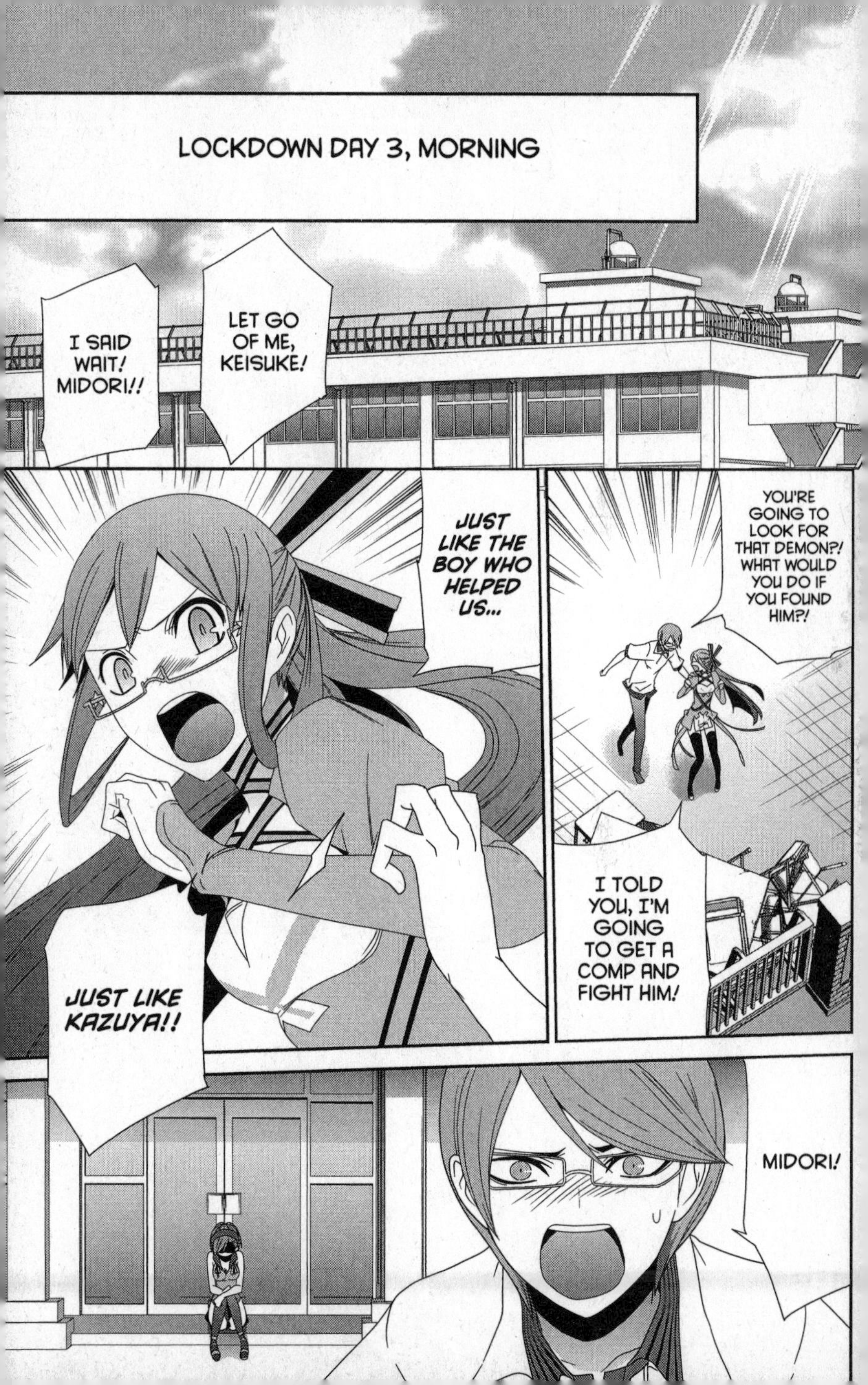
LOCKDOWN DAY 3, MORNING
LET GO OF ME, KEISUKE!
I SAID WAIT! MIDORI!!
YOU'RE GOING TO LOOK FOR THAT DEMON?! WHAT WOULD YOU DO IF YOU FOUND HIM?!
I TOLD YOU, I'M GOING TO GET A COMP AND FIGHT HIM!
JUST LIKE THE BOY WHO HELPED US...
JUST LIKE KAZUYA!!
MIDORI!

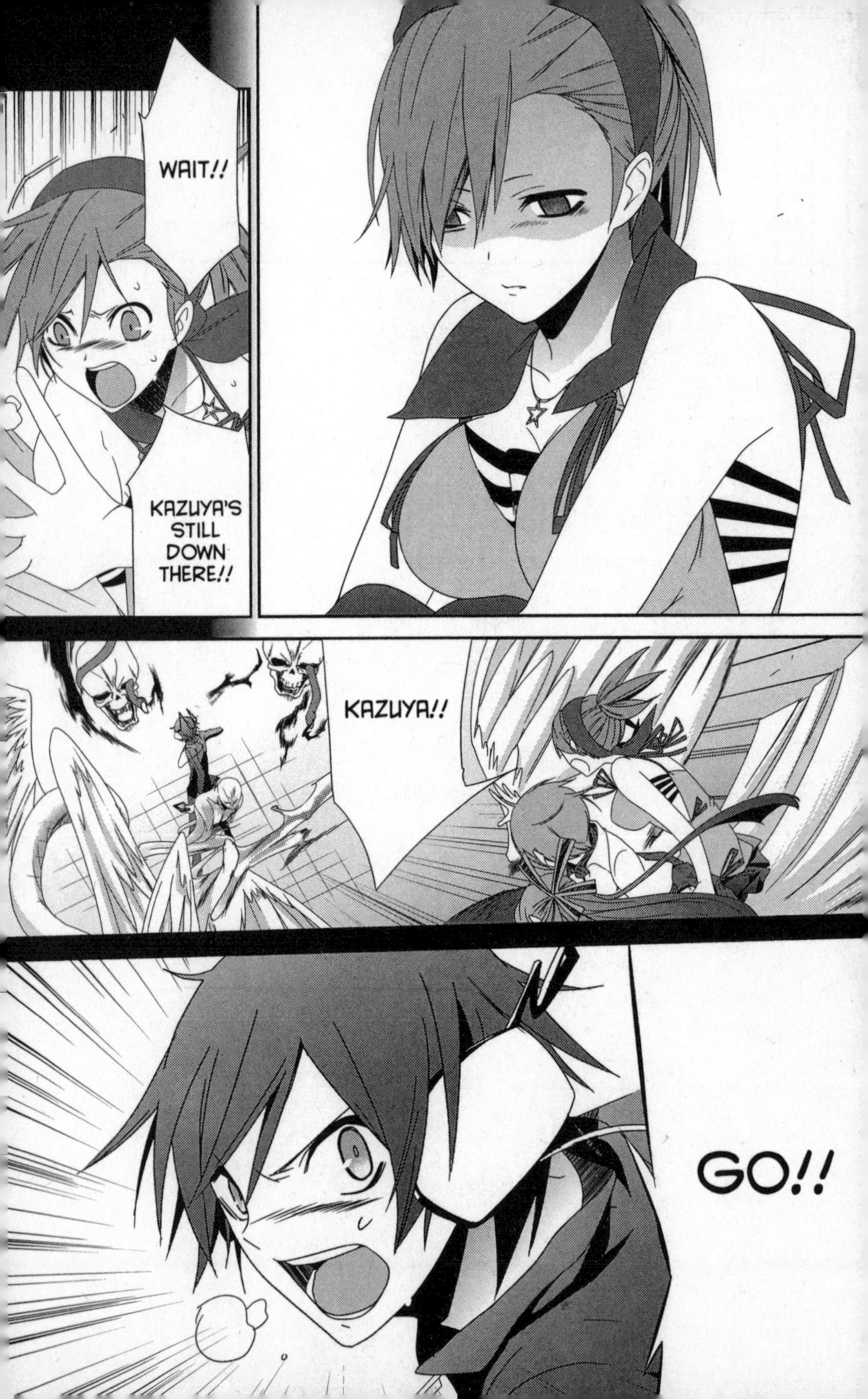
WAIT!!
KAZUYA'S STILL DOWN THERE!!
KAZUYA!!
GO!!

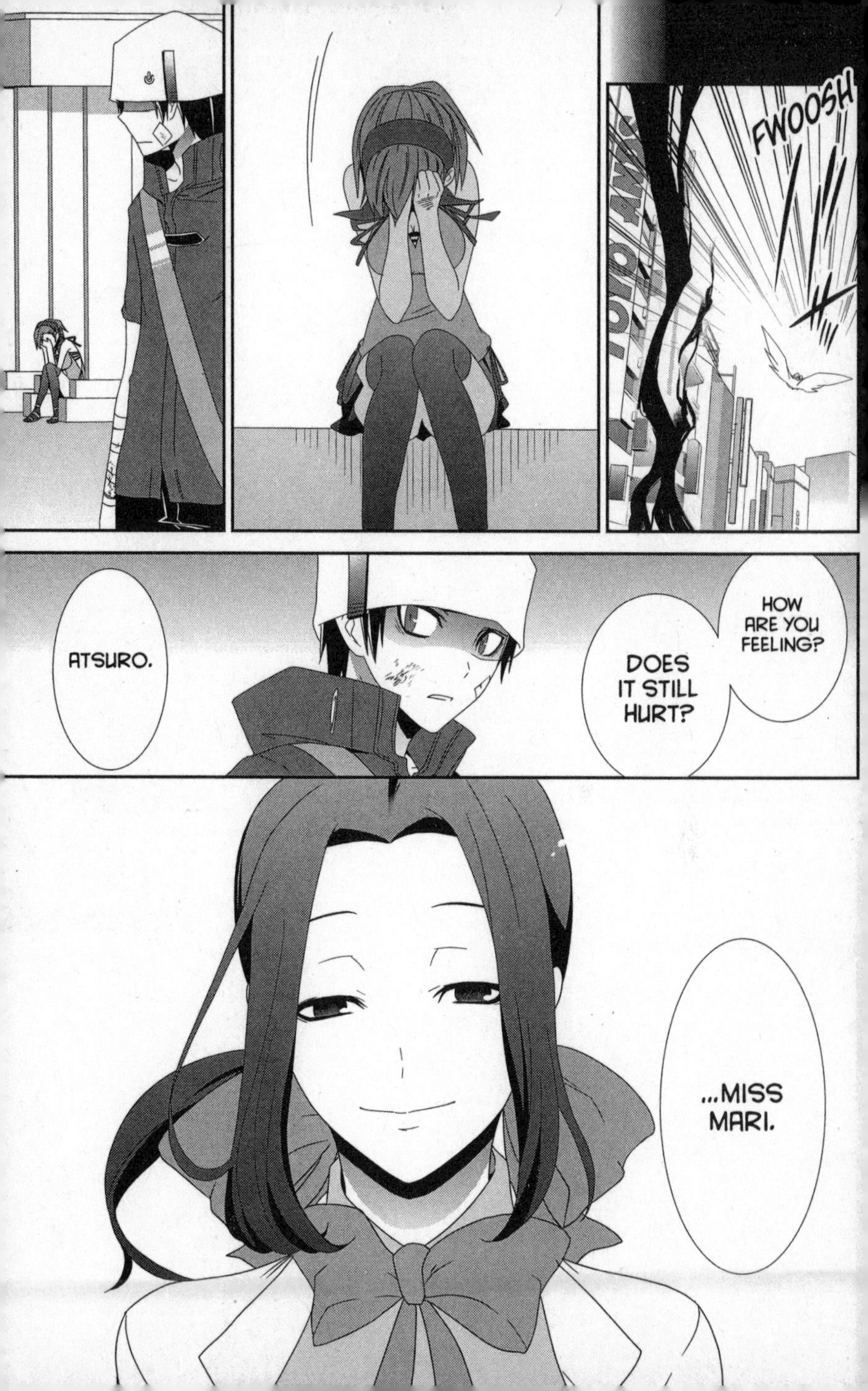
FWOOSH
HOW ARE YOU FEELING?
DOES IT STILL HURT?
ATSURO.
...MISS MARI.

SURVIVAL :11 THE DEVIL'S FUGE

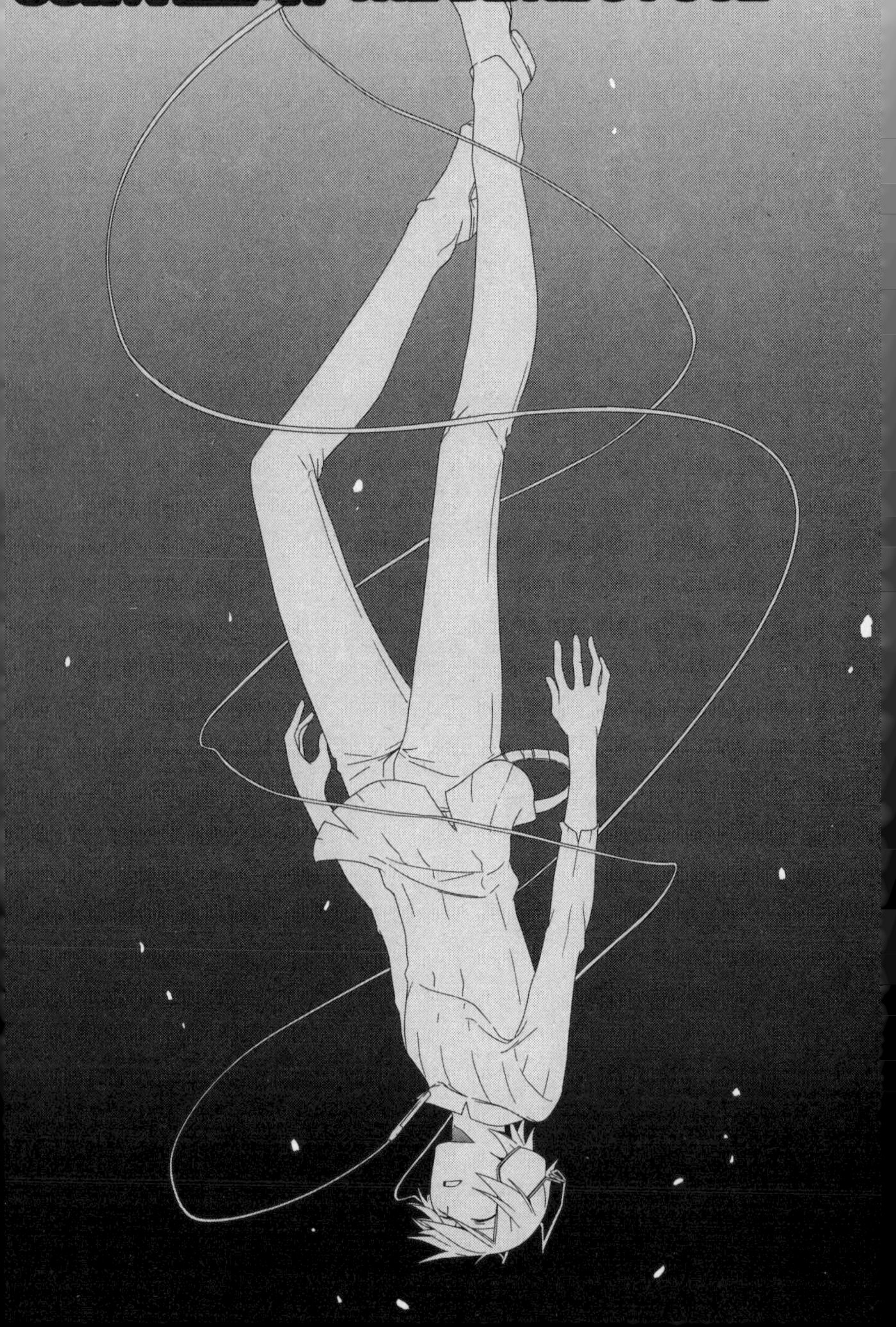

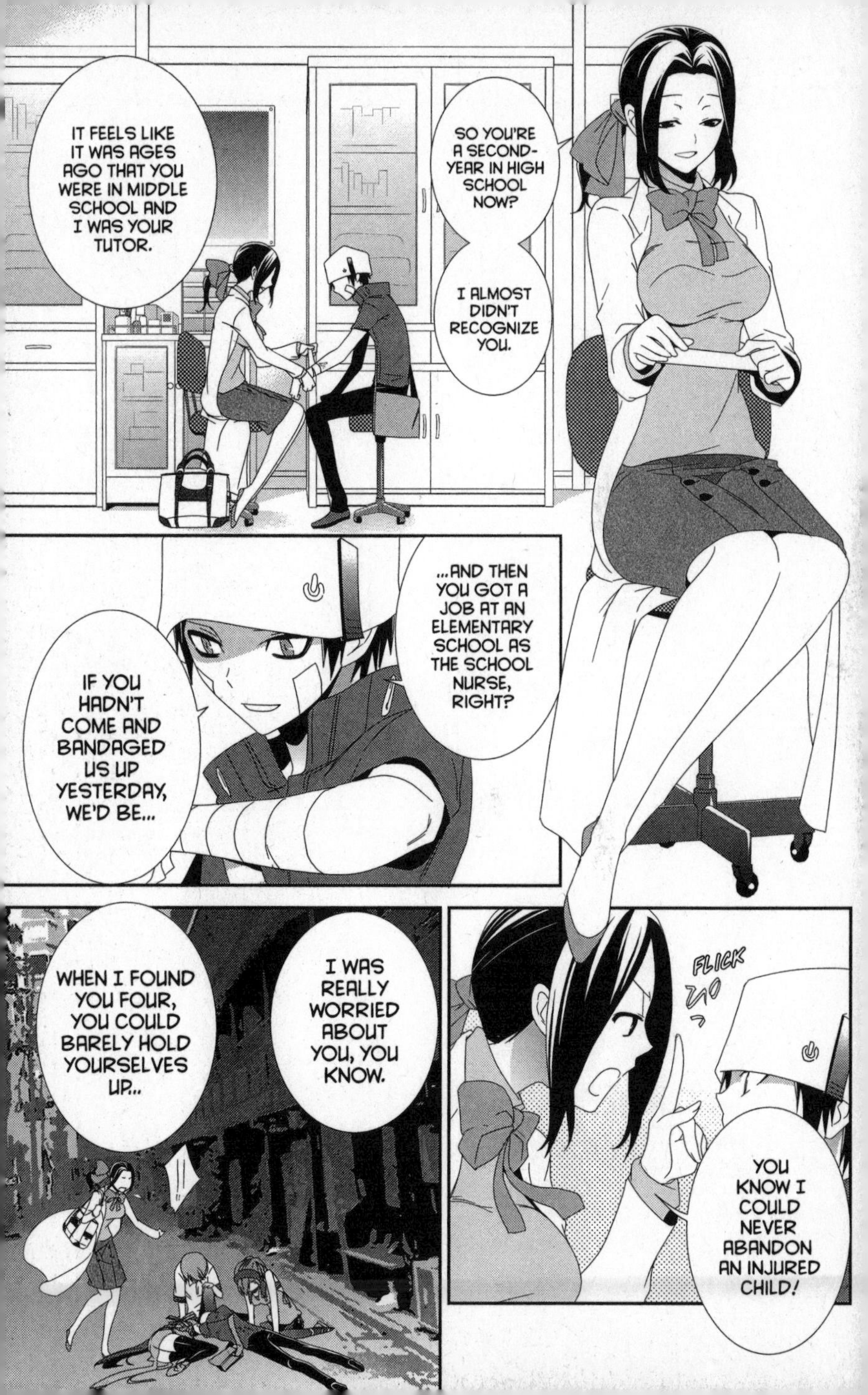
SO YOU'RE A SECOND-YEAR IN HIGH SCHOOL NOW?
I ALMOST DIDN'T RECOGNIZE YOU.
IT FEELS LIKE IT WAS AGES AGO THAT YOU WERE IN MIDDLE SCHOOL AND I WAS YOUR TUTOR.
...AND THEN YOU GOT A JOB AT AN ELEMENTARY SCHOOL AS THE SCHOOL NURSE, RIGHT?
IF YOU HADN'T COME AND BANDAGED US UP YESTERDAY, WE'D BE...
FLICK
YOU KNOW I COULD NEVER ABANDON AN INJURED CHILD!
I WAS REALLY WORRIED ABOUT YOU, YOU KNOW.
WHEN I FOUND YOU FOUR, YOU COULD BARELY HOLD YOURSELVES UP...
!

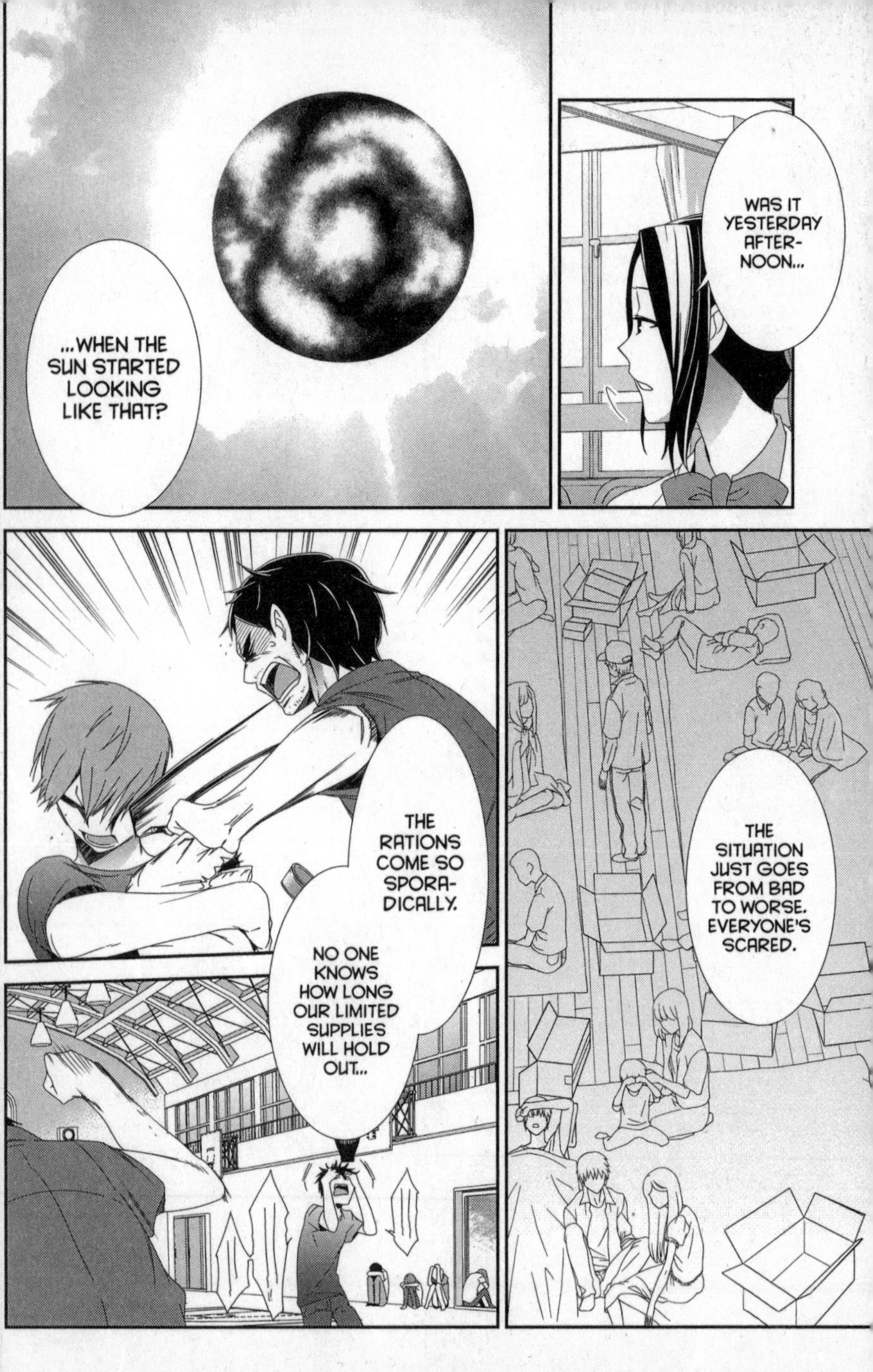
WAS IT YESTERDAY AFTER-NOON...
...WHEN THE SUN STARTED LOOKING LIKE THAT?
THE SITUATION JUST GOES FROM BAD TO WORSE. EVERYONE'S SCARED.
THE RATIONS COME SO SPORA-DICALLY.
NO ONE KNOWS HOW LONG OUR LIMITED SUPPLIES WILL HOLD OUT...

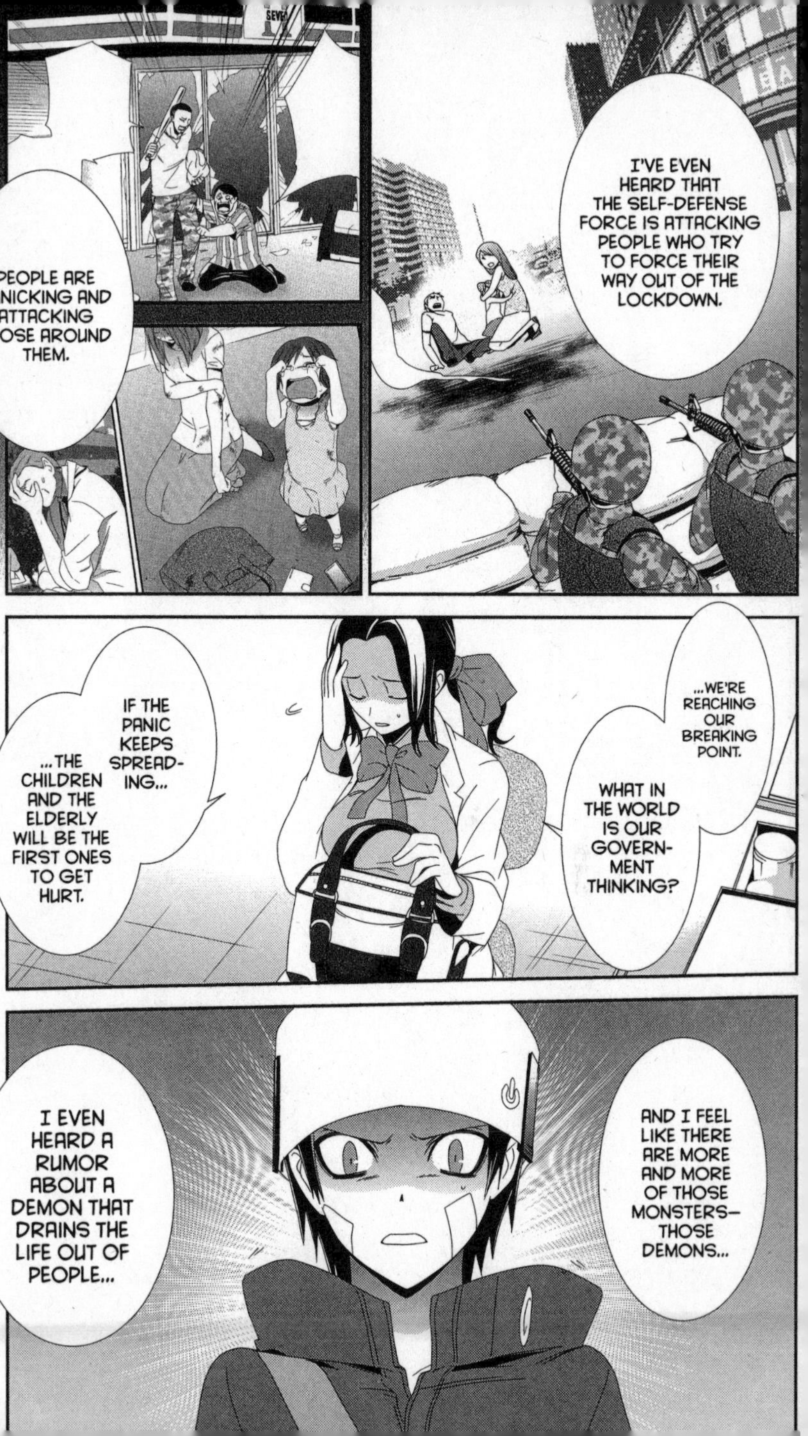
I'VE EVEN HEARD THAT THE SELF-DEFENSE FORCE IS ATTACKING PEOPLE WHO TRY TO FORCE THEIR WAY OUT OF THE LOCKDOWN.
PEOPLE ARE PANICKING AND ATTACKING THOSE AROUND THEM.
...WE'RE REACHING OUR BREAKING POINT.
WHAT IN THE WORLD IS OUR GOVERNMENT THINKING?
IF THE PANIC KEEPS SPREADING...
...THE CHILDREN AND THE ELDERLY WILL BE THE FIRST ONES TO GET HURT.
AND I FEEL LIKE THERE ARE MORE AND MORE OF THOSE MONSTERS—THOSE DEMONS...
I EVEN HEARD A RUMOR ABOUT A DEMON THAT DRAINS THE LIFE OUT OF PEOPLE...

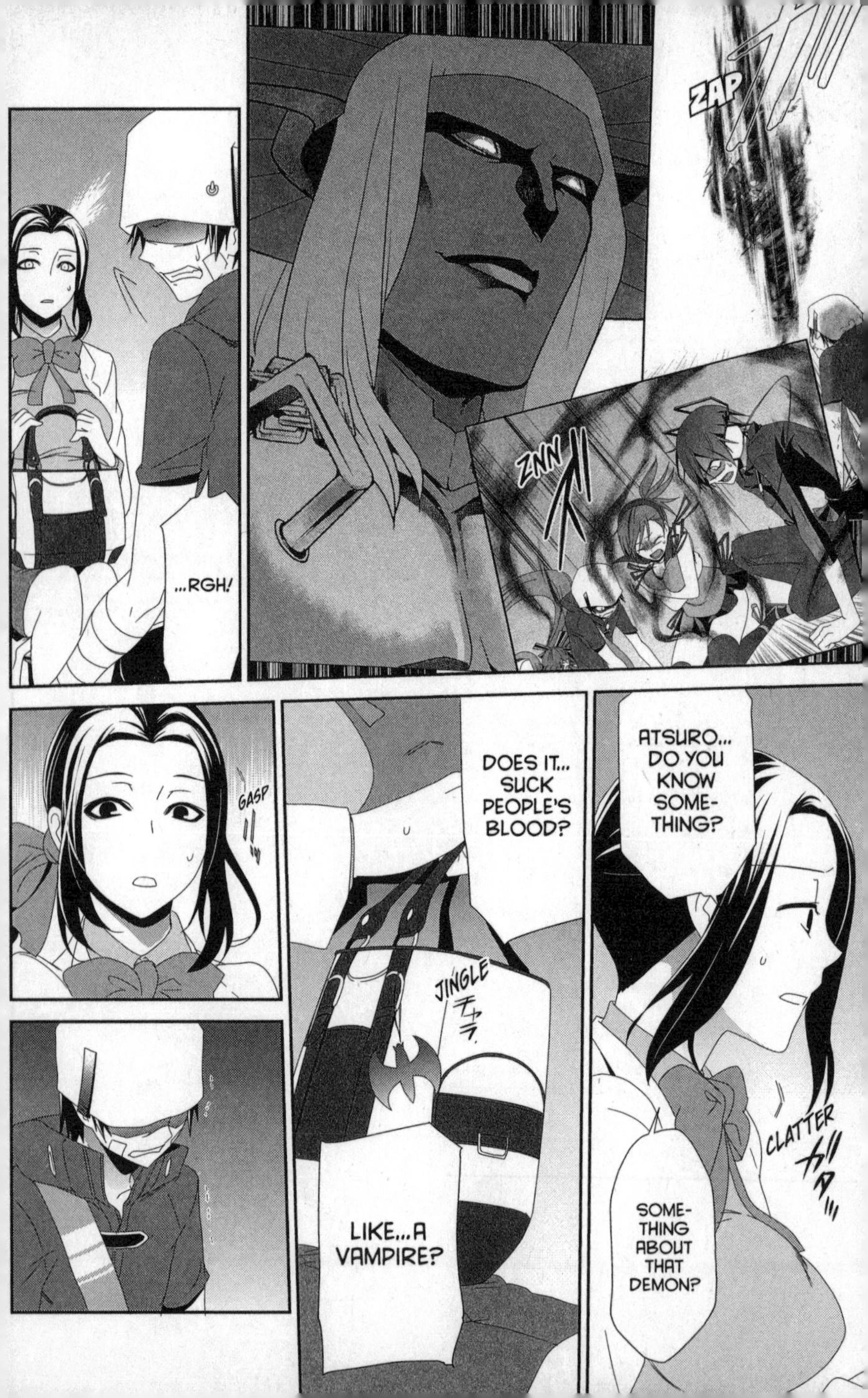
ZAP
ZNN
...RGH!
ATSURO... DO YOU KNOW SOME-THING?
CLATTER
SOME-THING ABOUT THAT DEMON?
DOES IT... SUCK PEOPLE'S BLOOD?
JINGLE
LIKE...A VAMPIRE?
GASP

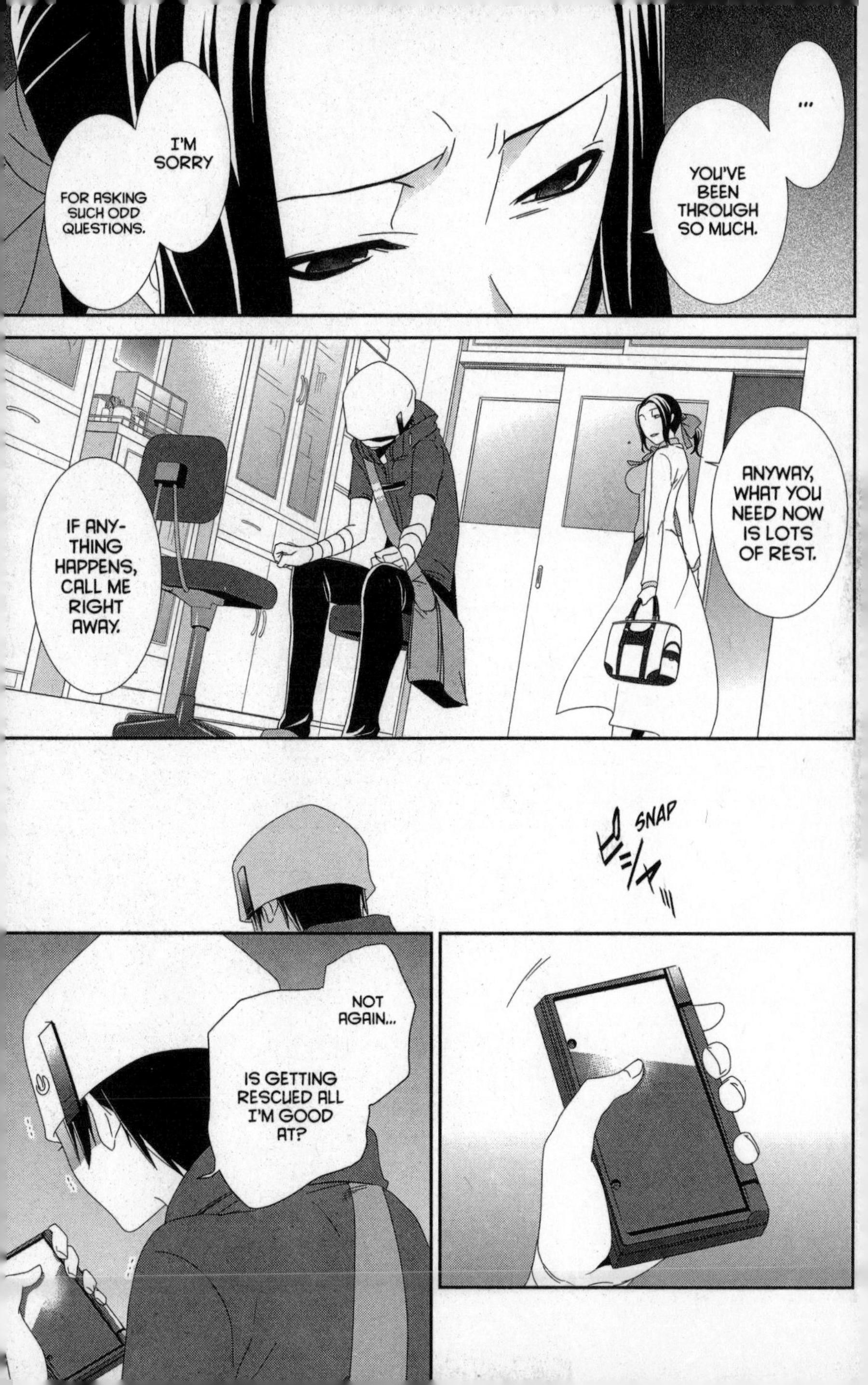
...
YOU'VE BEEN THROUGH SO MUCH.
I'M SORRY
FOR ASKING SUCH ODD QUESTIONS.
ANYWAY, WHAT YOU NEED NOW IS LOTS OF REST.
IF ANY-THING HAPPENS, CALL ME RIGHT AWAY.
SNAP
NOT AGAIN...
IS GETTING RESCUED ALL I'M GOOD AT?

IF YOU DIE...

HOW AM I SUPPOSED TO REPAY YOU?!

KAZUYA...!!

BLINK BLINK

OF COURSE, TODAY WOULD BE THE ONE DAY IT COMES EARLY...

...HEH.

FROM:	THE OBSERVER
SUBJECT:	LAPLACE MAIL

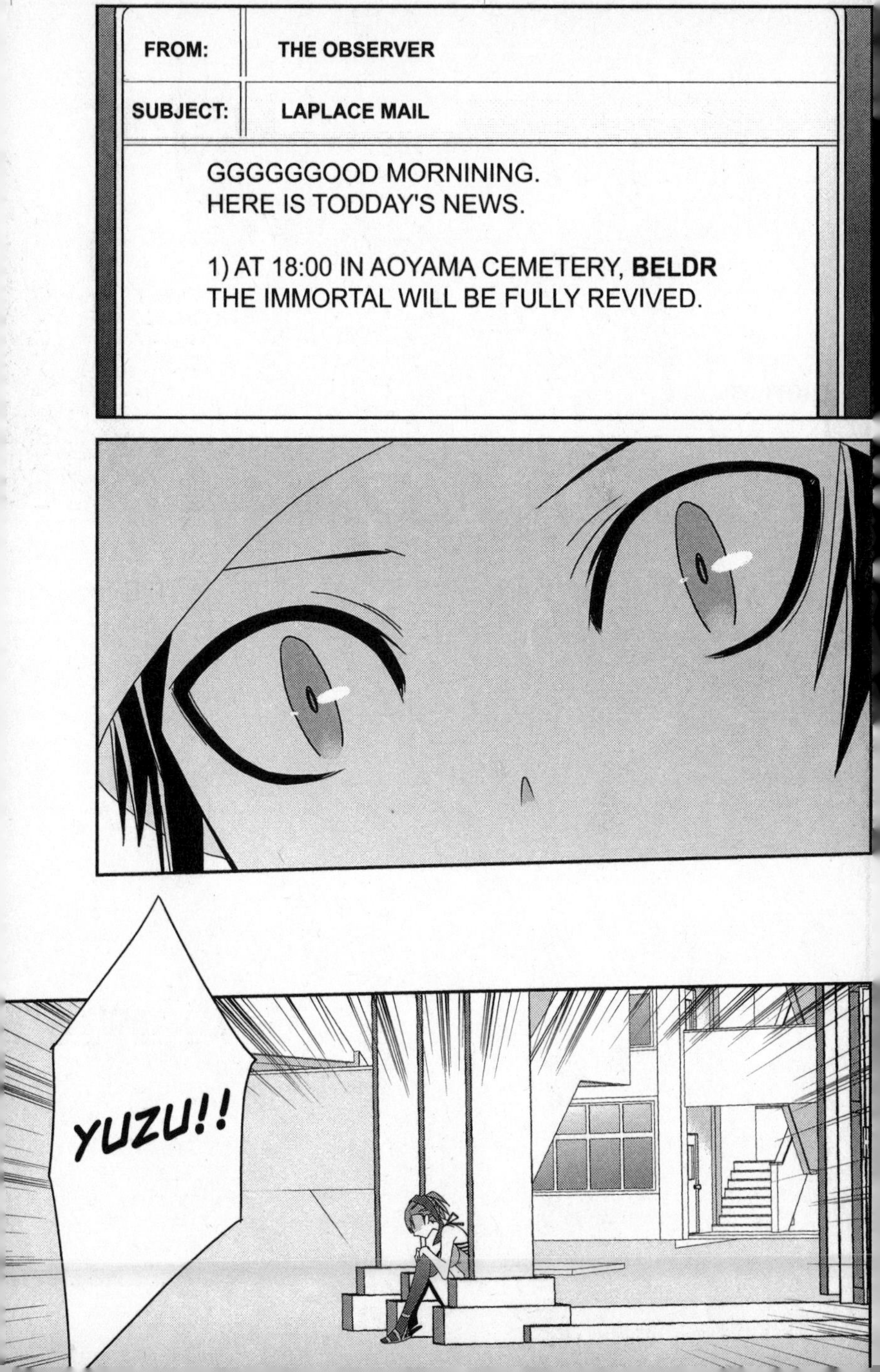
FROM:
THE OBSERVER
SUBJECT:
LAPLACE MAIL
GGGGGGOOD MORNINING.
HERE IS TODDAY'S NEWS.
1) AT 18:00 IN AOYAMA CEMETERY, BELDR THE IMMORTAL WILL BE FULLY REVIVED.
YUZU!!

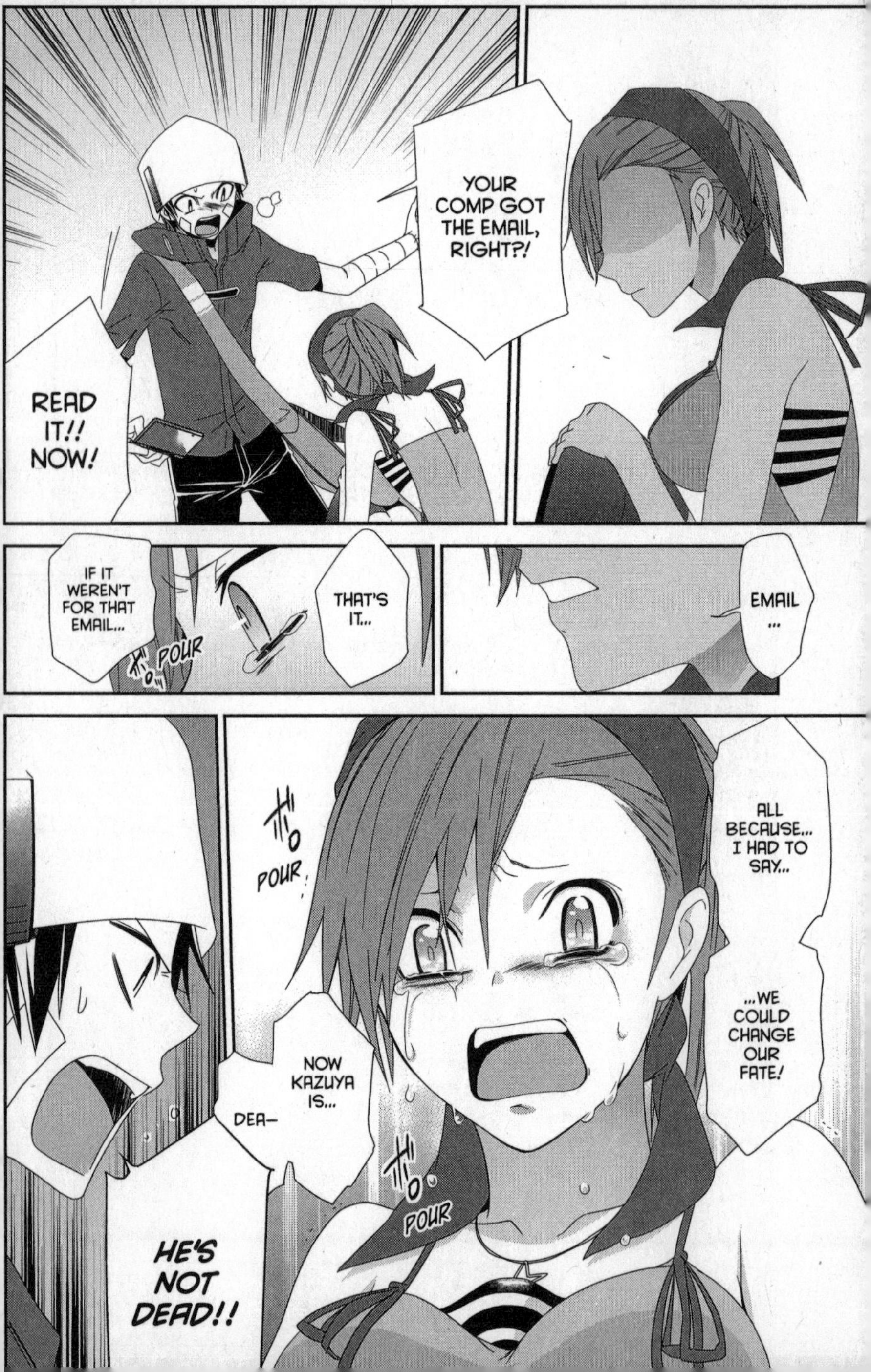
YOUR COMP GOT THE EMAIL, RIGHT?!
READ IT!! NOW!
EMAIL ...
THAT'S IT...
IF IT WEREN'T FOR THAT EMAIL...
POUR
ALL BECAUSE... I HAD TO SAY...
...WE COULD CHANGE OUR FATE!
POUR
NOW KAZUYA IS...
DEA—
POUR
HE'S NOT DEAD!!

FROM:	THE OBSERVER
SUBJECT:	LAPLACE MAIL

GGGGGGOOD MORNINING.
HERE IS TODDAY'S NEWS.

1) AT 18:00 IN AOYAMA CEMETERY, **BELDR**
THE IMMORTAL WILL BE FULLY REVIVED.
THERE WILL BE OVER 300 CASUALTIES,
INCLUDING KAZUYA MINEGISHI.

█VE A N█CE DAY.

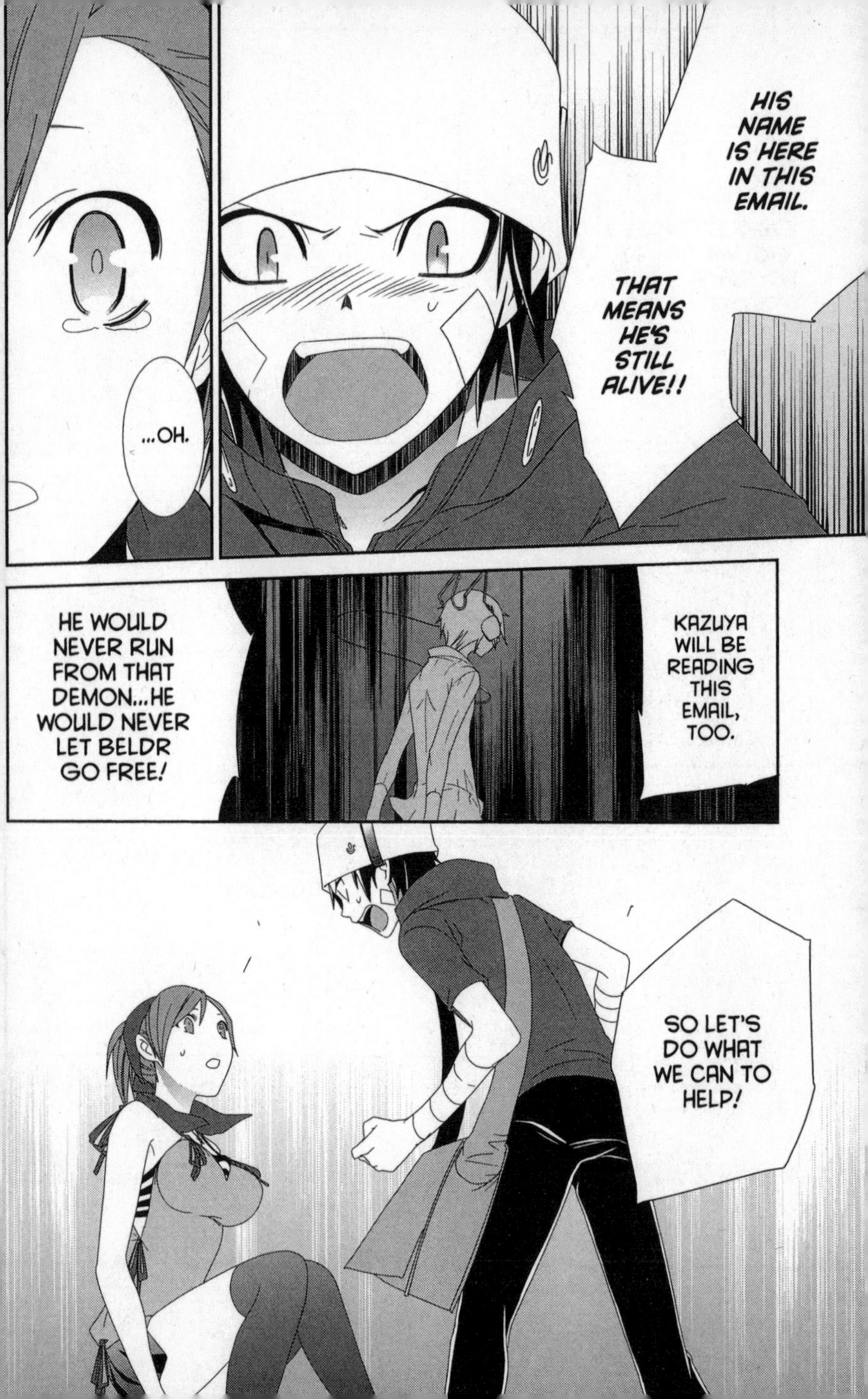
HIS NAME IS HERE IN THIS EMAIL.
THAT MEANS HE'S STILL ALIVE!!
...OH.
KAZUYA WILL BE READING THIS EMAIL, TOO.
HE WOULD NEVER RUN FROM THAT DEMON...HE WOULD NEVER LET BELDR GO FREE!
SO LET'S DO WHAT WE CAN TO HELP!

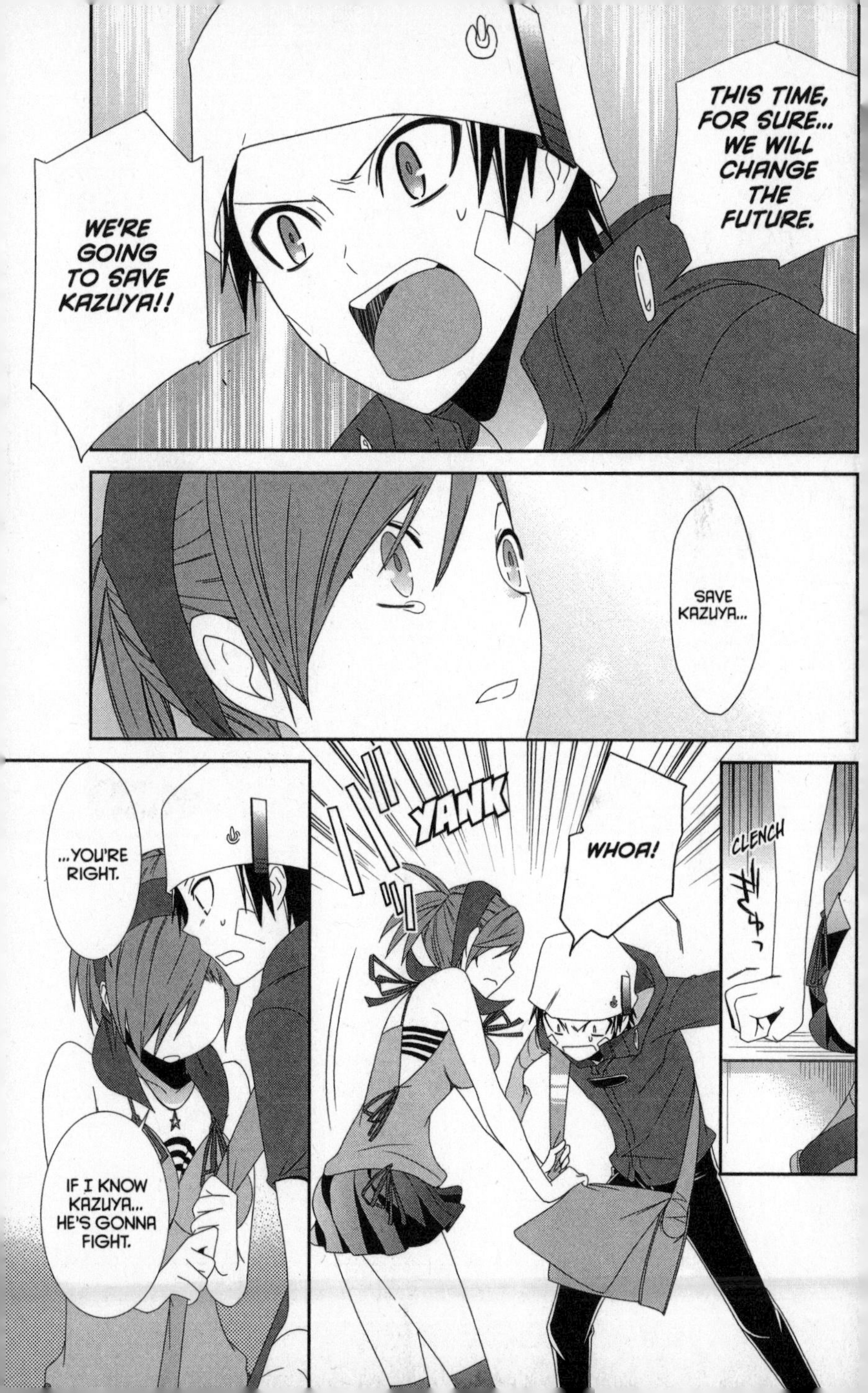
THIS TIME, FOR SURE... WE WILL CHANGE THE FUTURE.
WE'RE GOING TO SAVE KAZUYA!!
SAVE KAZUYA...
CLENCH
YANK
WHOA!
...YOU'RE RIGHT.
IF I KNOW KAZUYA... HE'S GONNA FIGHT.

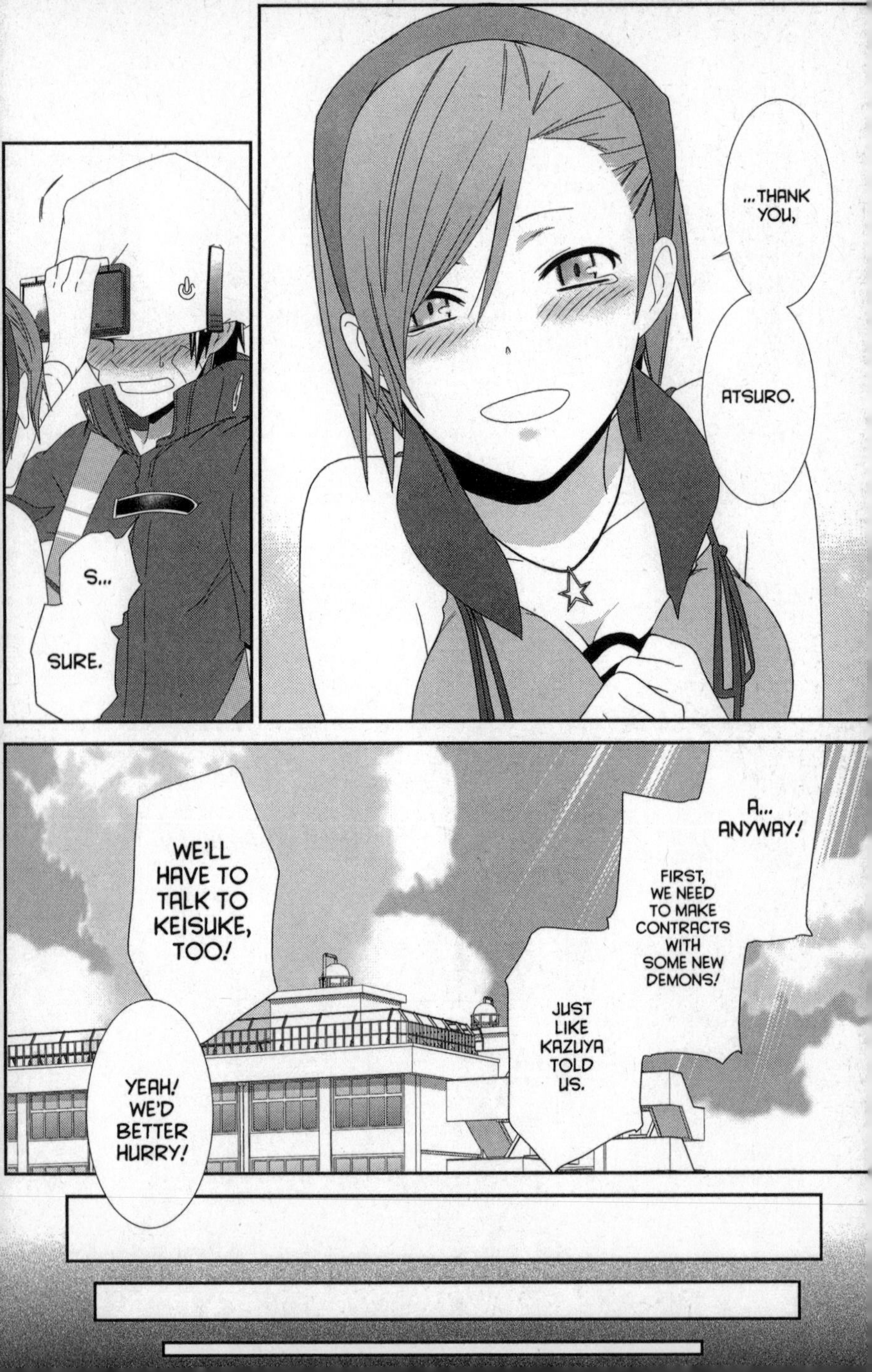
...THANK YOU,
ATSURO.
S...
SURE.
A... ANYWAY!
FIRST, WE NEED TO MAKE CONTRACTS WITH SOME NEW DEMONS!
JUST LIKE KAZUYA TOLD US.
WE'LL HAVE TO TALK TO KEISUKE, TOO!
YEAH! WE'D BETTER HURRY!

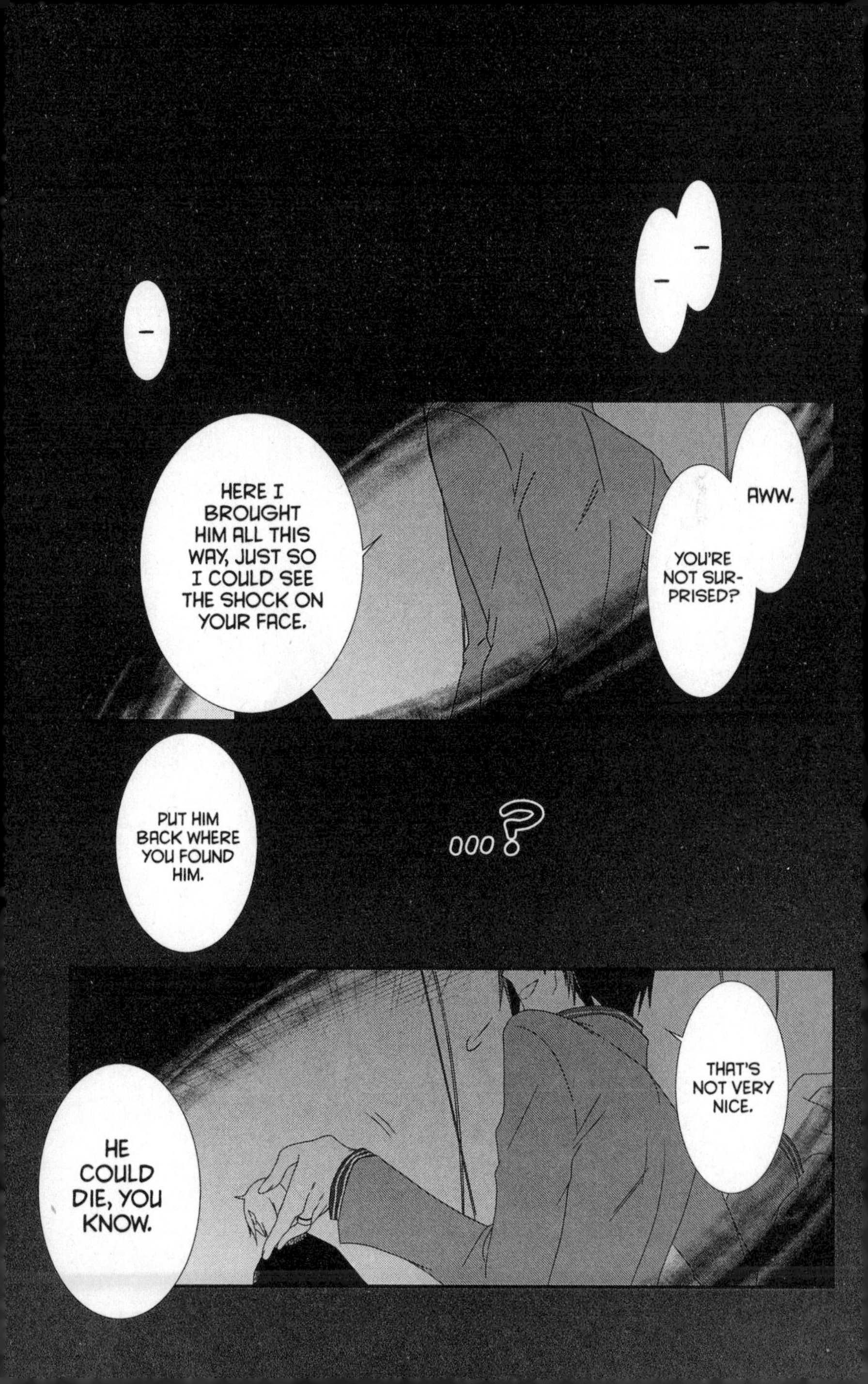
—
—
—
AWW.
YOU'RE NOT SUR-PRISED?
HERE I BROUGHT HIM ALL THIS WAY, JUST SO I COULD SEE THE SHOCK ON YOUR FACE.
ooo?
PUT HIM BACK WHERE YOU FOUND HIM.
THAT'S NOT VERY NICE.
HE COULD DIE, YOU KNOW.

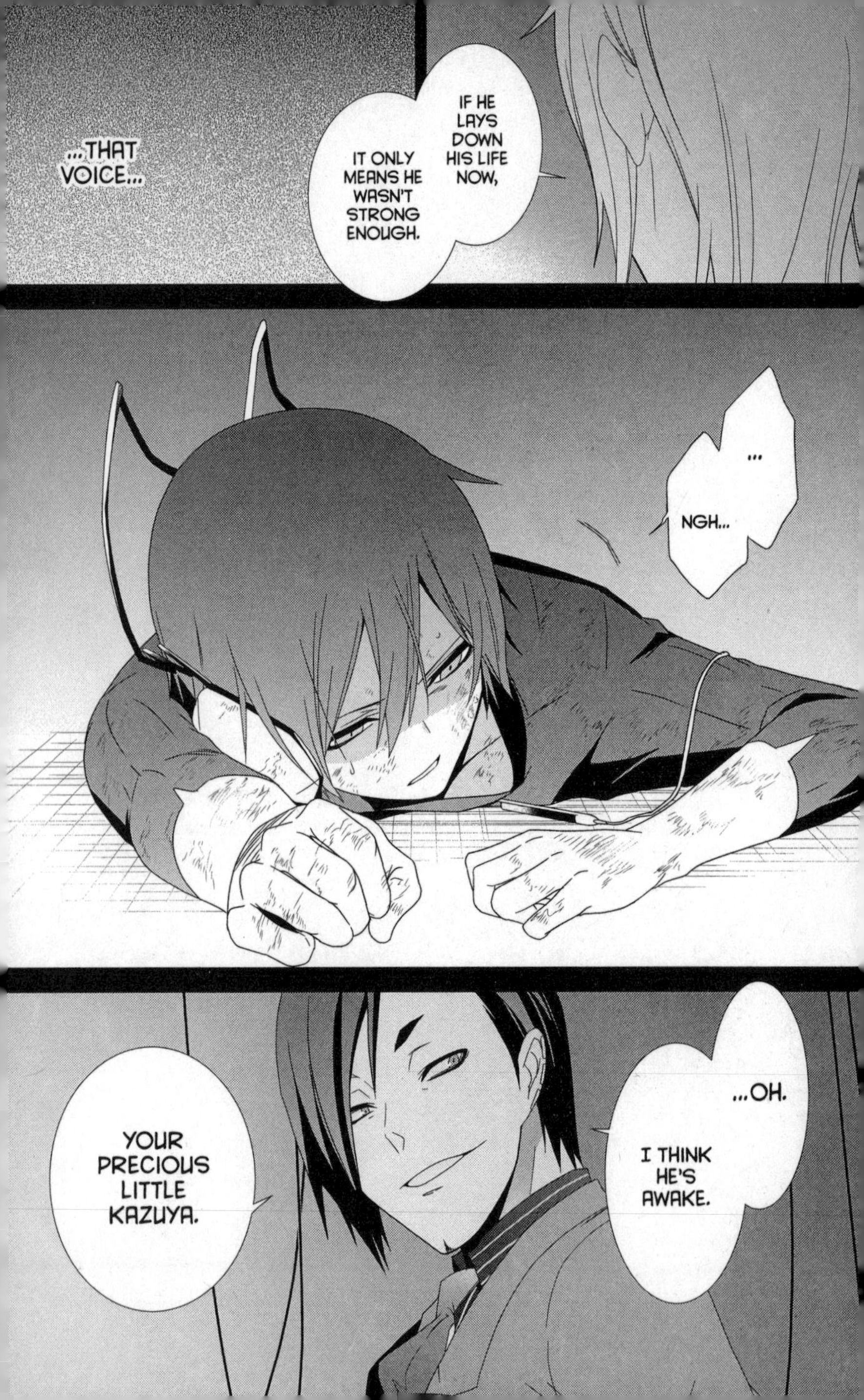
IF HE LAYS DOWN HIS LIFE NOW,
IT ONLY MEANS HE WASN'T STRONG ENOUGH.
...THAT VOICE...
...
NGH...
...OH.
I THINK HE'S AWAKE.
YOUR PRECIOUS LITTLE KAZUYA.

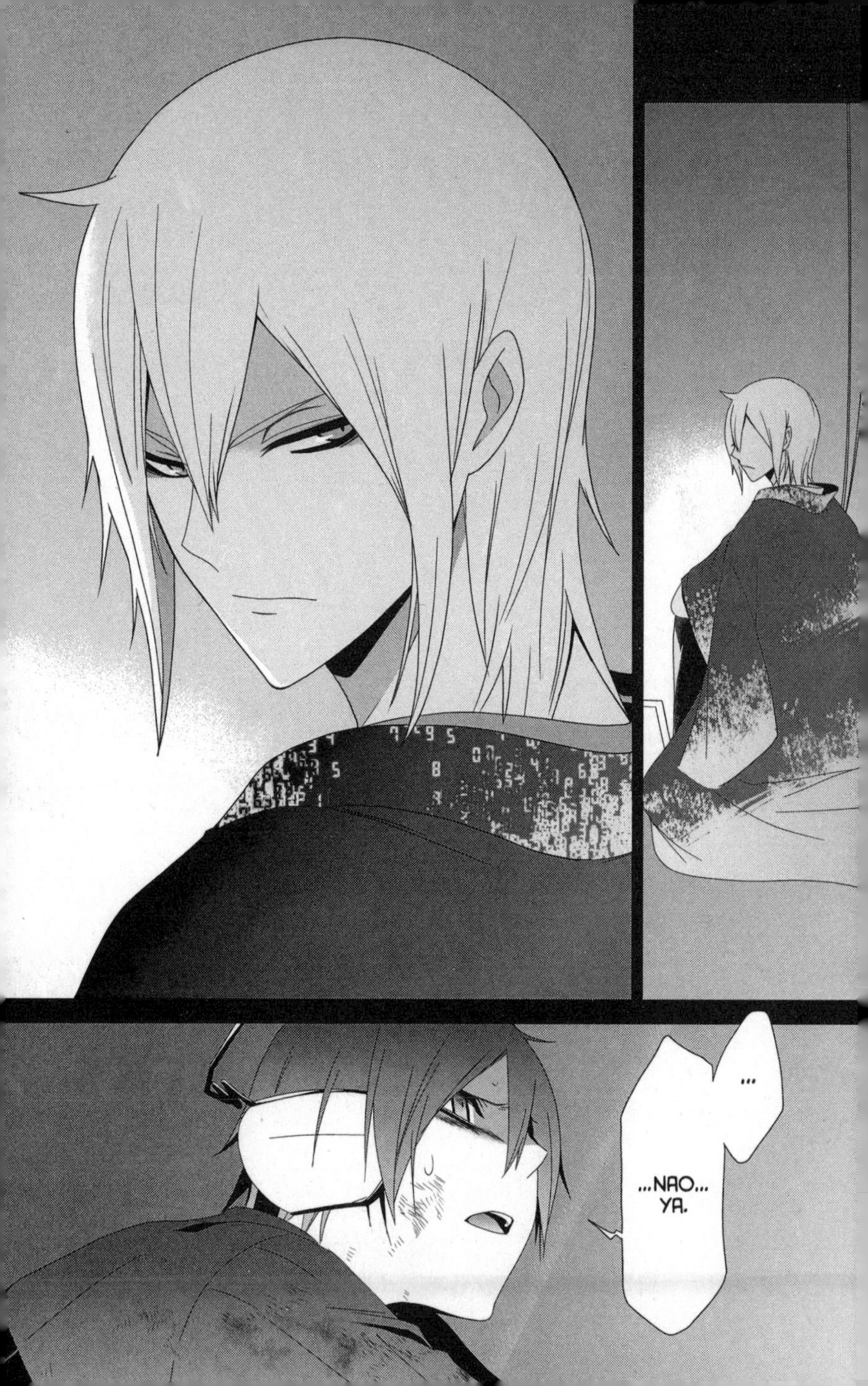
...
...NAO... YA.

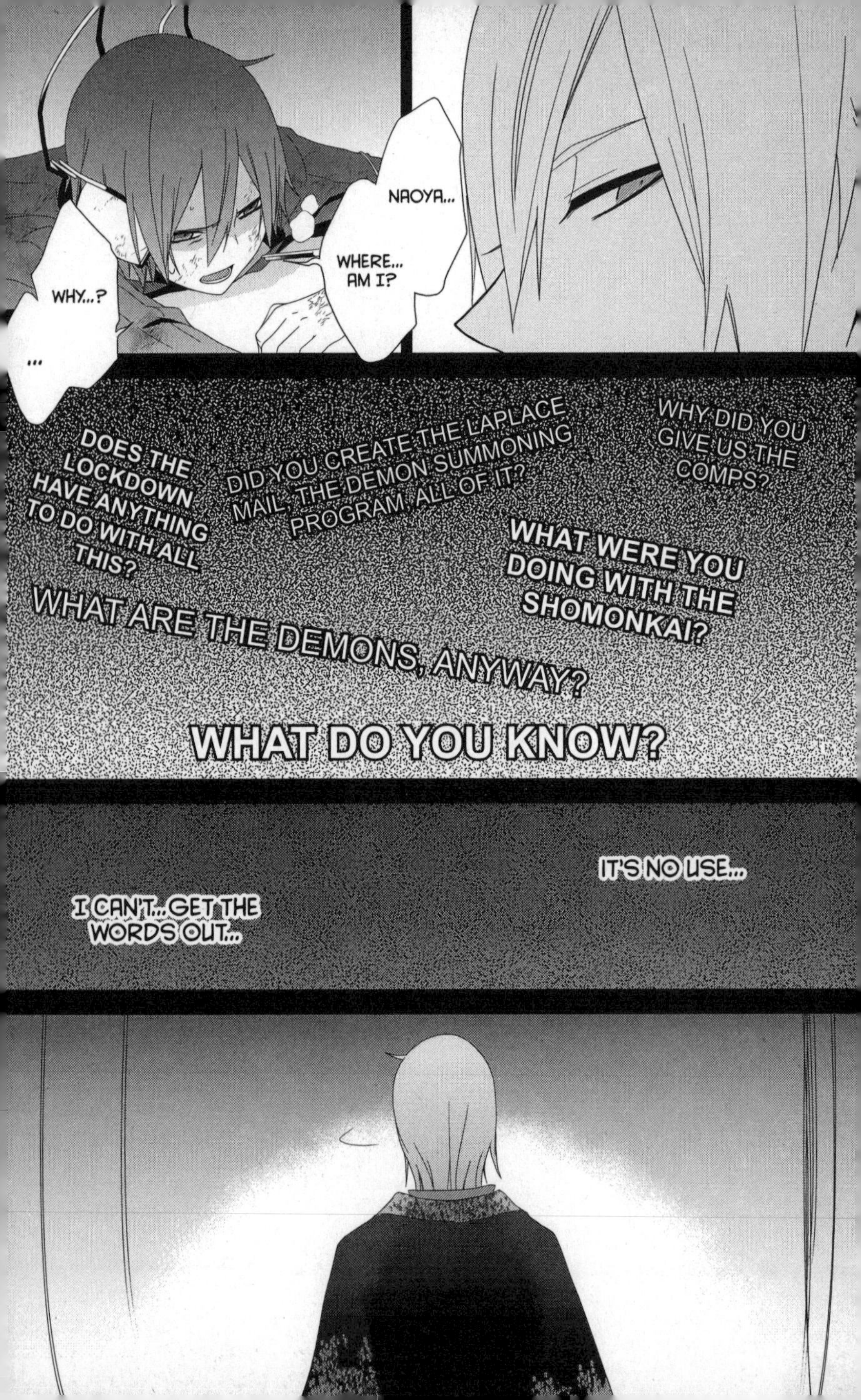

NAOYA...
WHERE... AM I?
WHY...?
...
WHY DID YOU GIVE US THE COMPS?
DID YOU CREATE THE LAPLACE MAIL, THE DEMON SUMMONING PROGRAM, ALL OF IT?
DOES THE LOCKDOWN HAVE ANYTHING TO DO WITH ALL THIS?
WHAT WERE YOU DOING WITH THE SHOMONKAI?
WHAT ARE THE DEMONS, ANYWAY?
WHAT DO YOU KNOW?
IT'S NO USE...
I CAN'T...GET THE WORDS OUT...

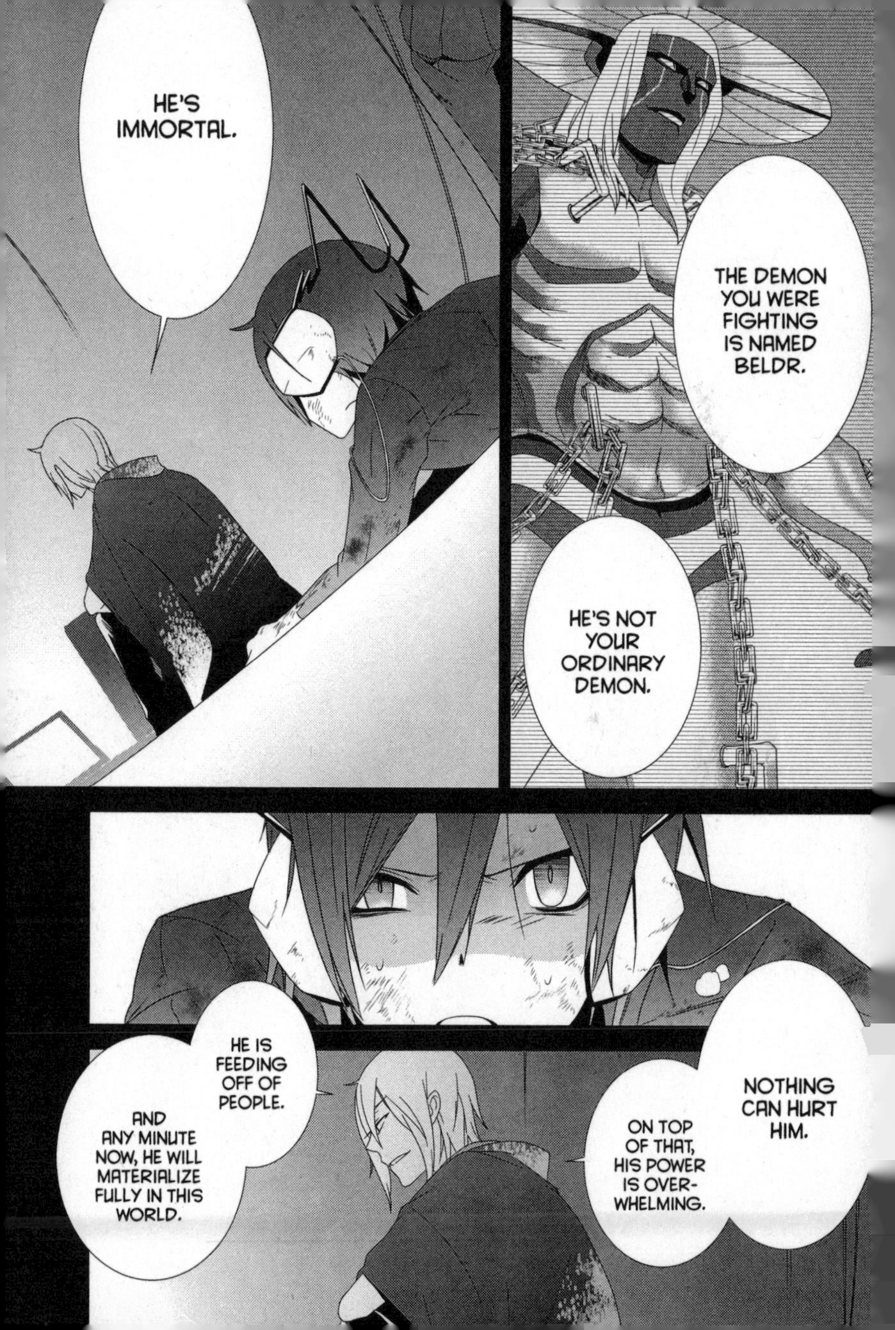
THE DEMON YOU WERE FIGHTING IS NAMED BELDR.
HE'S NOT YOUR ORDINARY DEMON.
HE'S IMMORTAL.
NOTHING CAN HURT HIM.
ON TOP OF THAT, HIS POWER IS OVER-WHELMING.
HE IS FEEDING OFF OF PEOPLE.
AND ANY MINUTE NOW, HE WILL MATERIALIZE FULLY IN THIS WORLD.

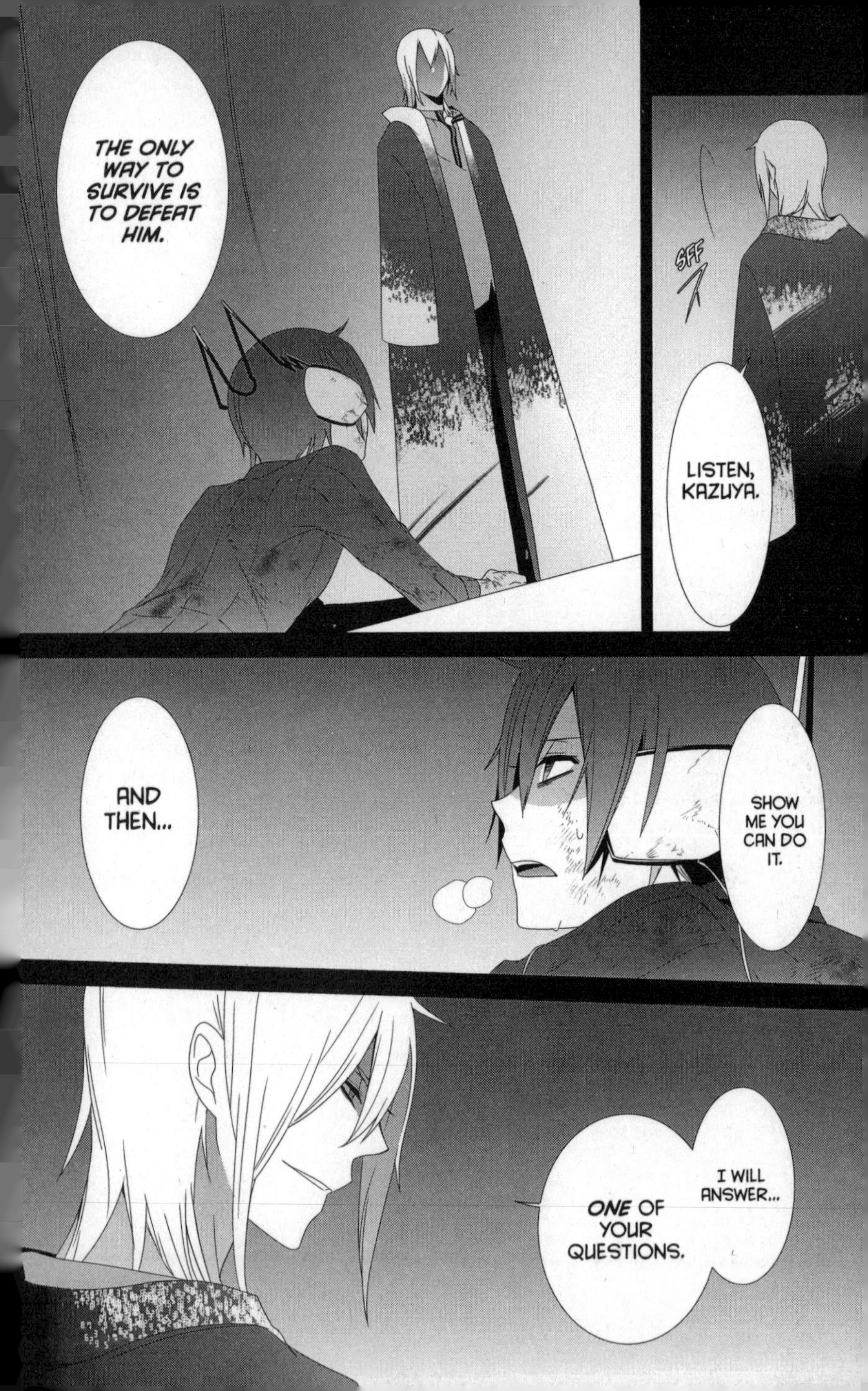
SFF
LISTEN, KAZUYA.
THE ONLY WAY TO SURVIVE IS TO DEFEAT HIM.
SHOW ME YOU CAN DO IT.
AND THEN...
I WILL ANSWER...
ONE OF YOUR QUESTIONS.

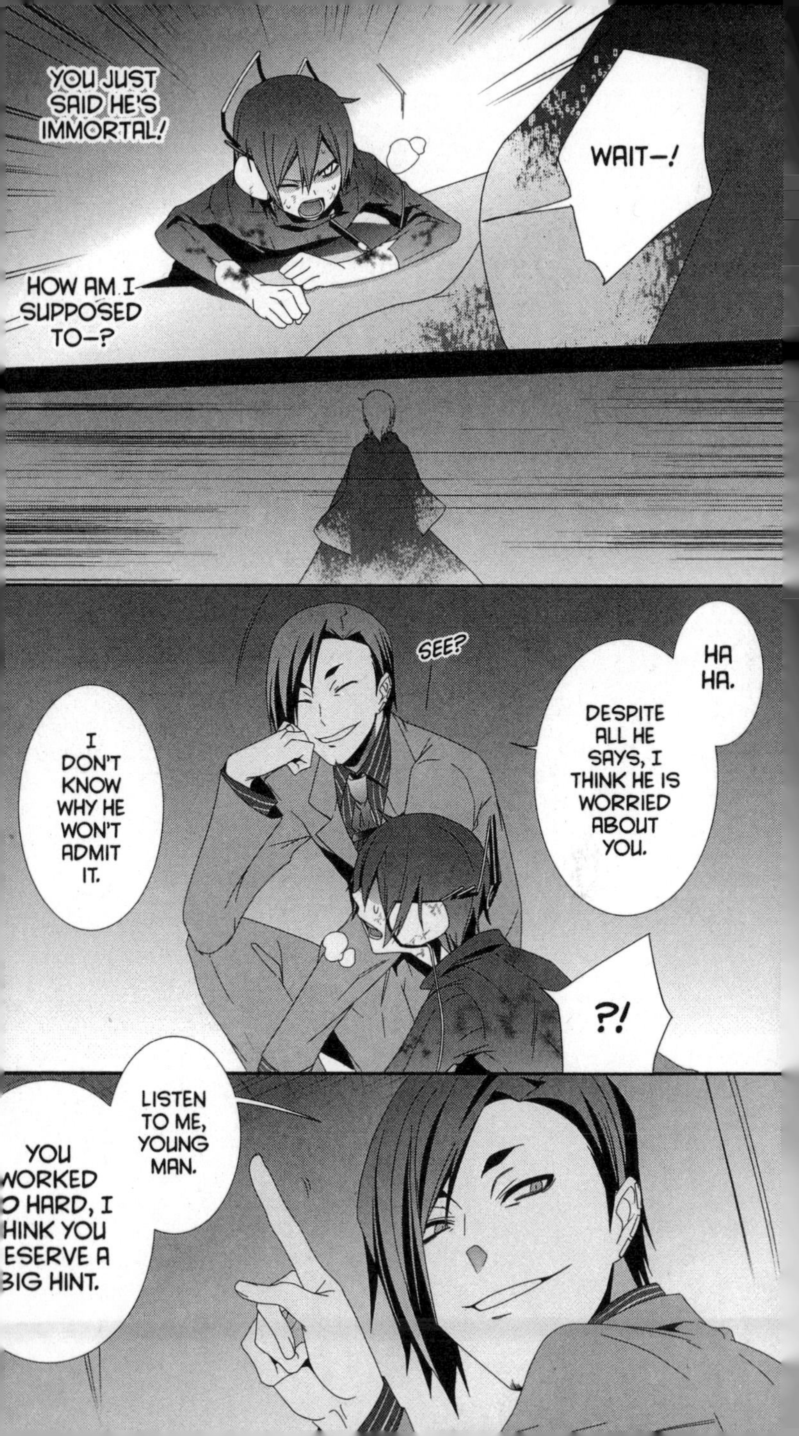
WAIT—!
YOU JUST SAID HE'S IMMORTAL!
HOW AM I SUPPOSED TO—?
HA HA.
DESPITE ALL HE SAYS, I THINK HE IS WORRIED ABOUT YOU.
SEE?
I DON'T KNOW WHY HE WON'T ADMIT IT.
?!
LISTEN TO ME, YOUNG MAN.
YOU WORKED O HARD, I HINK YOU ESERVE A BIG HINT.

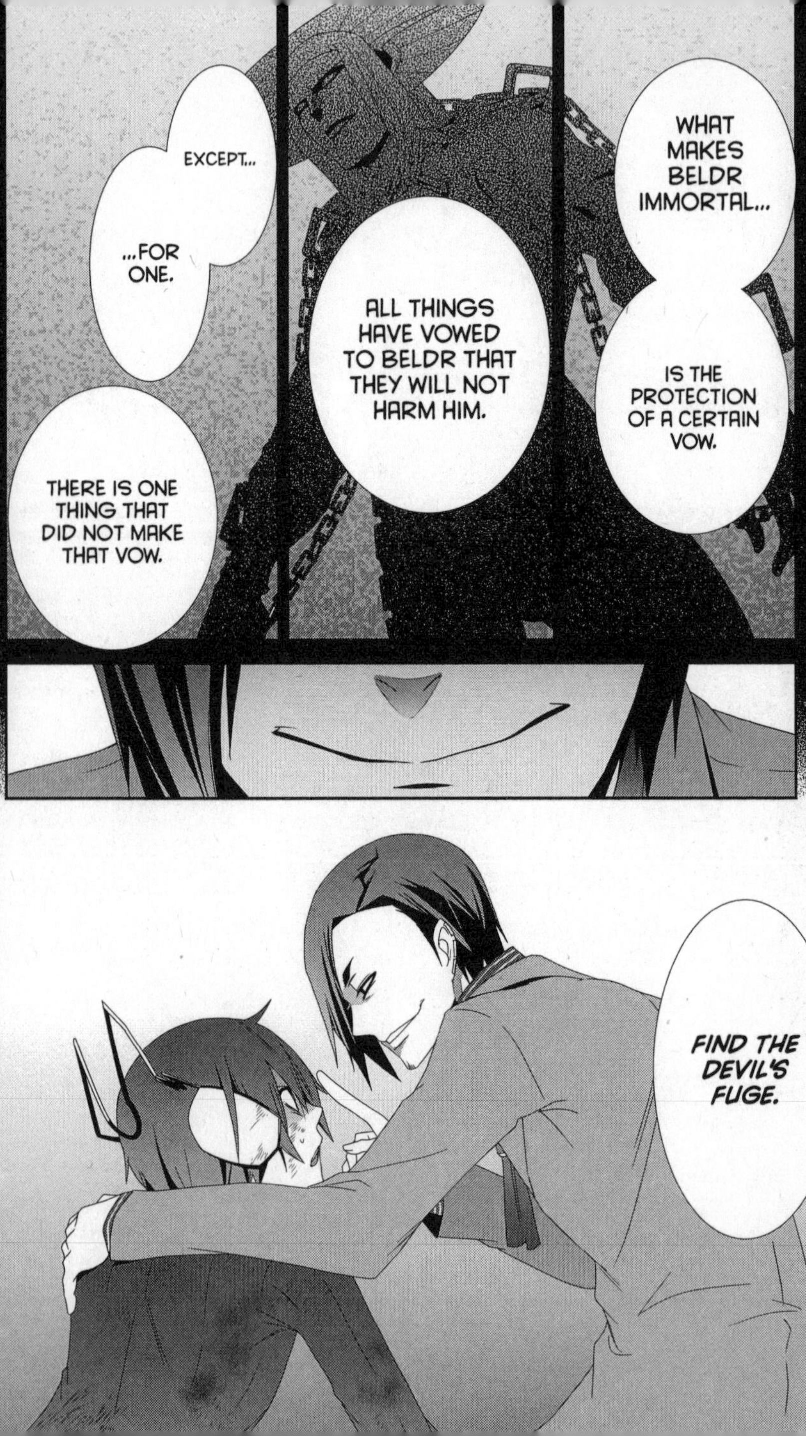
WHAT MAKES BELDR IMMORTAL...
IS THE PROTECTION OF A CERTAIN VOW.
ALL THINGS HAVE VOWED TO BELDR THAT THEY WILL NOT HARM HIM.
EXCEPT...
...FOR ONE.
THERE IS ONE THING THAT DID NOT MAKE THAT VOW.
FIND THE DEVIL'S FUGE.

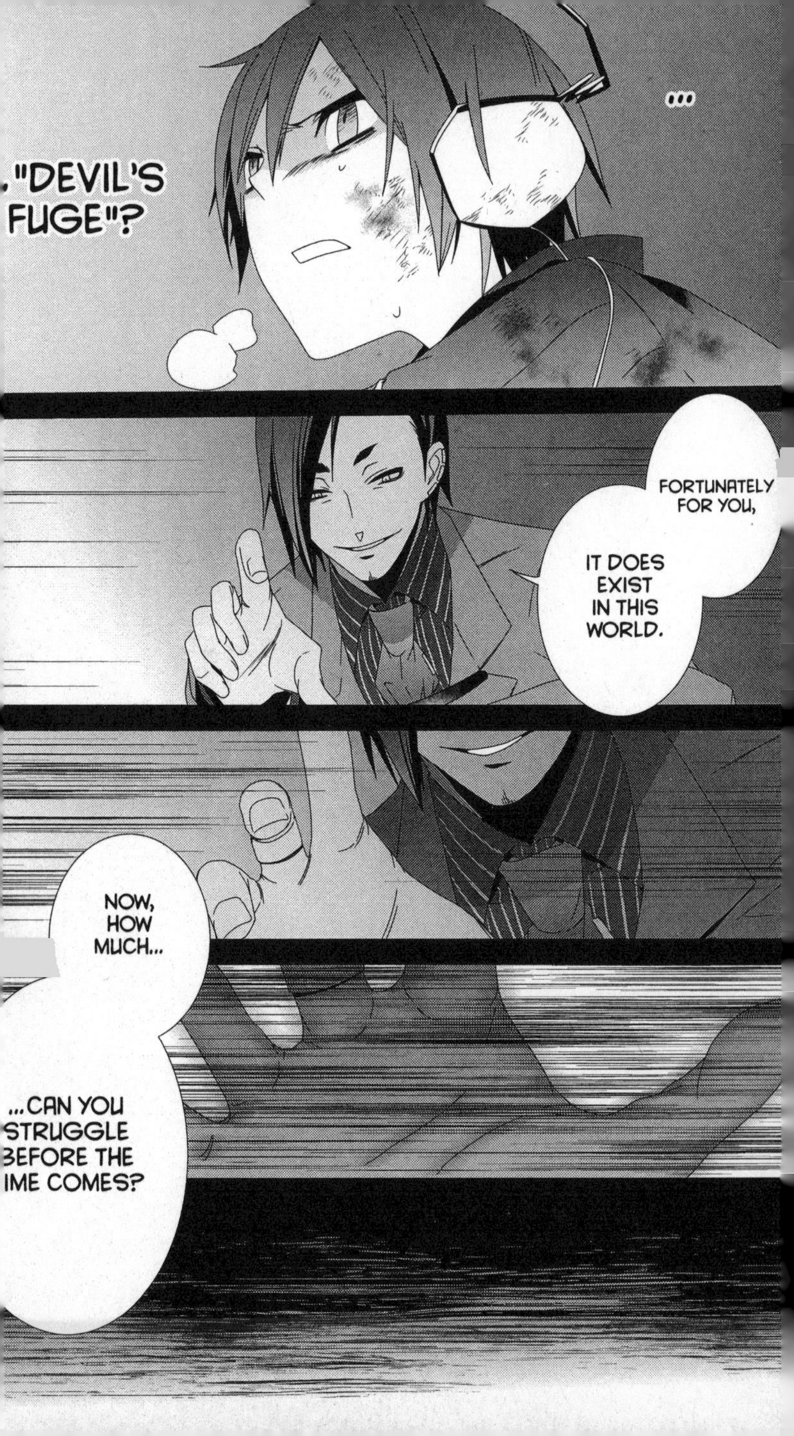
...
"DEVIL'S FUGE"?
FORTUNATELY FOR YOU,
IT DOES EXIST IN THIS WORLD.
NOW, HOW MUCH...
...CAN YOU STRUGGLE BEFORE THE IME COMES?

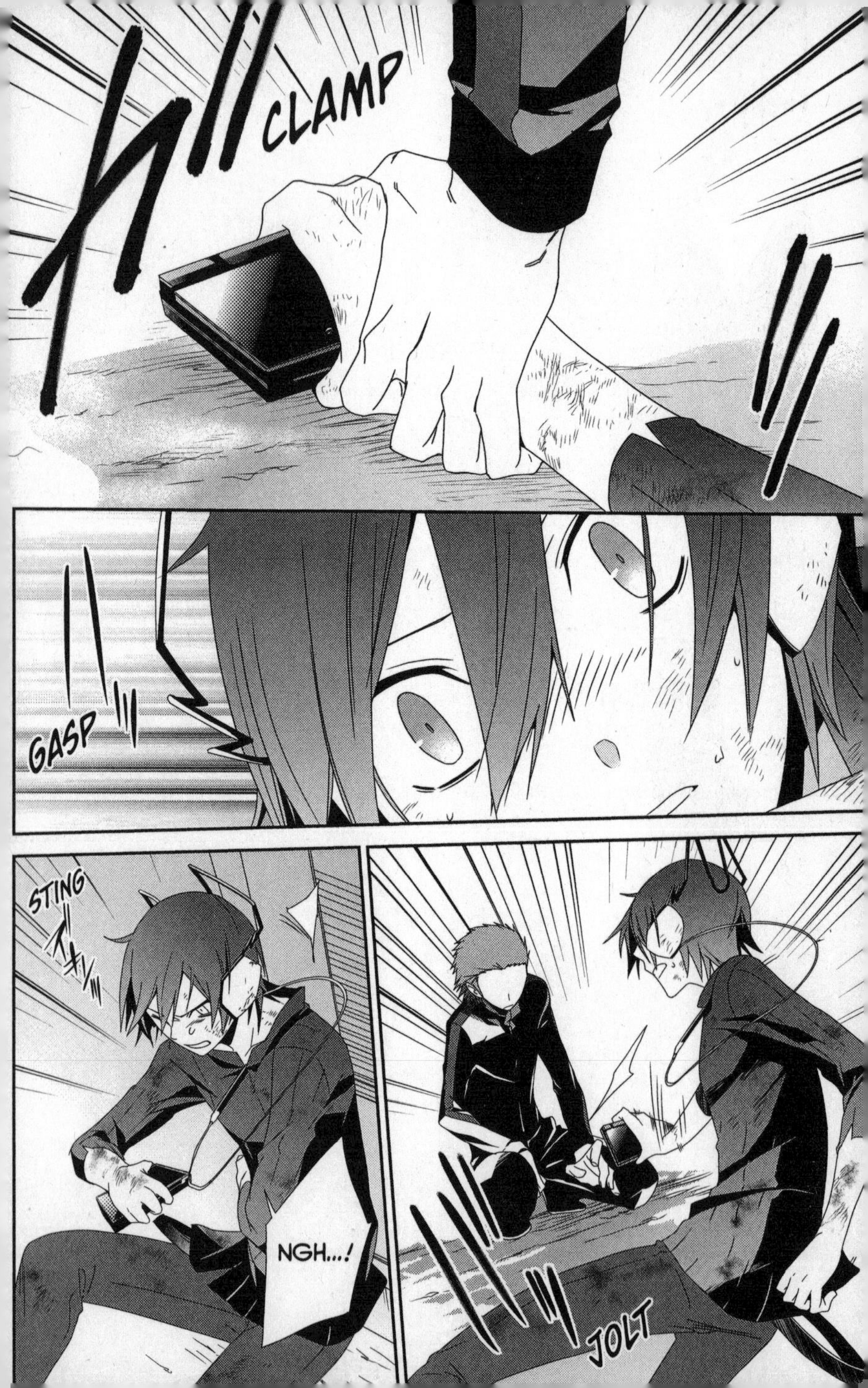
CLAMP
GASP
JOLT
STING
NGH...!

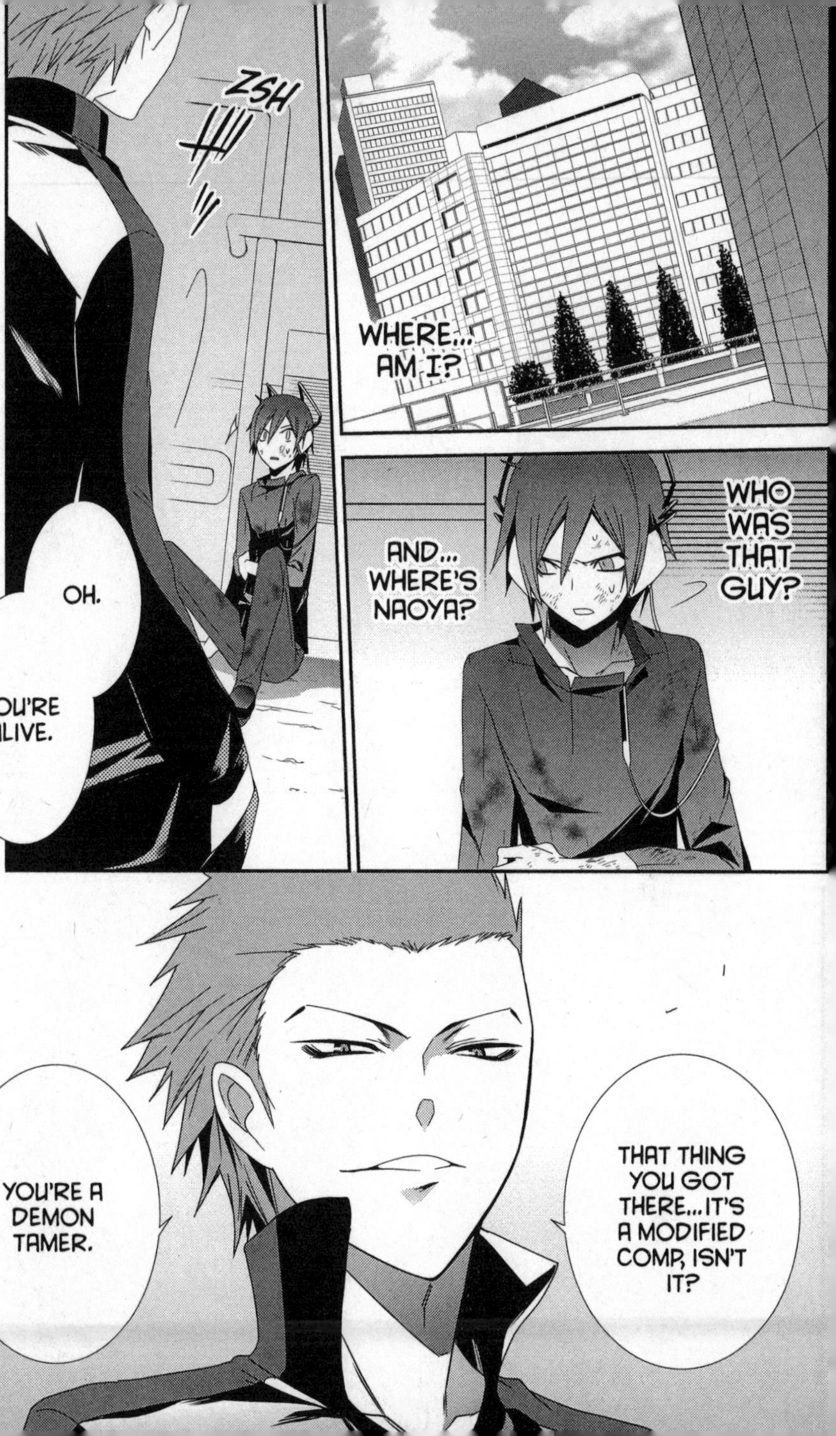
WHERE... AM I?
WHO WAS THAT GUY?
AND... WHERE'S NAOYA?
ZSH
OH.
YOU'RE ALIVE.
THAT THING YOU GOT THERE...IT'S A MODIFIED COMP, ISN'T IT?
YOU'RE A DEMON TAMER.

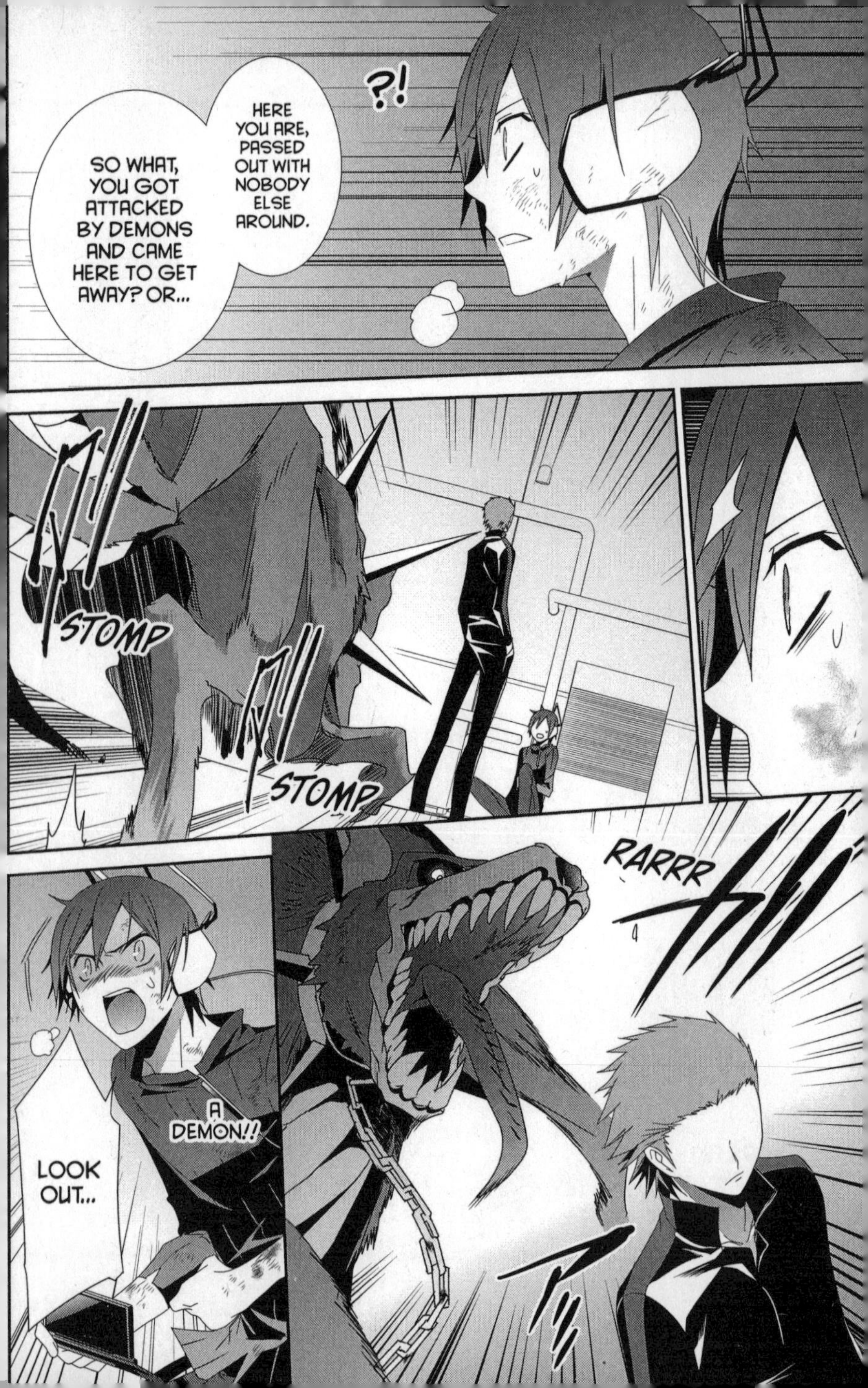
?!
HERE YOU ARE, PASSED OUT WITH NOBODY ELSE AROUND.
SO WHAT, YOU GOT ATTACKED BY DEMONS AND CAME HERE TO GET AWAY? OR...
STOMP
STOMP
RARRR
A DEMON!!
LOOK OUT...

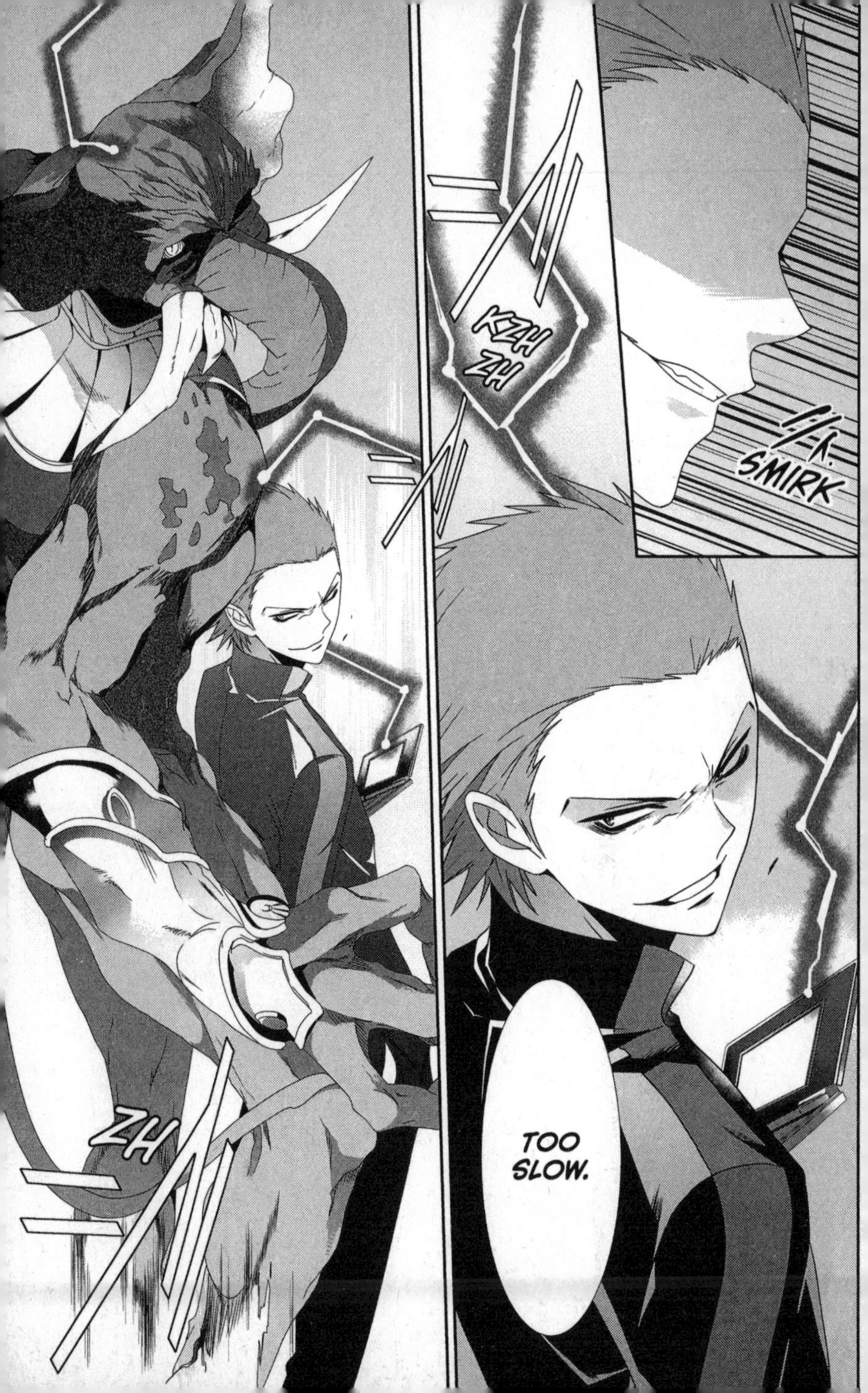
SMIRK
KZH ZH
TOO SLOW.
ZH

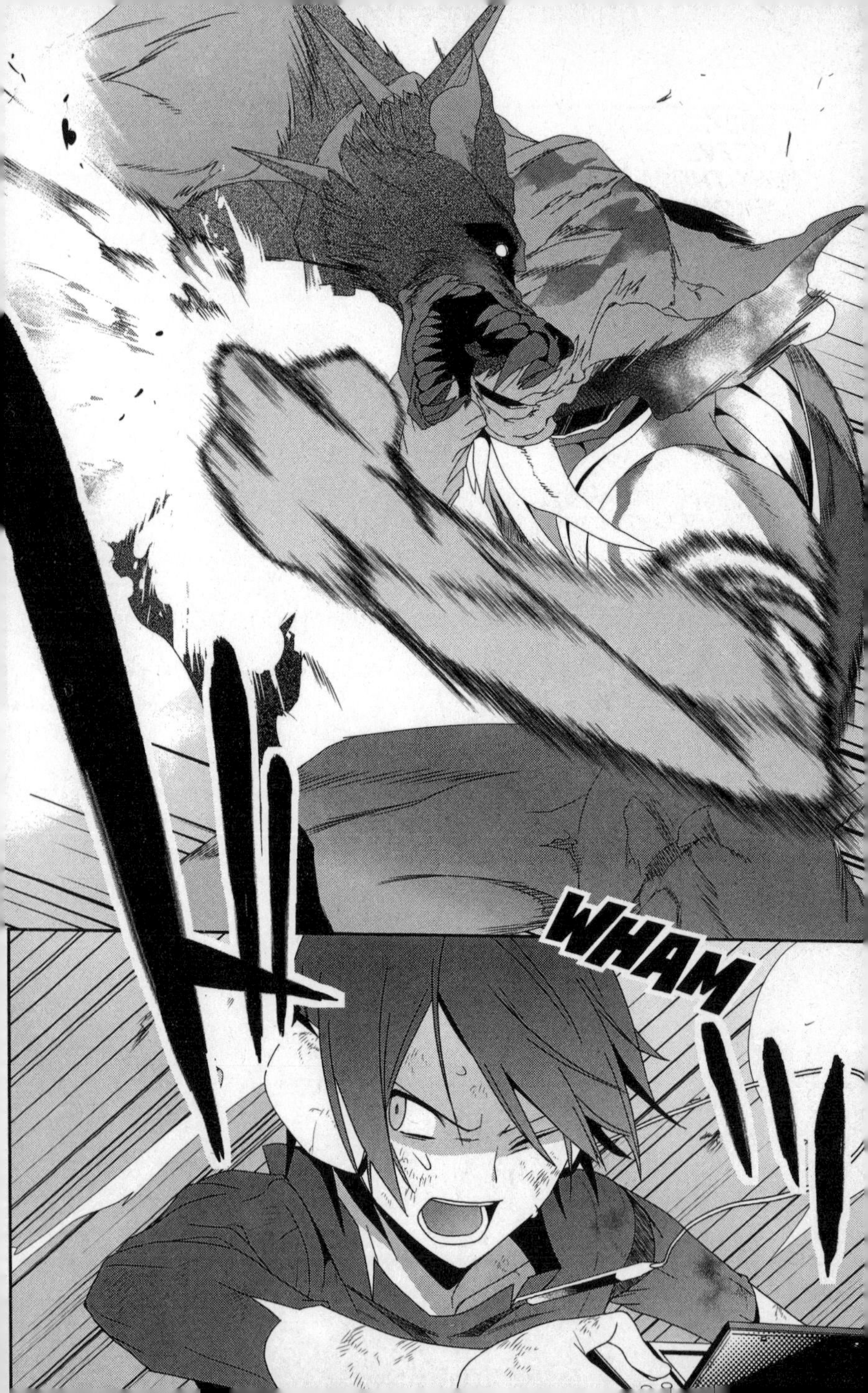
WHAM

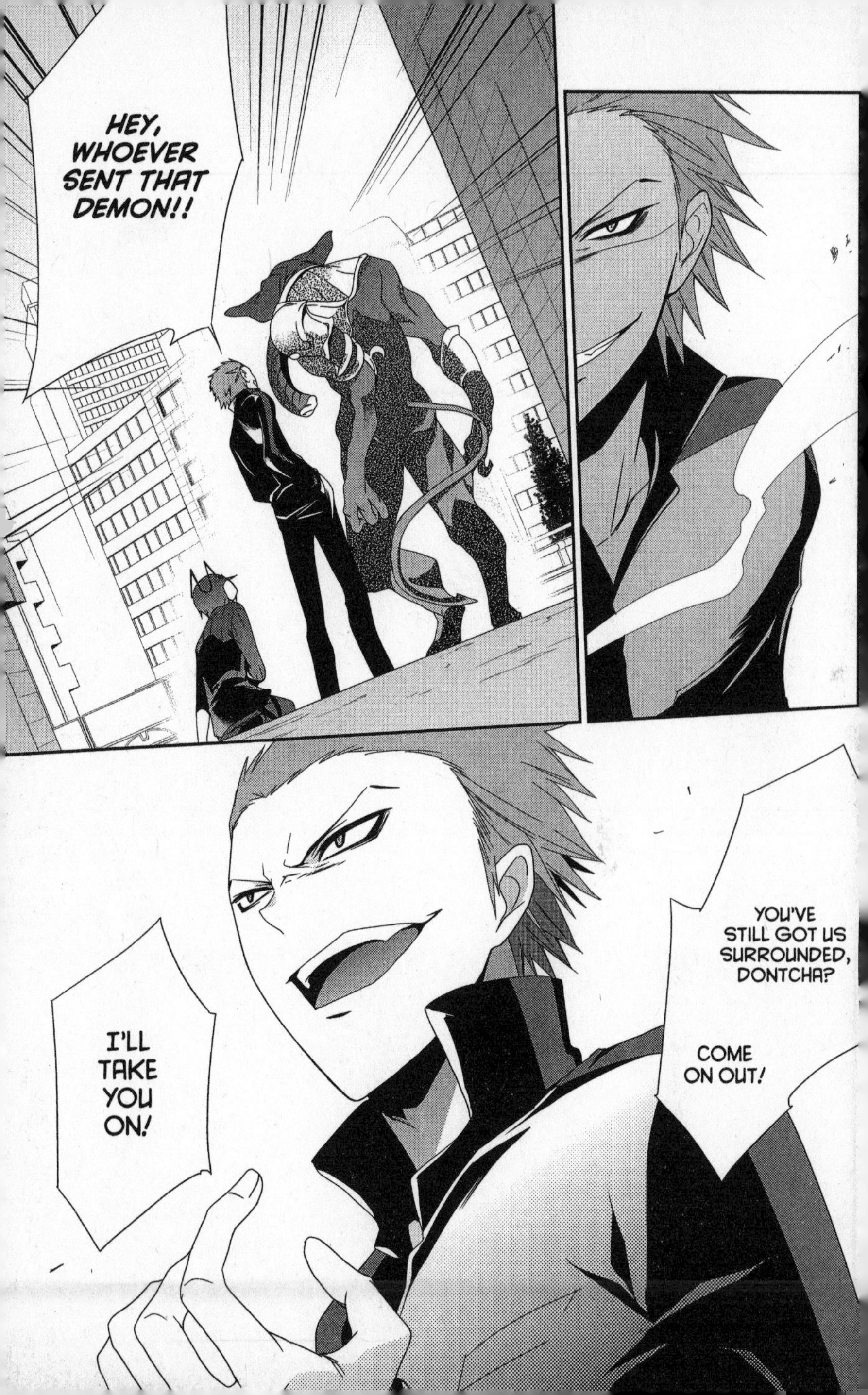
HEY, WHOEVER SENT THAT DEMON!!
YOU'VE STILL GOT US SURROUNDED, DONTCHA?
COME ON OUT!
I'LL TAKE YOU ON!

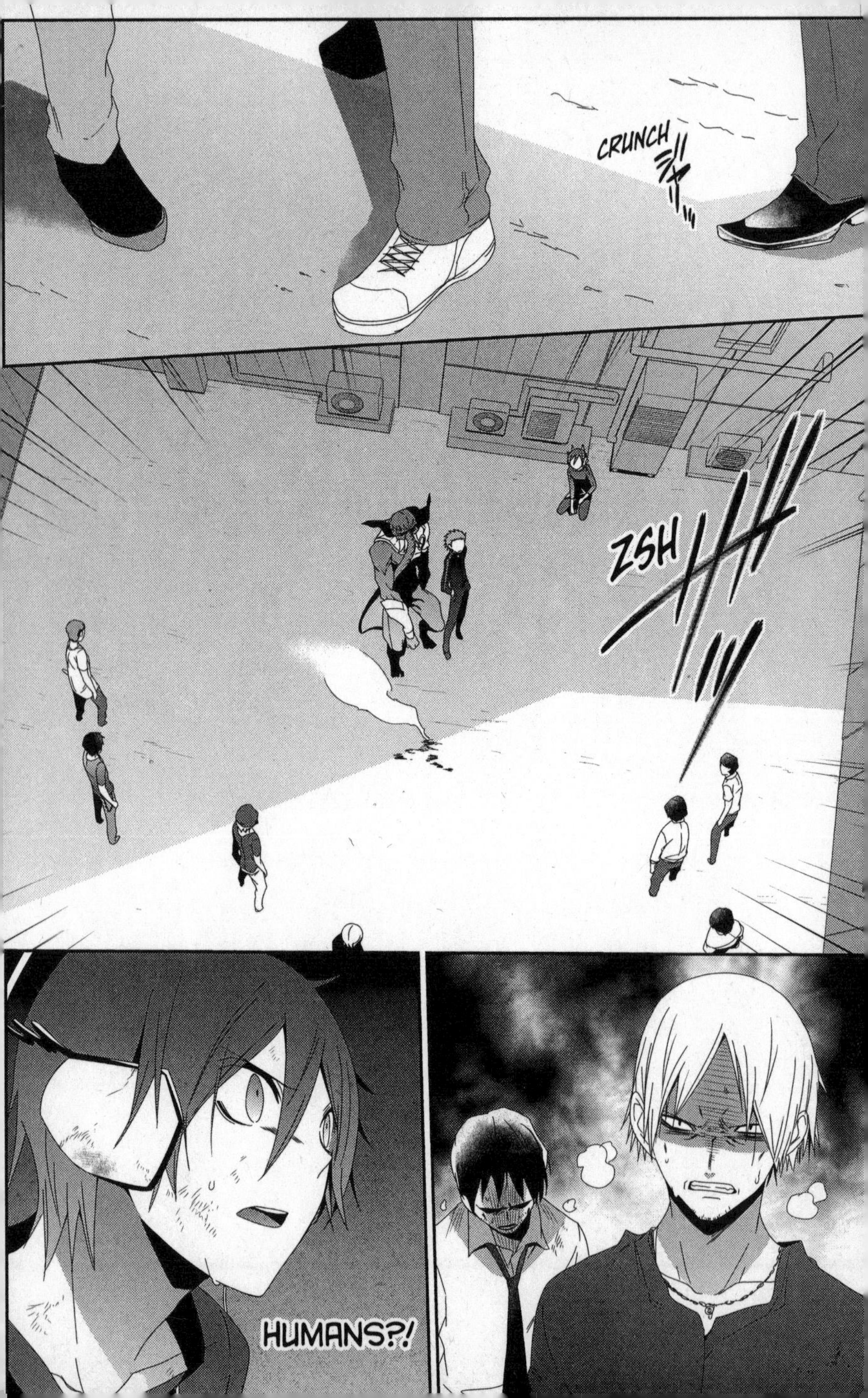
CRUNCH
ZSH
HUMANS?!

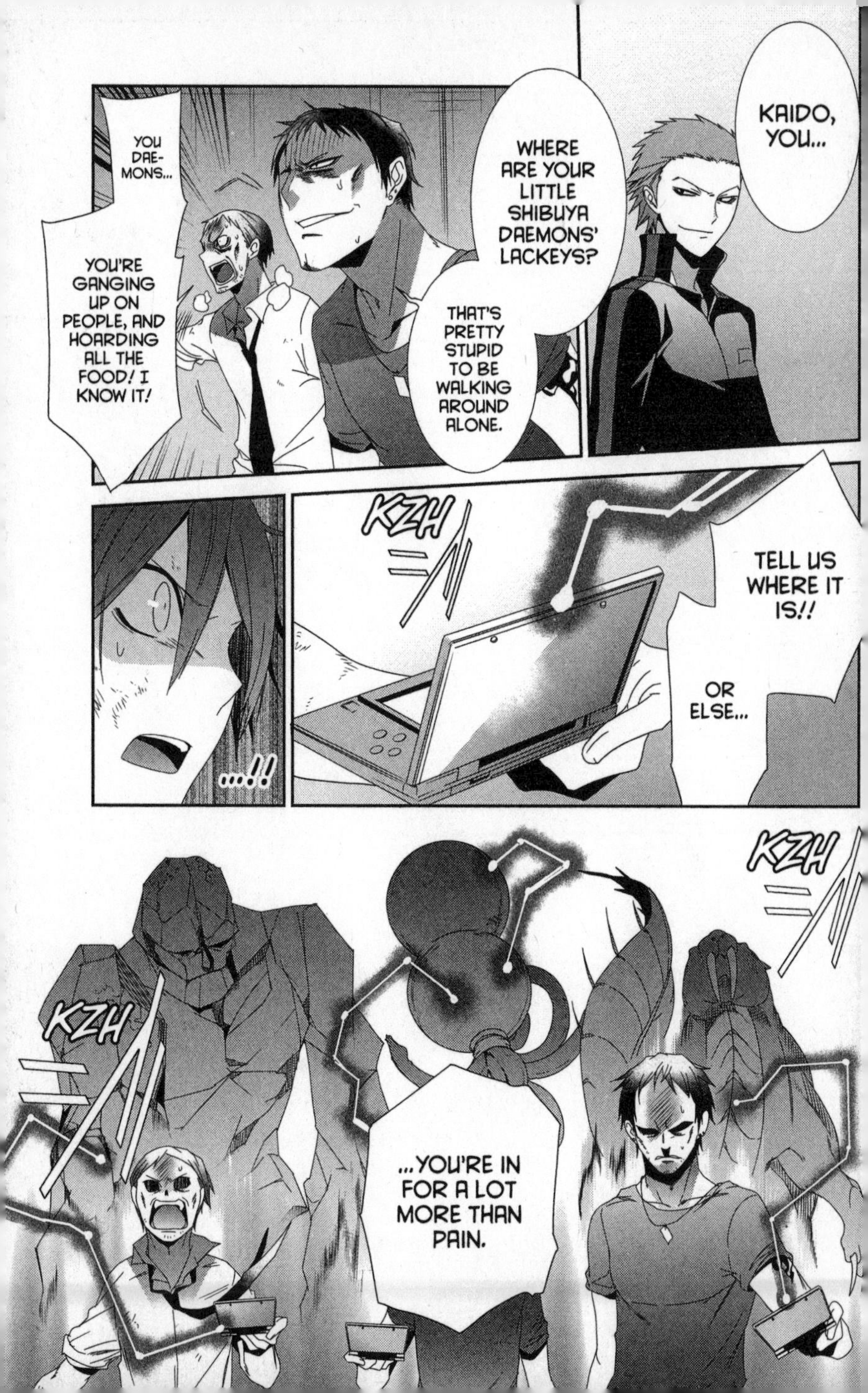
KAIDO, YOU...
WHERE ARE YOUR LITTLE SHIBUYA DAEMONS' LACKEYS?
THAT'S PRETTY STUPID TO BE WALKING AROUND ALONE.
YOU DAEMONS...
YOU'RE GANGING UP ON PEOPLE, AND HOARDING ALL THE FOOD! I KNOW IT!
TELL US WHERE IT IS!!
OR ELSE...
KZH
...!!
KZH
...YOU'RE IN FOR A LOT MORE THAN PAIN.
KZH

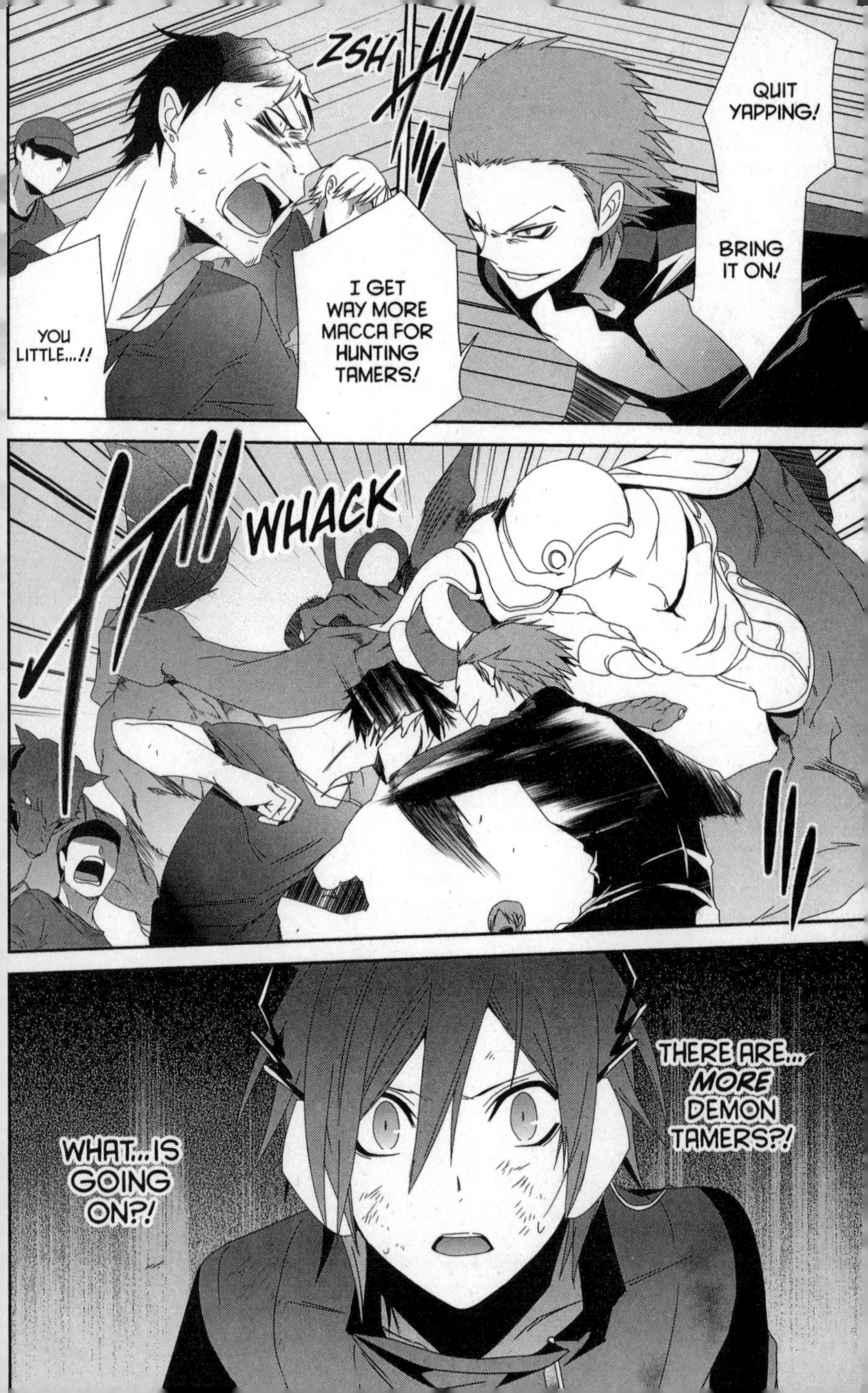
QUIT YAPPING!
BRING IT ON!
ZSH
I GET WAY MORE MACCA FOR HUNTING TAMERS!
YOU LITTLE...!!
WHACK
THERE ARE... MORE DEMON TAMERS?!
WHAT...IS GOING ON?!

NALAGIRI

AN EVIL ELEPHANT KING FROM SRI LANKAN
LORE. IN HINDUISM, ELEPHANTS ARE HOLY
CREATURES THAT WOULD NEVER BE TREATED
AS EVIL, BUT THERE WAS A TIME IN SRI LANKAN
HISTORY WHEN HINDUISM WAS SEEN AS A
HERETICAL RELIGION, WHICH MAY BE WHY
ELEPHANTS WERE LOOKED DOWN UPON AS
WICKED CREATURES.

DEVIL SURVIVOR
デビルサバイバー

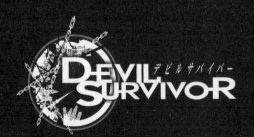

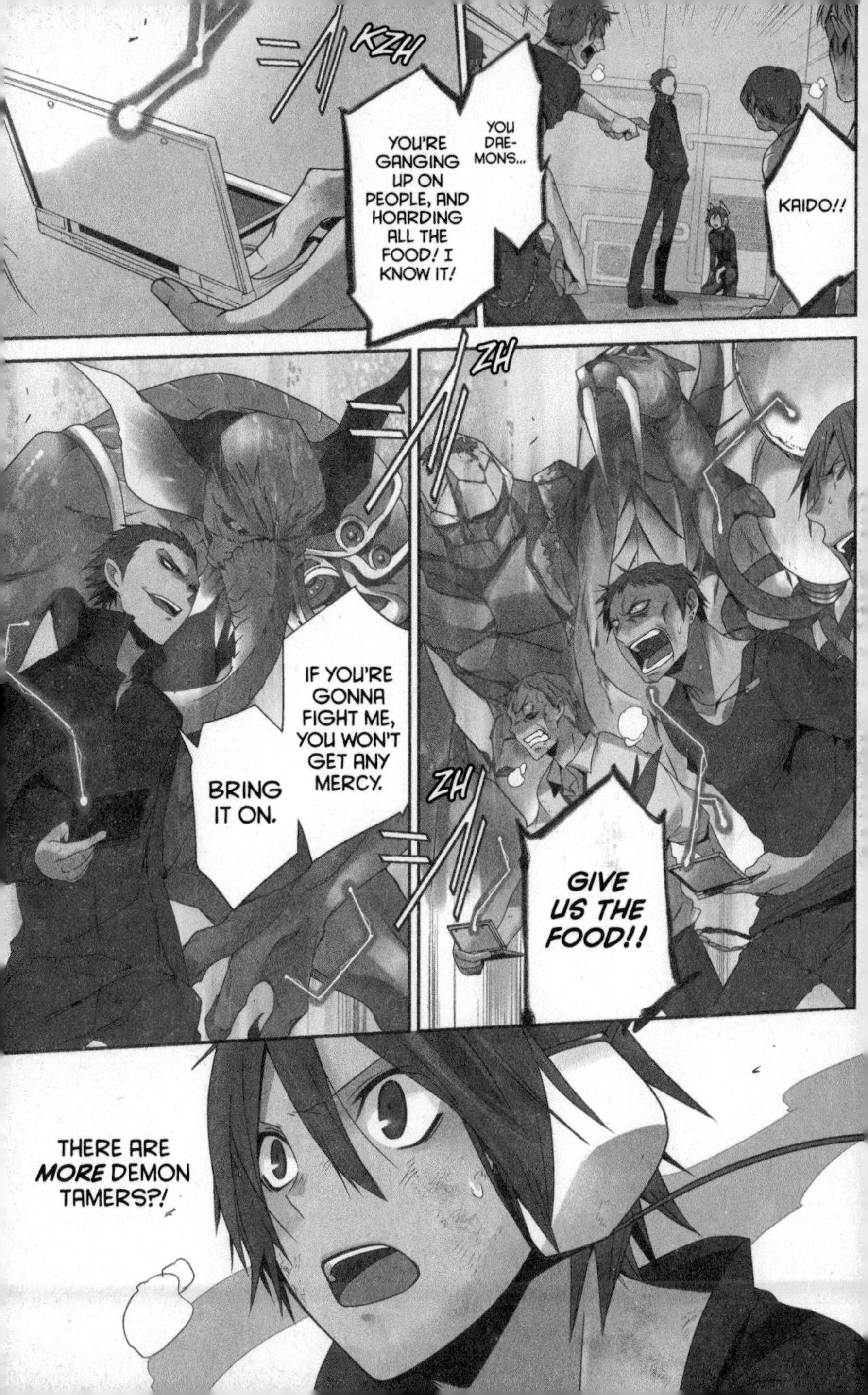
KAIDO!!
YOU DAEMONS...
YOU'RE GANGING UP ON PEOPLE, AND HOARDING ALL THE FOOD! I KNOW IT!
KZH
ZH
ZH
GIVE US THE FOOD!!
IF YOU'RE GONNA FIGHT ME, YOU WON'T GET ANY MERCY.
BRING IT ON.
THERE ARE MORE DEMON TAMERS?!

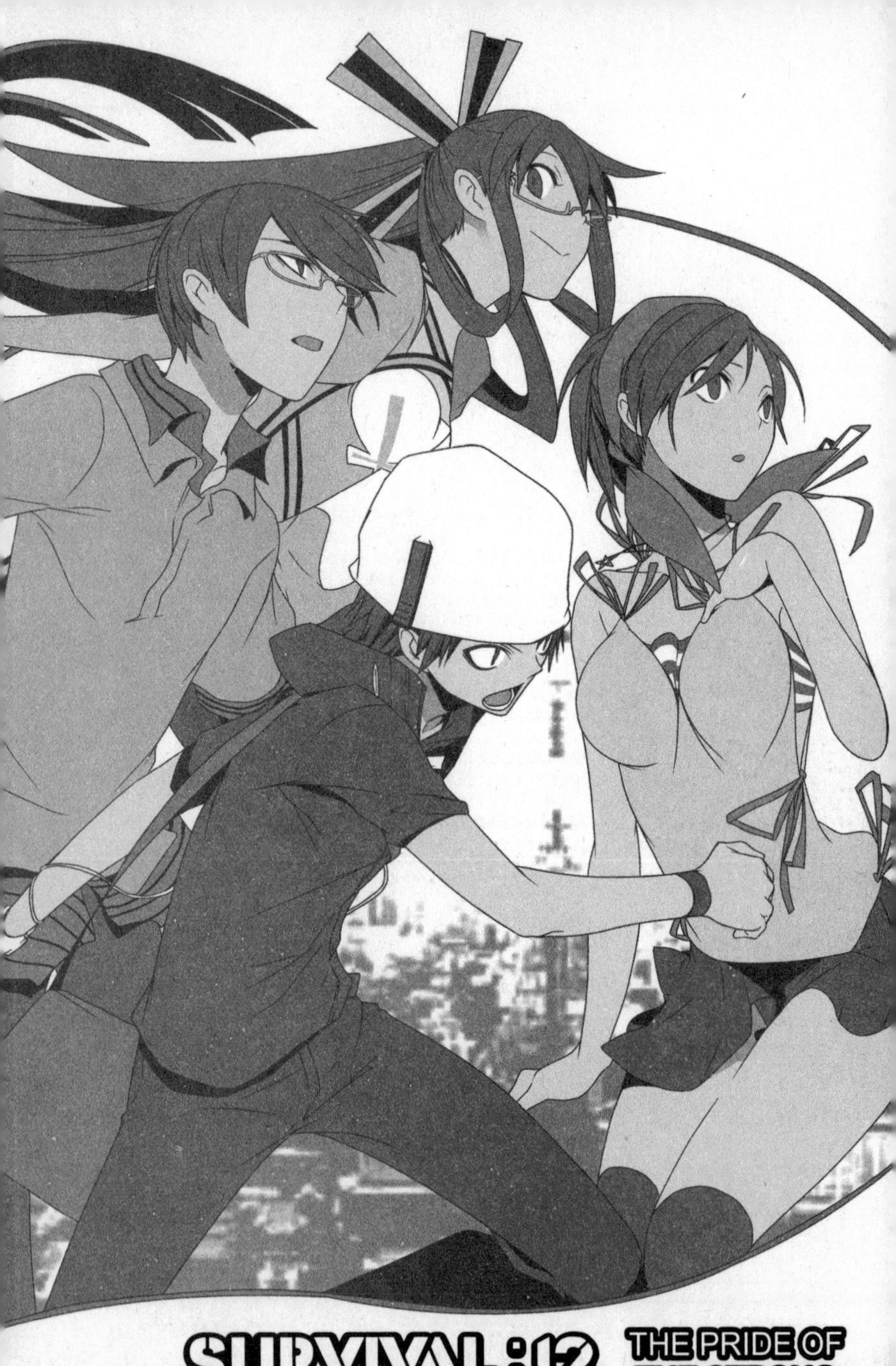

SURVIVAL : 12 THE PRIDE OF THE STRONG

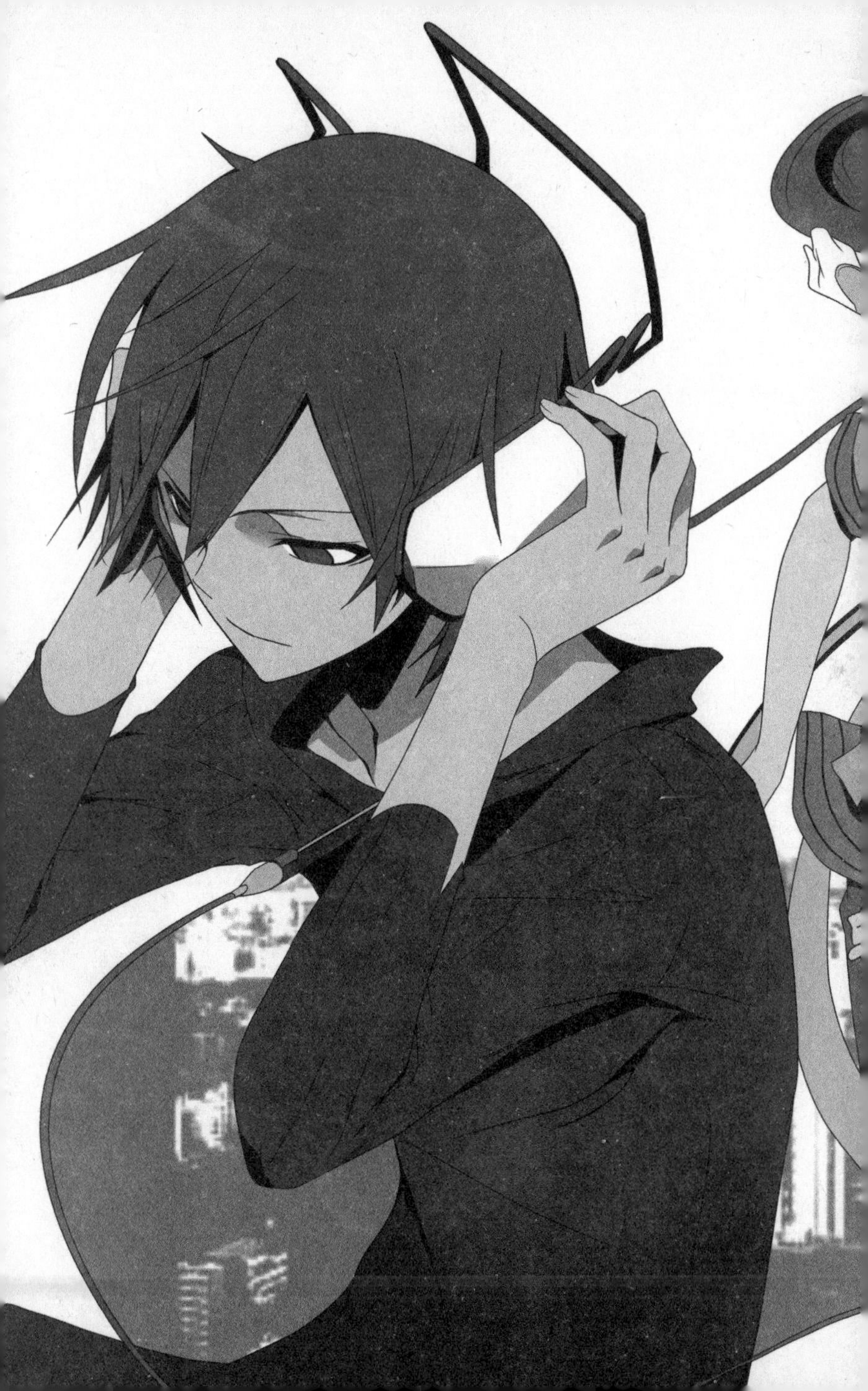

DEVIL SURVIVOR
デビルサバイバー

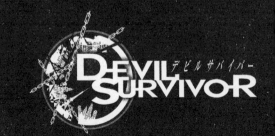

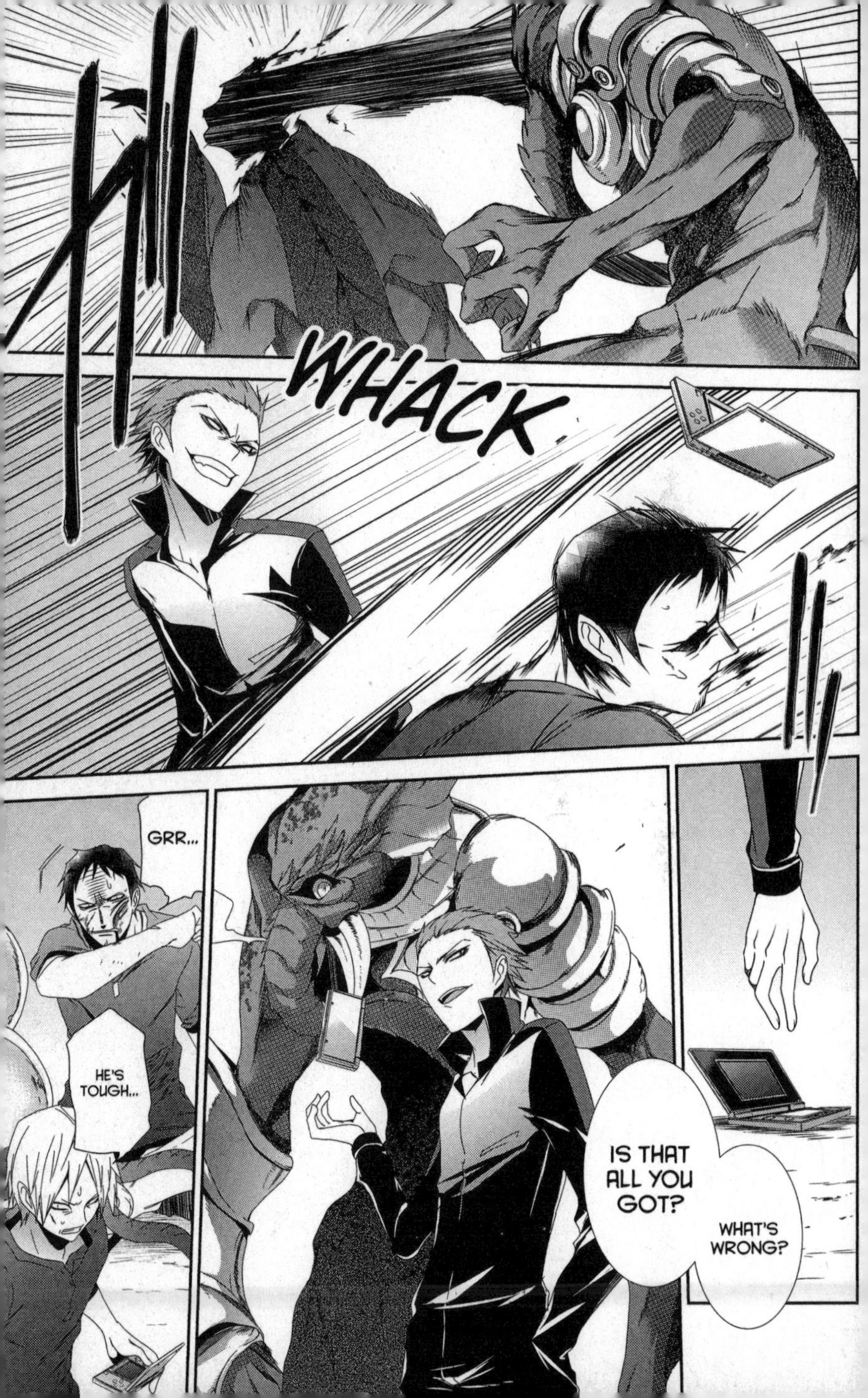
WHACK
GRR...
IS THAT ALL YOU GOT?
WHAT'S WRONG?
HE'S TOUGH...

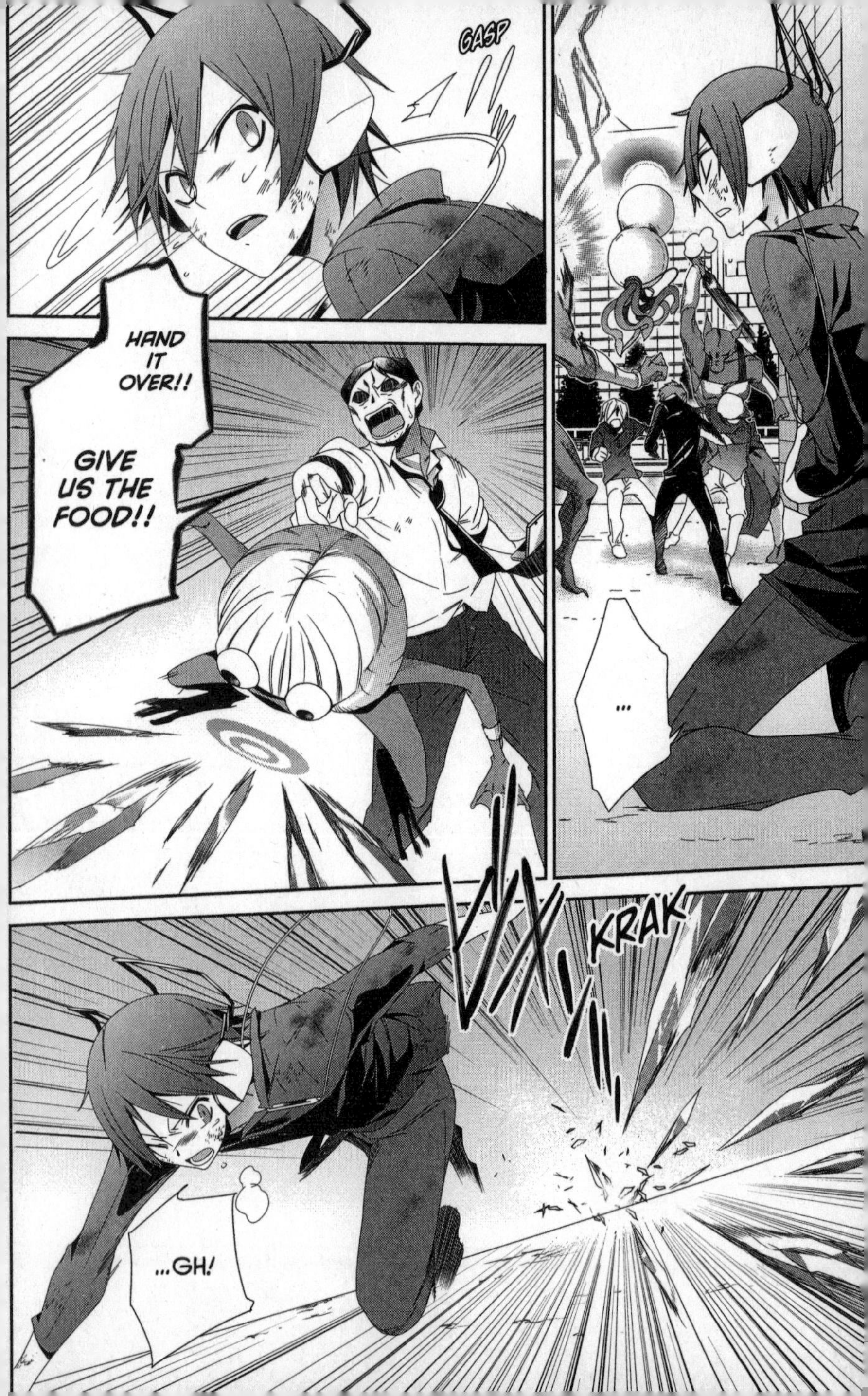
...
GASP
HAND IT OVER!!
GIVE US THE FOOD!!
KRAK
...GH!

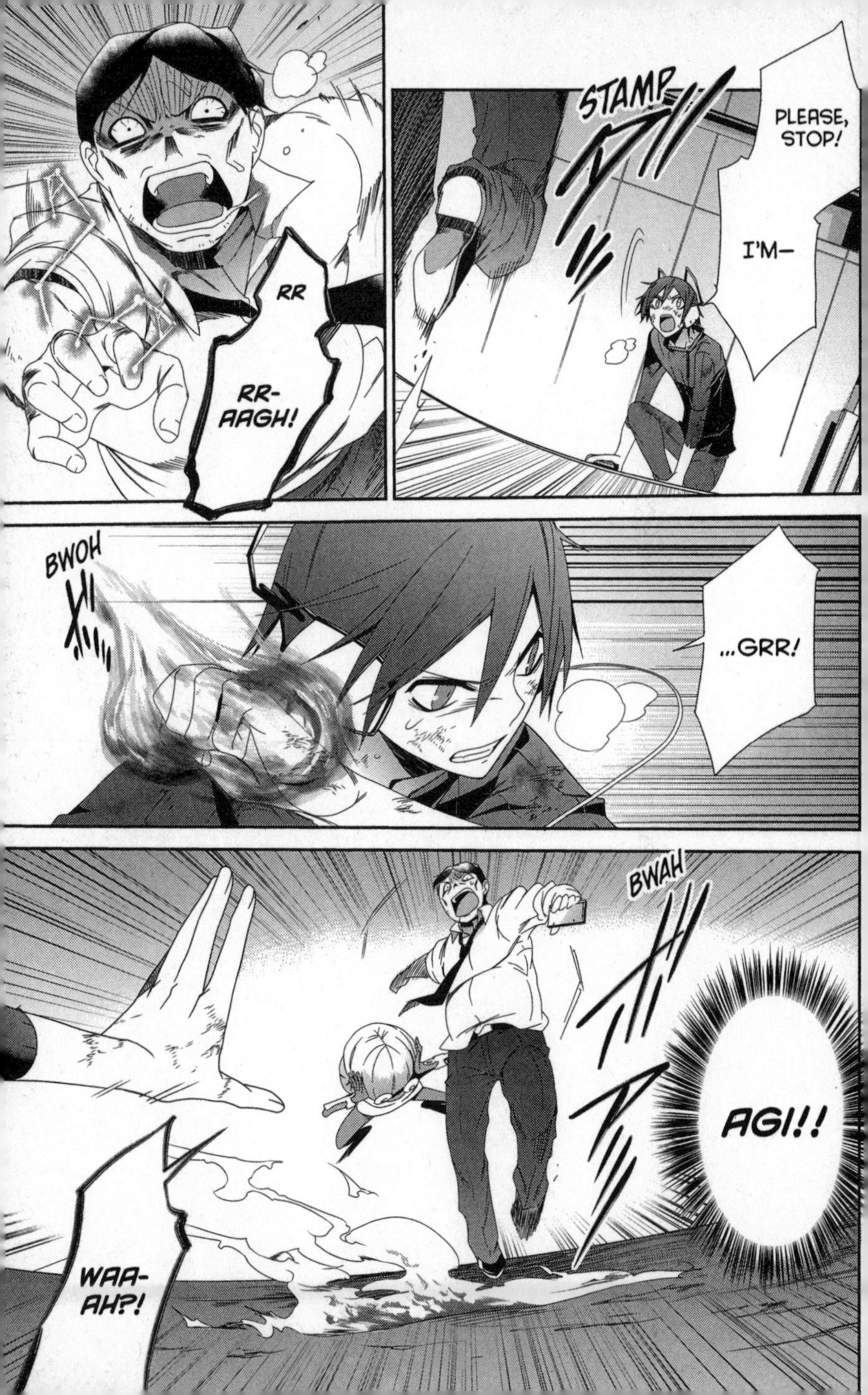

PLEASE, STOP!
I'M—
STAMP
RR
RR-AAGH!
...GRR!
BWOH
BWAH
AGI!!
WAA-AH?!

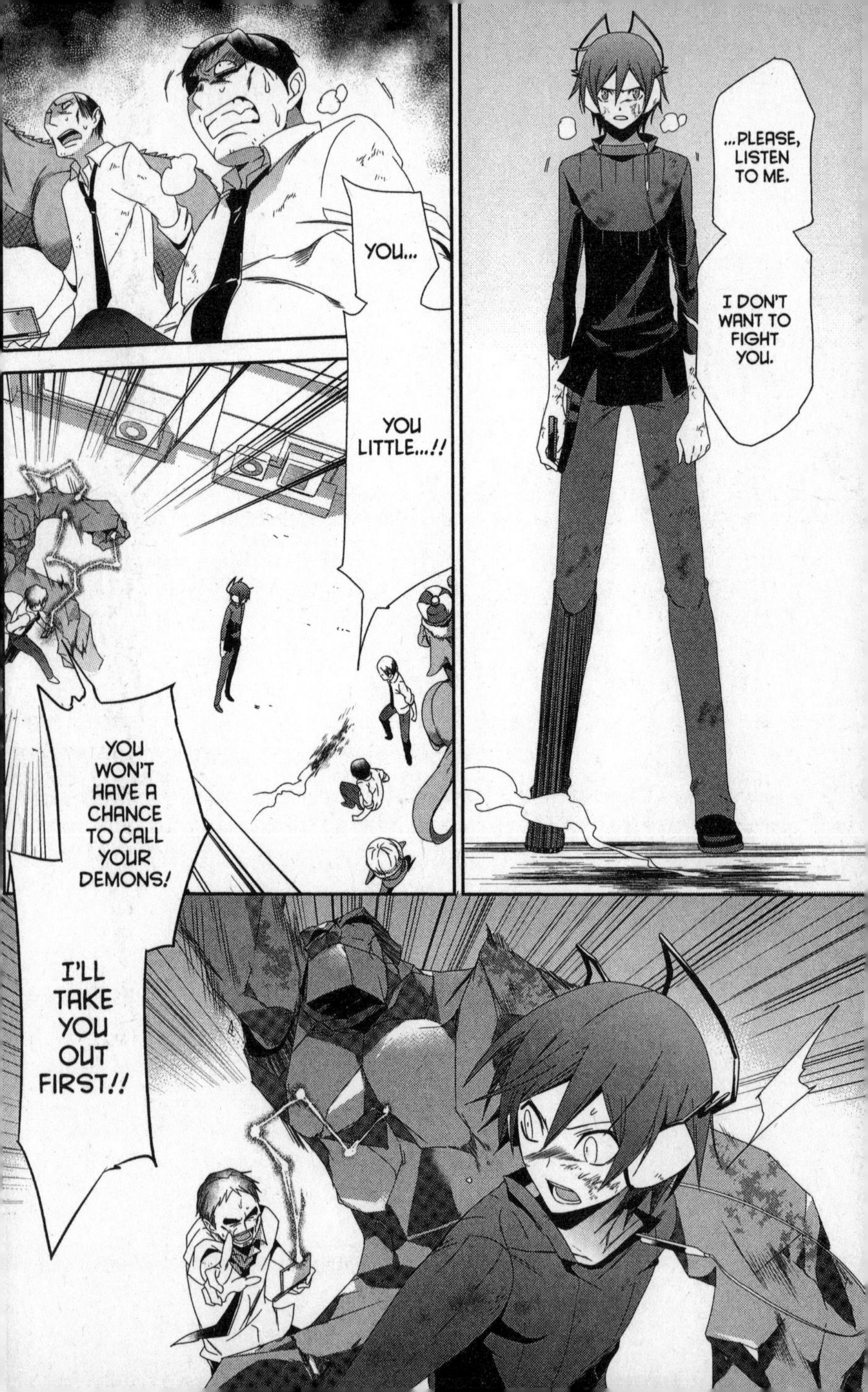
...PLEASE, LISTEN TO ME.
I DON'T WANT TO FIGHT YOU.
YOU...
YOU LITTLE...!!
YOU WON'T HAVE A CHANCE TO CALL YOUR DEMONS!
I'LL TAKE YOU OUT FIRST!!

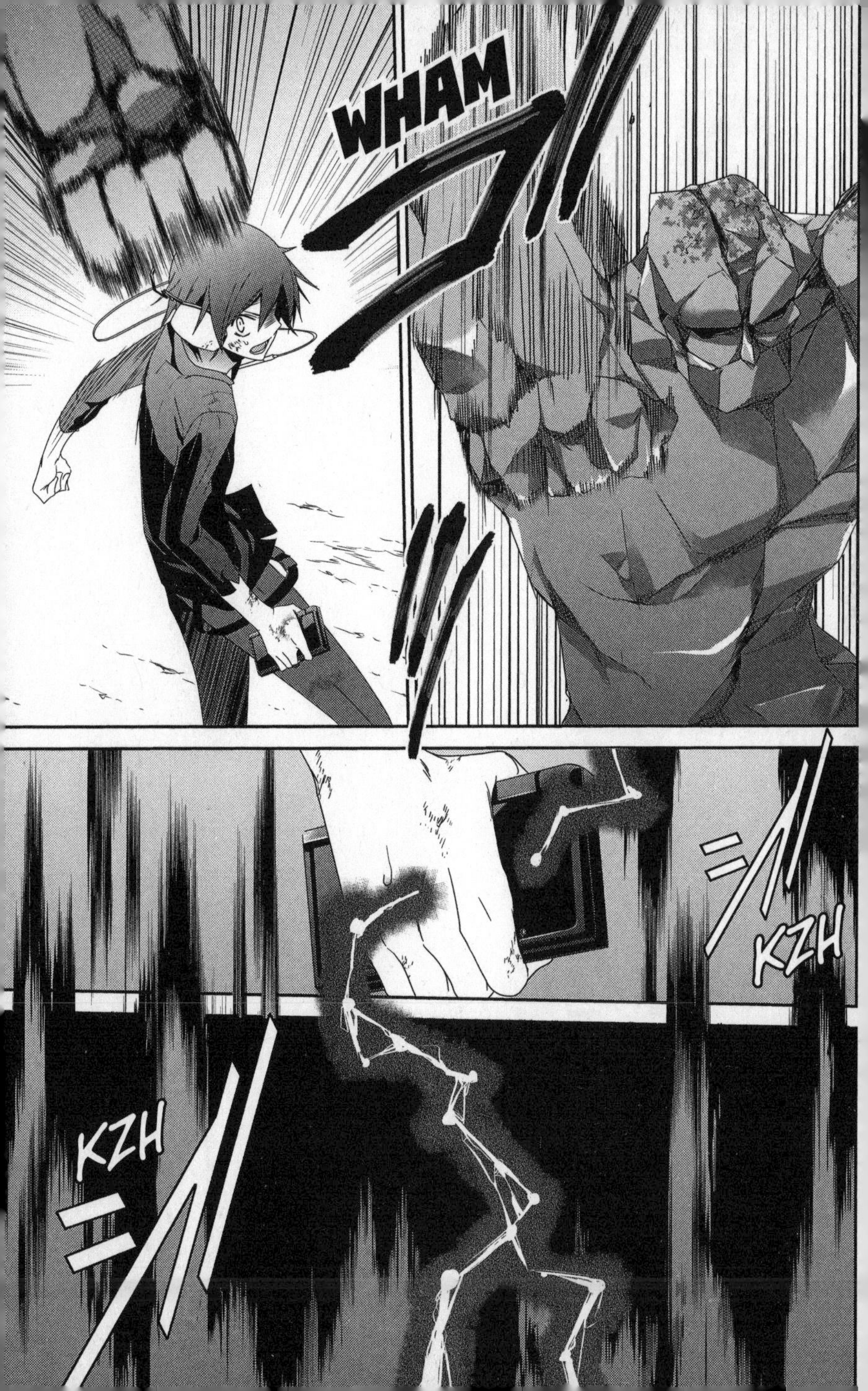
WHAM
KZH
KZH

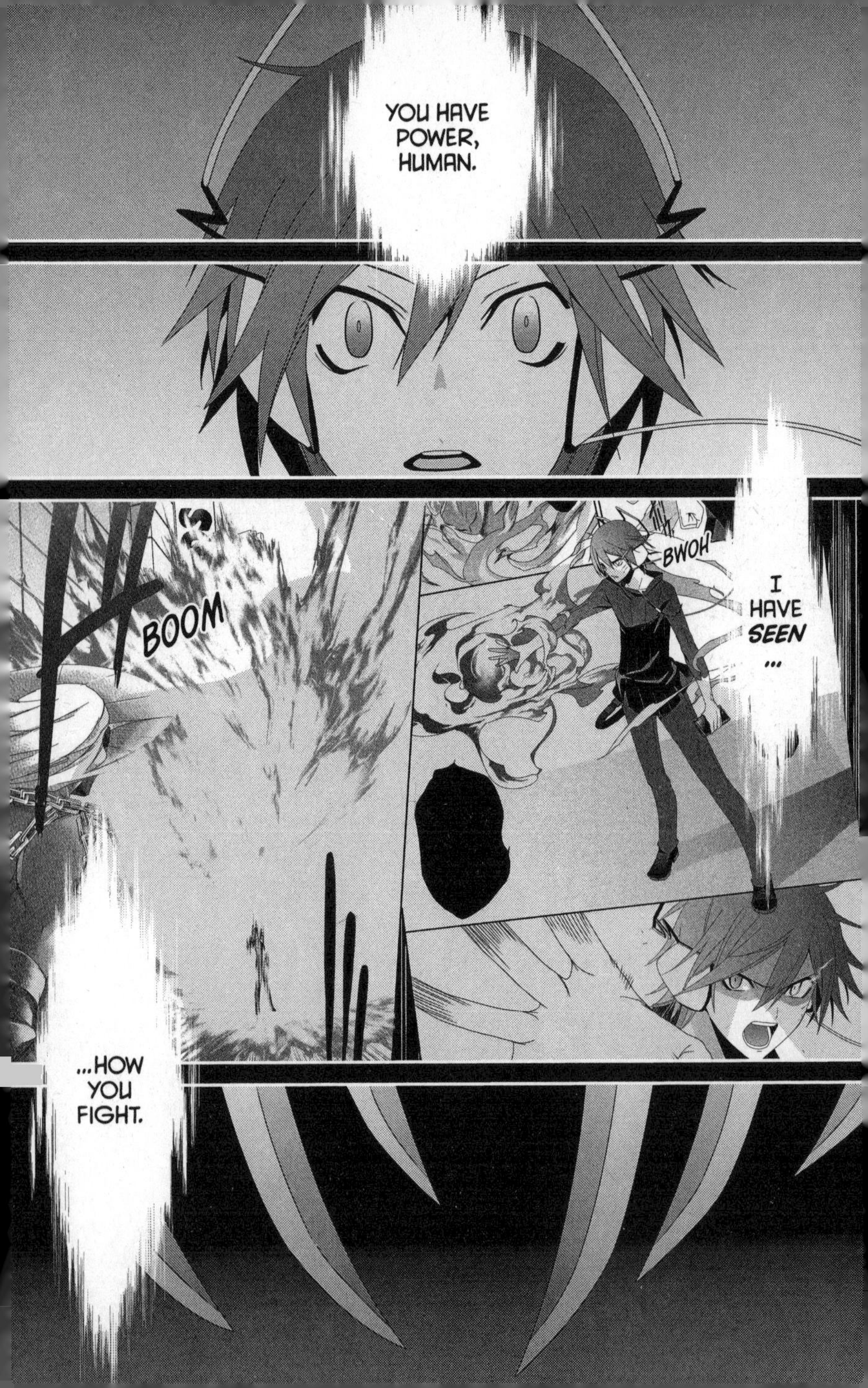
YOU HAVE POWER, HUMAN.
BWOH
I HAVE SEEN ...
BOOM
...HOW YOU FIGHT.

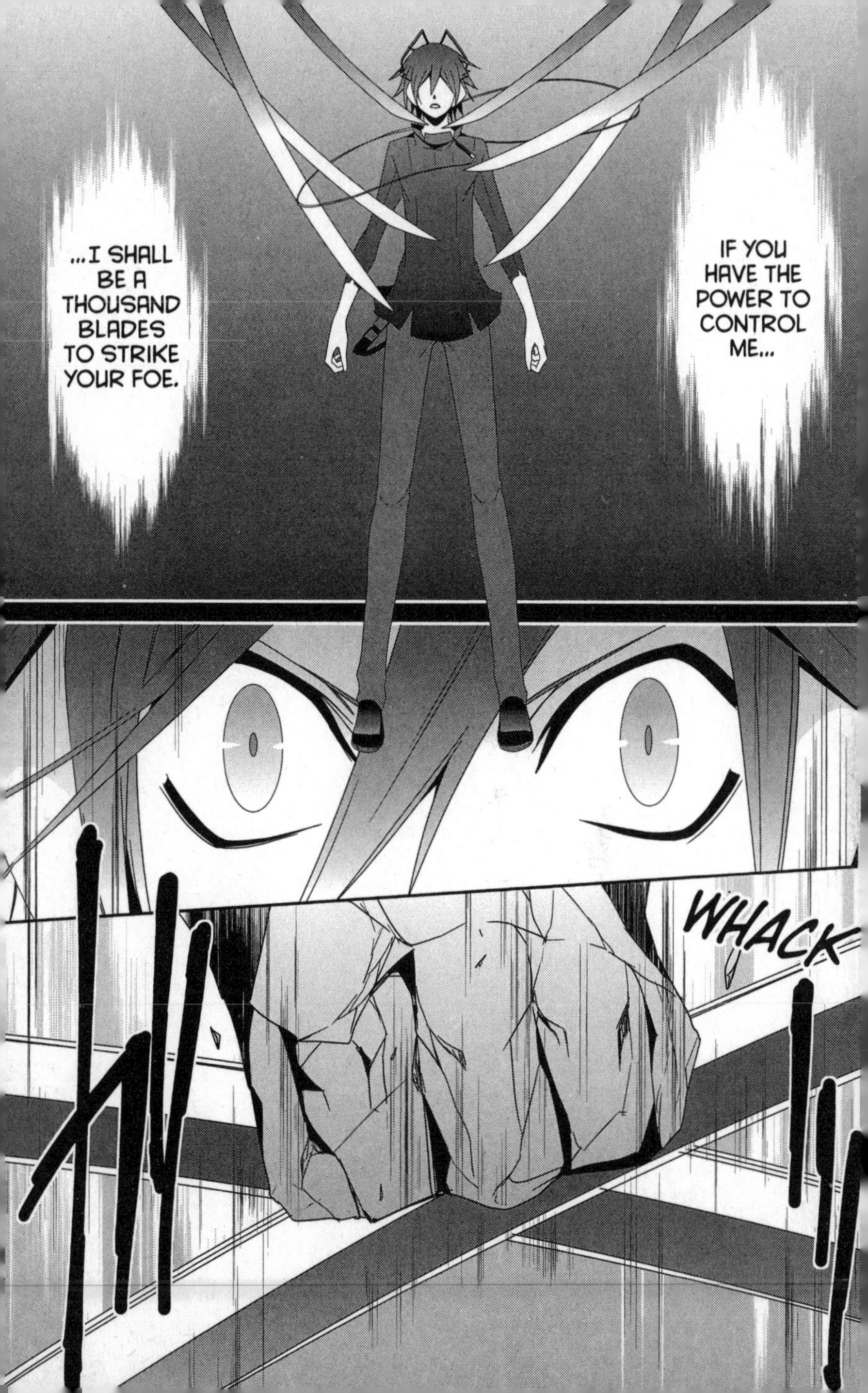
IF YOU HAVE THE POWER TO CONTROL ME...
...I SHALL BE A THOUSAND BLADES TO STRIKE YOUR FOE.
WHACK

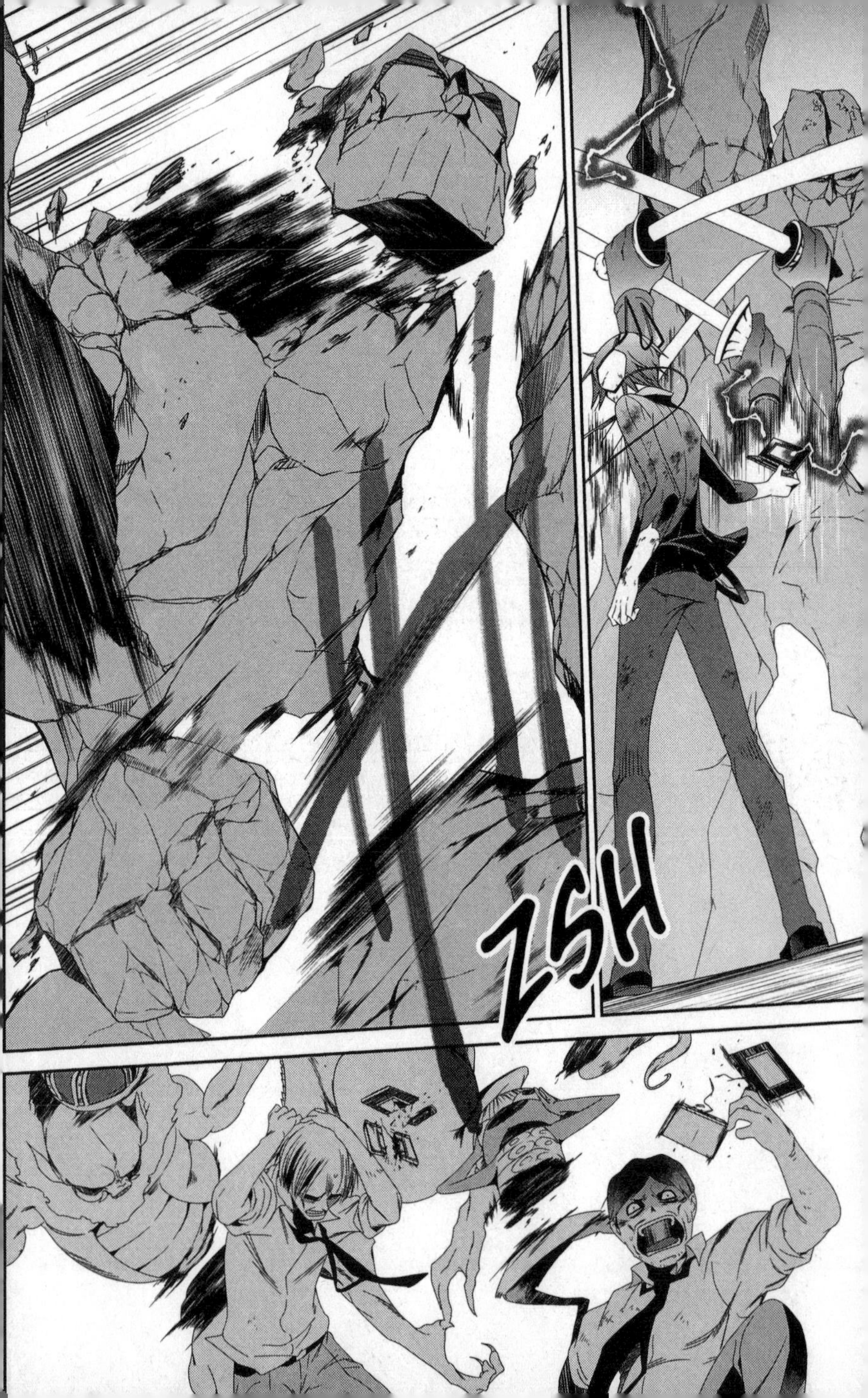
ZSH

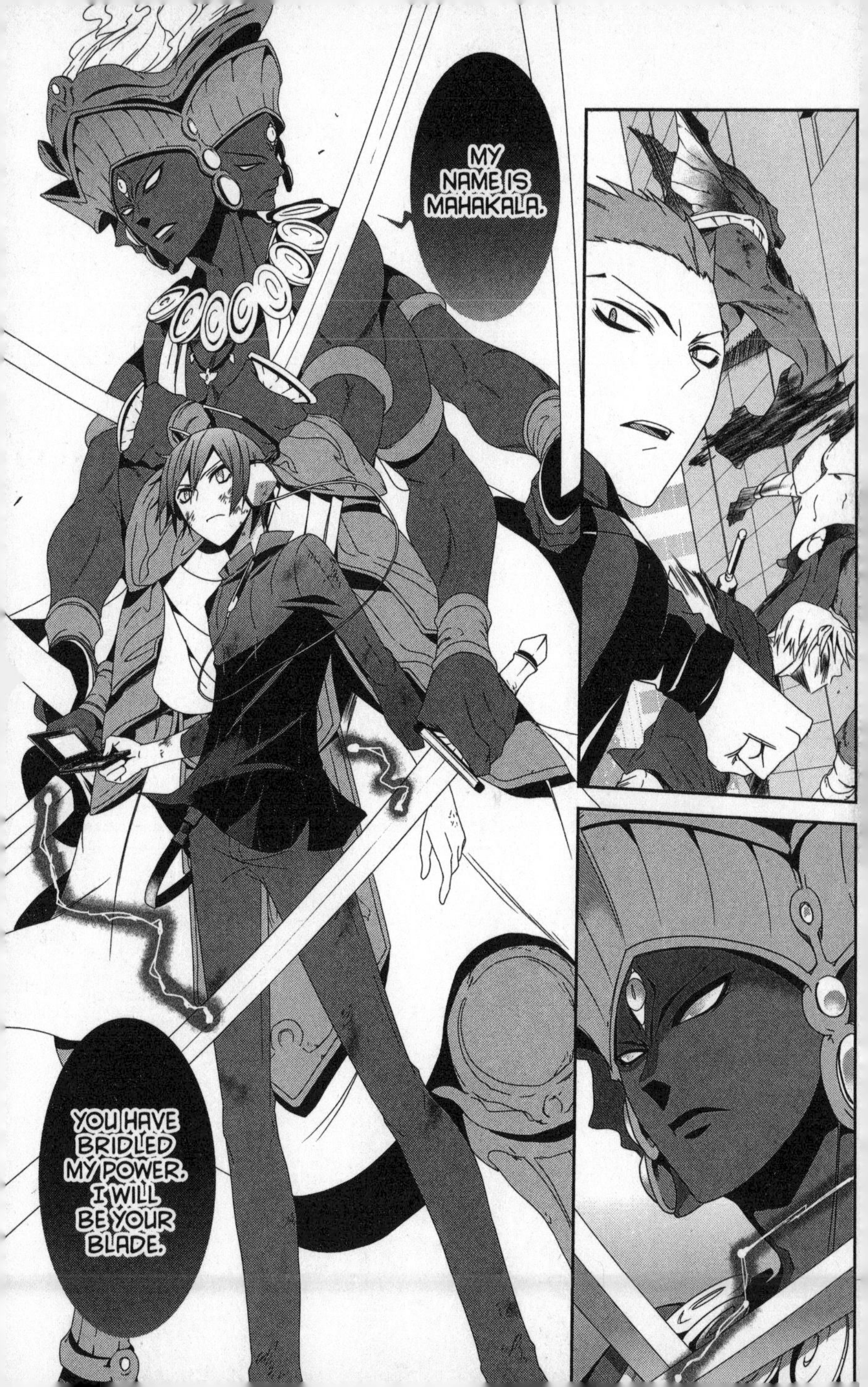
MY NAME IS MAHAKALA.
YOU HAVE BRIDLED MY POWER. I WILL BE YOUR BLADE.

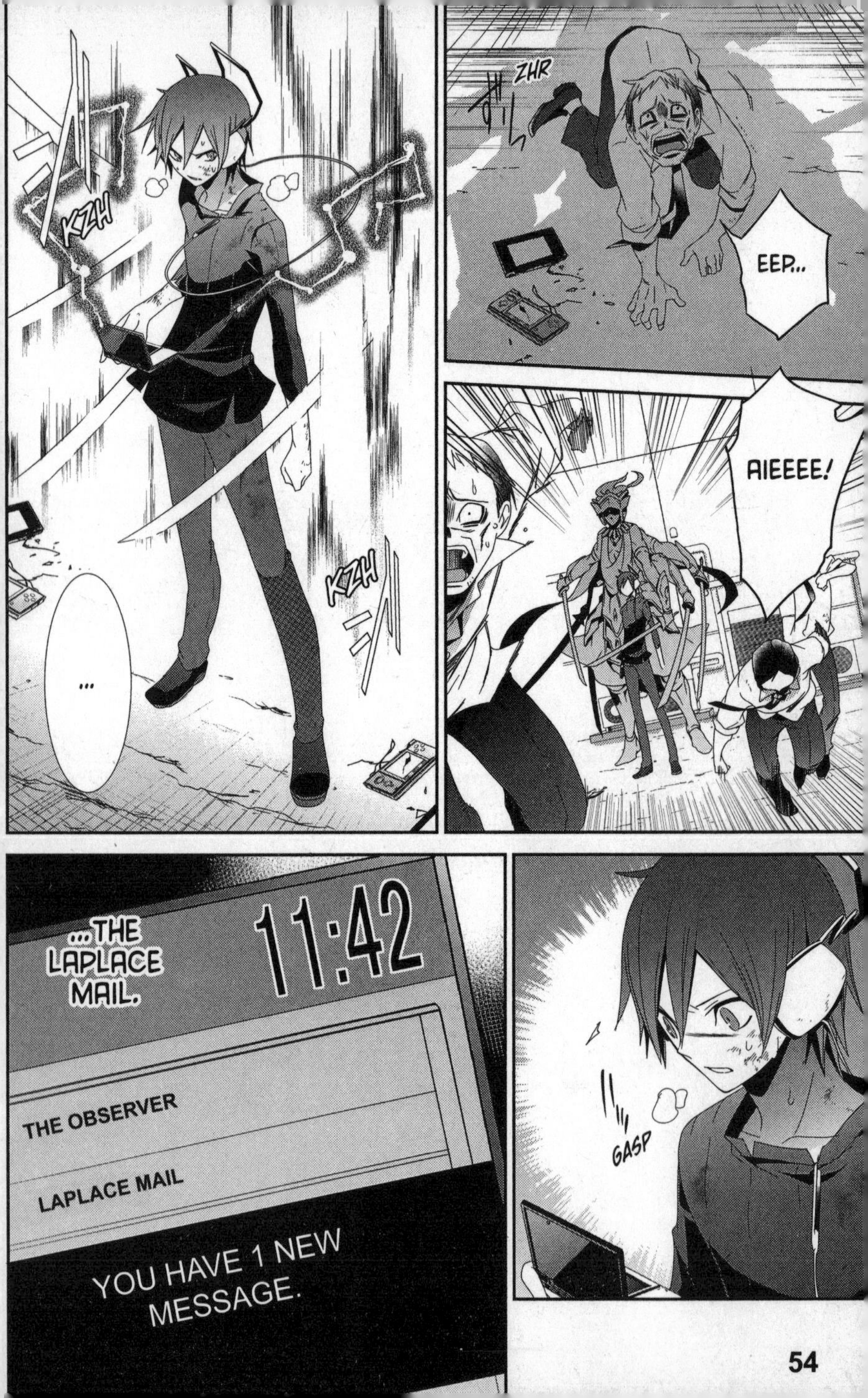
ZHR
EEP...
AIEEEE!
KZH
KZH
...
GASP
...THE LAPLACE MAIL.
11:42
THE OBSERVER
LAPLACE MAIL
YOU HAVE 1 NEW MESSAGE.

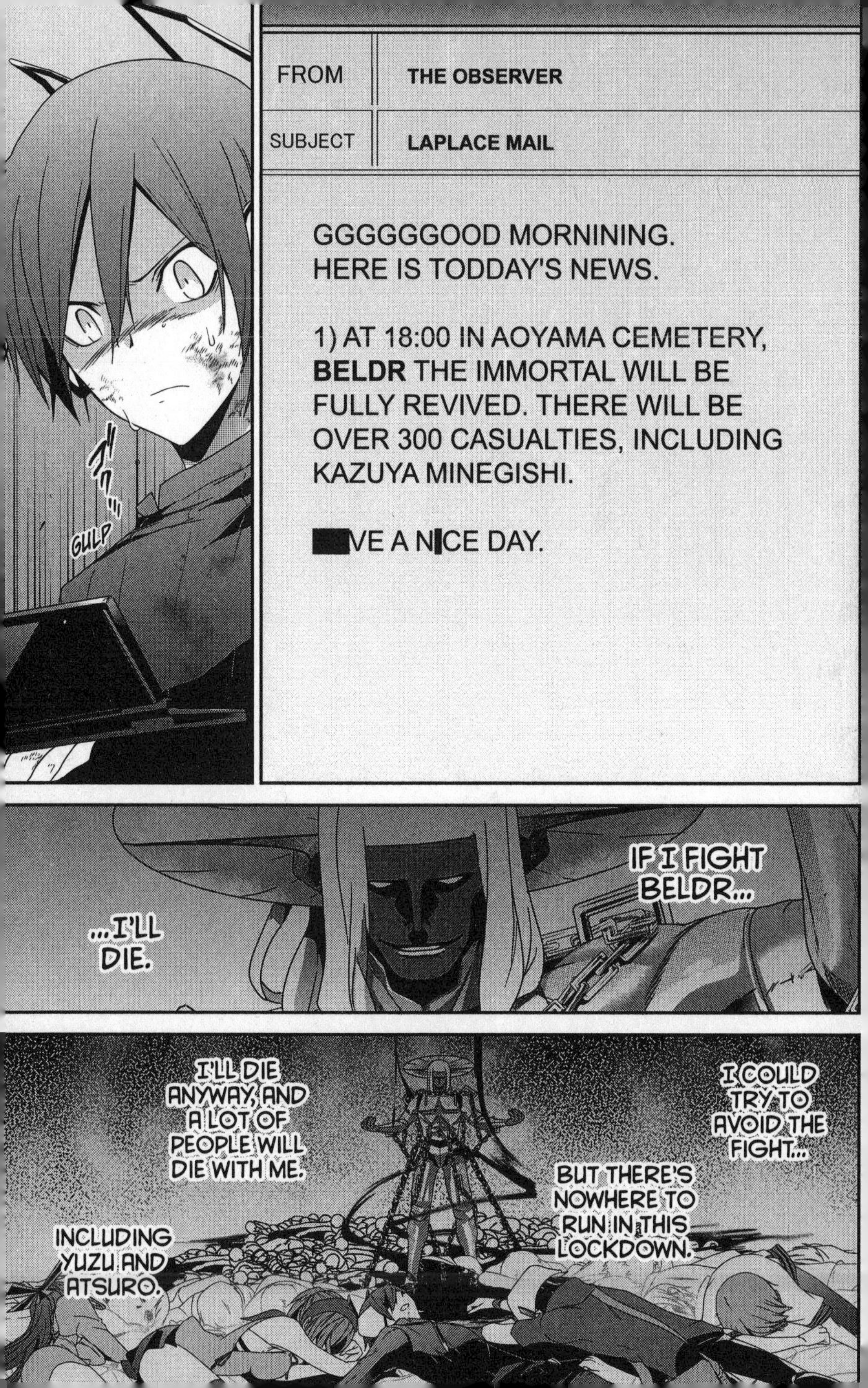
FROM
THE OBSERVER
SUBJECT
LAPLACE MAIL
GGGGGGOOD MORNINING.
HERE IS TODDAY'S NEWS.
1) AT 18:00 IN AOYAMA CEMETERY, BELDR THE IMMORTAL WILL BE FULLY REVIVED. THERE WILL BE OVER 300 CASUALTIES, INCLUDING KAZUYA MINEGISHI.
[redacted]VE A N[redacted]CE DAY.
GULP
IF I FIGHT BELDR...
...I'LL DIE.
I COULD TRY TO AVOID THE FIGHT...
BUT THERE'S NOWHERE TO RUN IN THIS LOCKDOWN.
I'LL DIE ANYWAY, AND A LOT OF PEOPLE WILL DIE WITH ME.
INCLUDING YUZU AND ATSURO.

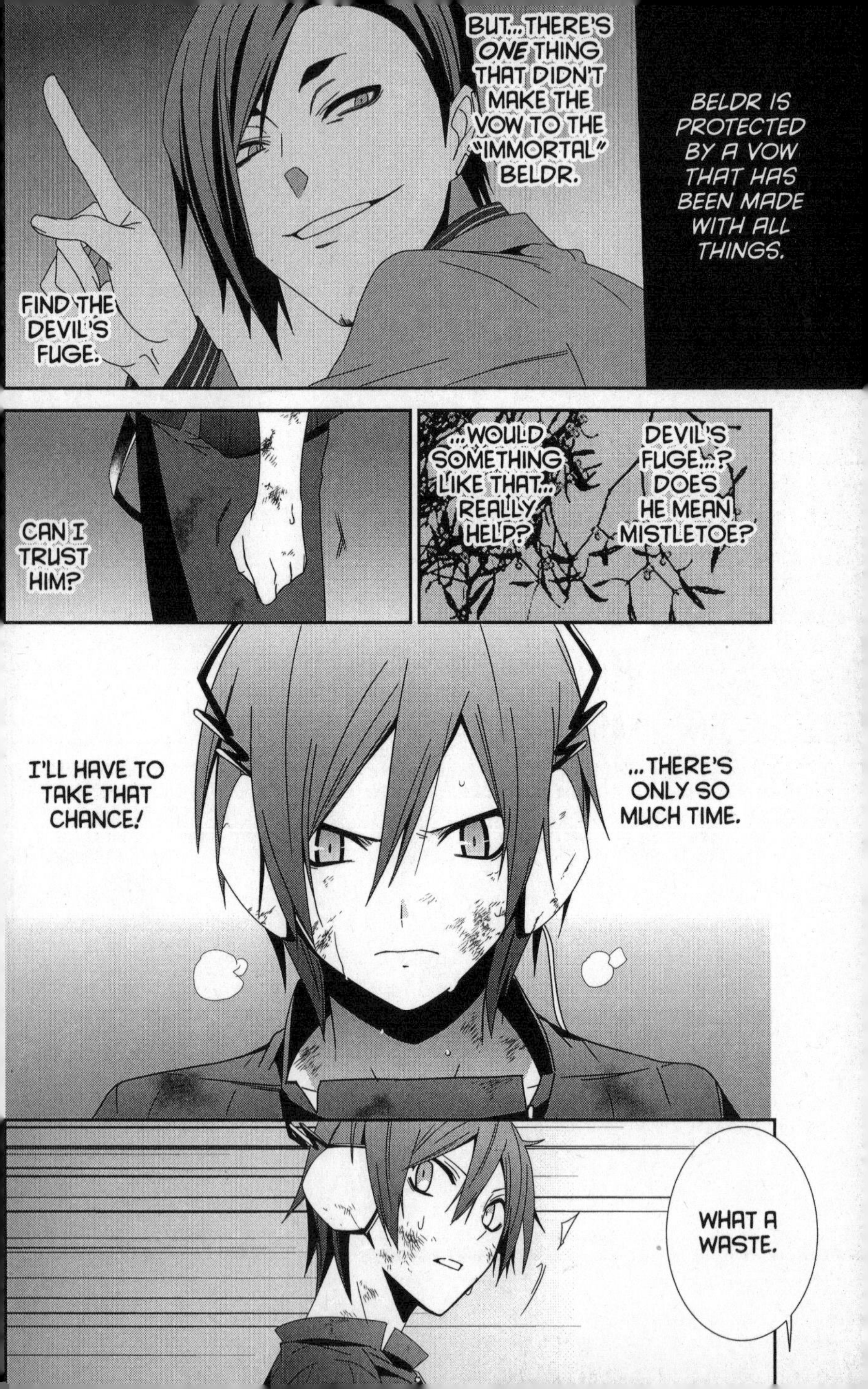
BELDR IS PROTECTED BY A VOW THAT HAS BEEN MADE WITH ALL THINGS.
BUT... THERE'S *ONE* THING THAT DIDN'T MAKE THE VOW TO THE "IMMORTAL" BELDR.
FIND THE DEVIL'S FUGE.
DEVIL'S FUGE...? DOES HE MEAN MISTLETOE?
...WOULD SOMETHING LIKE THAT... REALLY HELP?
CAN I TRUST HIM?
...THERE'S ONLY SO MUCH TIME.
I'LL HAVE TO TAKE THAT CHANCE!
WHAT A WASTE.

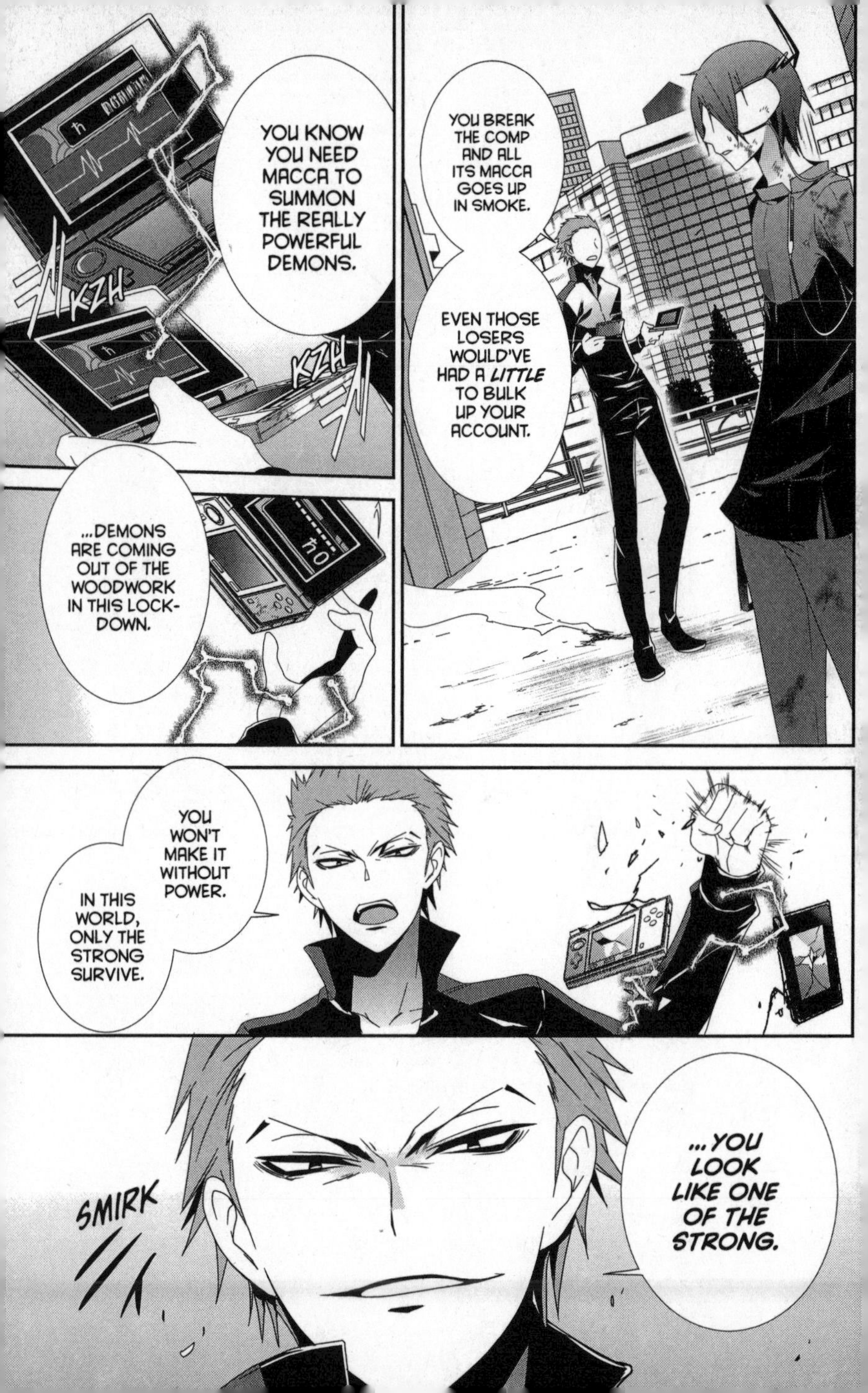
YOU BREAK THE COMP AND ALL ITS MACCA GOES UP IN SMOKE.
EVEN THOSE LOSERS WOULD'VE HAD A *LITTLE* TO BULK UP YOUR ACCOUNT.
YOU KNOW YOU NEED MACCA TO SUMMON THE REALLY POWERFUL DEMONS.
KZH
KZH
...DEMONS ARE COMING OUT OF THE WOODWORK IN THIS LOCK-DOWN.
YOU WON'T MAKE IT WITHOUT POWER.
IN THIS WORLD, ONLY THE STRONG SURVIVE.
...YOU LOOK LIKE ONE OF THE STRONG.
SMIRK

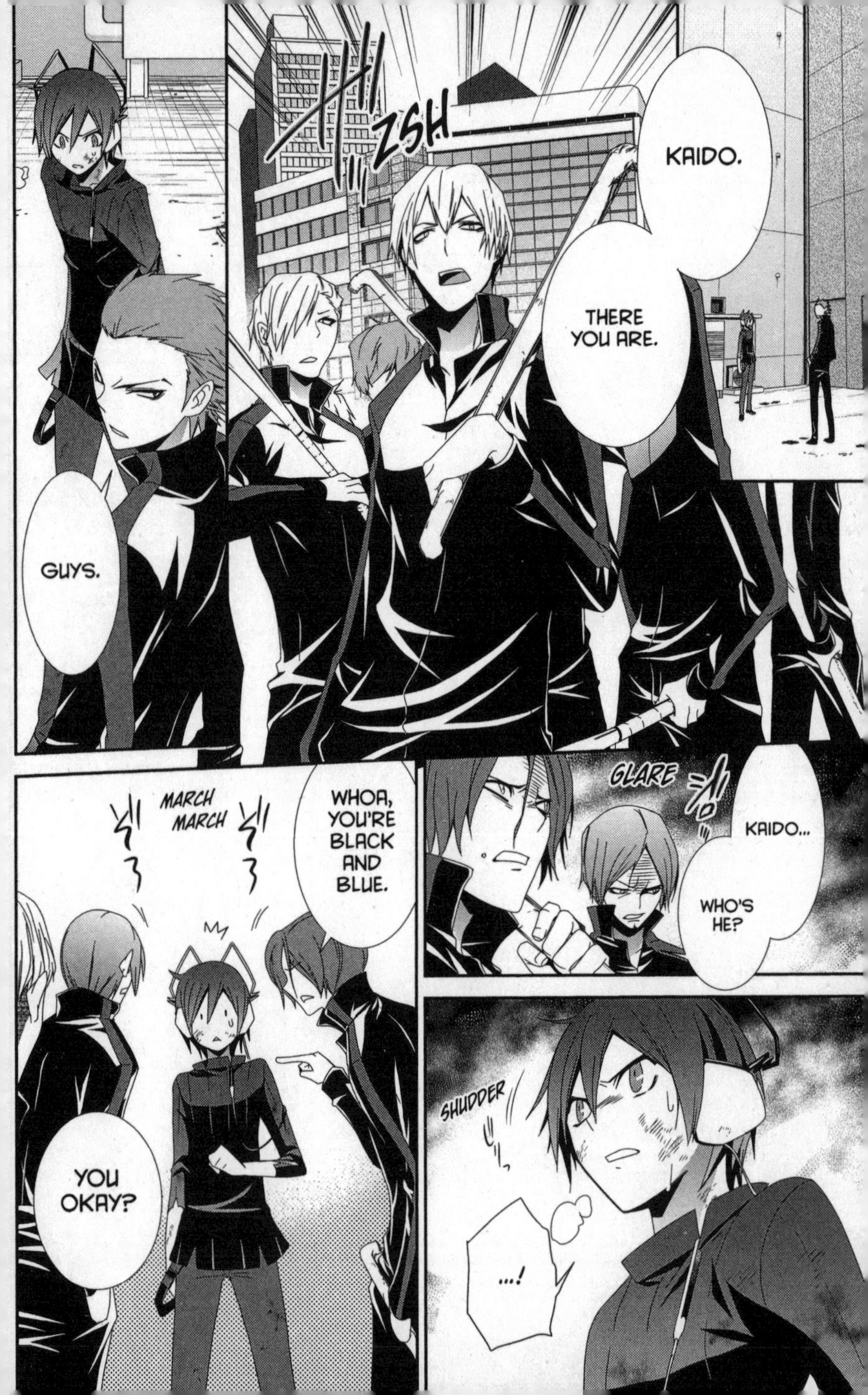
ZSH
KAIDO.
THERE YOU ARE.
GUYS.
GLARE
KAIDO...
WHO'S HE?
SHUDDER
...!
WHOA, YOU'RE BLACK AND BLUE.
MARCH MARCH
YOU OKAY?

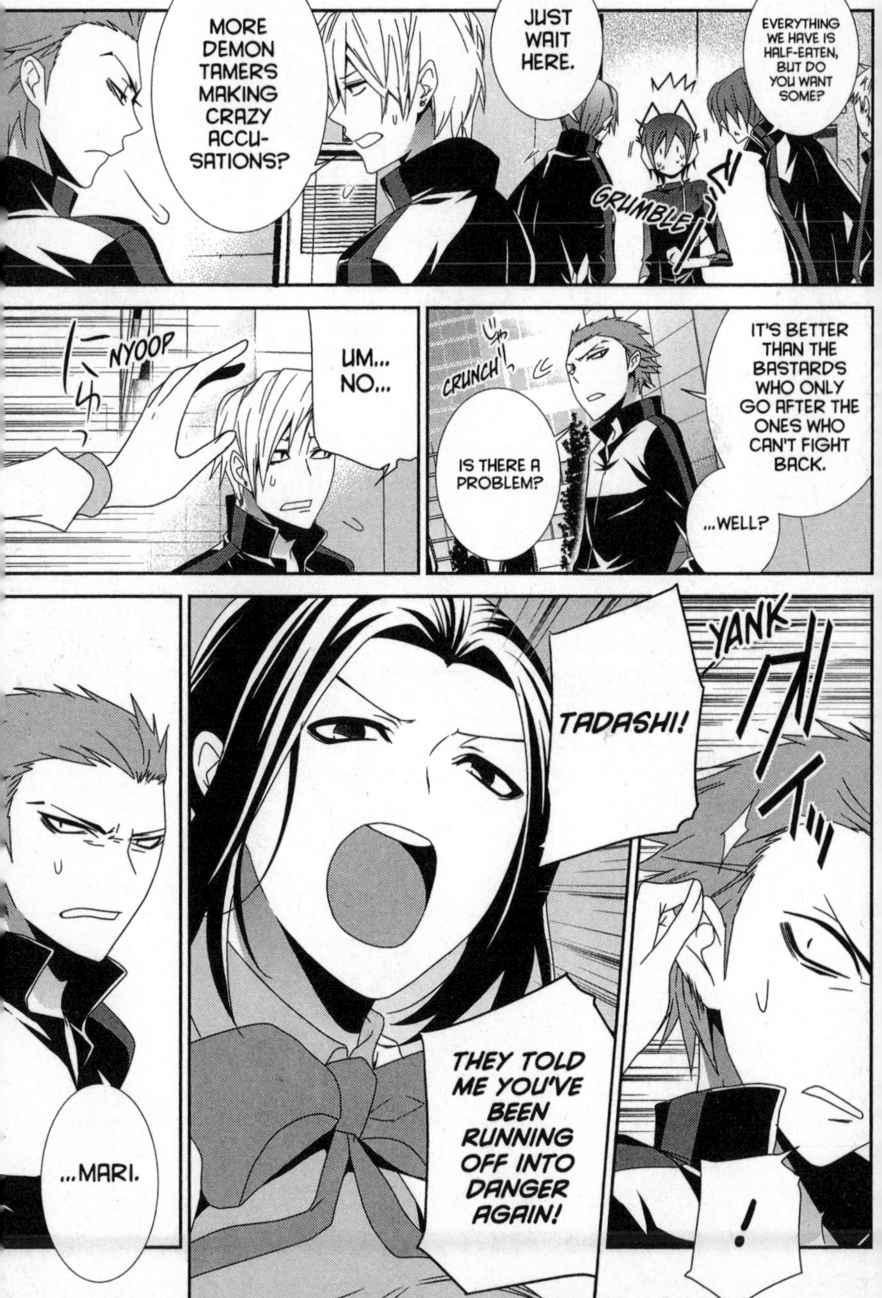
EVERYTHING WE HAVE IS HALF-EATEN, BUT DO YOU WANT SOME?
GRUMBLE
JUST WAIT HERE.
MORE DEMON TAMERS MAKING CRAZY ACCUSATIONS?
IT'S BETTER THAN THE BASTARDS WHO ONLY GO AFTER THE ONES WHO CAN'T FIGHT BACK.
CRUNCH
IS THERE A PROBLEM?
...WELL?
NYOOP
UM... NO...
YANK
TADASHI!
THEY TOLD ME YOU'VE BEEN RUNNING OFF INTO DANGER AGAIN!
!
...MARI.

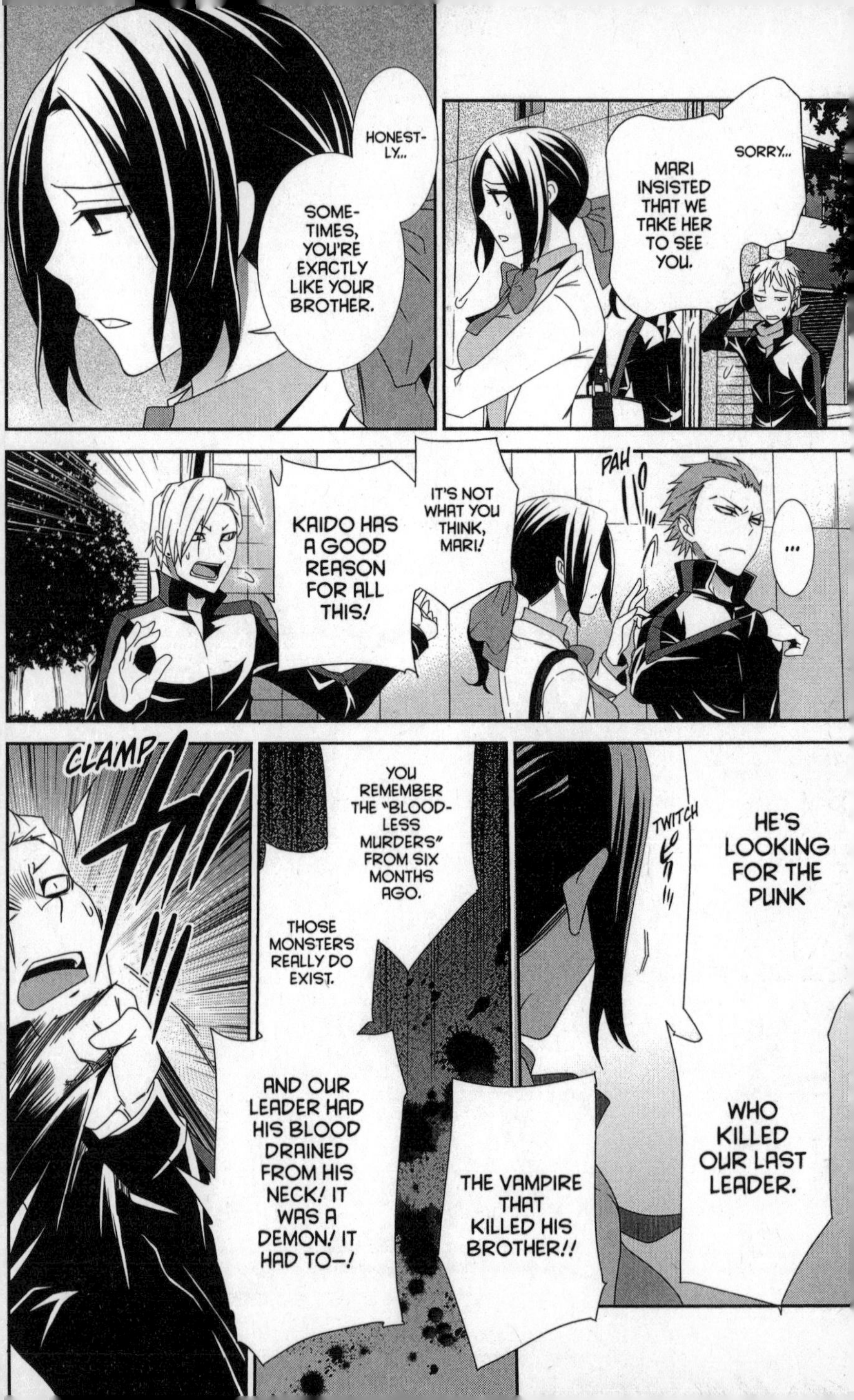
SORRY...
MARI INSISTED THAT WE TAKE HER TO SEE YOU.
HONEST-LY...
SOME-TIMES, YOU'RE EXACTLY LIKE YOUR BROTHER.
PAH
...
IT'S NOT WHAT YOU THINK, MARI!
KAIDO HAS A GOOD REASON FOR ALL THIS!
TWITCH
HE'S LOOKING FOR THE PUNK
WHO KILLED OUR LAST LEADER.
YOU REMEMBER THE "BLOOD-LESS MURDERS" FROM SIX MONTHS AGO.
THOSE MONSTERS REALLY DO EXIST.
THE VAMPIRE THAT KILLED HIS BROTHER!!
CLAMP
AND OUR LEADER HAD HIS BLOOD DRAINED FROM HIS NECK! IT WAS A DEMON! IT HAD TO—!

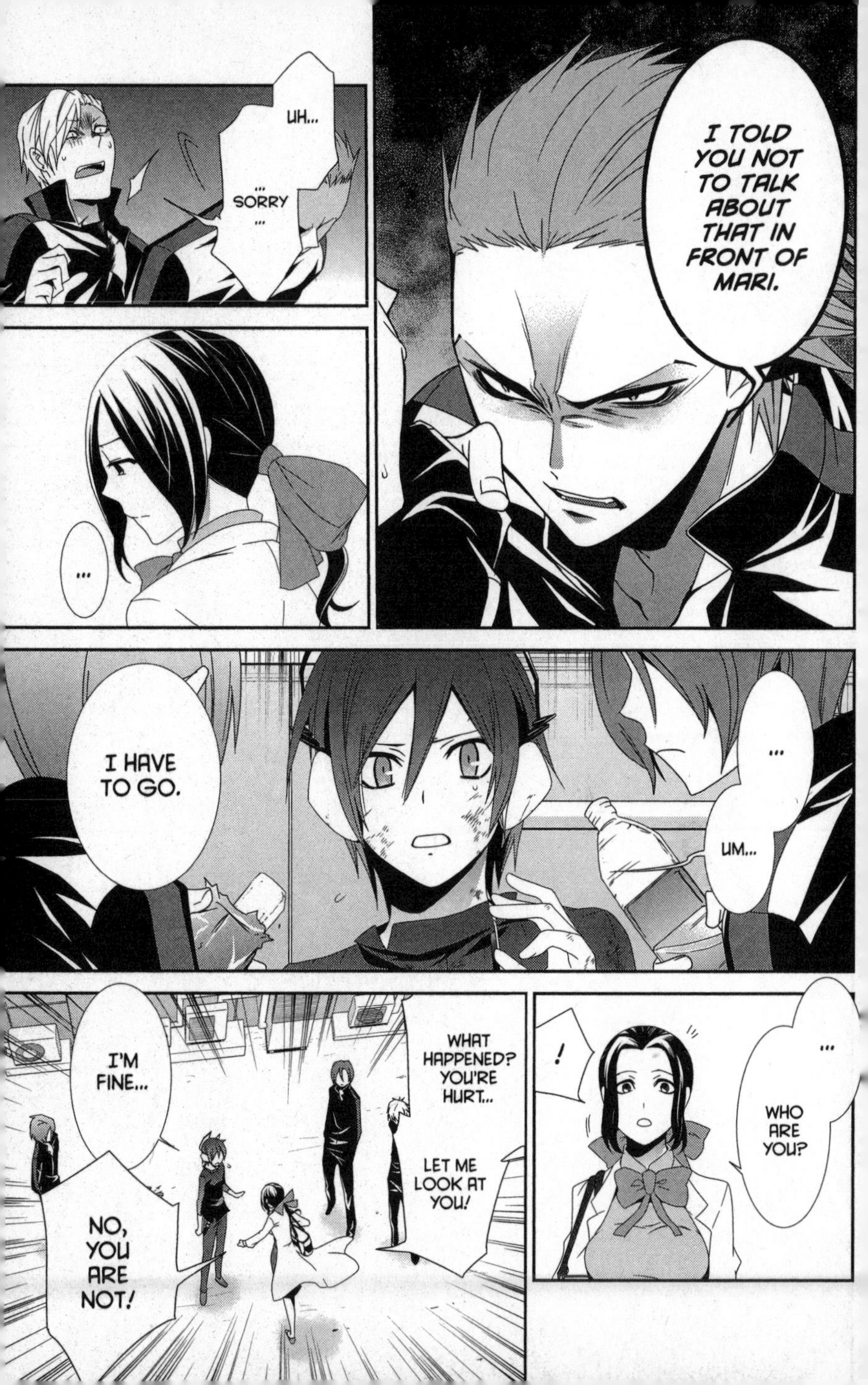
I TOLD YOU NOT TO TALK ABOUT THAT IN FRONT OF MARI.
UH...
... SORRY ...
...
...
UM...
I HAVE TO GO.
...
WHO ARE YOU?
!
WHAT HAPPENED? YOU'RE HURT...
LET ME LOOK AT YOU!
I'M FINE...
NO, YOU ARE NOT!

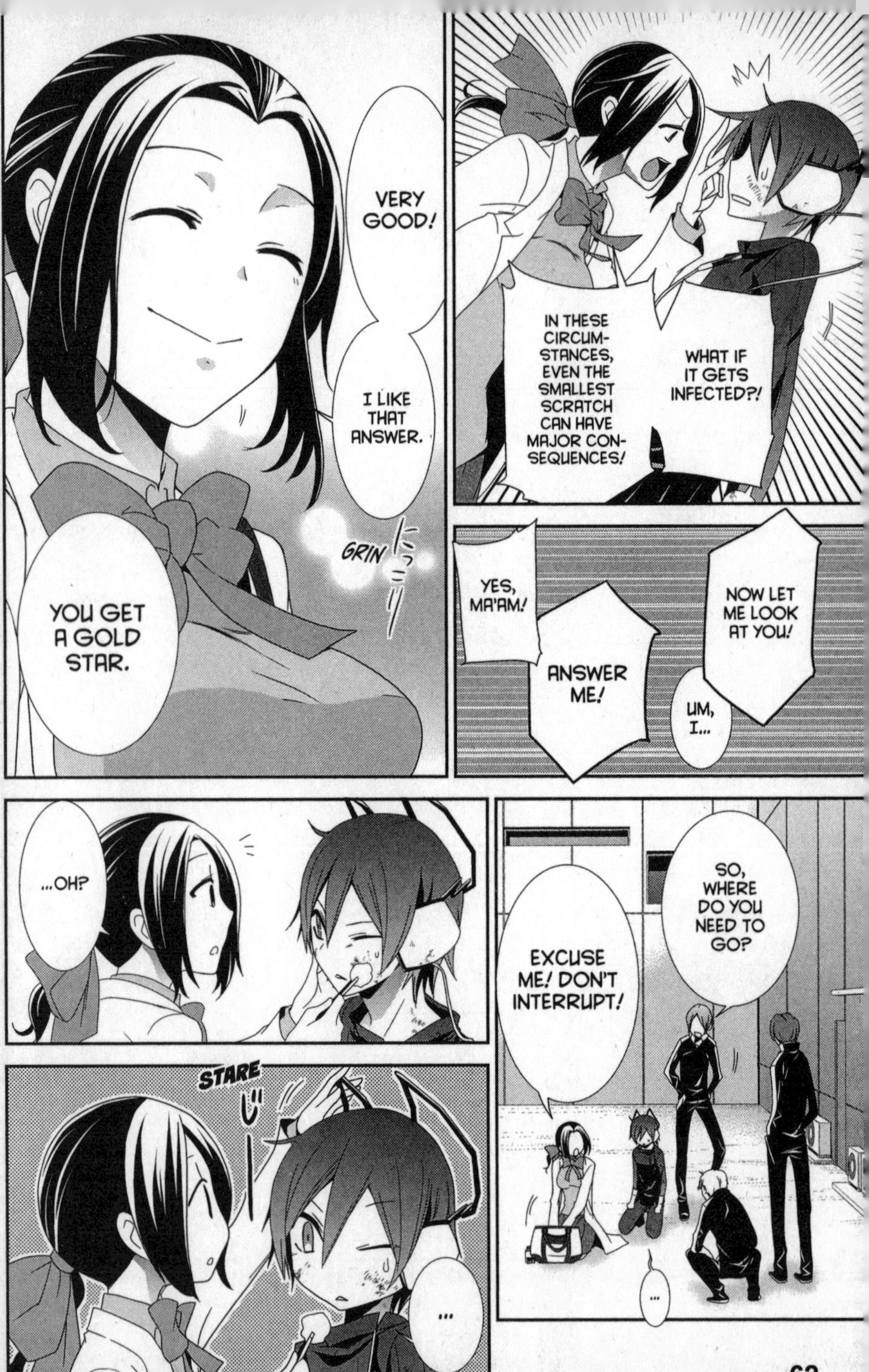
WHAT IF IT GETS INFECTED?!
IN THESE CIRCUM-STANCES, EVEN THE SMALLEST SCRATCH CAN HAVE MAJOR CON-SEQUENCES!
NOW LET ME LOOK AT YOU!
UM, I...
ANSWER ME!
YES, MA'AM!
VERY GOOD!
I LIKE THAT ANSWER.
GRIN
YOU GET A GOLD STAR.
SO, WHERE DO YOU NEED TO GO?
EXCUSE ME! DON'T INTERRUPT!
...
...OH?
STARE
...

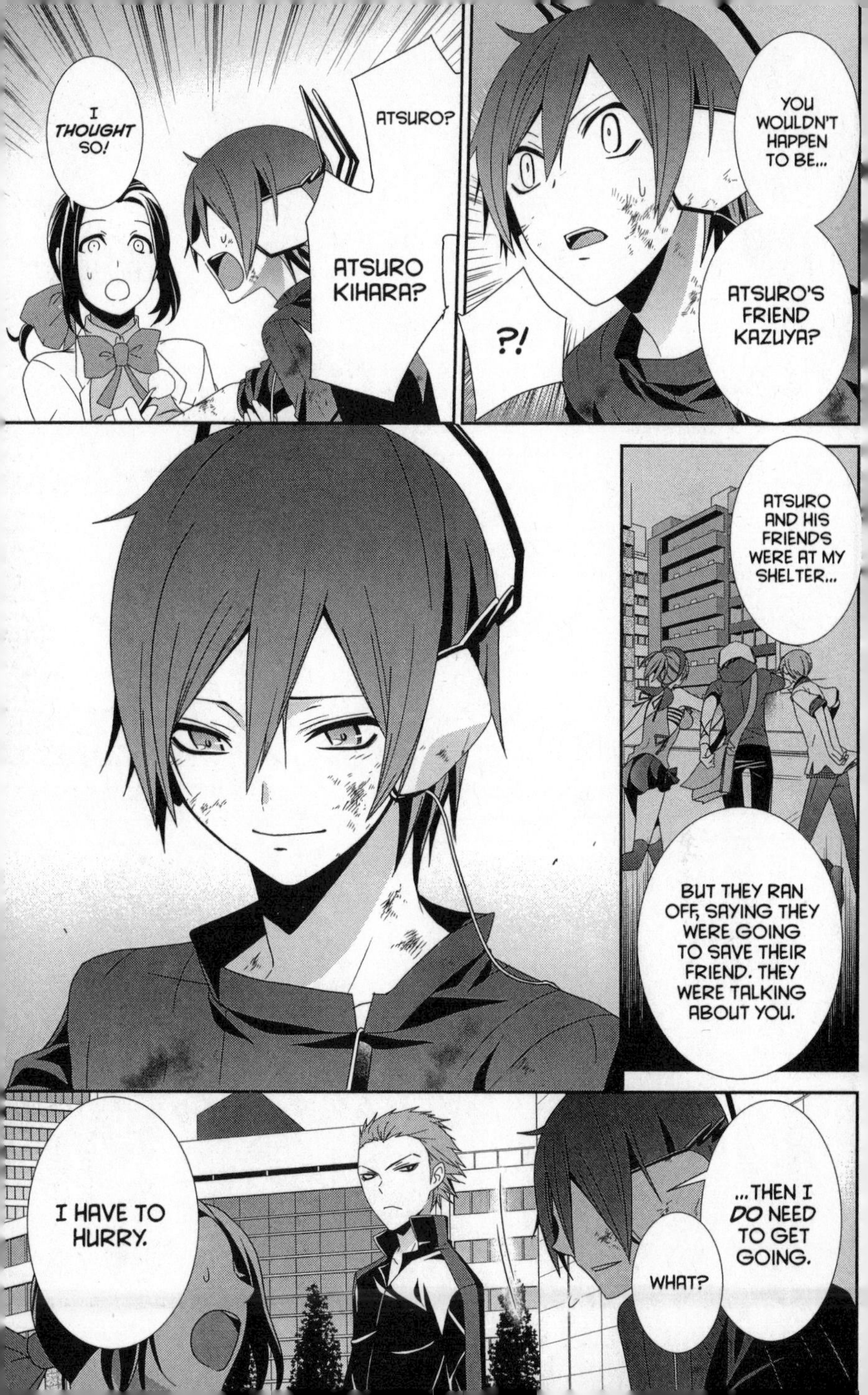
YOU WOULDN'T HAPPEN TO BE...
ATSURO'S FRIEND KAZUYA?
?!
ATSURO?
ATSURO KIHARA?
I *THOUGHT* SO!
ATSURO AND HIS FRIENDS WERE AT MY SHELTER...
BUT THEY RAN OFF, SAYING THEY WERE GOING TO SAVE THEIR FRIEND. THEY WERE TALKING ABOUT YOU.
...THEN I *DO* NEED TO GET GOING.
WHAT?
I HAVE TO HURRY.

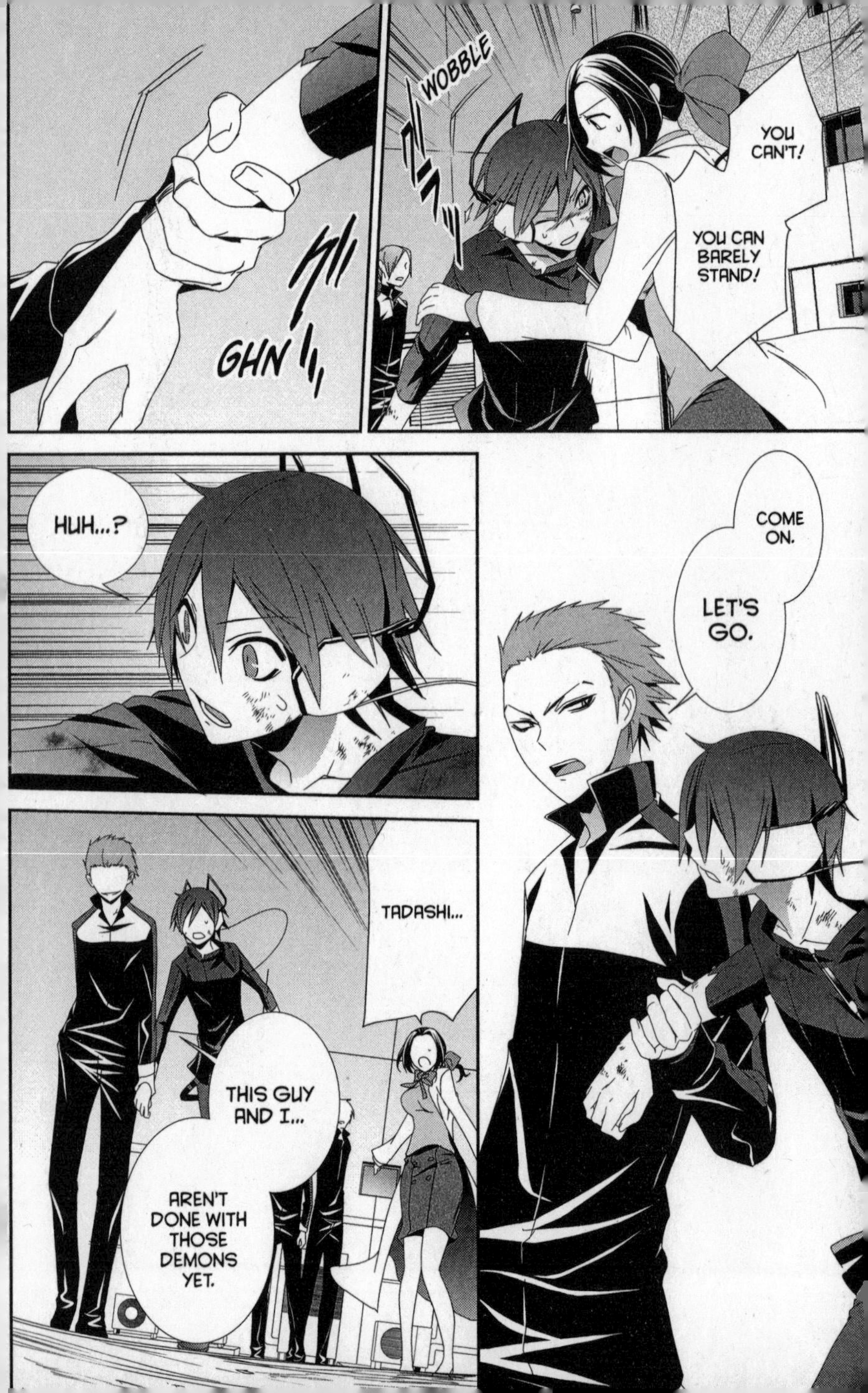
WOBBLE
YOU CAN'T!
YOU CAN BARELY STAND!
GHN
COME ON.
LET'S GO.
HUH...?
TADASHI...
THIS GUY AND I...
AREN'T DONE WITH THOSE DEMONS YET.

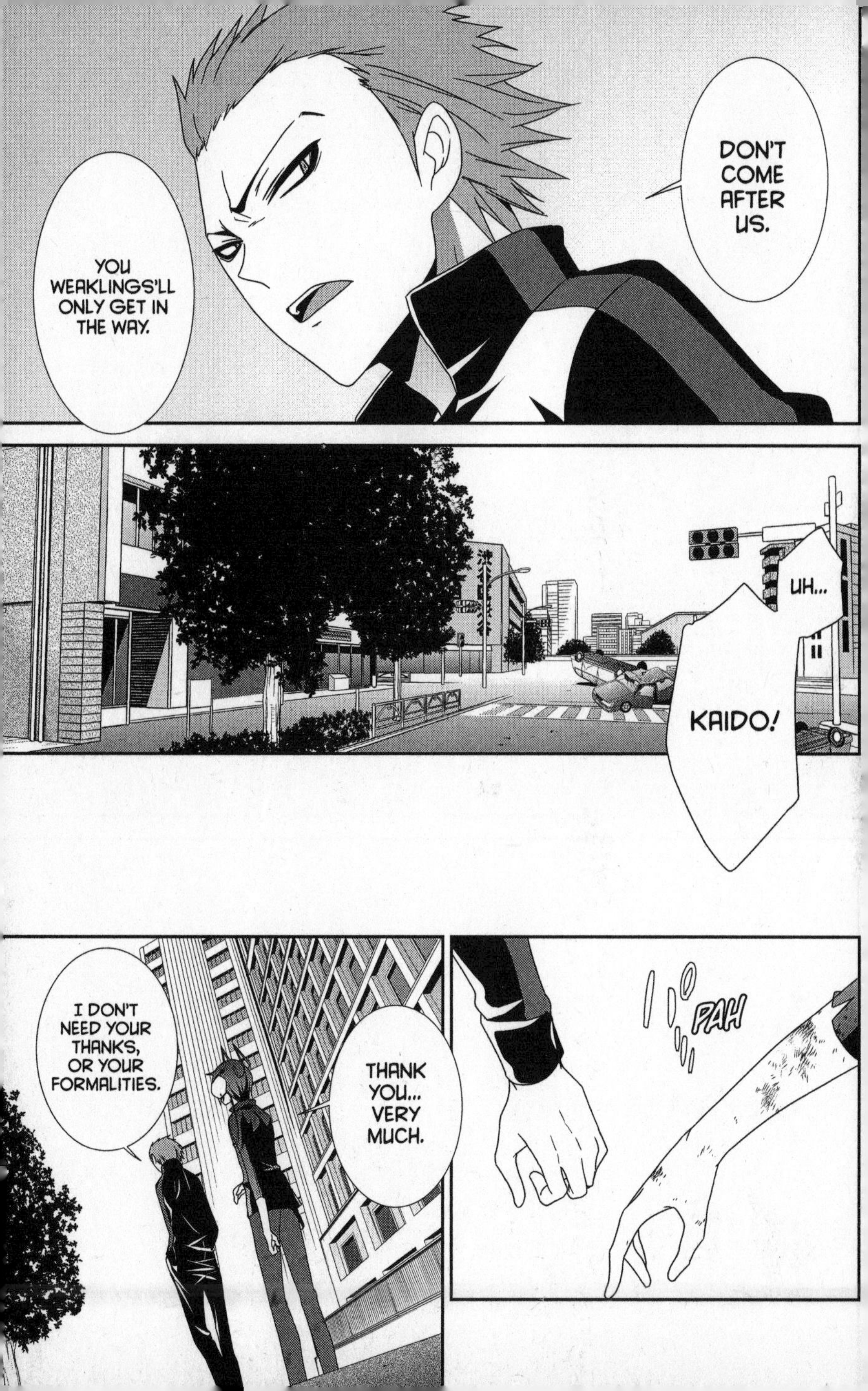
DON'T COME AFTER US.
YOU WEAKLINGS'LL ONLY GET IN THE WAY.
UH... KAIDO!
PAH
THANK YOU... VERY MUCH.
I DON'T NEED YOUR THANKS, OR YOUR FORMALITIES.

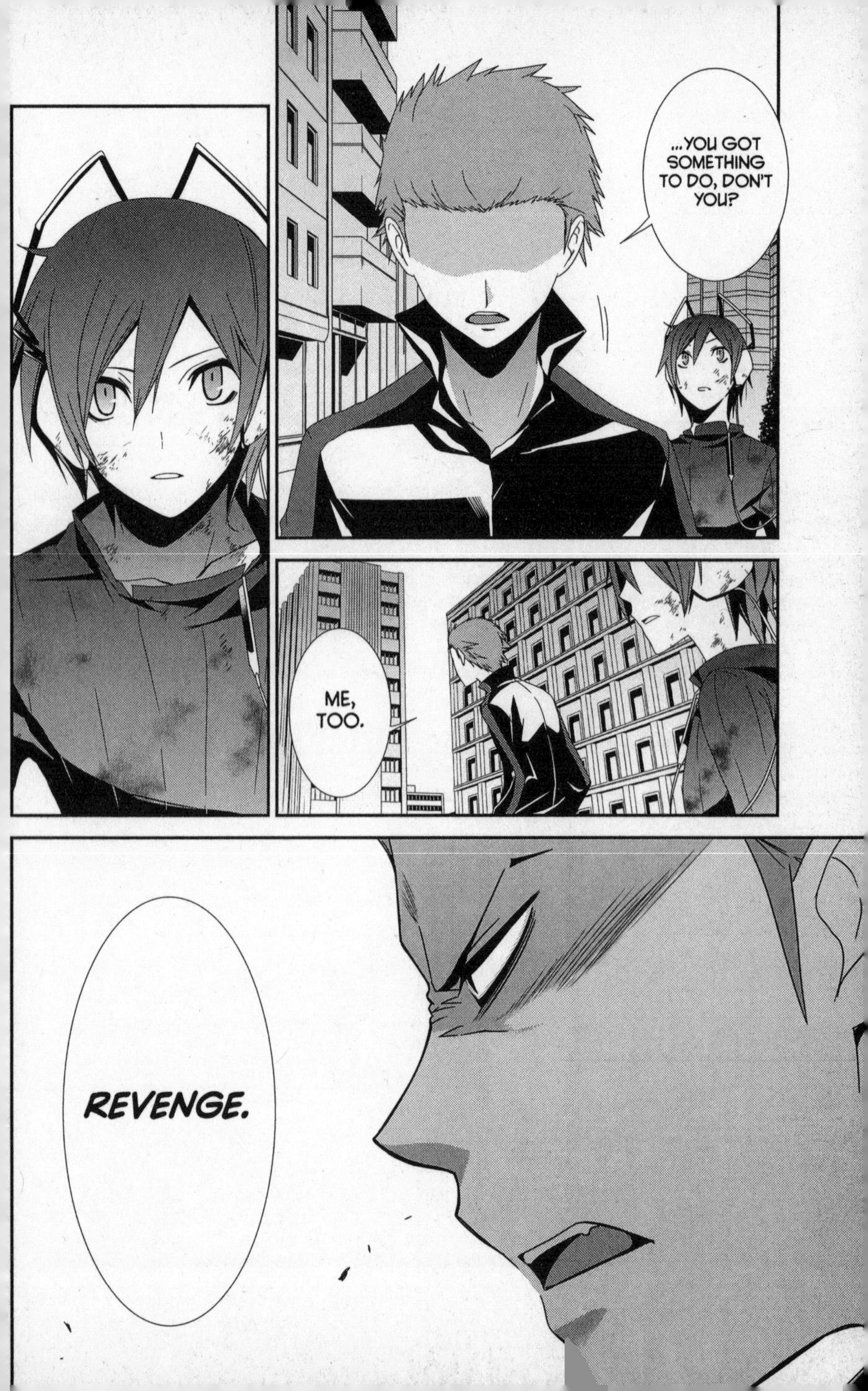
...YOU GOT SOMETHING TO DO, DON'T YOU?
ME, TOO.
REVENGE.

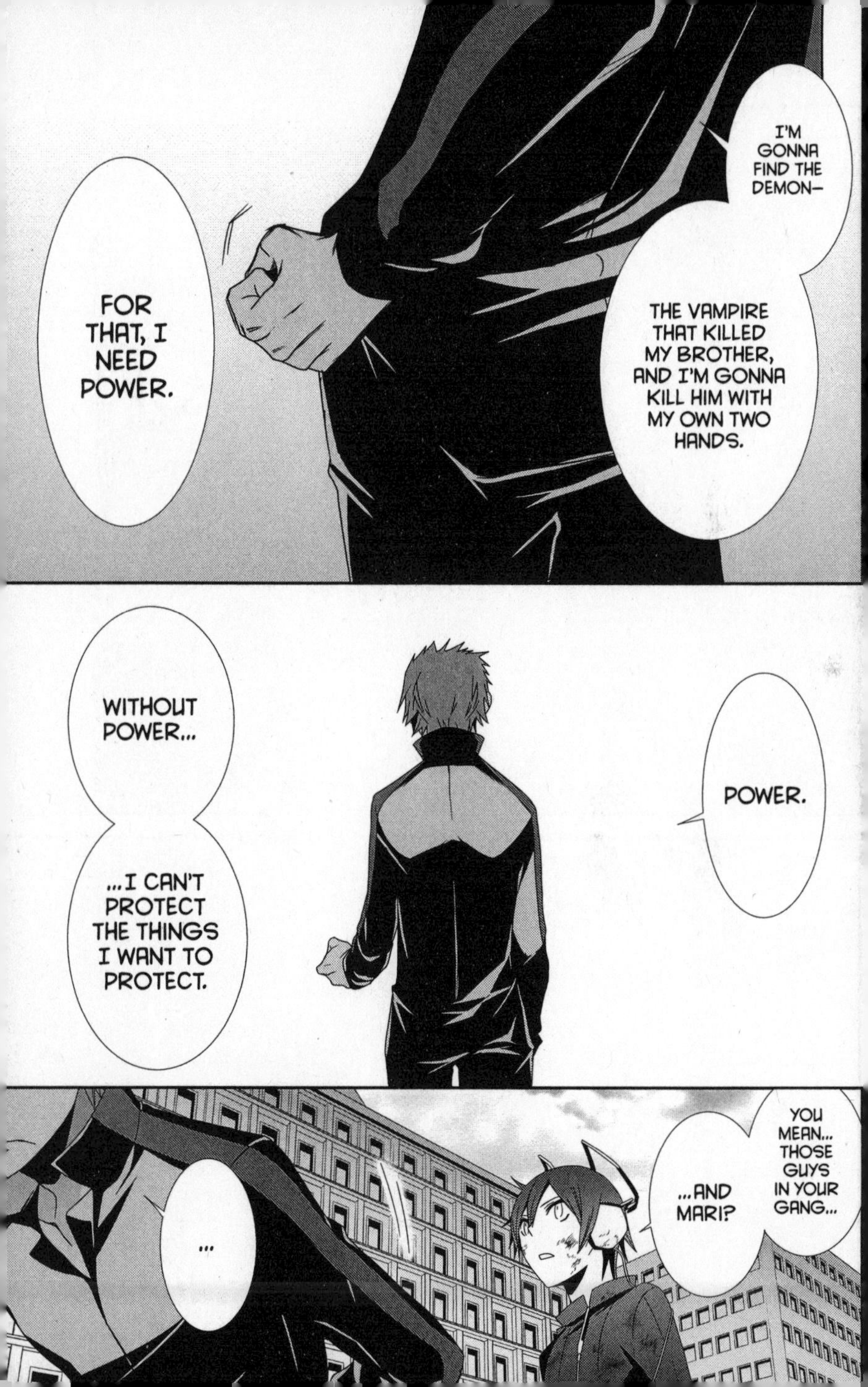
I'M GONNA FIND THE DEMON—
THE VAMPIRE THAT KILLED MY BROTHER, AND I'M GONNA KILL HIM WITH MY OWN TWO HANDS.
FOR THAT, I NEED POWER.
POWER.
WITHOUT POWER...
...I CAN'T PROTECT THE THINGS I WANT TO PROTECT.
YOU MEAN... THOSE GUYS IN YOUR GANG...
...AND MARI?
...

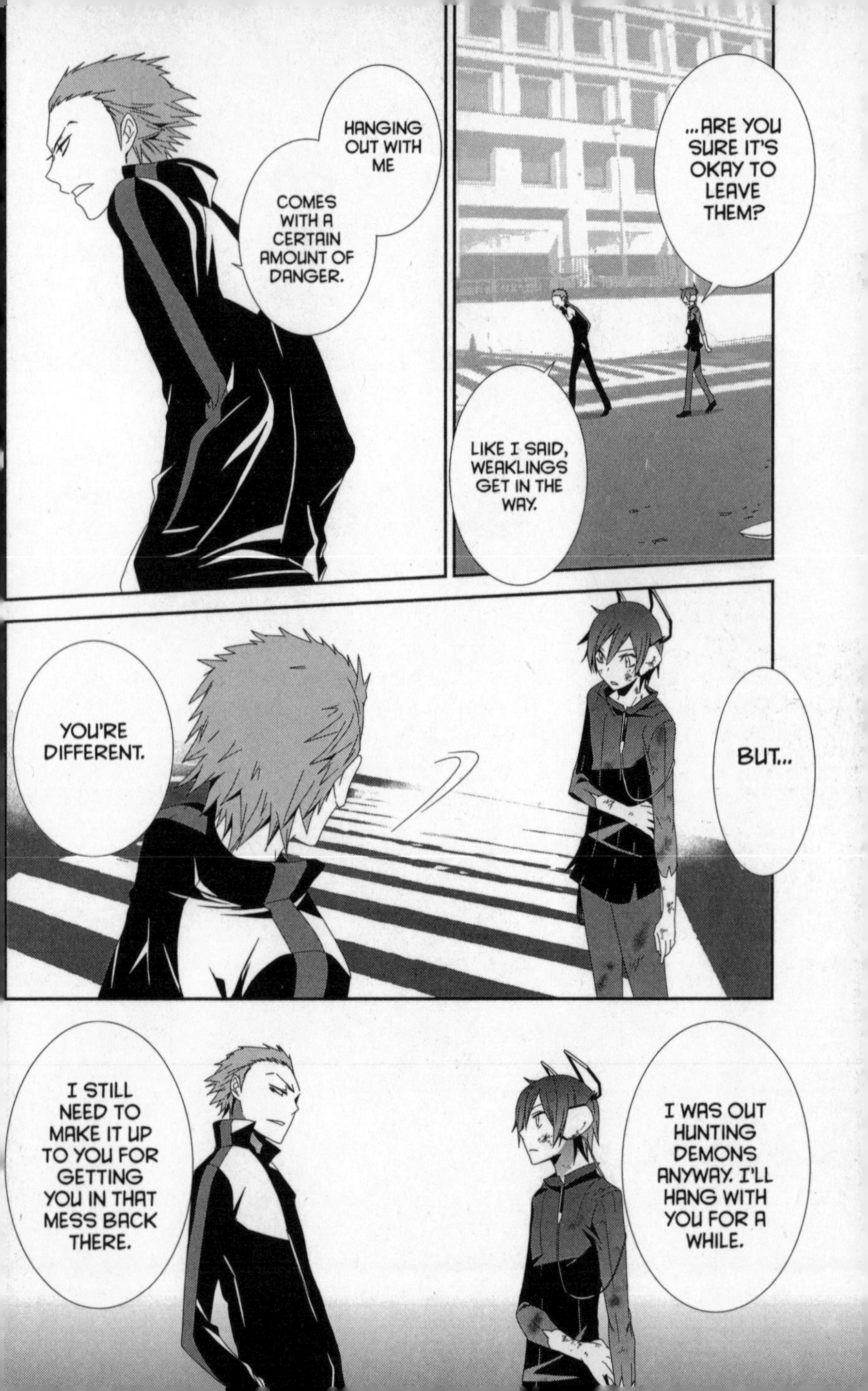
...ARE YOU SURE IT'S OKAY TO LEAVE THEM?
LIKE I SAID, WEAKLINGS GET IN THE WAY.
HANGING OUT WITH ME
COMES WITH A CERTAIN AMOUNT OF DANGER.
BUT...
YOU'RE DIFFERENT.
I WAS OUT HUNTING DEMONS ANYWAY. I'LL HANG WITH YOU FOR A WHILE.
I STILL NEED TO MAKE IT UP TO YOU FOR GETTING YOU IN THAT MESS BACK THERE.

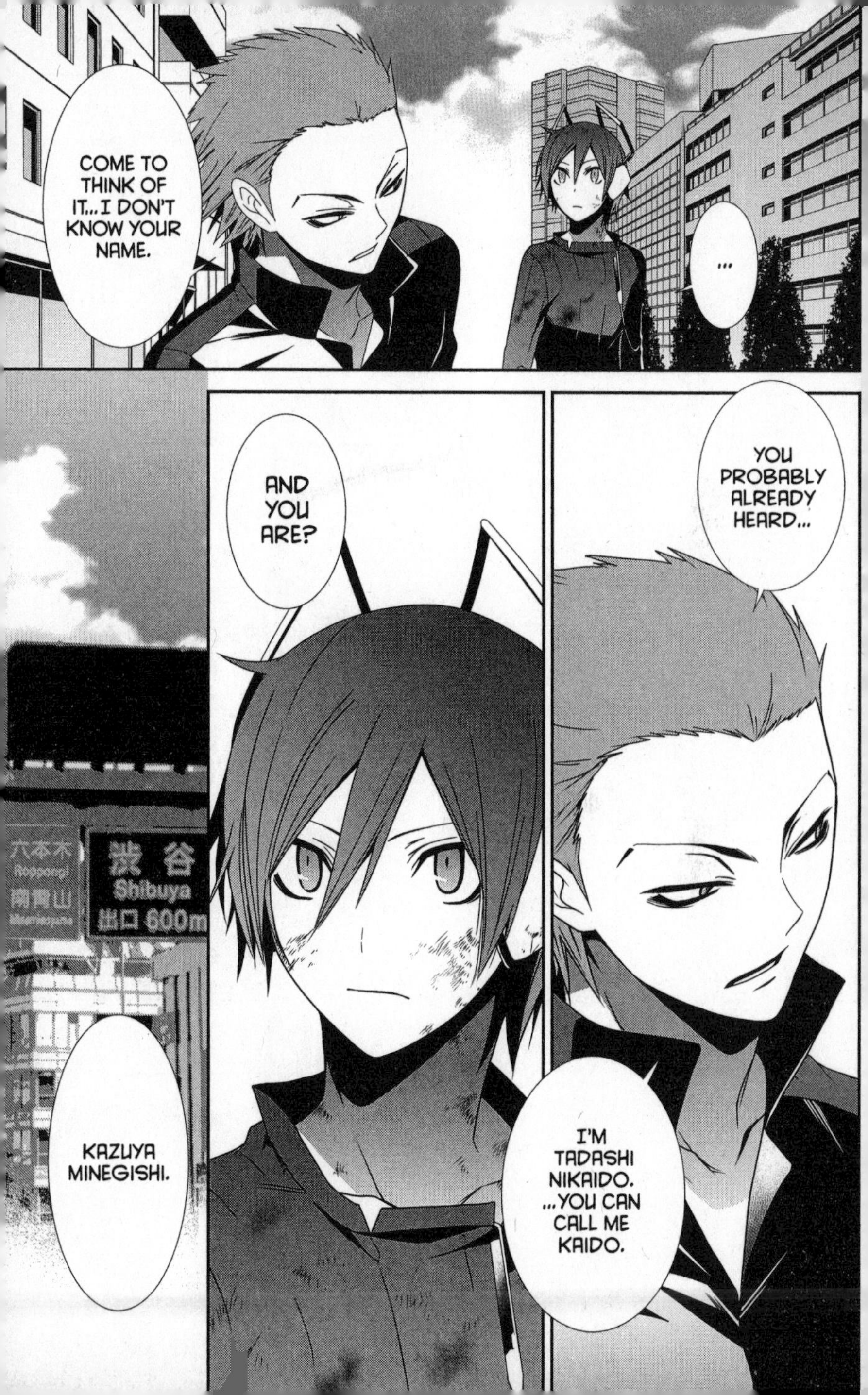
COME TO THINK OF IT...I DON'T KNOW YOUR NAME.
...
YOU PROBABLY ALREADY HEARD...
I'M TADASHI NIKAIDO. ...YOU CAN CALL ME KAIDO.
AND YOU ARE?
KAZUYA MINEGISHI.
六本木
Roppongi
南青山
渋谷
Shibuya
出口 600m

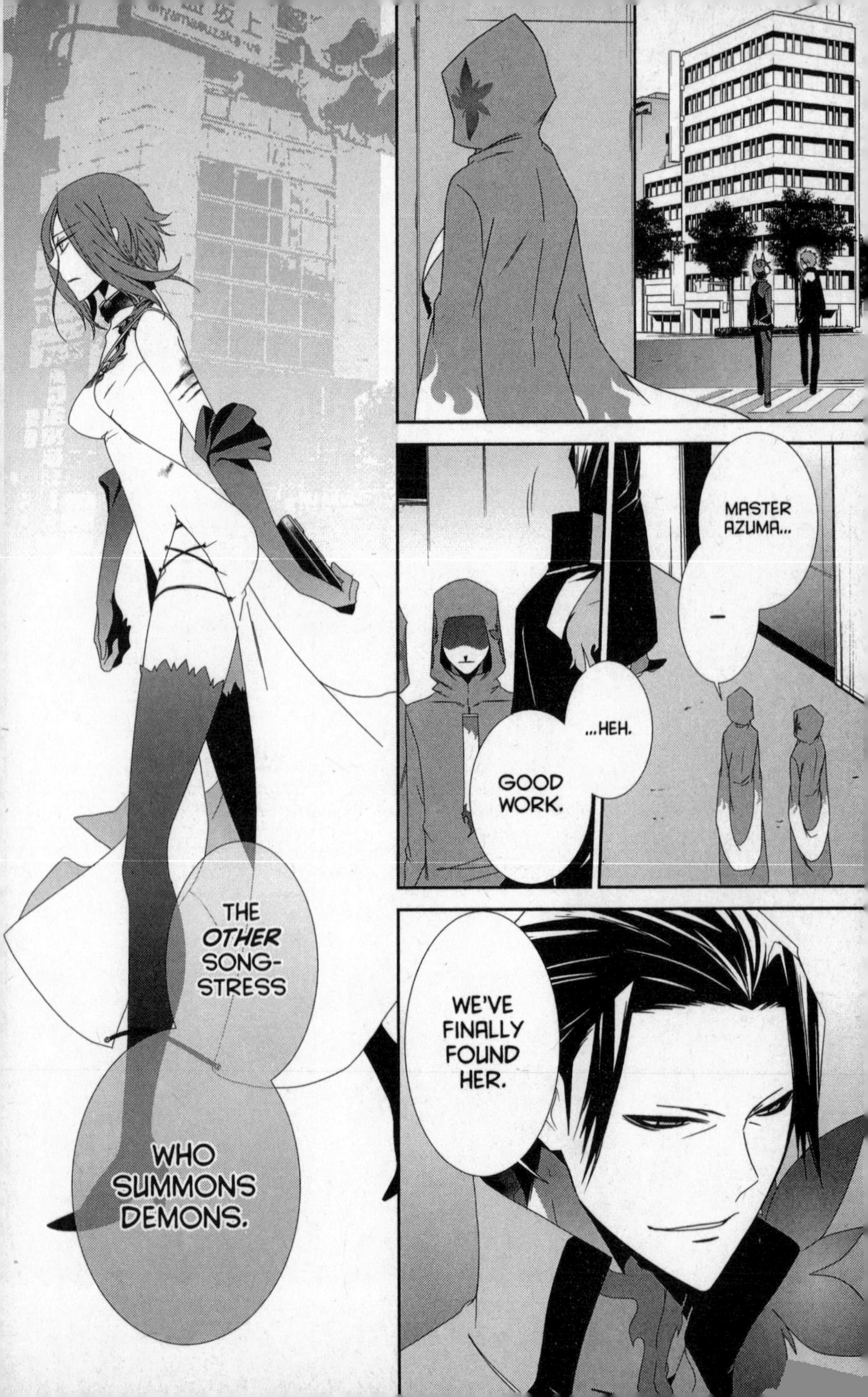
MASTER AZUMA...
–
...HEH.
GOOD WORK.
WE'VE FINALLY FOUND HER.
THE *OTHER* SONG-STRESS
WHO SUMMONS DEMONS.

PROFILE

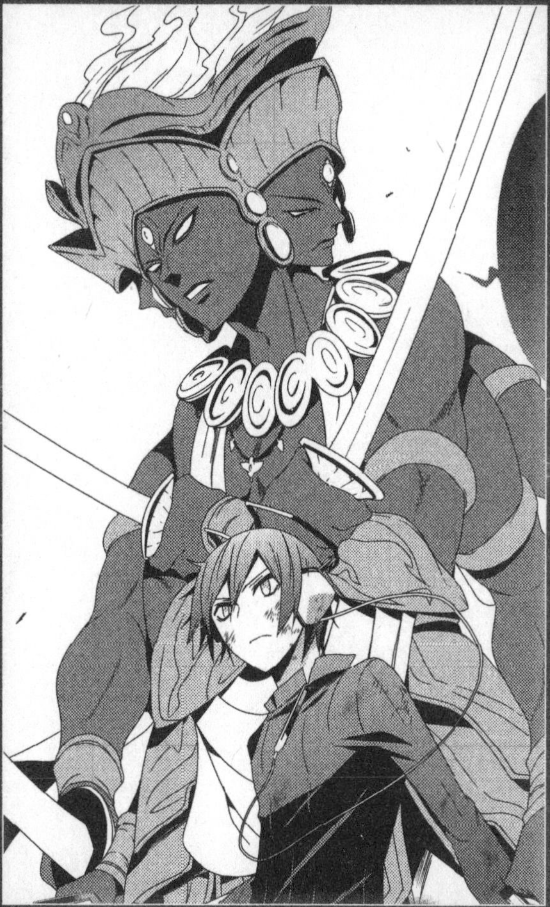

MAHAKALA

AN INDIAN DEITY WITH A WRATHFUL COUNTENANCE WHO WARDS OFF EVIL. HE HAS BEEN ADOPTED INTO BUDDHISM AND IS KNOWN IN JAPAN BY THE NAME DAIKOKUTEN. SWORDS IN HAND, HE IS FEARSOME TO BEHOLD, BUT IF PAID PROPER TRIBUTE AND REVERENCE, HE WILL BESTOW GREAT FORTUNE AND WEALTH UPON HIS BELIEVERS. ONE THEORY HOLDS THAT HE IS AN INCARNATION OF SHIVA, THE DESTROYER.

DEVIL SURVIVOR
デビルサバイバー

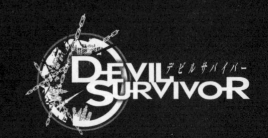

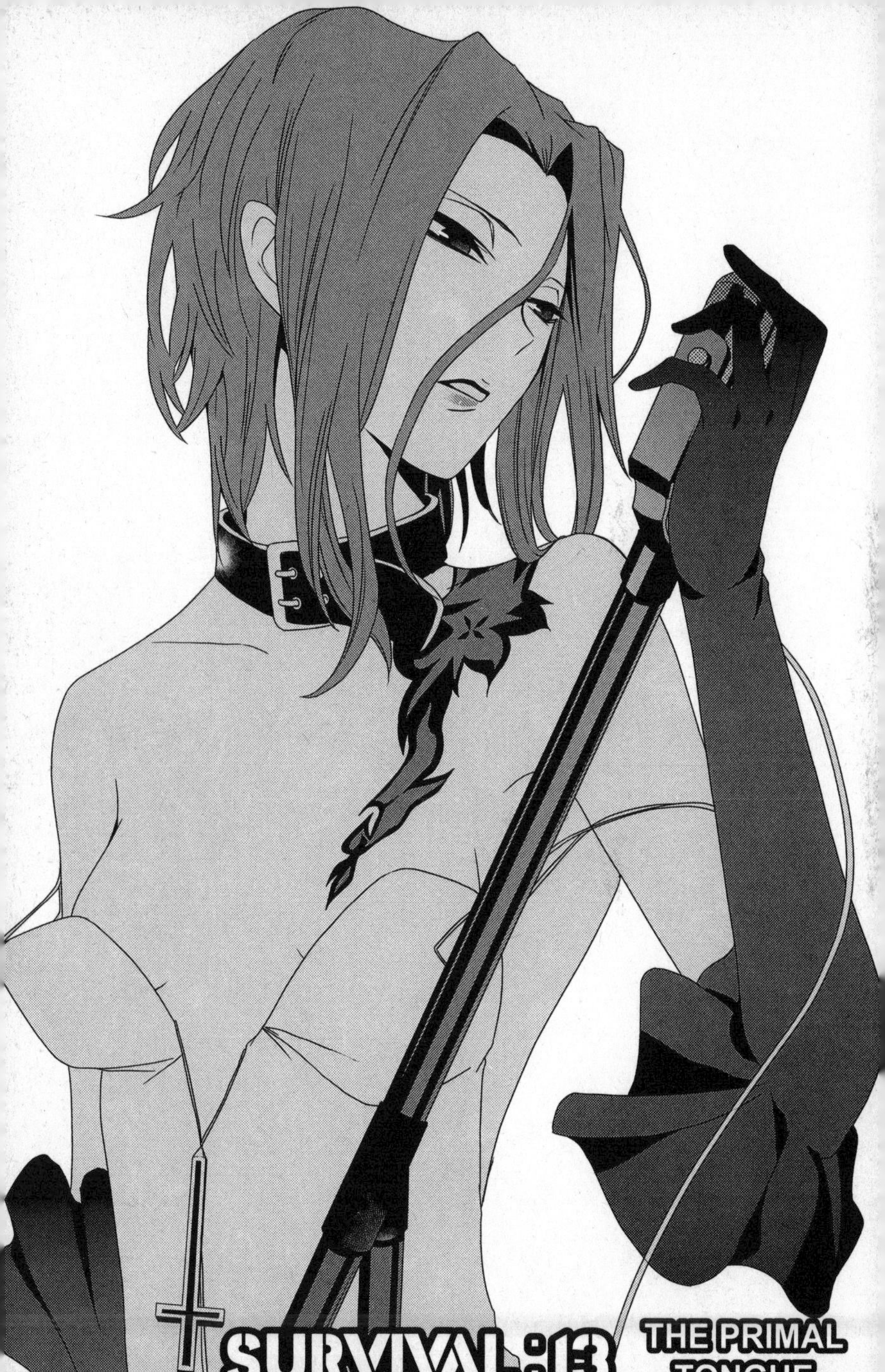

SURVIVAL:13 THE PRIMAL TONGUE

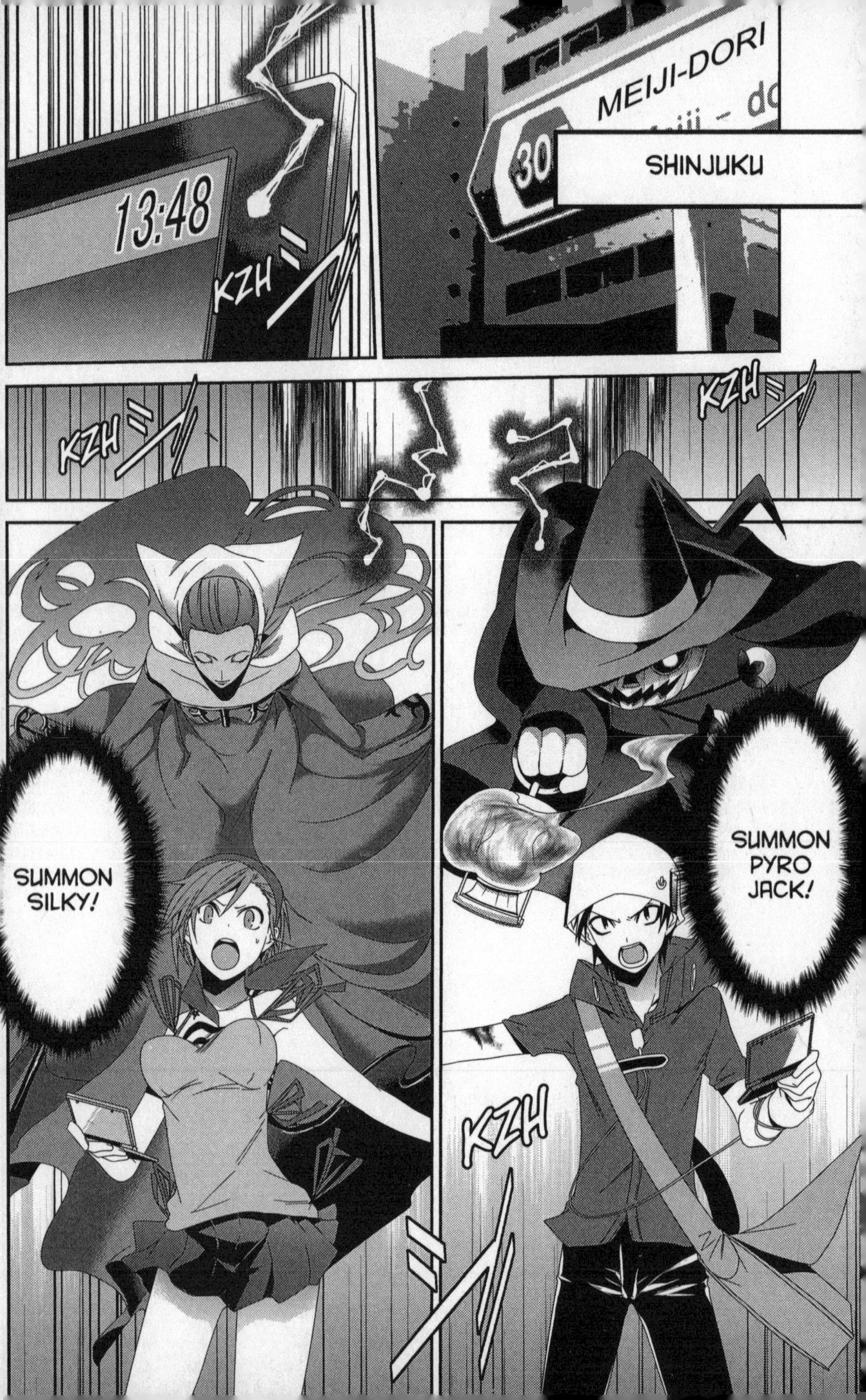
MEIJI-DORI
30
SHINJUKU
13:48
KZH
KZH
KZH
SUMMON PYRO JACK!
KZH
SUMMON SILKY!

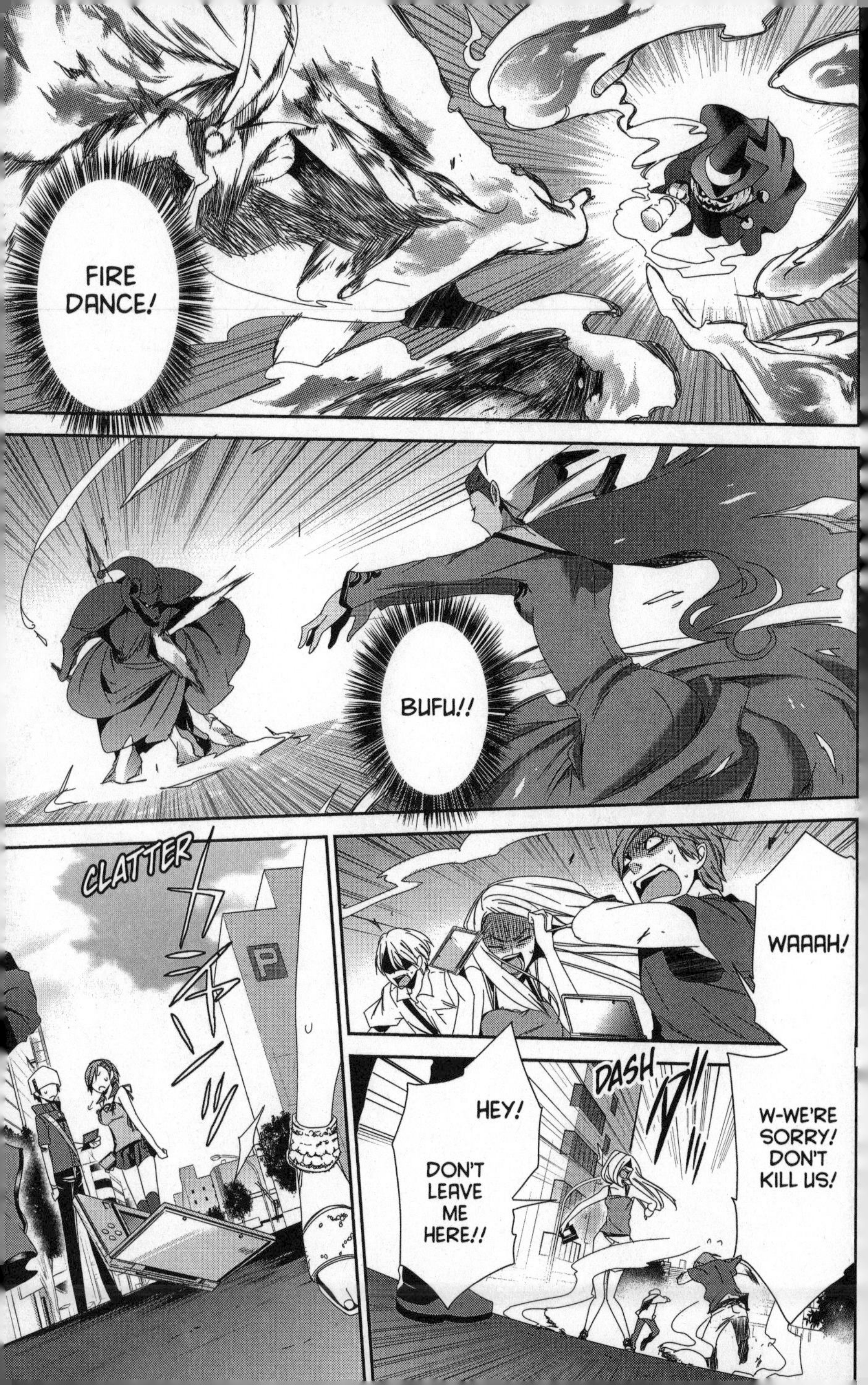
FIRE DANCE!
BUFU!!
WAAAH!
W-WE'RE SORRY! DON'T KILL US!
DASH
HEY!
DON'T LEAVE ME HERE!!
CLATTER

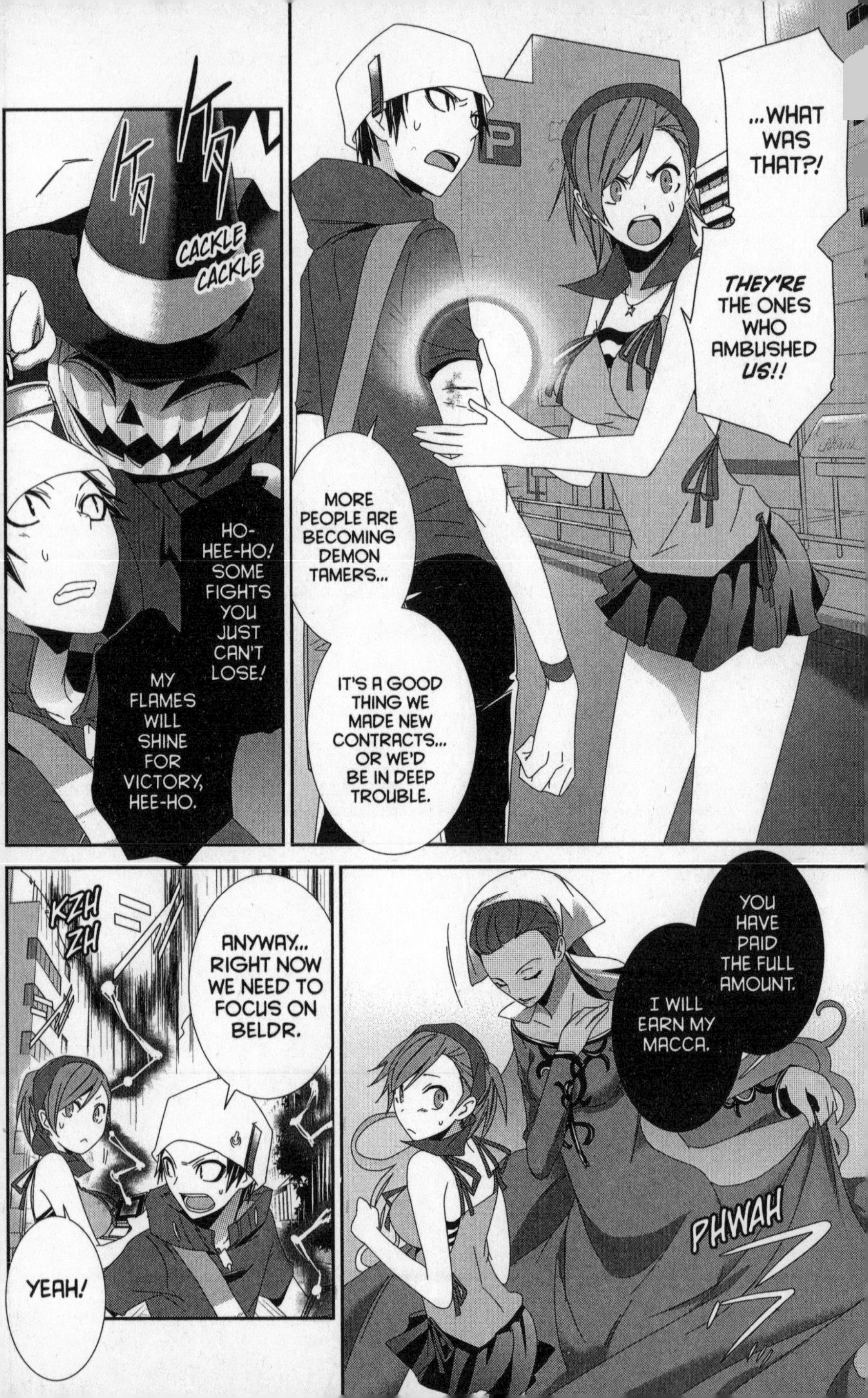
...WHAT WAS THAT?!
THEY'RE THE ONES WHO AMBUSHED *US!!*
MORE PEOPLE ARE BECOMING DEMON TAMERS...
IT'S A GOOD THING WE MADE NEW CONTRACTS... OR WE'D BE IN DEEP TROUBLE.
CACKLE CACKLE
HO-HEE-HO! SOME FIGHTS YOU JUST CAN'T LOSE!
MY FLAMES WILL SHINE FOR VICTORY, HEE-HO.
YOU HAVE PAID THE FULL AMOUNT.
I WILL EARN MY MACCA.
PHWAH
KZH ZH
ANYWAY... RIGHT NOW WE NEED TO FOCUS ON BELDR.
YEAH!

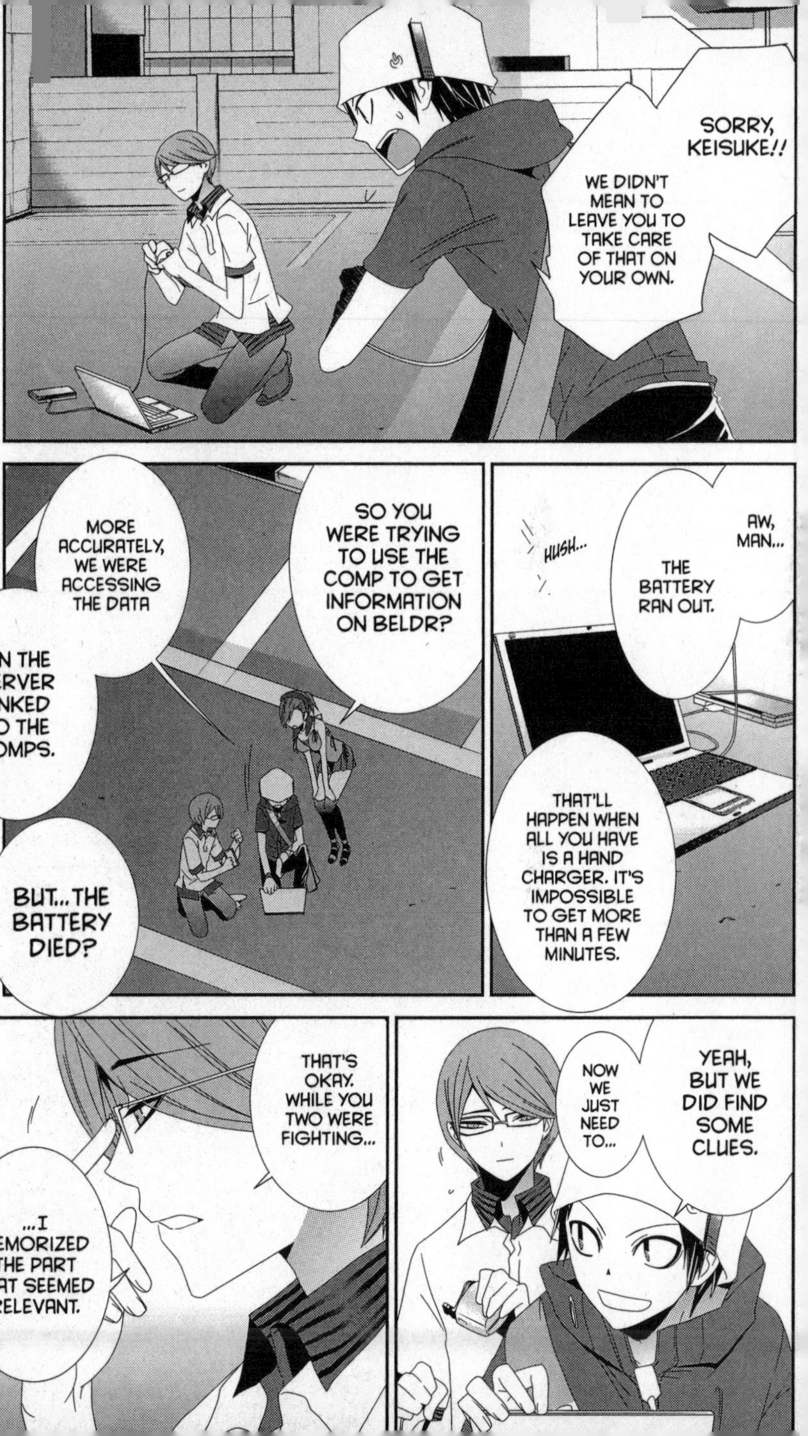
SORRY, KEISUKE!!
WE DIDN'T MEAN TO LEAVE YOU TO TAKE CARE OF THAT ON YOUR OWN.
AW, MAN...
THE BATTERY RAN OUT.
HUSH...
THAT'LL HAPPEN WHEN ALL YOU HAVE IS A HAND CHARGER. IT'S IMPOSSIBLE TO GET MORE THAN A FEW MINUTES.
SO YOU WERE TRYING TO USE THE COMP TO GET INFORMATION ON BELDR?
MORE ACCURATELY, WE WERE ACCESSING THE DATA
ON THE SERVER LINKED TO THE COMPS.
BUT...THE BATTERY DIED?
YEAH, BUT WE DID FIND SOME CLUES.
NOW WE JUST NEED TO...
THAT'S OKAY. WHILE YOU TWO WERE FIGHTING...
...I MEMORIZED THE PART THAT SEEMED RELEVANT.

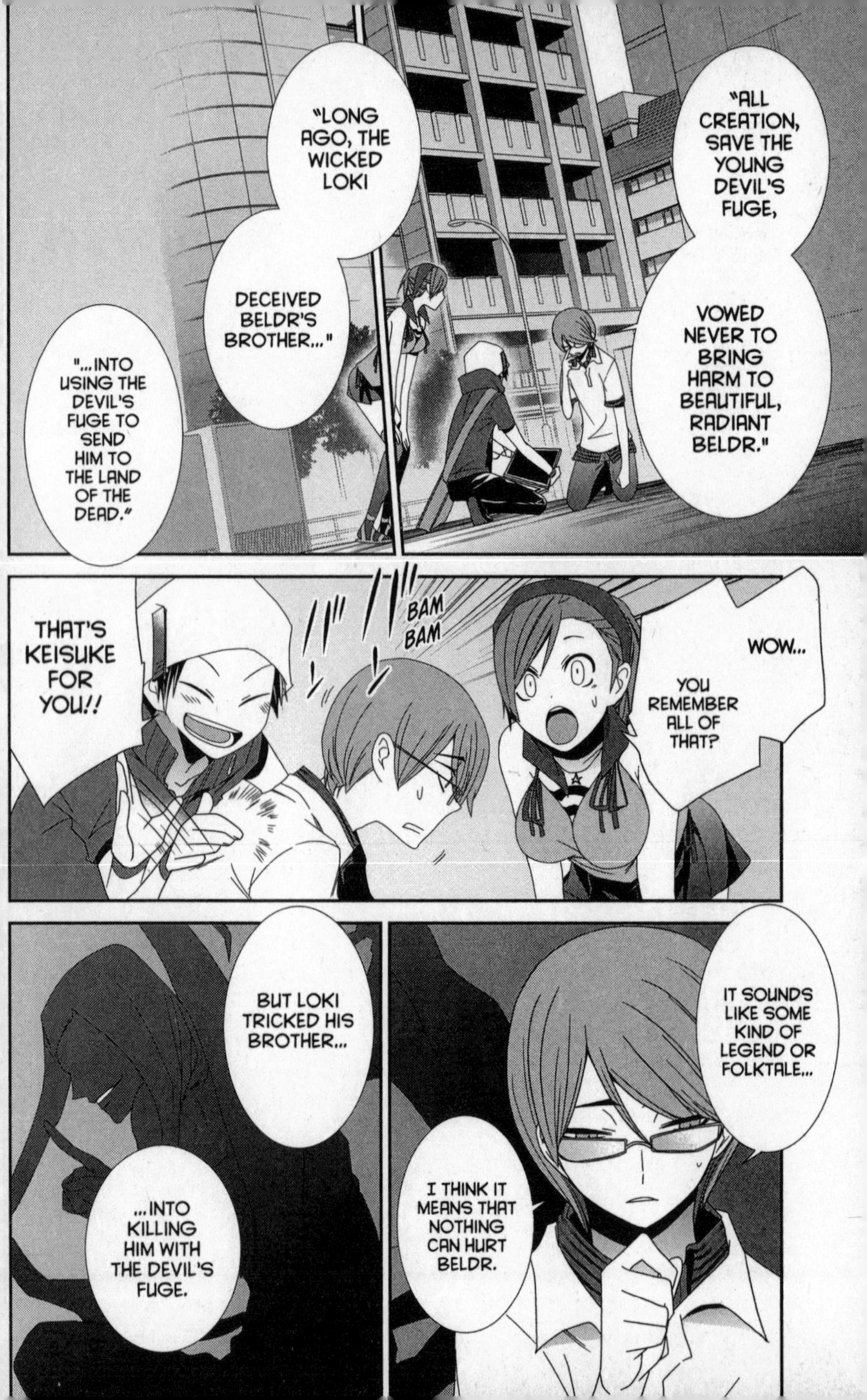
"ALL CREATION, SAVE THE YOUNG DEVIL'S FUGE,
VOWED NEVER TO BRING HARM TO BEAUTIFUL, RADIANT BELDR."
"LONG AGO, THE WICKED LOKI
DECEIVED BELDR'S BROTHER..."
"...INTO USING THE DEVIL'S FUGE TO SEND HIM TO THE LAND OF THE DEAD."
WOW...
YOU REMEMBER ALL OF THAT?
BAM BAM
THAT'S KEISUKE FOR YOU!!
IT SOUNDS LIKE SOME KIND OF LEGEND OR FOLKTALE...
I THINK IT MEANS THAT NOTHING CAN HURT BELDR.
BUT LOKI TRICKED HIS BROTHER...
...INTO KILLING HIM WITH THE DEVIL'S FUGE.

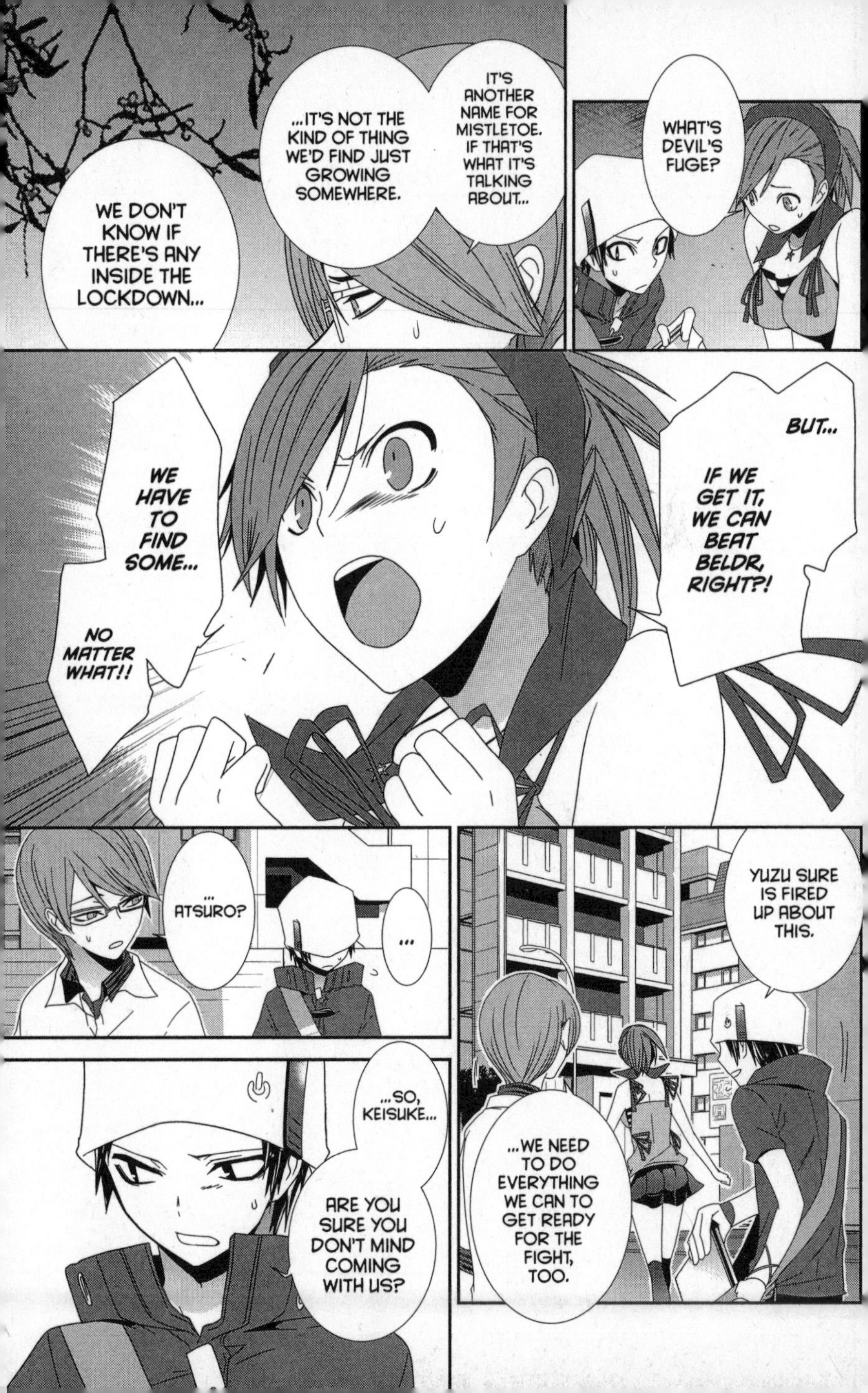
WHAT'S DEVIL'S FUGE?
IT'S ANOTHER NAME FOR MISTLETOE. IF THAT'S WHAT IT'S TALKING ABOUT...
...IT'S NOT THE KIND OF THING WE'D FIND JUST GROWING SOMEWHERE.
WE DON'T KNOW IF THERE'S ANY INSIDE THE LOCKDOWN...
BUT...
IF WE GET IT, WE CAN BEAT BELDR, RIGHT?!
WE HAVE TO FIND SOME...
NO MATTER WHAT!!
YUZU SURE IS FIRED UP ABOUT THIS.
...WE NEED TO DO EVERYTHING WE CAN TO GET READY FOR THE FIGHT, TOO.
... ATSURO?
...
...SO, KEISUKE...
ARE YOU SURE YOU DON'T MIND COMING WITH US?

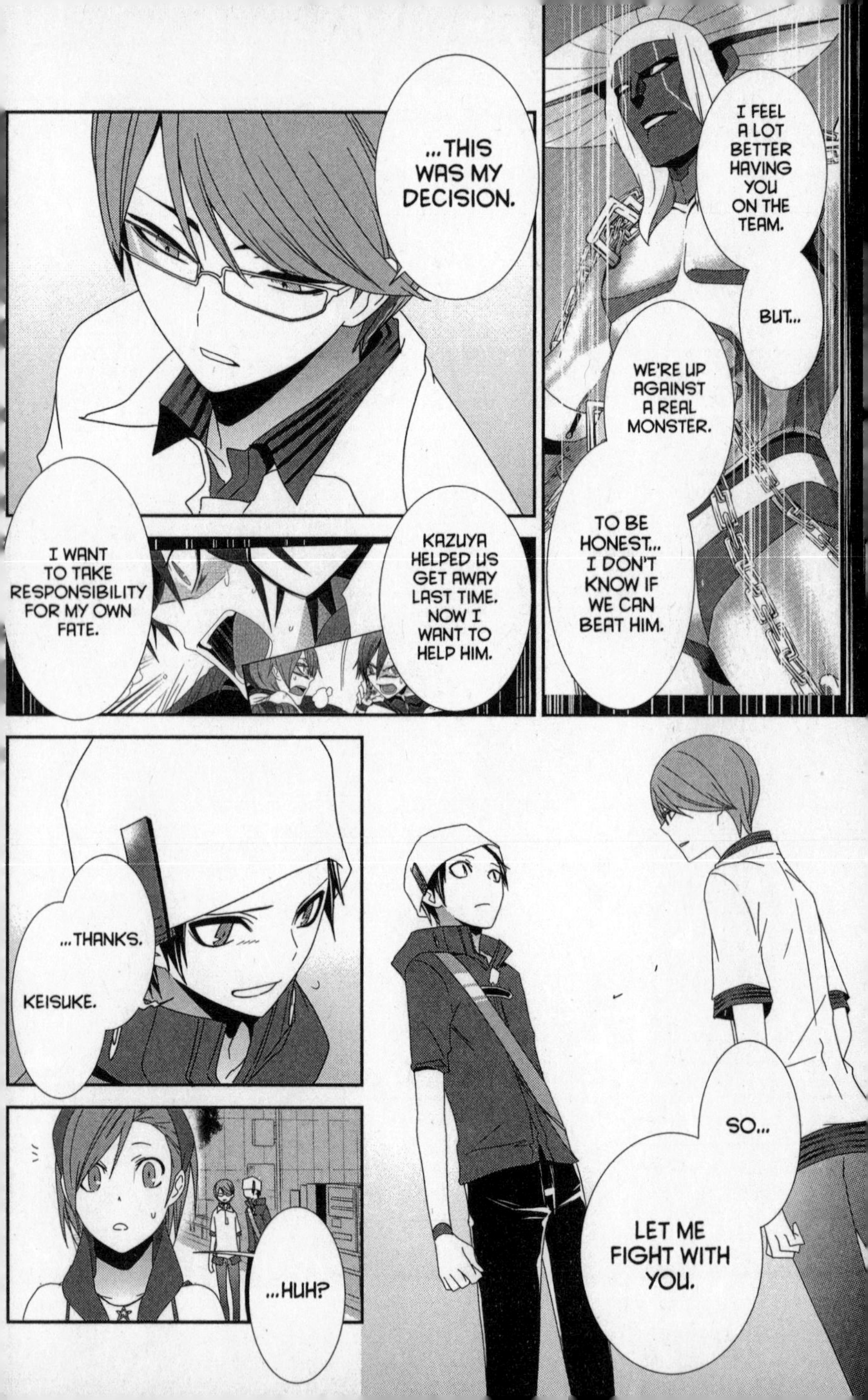
I FEEL A LOT BETTER HAVING YOU ON THE TEAM.
BUT...
WE'RE UP AGAINST A REAL MONSTER.
TO BE HONEST... I DON'T KNOW IF WE CAN BEAT HIM.
...THIS WAS MY DECISION.
KAZUYA HELPED US GET AWAY LAST TIME. NOW I WANT TO HELP HIM.
I WANT TO TAKE RESPONSIBILITY FOR MY OWN FATE.
SO...
LET ME FIGHT WITH YOU.
...THANKS.
KEISUKE.
...HUH?

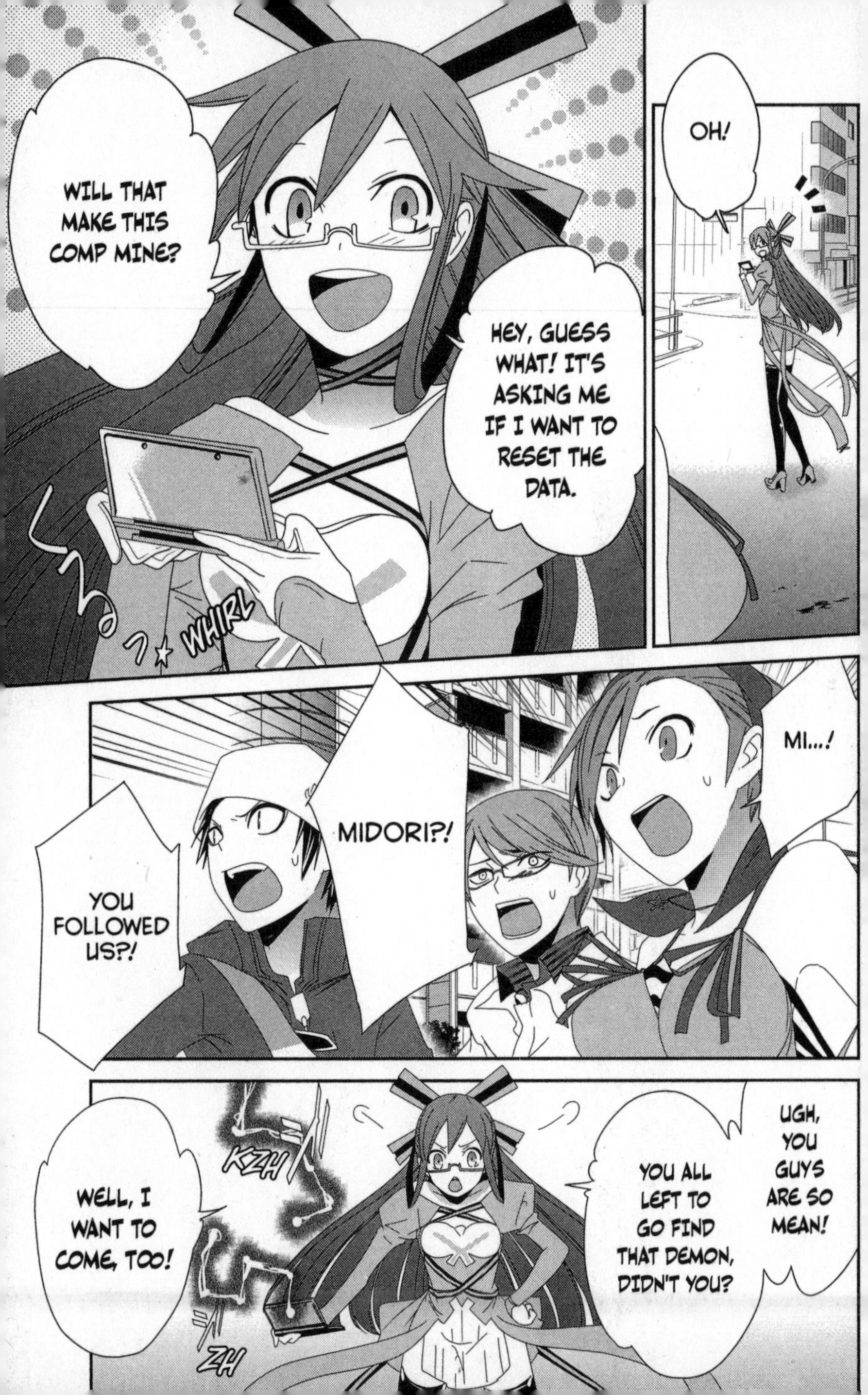
OH!
HEY, GUESS WHAT! IT'S ASKING ME IF I WANT TO RESET THE DATA.
WILL THAT MAKE THIS COMP MINE?
WHIRL
MI...!
MIDORI?!
YOU FOLLOWED US?!
UGH, YOU GUYS ARE SO MEAN!
YOU ALL LEFT TO GO FIND THAT DEMON, DIDN'T YOU?
WELL, I WANT TO COME, TOO!
KZH
ZH

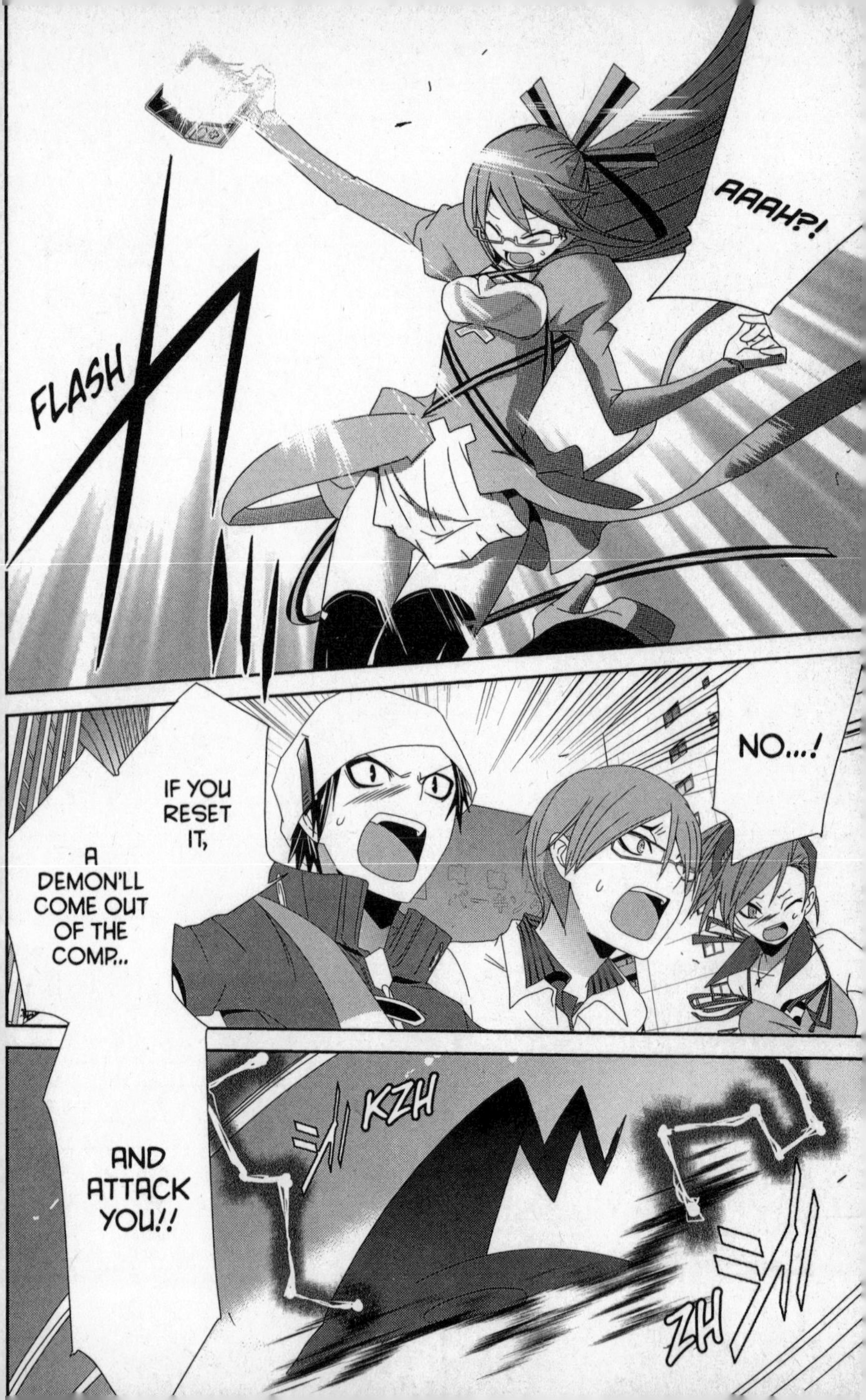
AAAH?!
FLASH
NO...!
IF YOU RESET IT,
A DEMON'LL COME OUT OF THE COMP...
ZH
KZH
AND ATTACK YOU!!

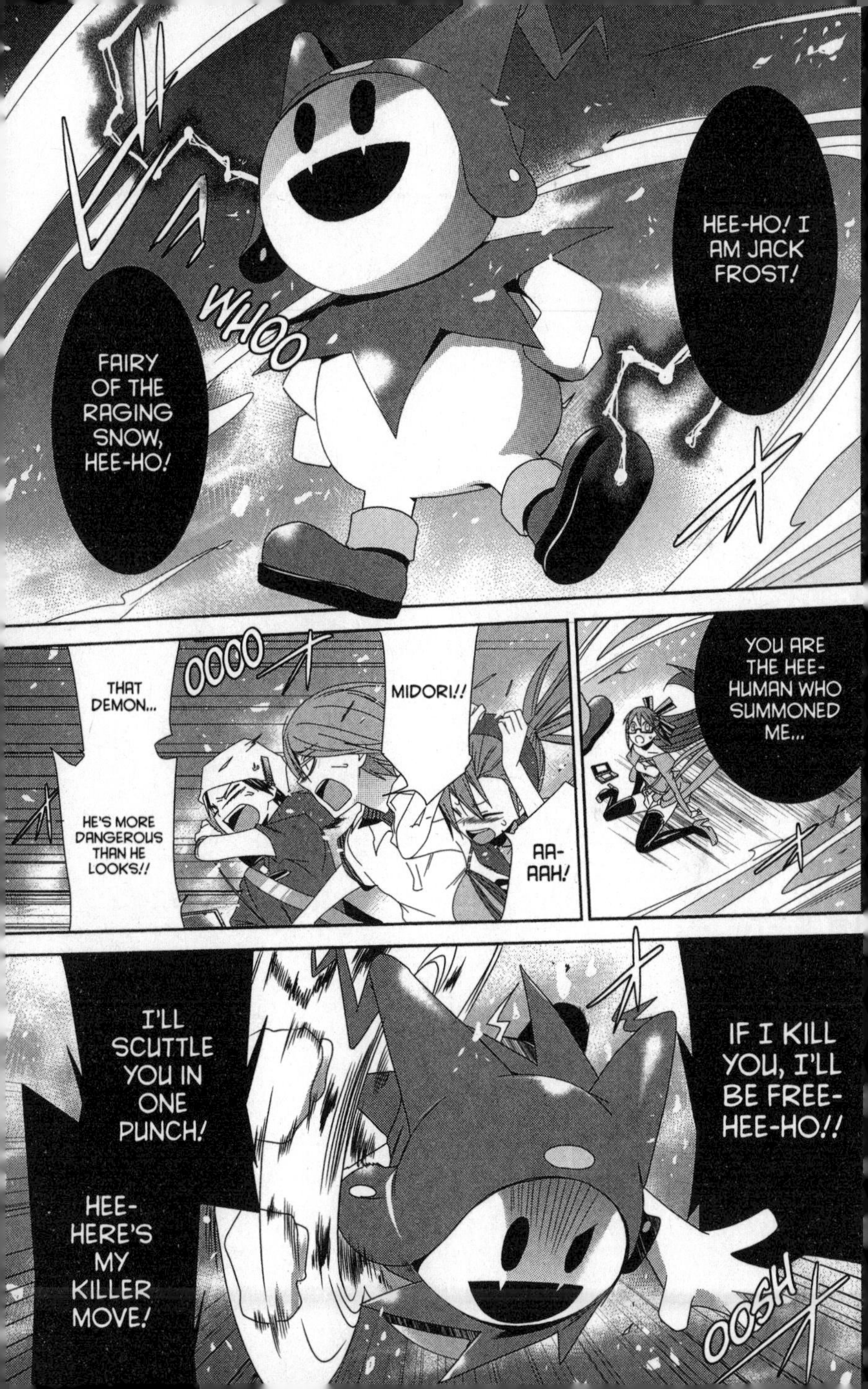

HEE-HO! I AM JACK FROST!
WHOO
FAIRY OF THE RAGING SNOW, HEE-HO!
YOU ARE THE HEE-HUMAN WHO SUMMONED ME...
MIDORI!!
OOOO
THAT DEMON...
AA-AAH!
HE'S MORE DANGEROUS THAN HE LOOKS!!
IF I KILL YOU, I'LL BE FREE-HEE-HO!!
I'LL SCUTTLE YOU IN ONE PUNCH!
OOSH
HEE-HERE'S MY KILLER MOVE!

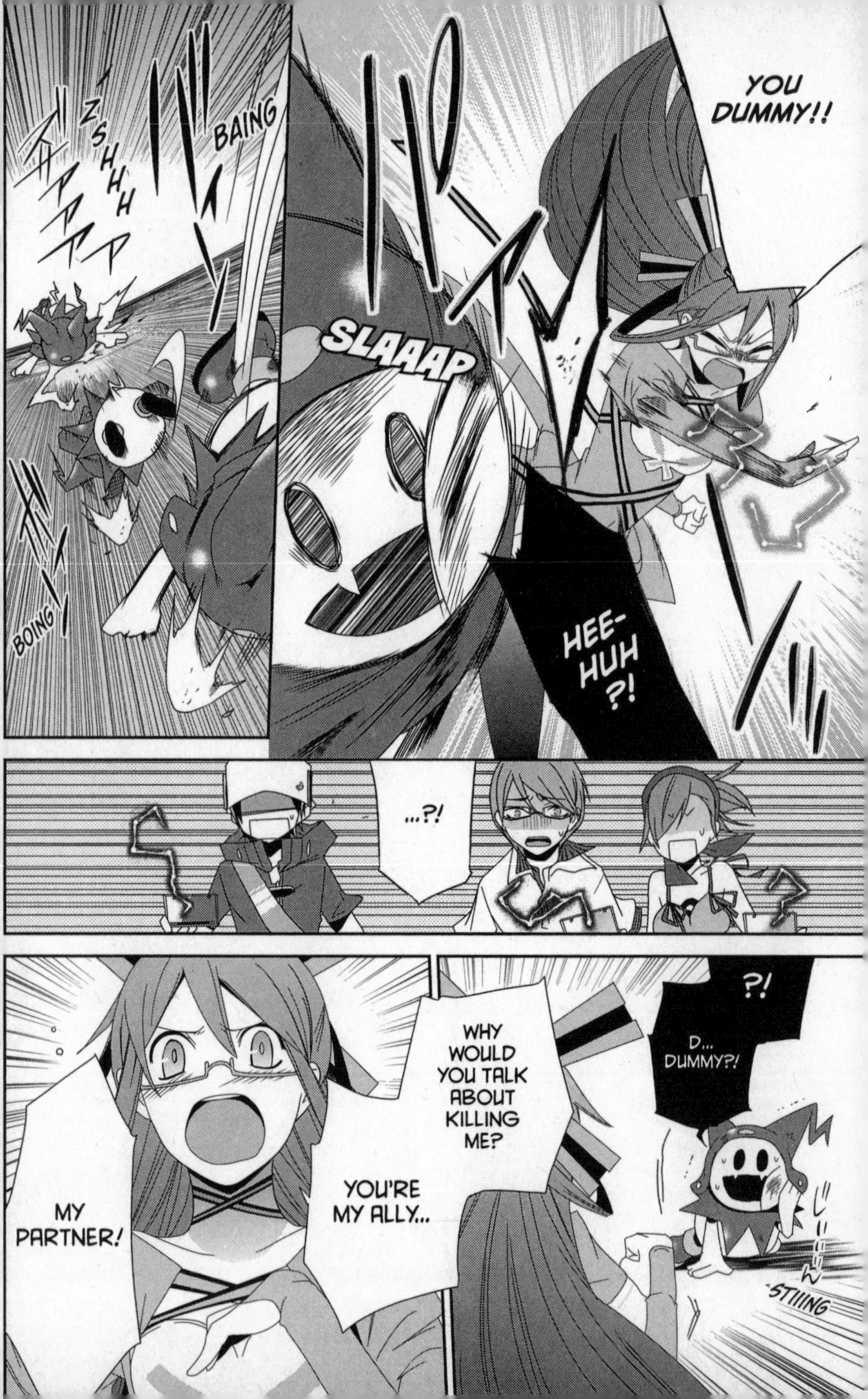
YOU DUMMY!!
SLAAAP
HEE-HUH?!
BAING
ZSHHH
BOING
...?!
?!
D... DUMMY?!
STIING
WHY WOULD YOU TALK ABOUT KILLING ME?
YOU'RE MY ALLY...
MY PARTNER!

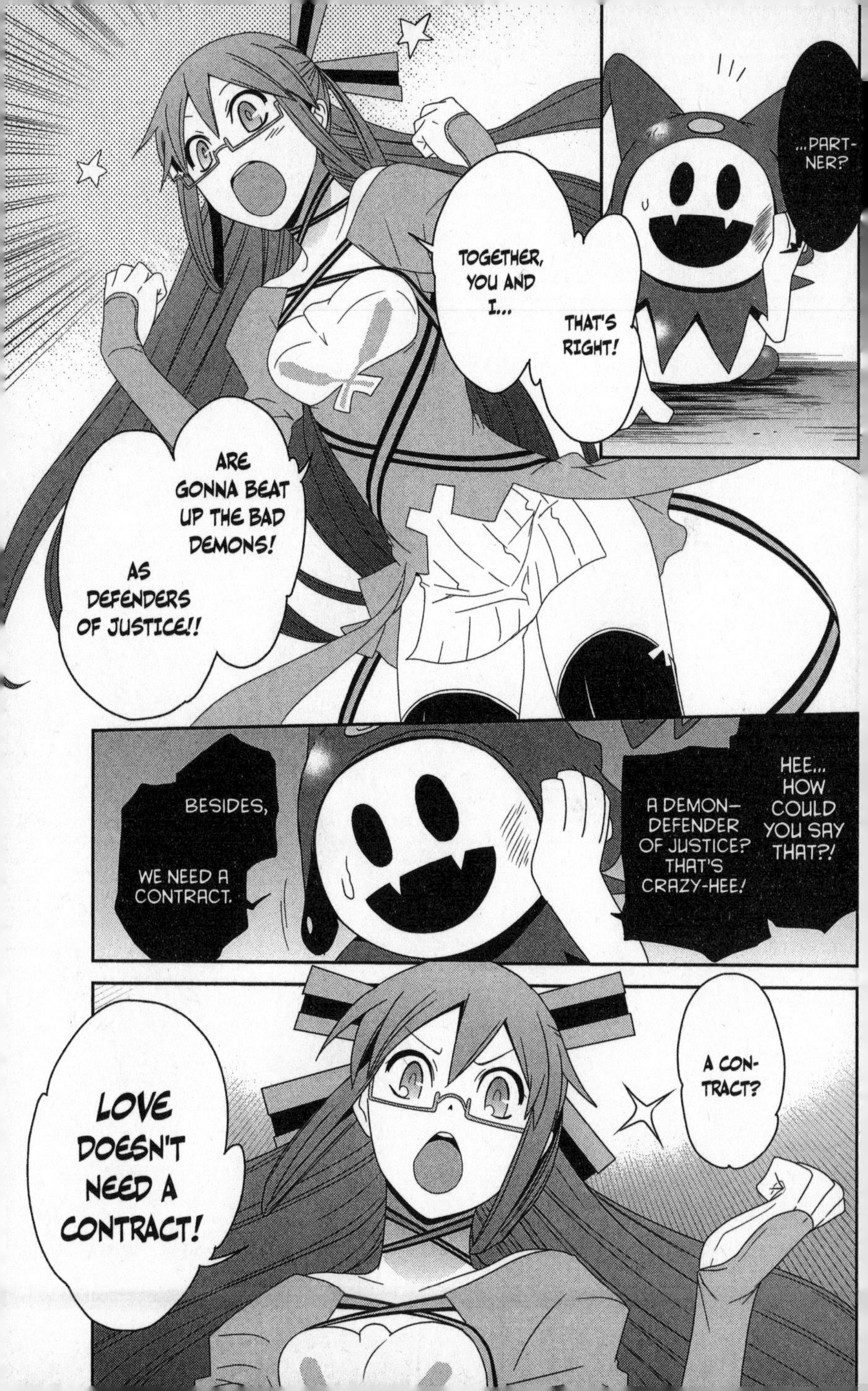

...PART-NER?
THAT'S RIGHT!
TOGETHER, YOU AND I...
ARE GONNA BEAT UP THE BAD DEMONS!
AS DEFENDERS OF JUSTICE!!
HEE... HOW COULD YOU SAY THAT?!
A DEMON-DEFENDER OF JUSTICE? THAT'S CRAZY-HEE!
BESIDES,
WE NEED A CONTRACT.
A CON-TRACT?
LOVE DOESN'T NEED A CONTRACT!

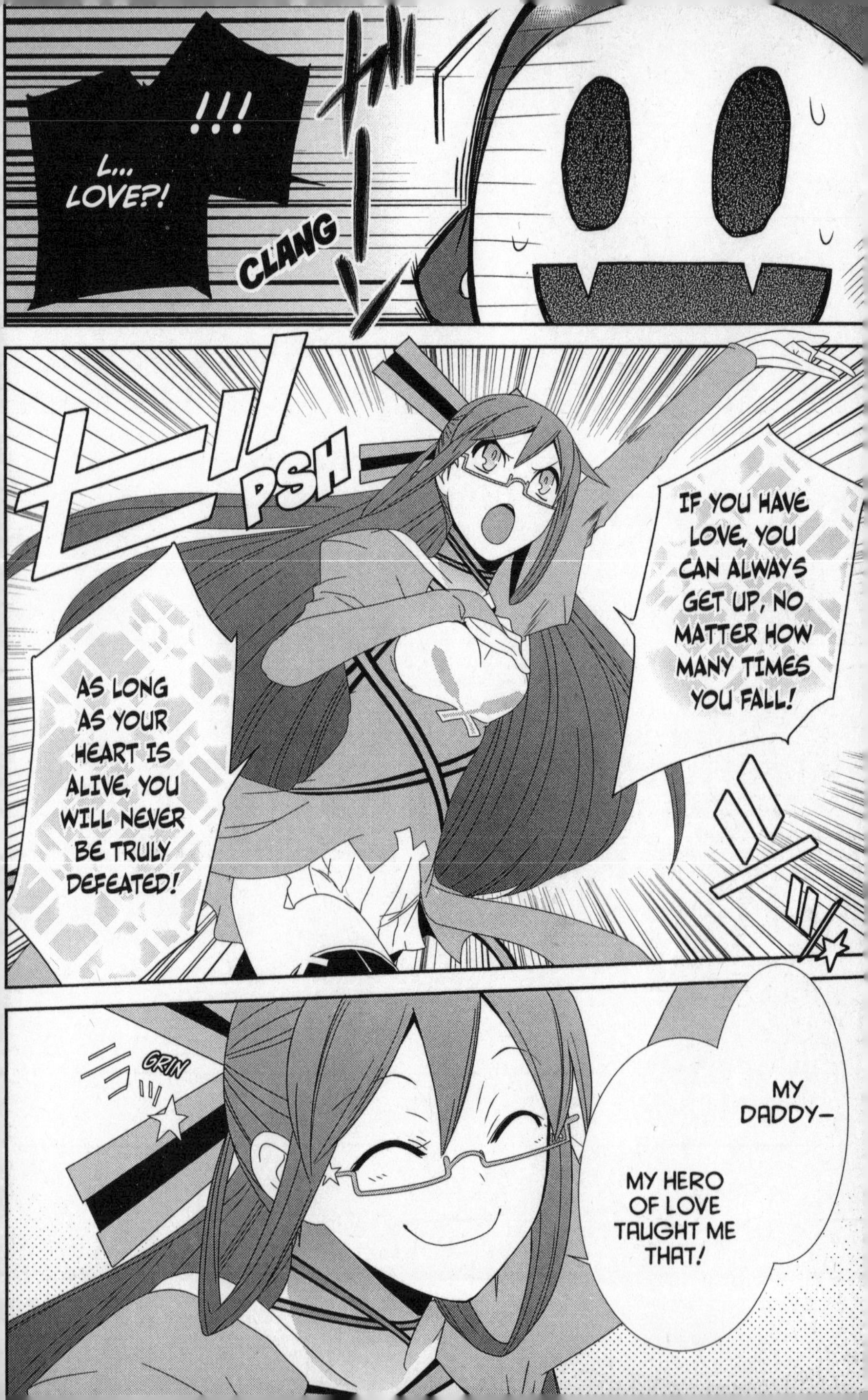
!!!
L... LOVE?!
CLANG
PSH
IF YOU HAVE LOVE, YOU CAN ALWAYS GET UP, NO MATTER HOW MANY TIMES YOU FALL!
AS LONG AS YOUR HEART IS ALIVE, YOU WILL NEVER BE TRULY DEFEATED!
GRIN
MY DADDY—
MY HERO OF LOVE TAUGHT ME THAT!

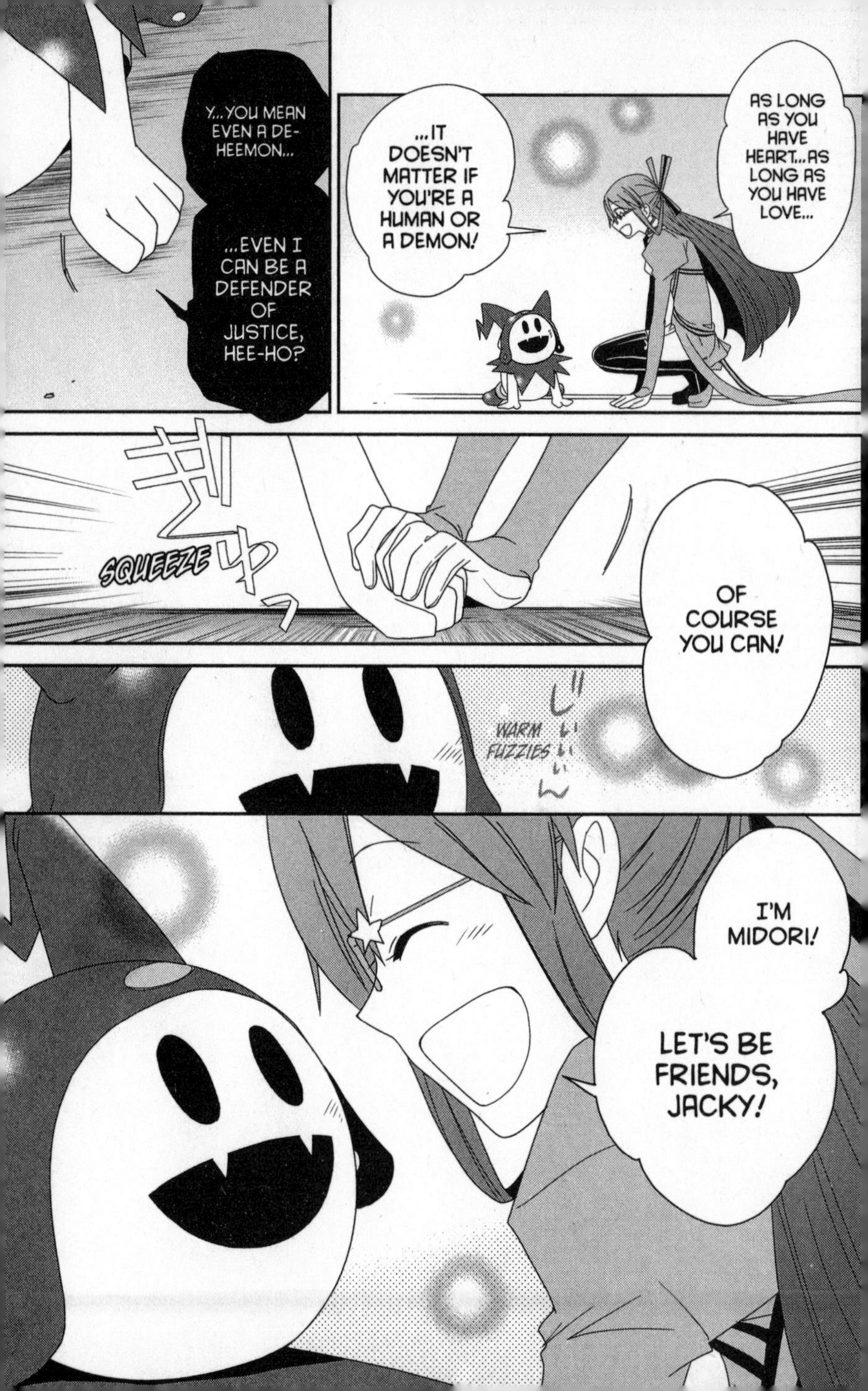
AS LONG AS YOU HAVE HEART...AS LONG AS YOU HAVE LOVE...
...IT DOESN'T MATTER IF YOU'RE A HUMAN OR A DEMON!
Y...YOU MEAN EVEN A DE-HEEMON...
...EVEN I CAN BE A DEFENDER OF JUSTICE, HEE-HO?
OF COURSE YOU CAN!
SQUEEZE
WARM FUZZIES
I'M MIDORI!
LET'S BE FRIENDS, JACKY!

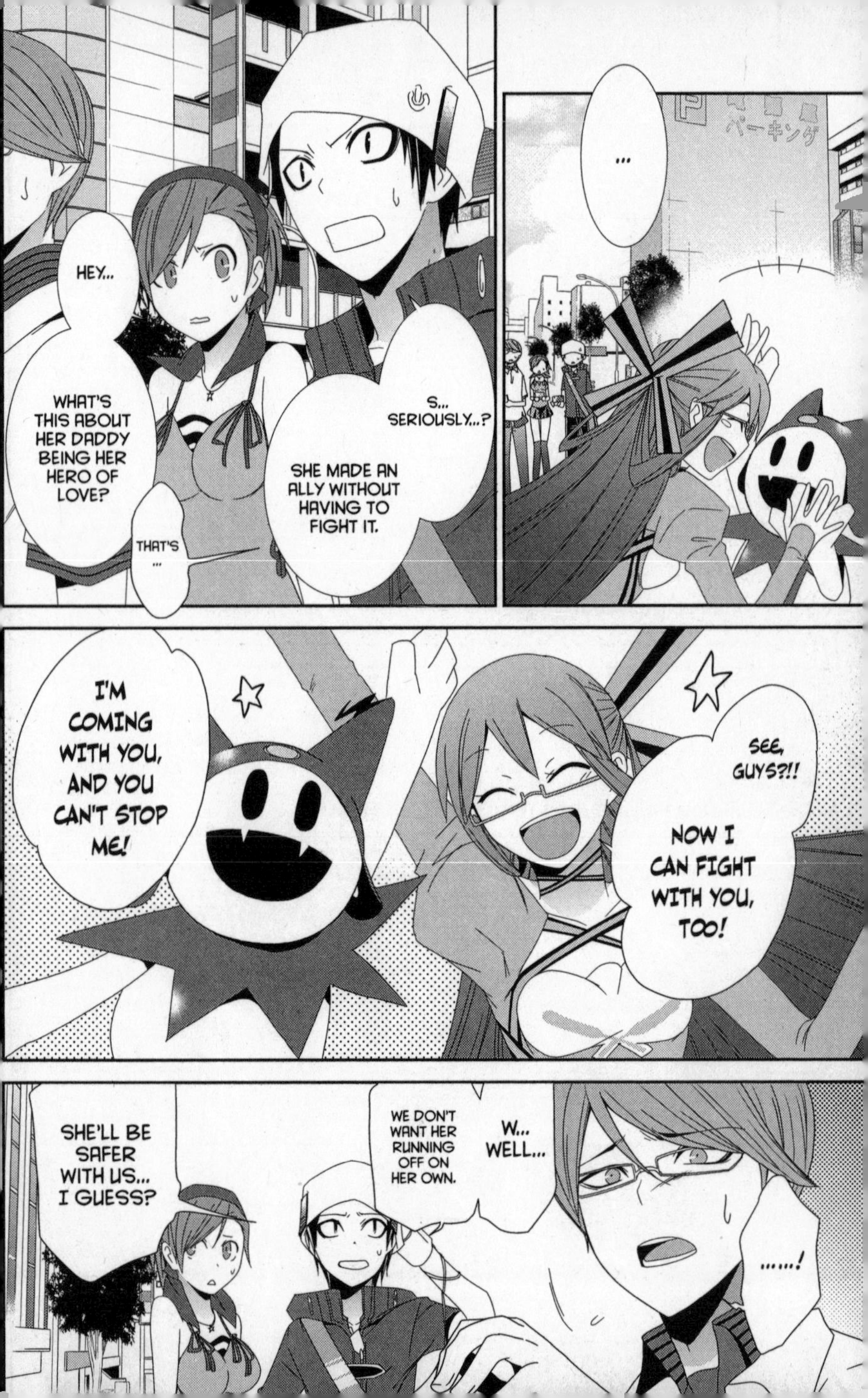
...
パーキング
S... SERIOUSLY...?
SHE MADE AN ALLY WITHOUT HAVING TO FIGHT IT.
HEY...
WHAT'S THIS ABOUT HER DADDY BEING HER HERO OF LOVE?
THAT'S ...
SEE, GUYS?!!
NOW I CAN FIGHT WITH YOU, TOO!
I'M COMING WITH YOU, AND YOU CAN'T STOP ME!
......!
W... WELL...
WE DON'T WANT HER RUNNING OFF ON HER OWN.
SHE'LL BE SAFER WITH US... I GUESS?

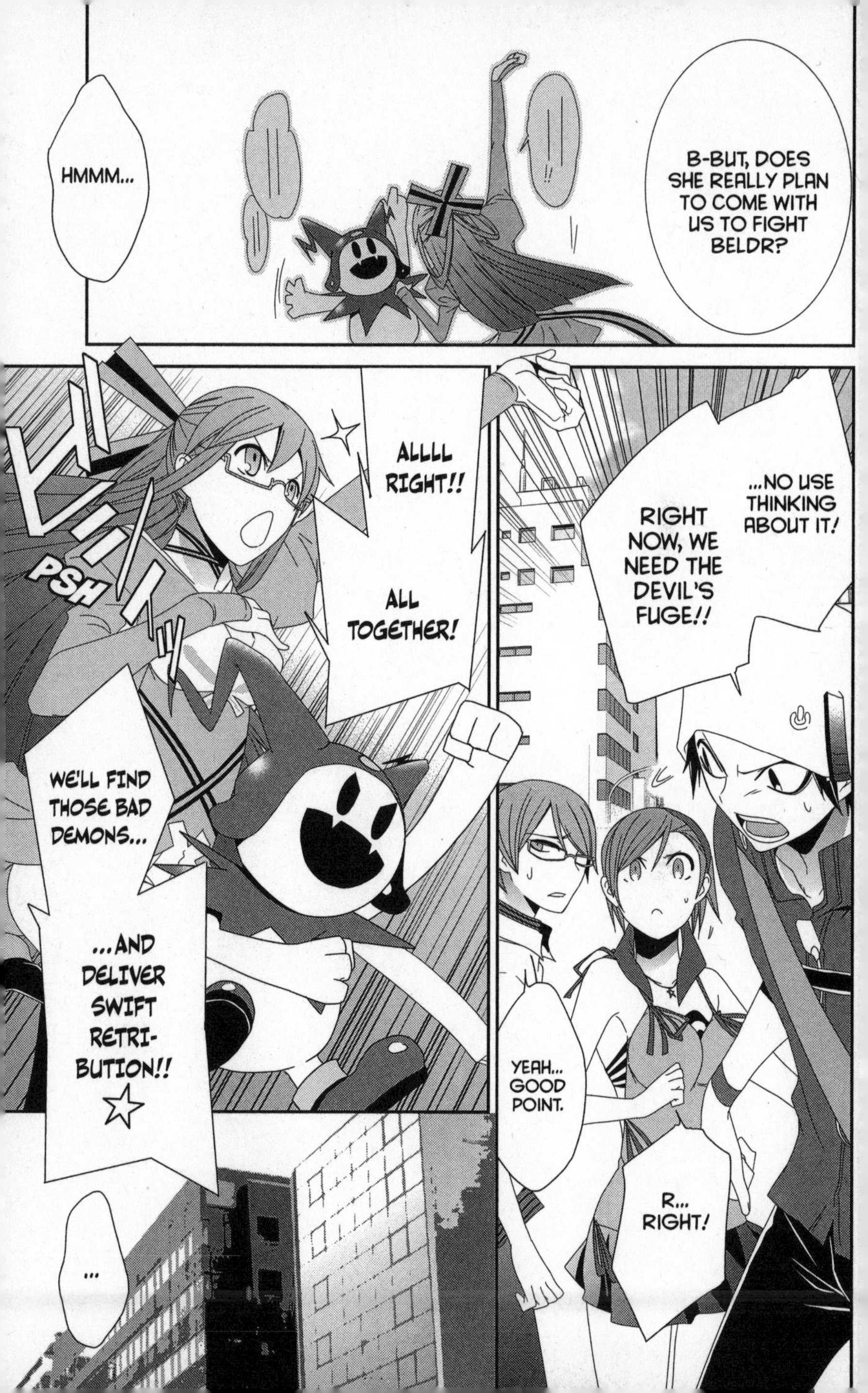
B-BUT, DOES SHE REALLY PLAN TO COME WITH US TO FIGHT BELDR?
!!
HMMM...
...NO USE THINKING ABOUT IT!
RIGHT NOW, WE NEED THE DEVIL'S FUGE!!
YEAH... GOOD POINT.
R... RIGHT!
ALLLL RIGHT!!
ALL TOGETHER!
PSH
WE'LL FIND THOSE BAD DEMONS...
...AND DELIVER SWIFT RETRI-BUTION!! ☆
...

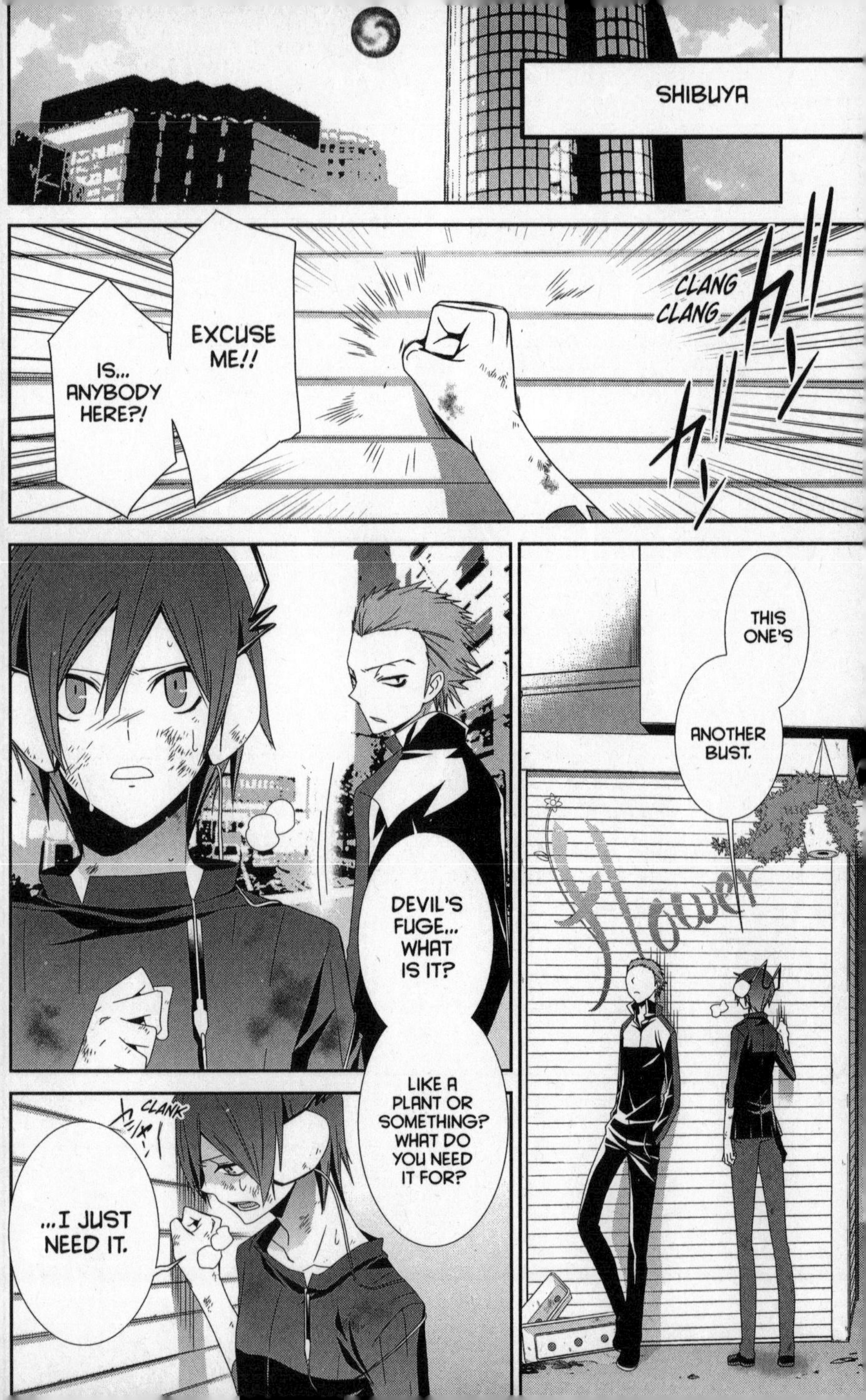
SHIBUYA
CLANG CLANG
EXCUSE ME!!
IS... ANYBODY HERE?!
THIS ONE'S ANOTHER BUST.
DEVIL'S FUGE... WHAT IS IT?
LIKE A PLANT OR SOMETHING? WHAT DO YOU NEED IT FOR?
CLANK
...I JUST NEED IT.

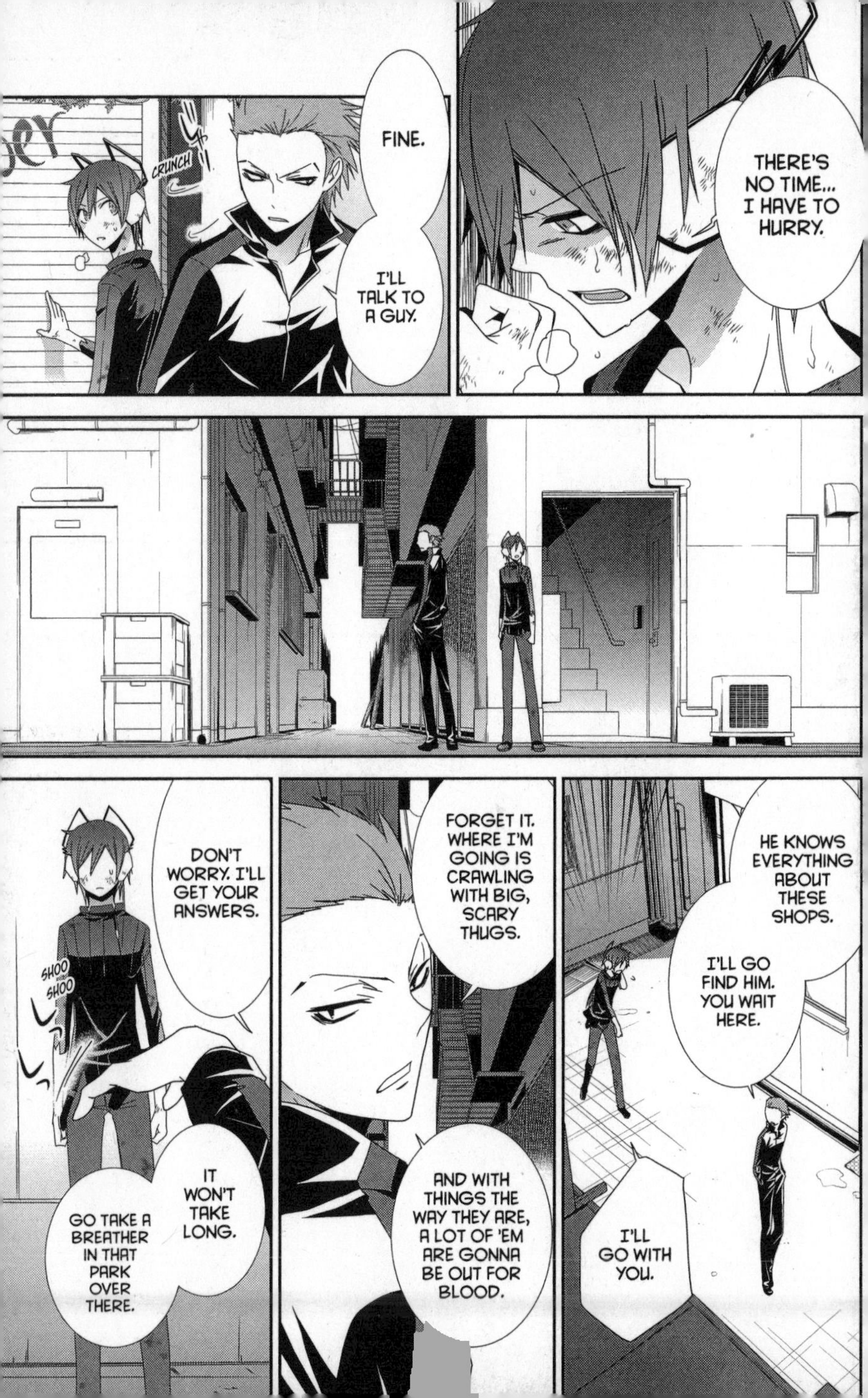
THERE'S NO TIME... I HAVE TO HURRY.
FINE.
I'LL TALK TO A GUY.
CRUNCH
HE KNOWS EVERYTHING ABOUT THESE SHOPS.
I'LL GO FIND HIM. YOU WAIT HERE.
I'LL GO WITH YOU.
FORGET IT. WHERE I'M GOING IS CRAWLING WITH BIG, SCARY THUGS.
AND WITH THINGS THE WAY THEY ARE, A LOT OF 'EM ARE GONNA BE OUT FOR BLOOD.
DON'T WORRY. I'LL GET YOUR ANSWERS.
IT WON'T TAKE LONG.
GO TAKE A BREATHER IN THAT PARK OVER THERE.
SHOO SHOO

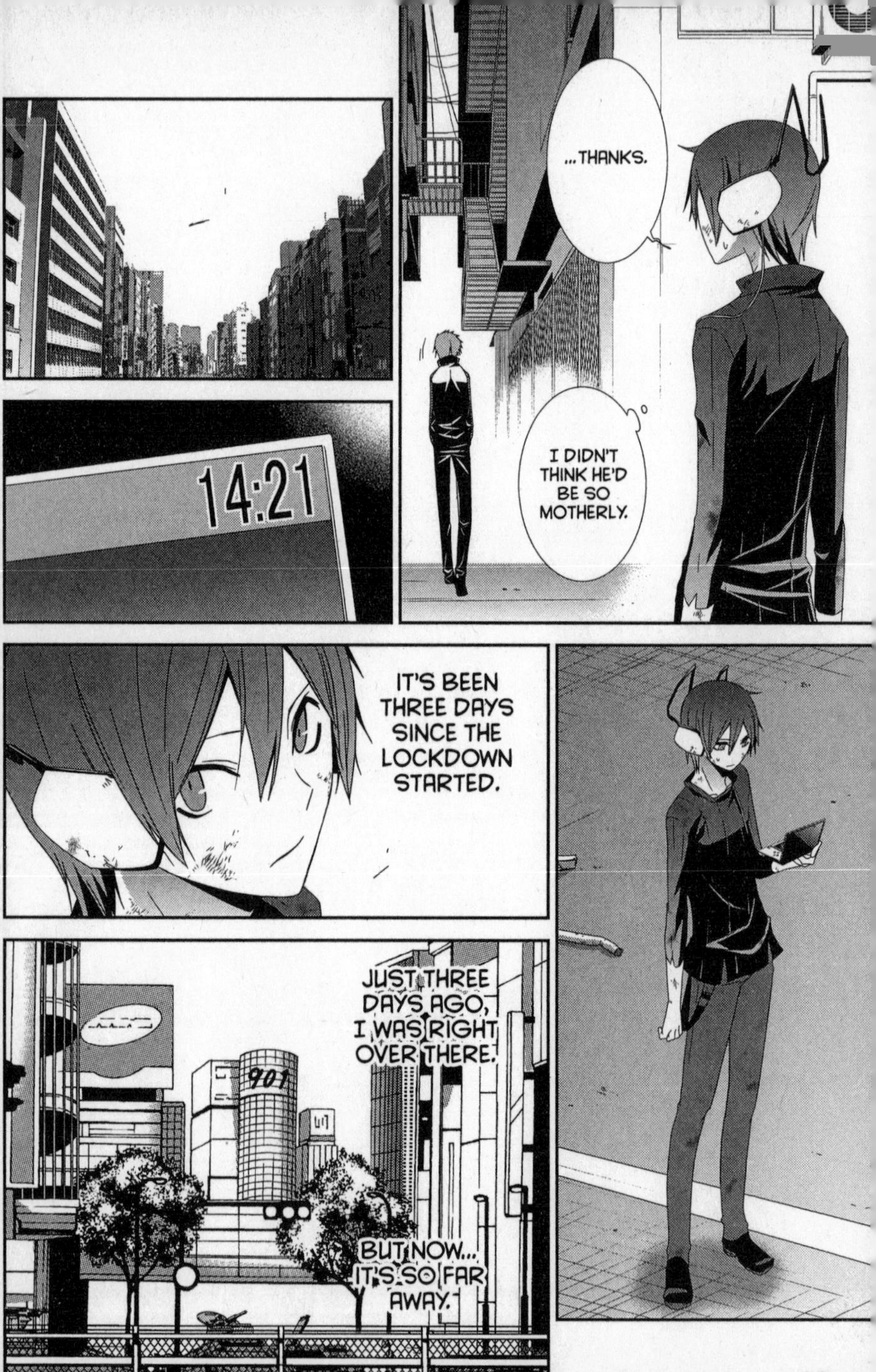
...THANKS.
I DIDN'T THINK HE'D BE SO MOTHERLY.
14:21
IT'S BEEN THREE DAYS SINCE THE LOCKDOWN STARTED.
JUST THREE DAYS AGO, I WAS RIGHT OVER THERE.
901
BUT NOW... IT'S SO FAR AWAY.

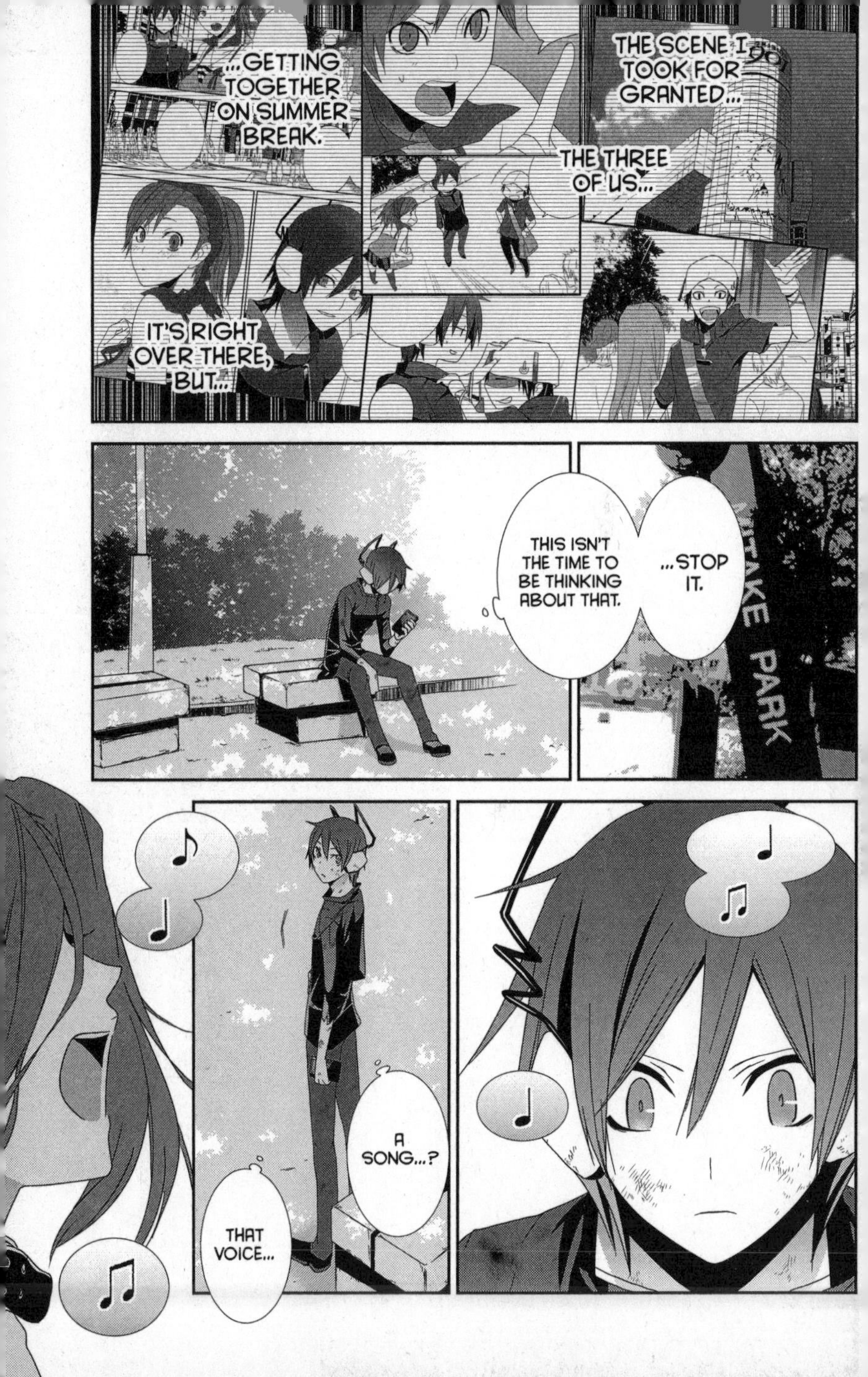
THE SCENE I TOOK FOR GRANTED...
THE THREE OF US...
...GETTING TOGETHER ON SUMMER BREAK.
IT'S RIGHT OVER THERE, BUT...
...STOP IT.
THIS ISN'T THE TIME TO BE THINKING ABOUT THAT.
PARK
A SONG...?
THAT VOICE...

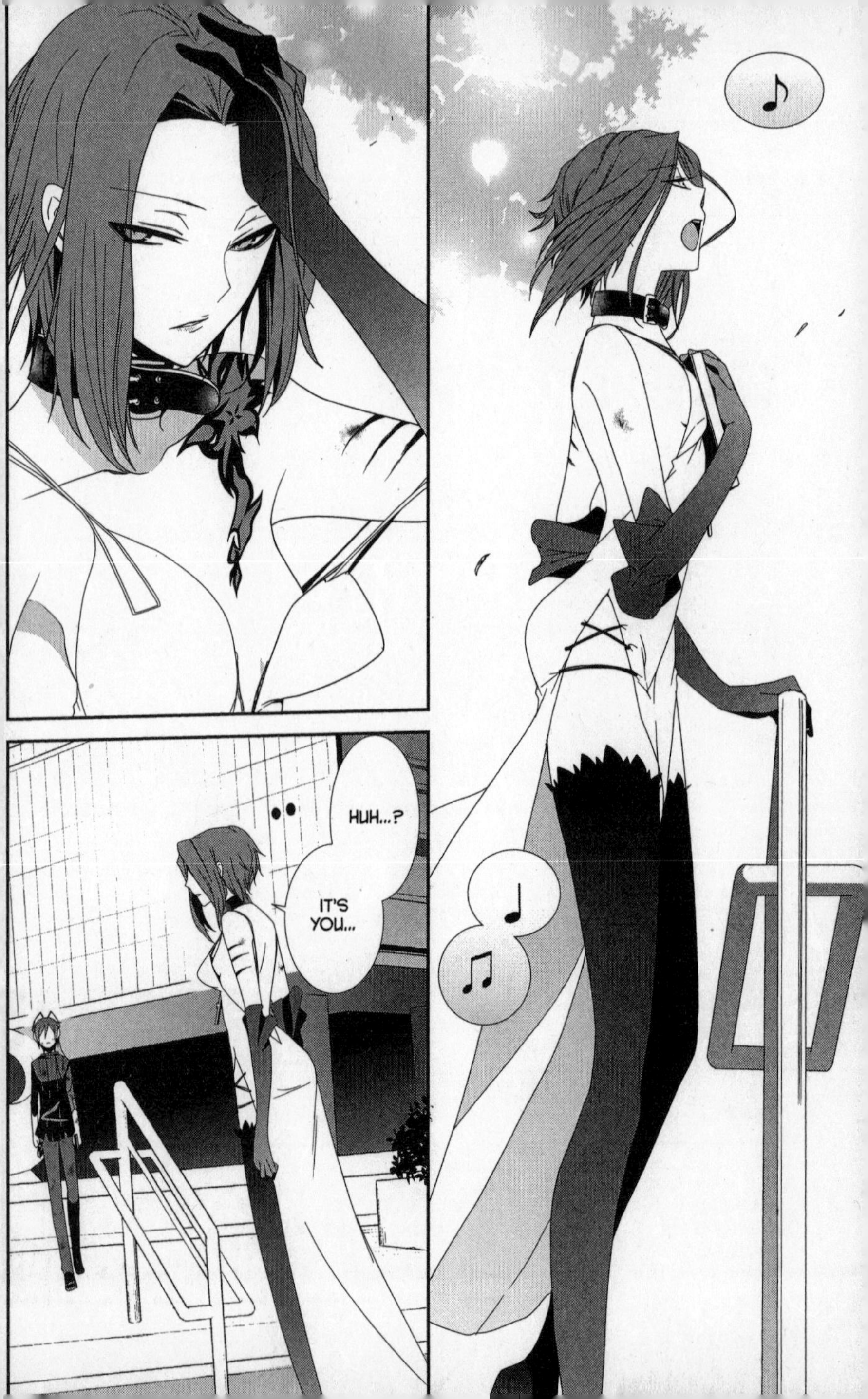
HUH...?
IT'S YOU...

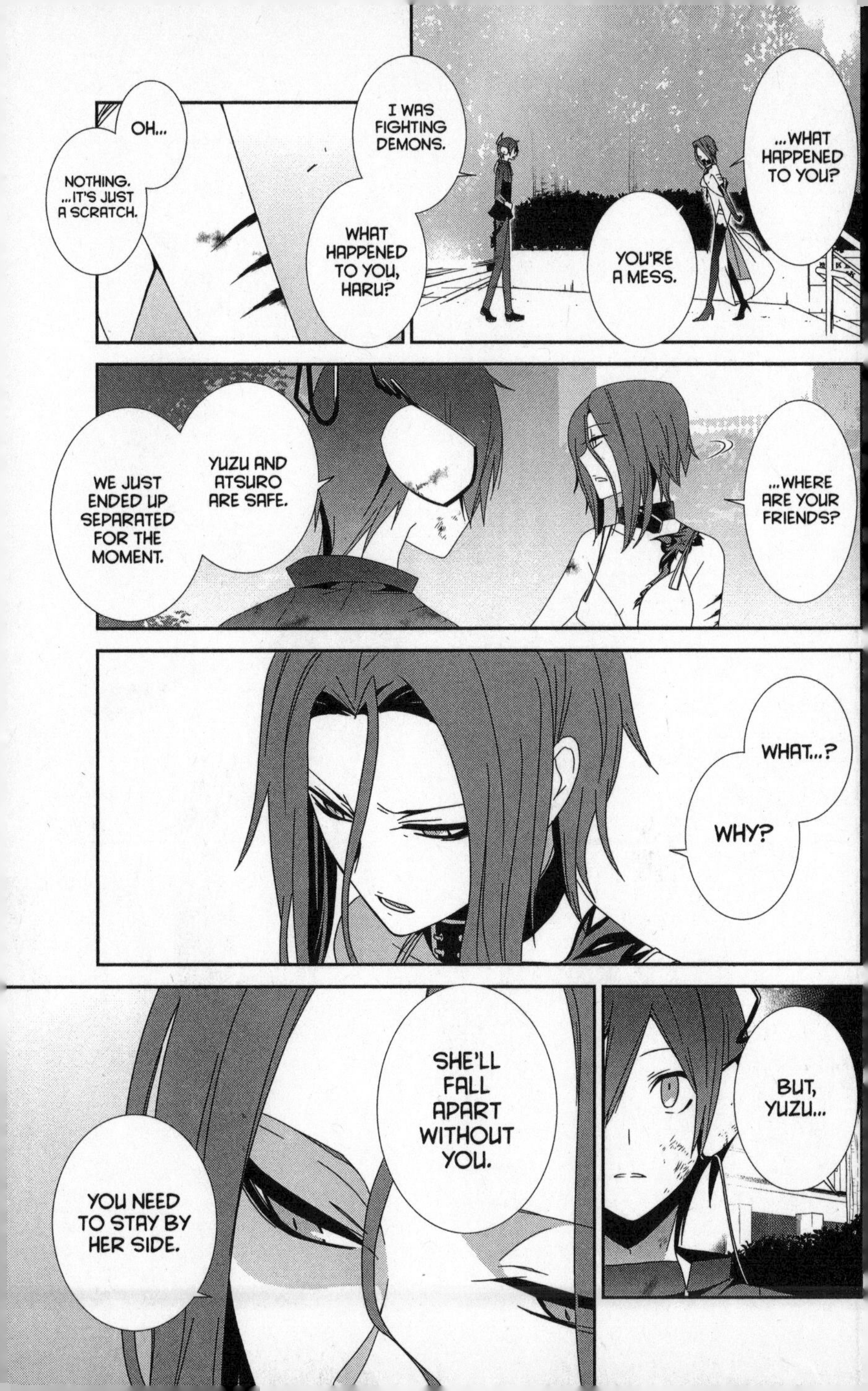
...WHAT HAPPENED TO YOU?
YOU'RE A MESS.
I WAS FIGHTING DEMONS.
WHAT HAPPENED TO YOU, HARU?
OH...
NOTHING. ...IT'S JUST A SCRATCH.
...WHERE ARE YOUR FRIENDS?
YUZU AND ATSURO ARE SAFE.
WE JUST ENDED UP SEPARATED FOR THE MOMENT.
WHAT...?
WHY?
BUT, YUZU...
SHE'LL FALL APART WITHOUT YOU.
YOU NEED TO STAY BY HER SIDE.

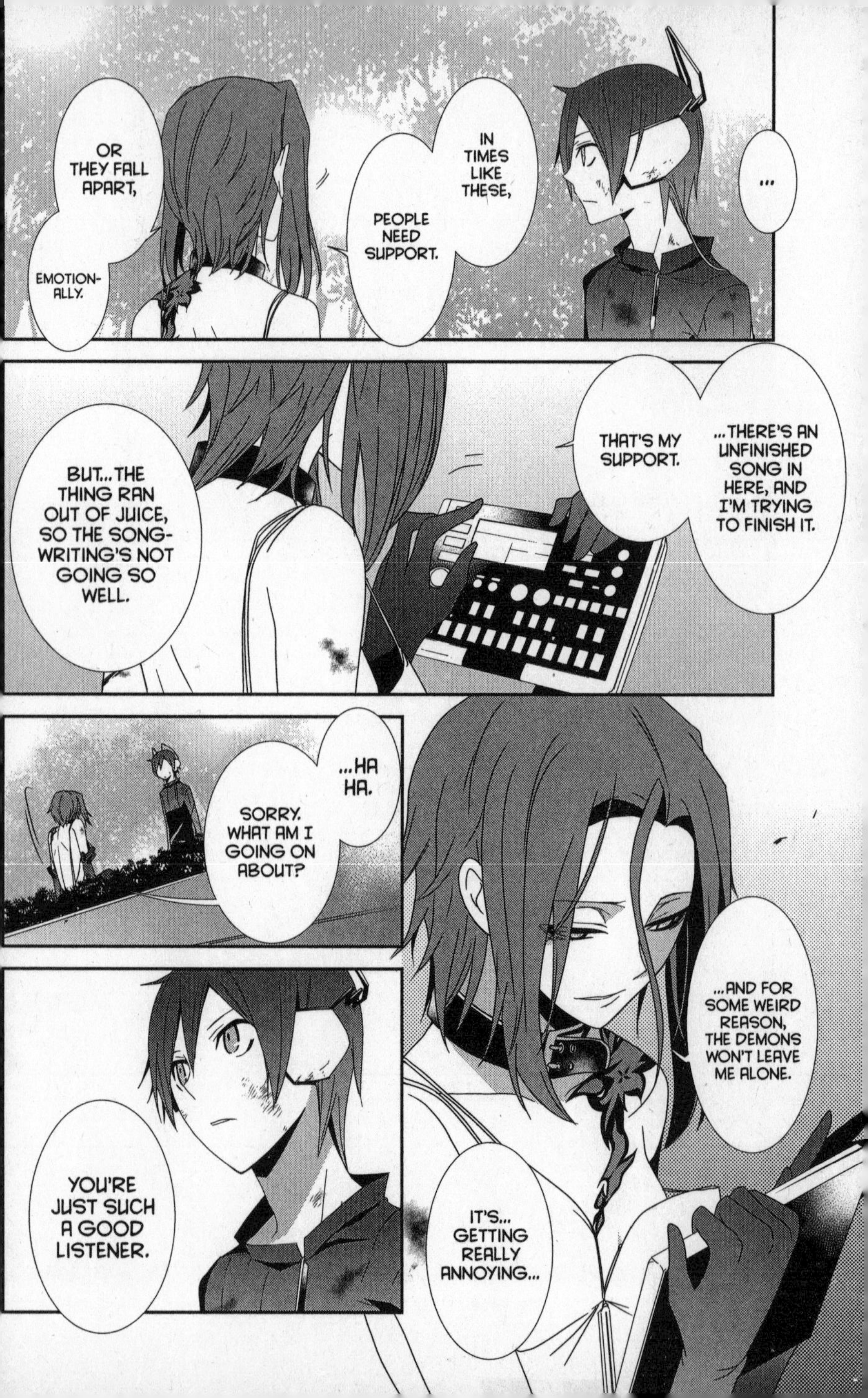
...
IN TIMES LIKE THESE,
PEOPLE NEED SUPPORT.
OR THEY FALL APART,
EMOTION-ALLY.
...THERE'S AN UNFINISHED SONG IN HERE, AND I'M TRYING TO FINISH IT.
THAT'S MY SUPPORT.
BUT...THE THING RAN OUT OF JUICE, SO THE SONG-WRITING'S NOT GOING SO WELL.
...AND FOR SOME WEIRD REASON, THE DEMONS WON'T LEAVE ME ALONE.
IT'S... GETTING REALLY ANNOYING...
...HA HA.
SORRY. WHAT AM I GOING ON ABOUT?
YOU'RE JUST SUCH A GOOD LISTENER.

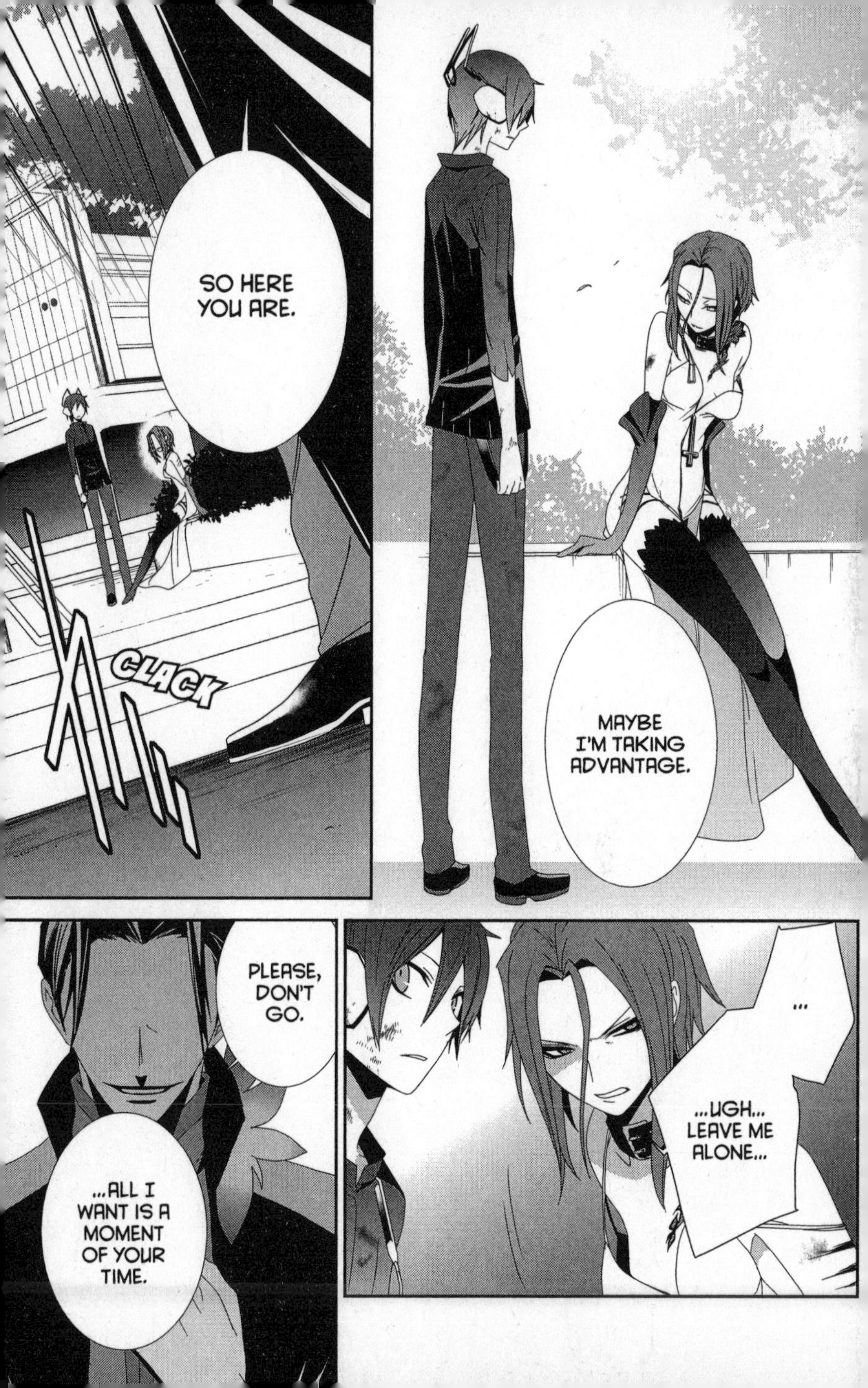
MAYBE I'M TAKING ADVANTAGE.
SO HERE YOU ARE.
CLACK
...
...UGH... LEAVE ME ALONE...
PLEASE, DON'T GO.
...ALL I WANT IS A MOMENT OF YOUR TIME.

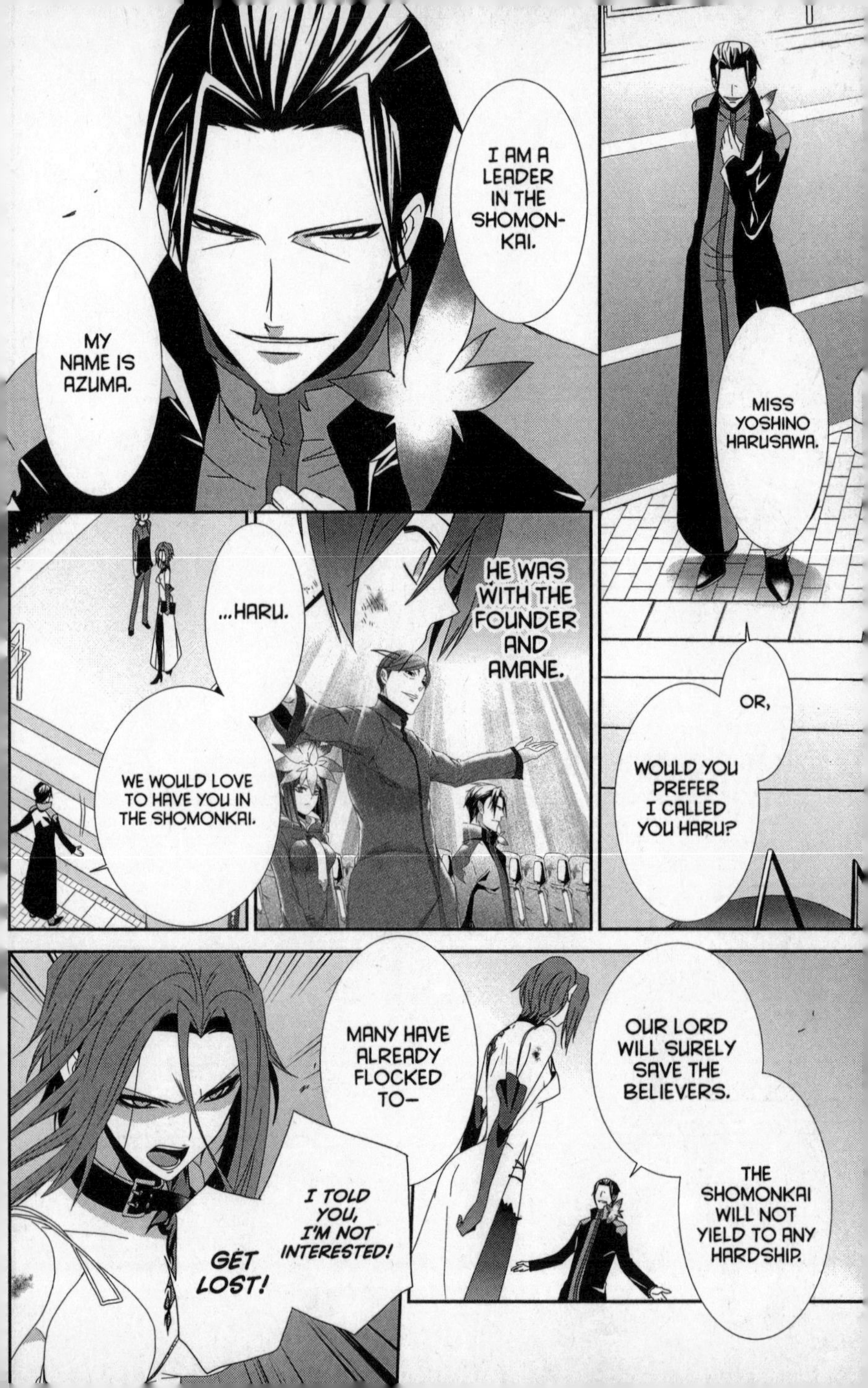
MISS YOSHINO HARUSAWA.
I AM A LEADER IN THE SHOMON-KAI.
MY NAME IS AZUMA.
OR,
WOULD YOU PREFER I CALLED YOU HARU?
HE WAS WITH THE FOUNDER AND AMANE.
...HARU.
WE WOULD LOVE TO HAVE YOU IN THE SHOMONKAI.
OUR LORD WILL SURELY SAVE THE BELIEVERS.
MANY HAVE ALREADY FLOCKED TO—
THE SHOMONKAI WILL NOT YIELD TO ANY HARDSHIP.
I TOLD YOU, I'M NOT INTERESTED!
GET LOST!

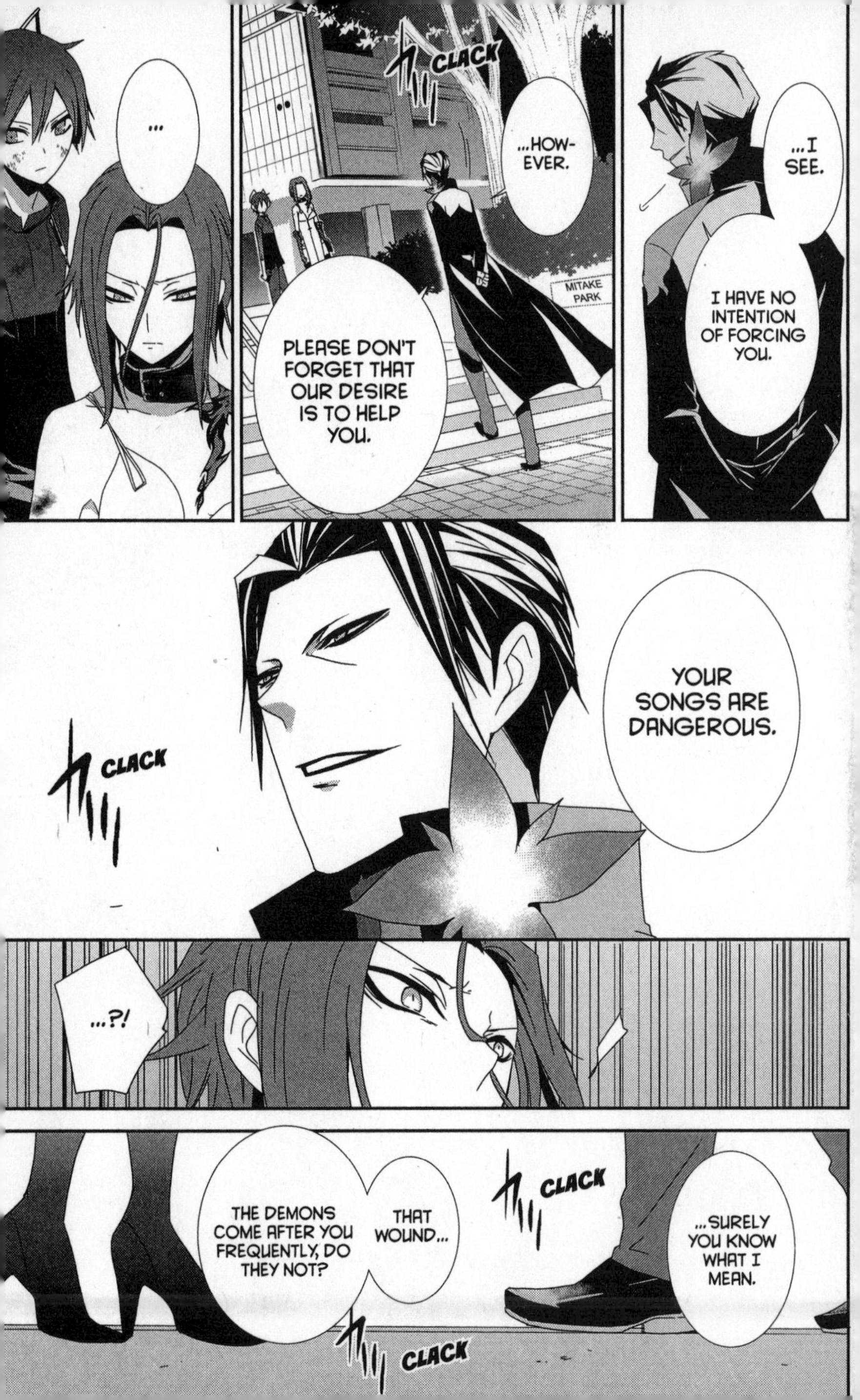
...I SEE.
I HAVE NO INTENTION OF FORCING YOU.
CLACK
...HOW-EVER.
MITAKE PARK
PLEASE DON'T FORGET THAT OUR DESIRE IS TO HELP YOU.
...
YOUR SONGS ARE DANGEROUS.
CLACK
...?!
...SURELY YOU KNOW WHAT I MEAN.
CLACK
THAT WOUND...
THE DEMONS COME AFTER YOU FREQUENTLY, DO THEY NOT?
CLACK

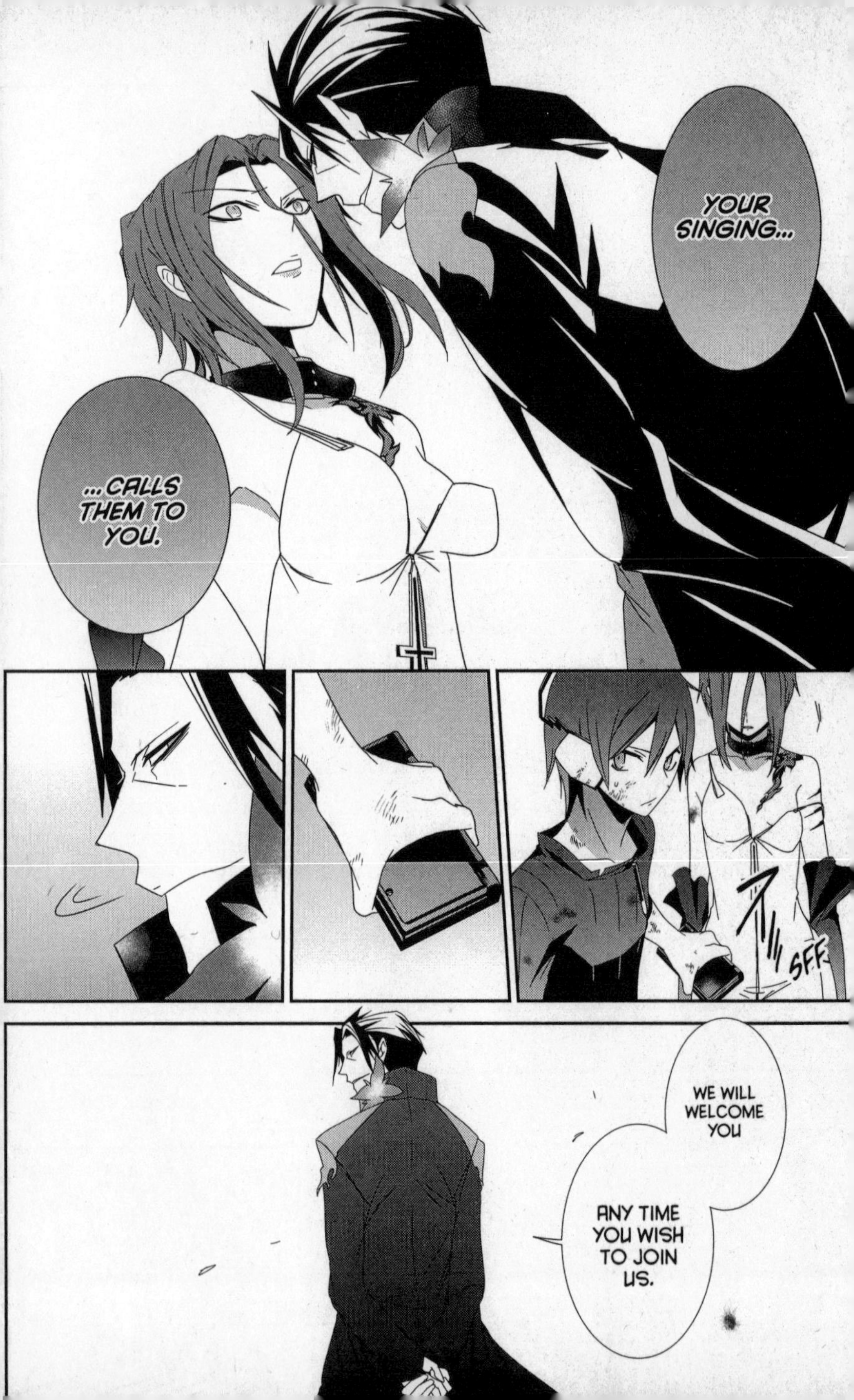
YOUR SINGING...
...CALLS THEM TO YOU.
SFF
WE WILL WELCOME YOU
ANY TIME YOU WISH TO JOIN US.

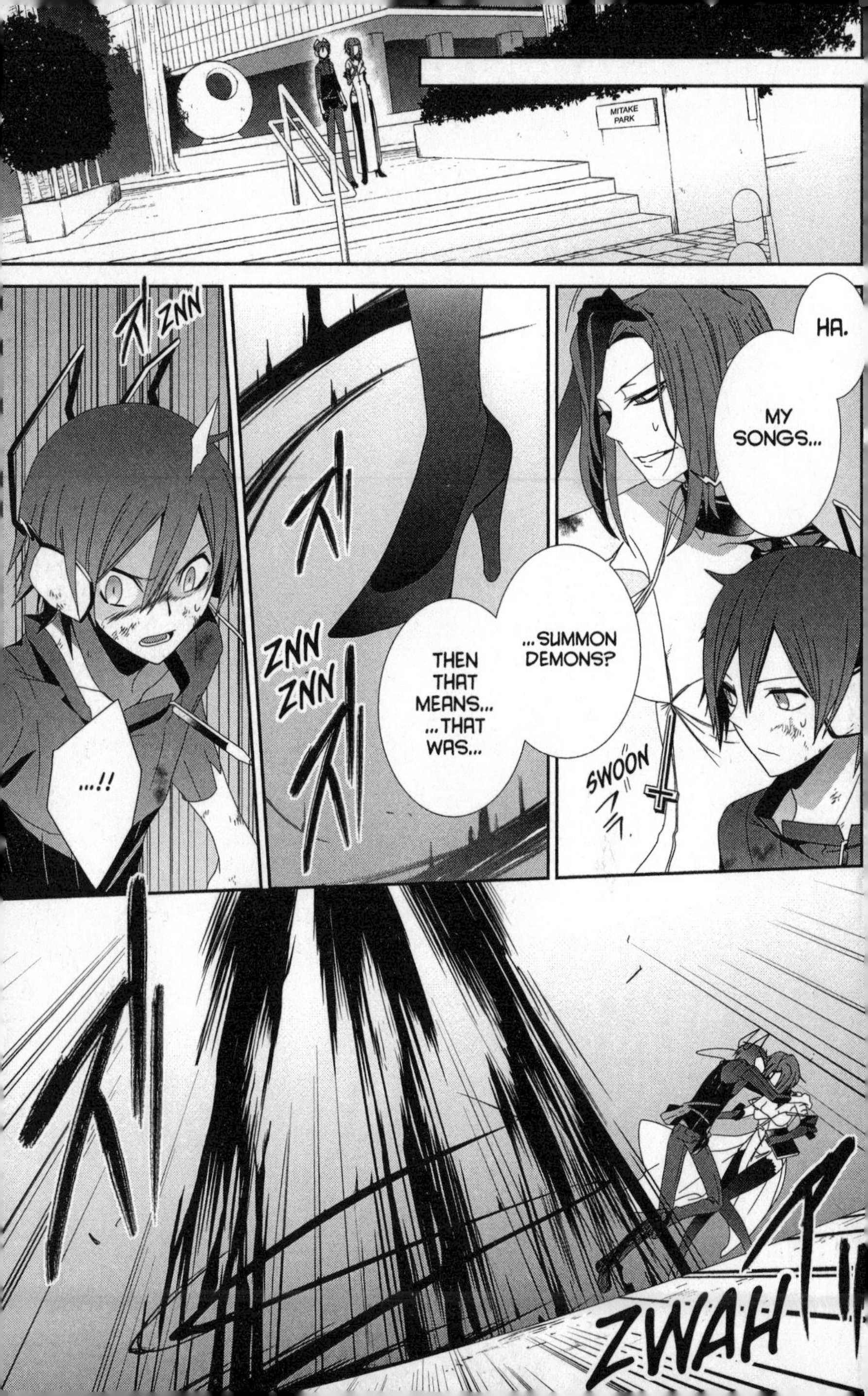
MITAKE PARK
HA.
MY SONGS...
...SUMMON DEMONS?
THEN THAT MEANS... ...THAT WAS...
SWOON
ZNN ZNN
ZNN
...!!
ZWAH

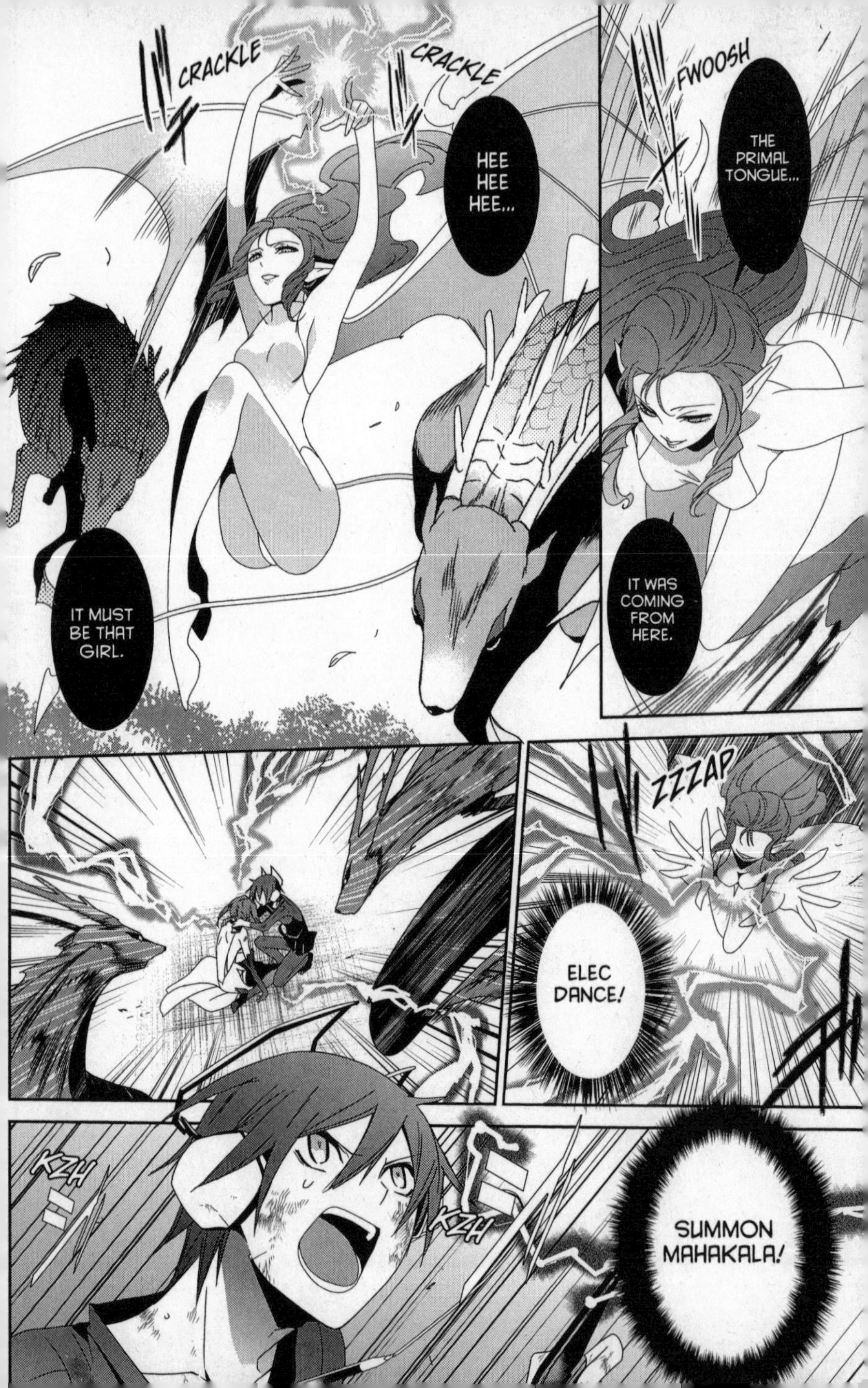
FWOOSH
THE PRIMAL TONGUE...
IT WAS COMING FROM HERE.
CRACKLE
CRACKLE
HEE HEE HEE...
IT MUST BE THAT GIRL.
ZZZAP
ELEC DANCE!
SUMMON MAHAKALA!
KZH
KZH

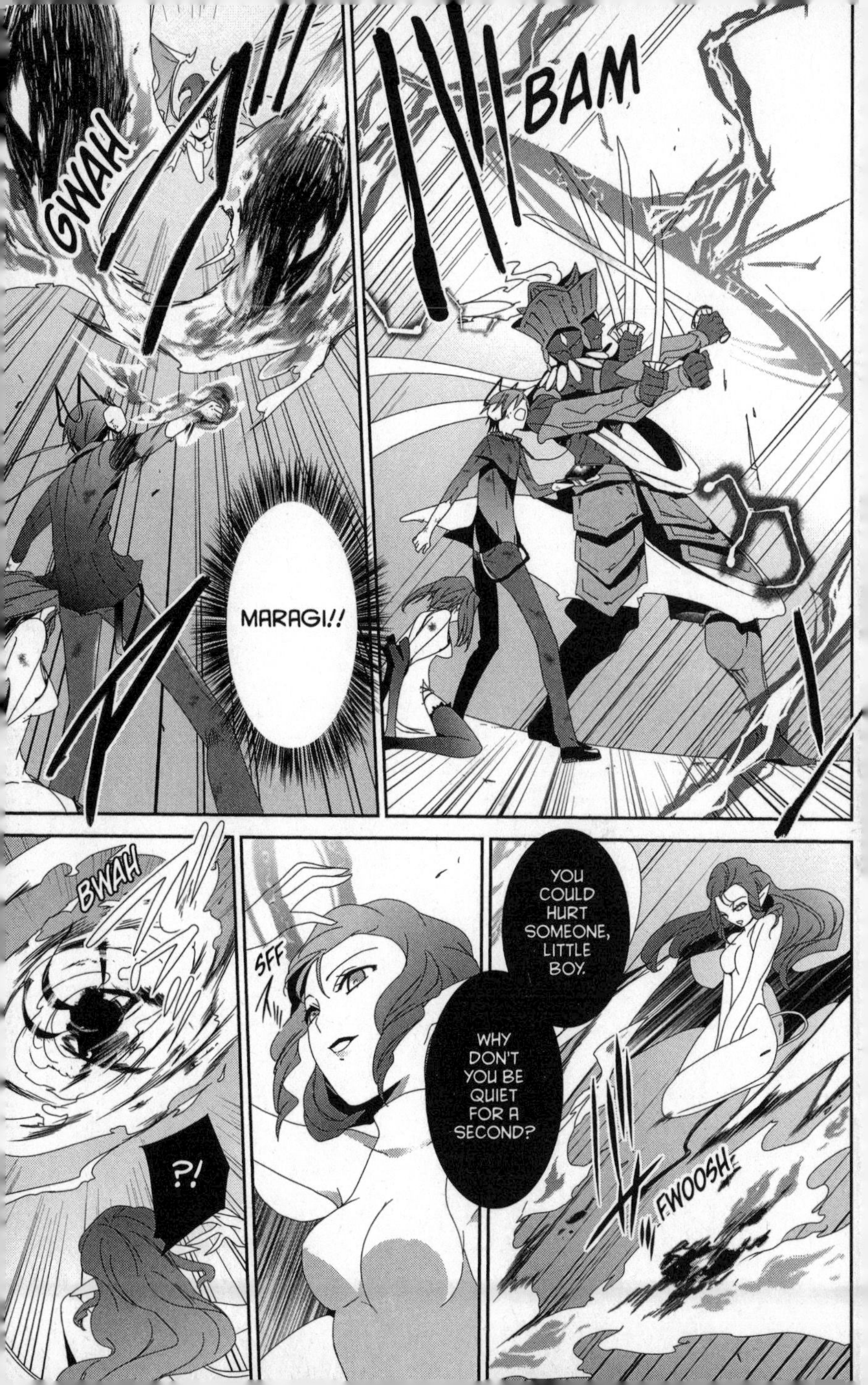
BAM
GWAH
MARAGI!!
YOU COULD HURT SOMEONE, LITTLE BOY.
FWOOSH
WHY DON'T YOU BE QUIET FOR A SECOND?
SFF
BWAH
?!

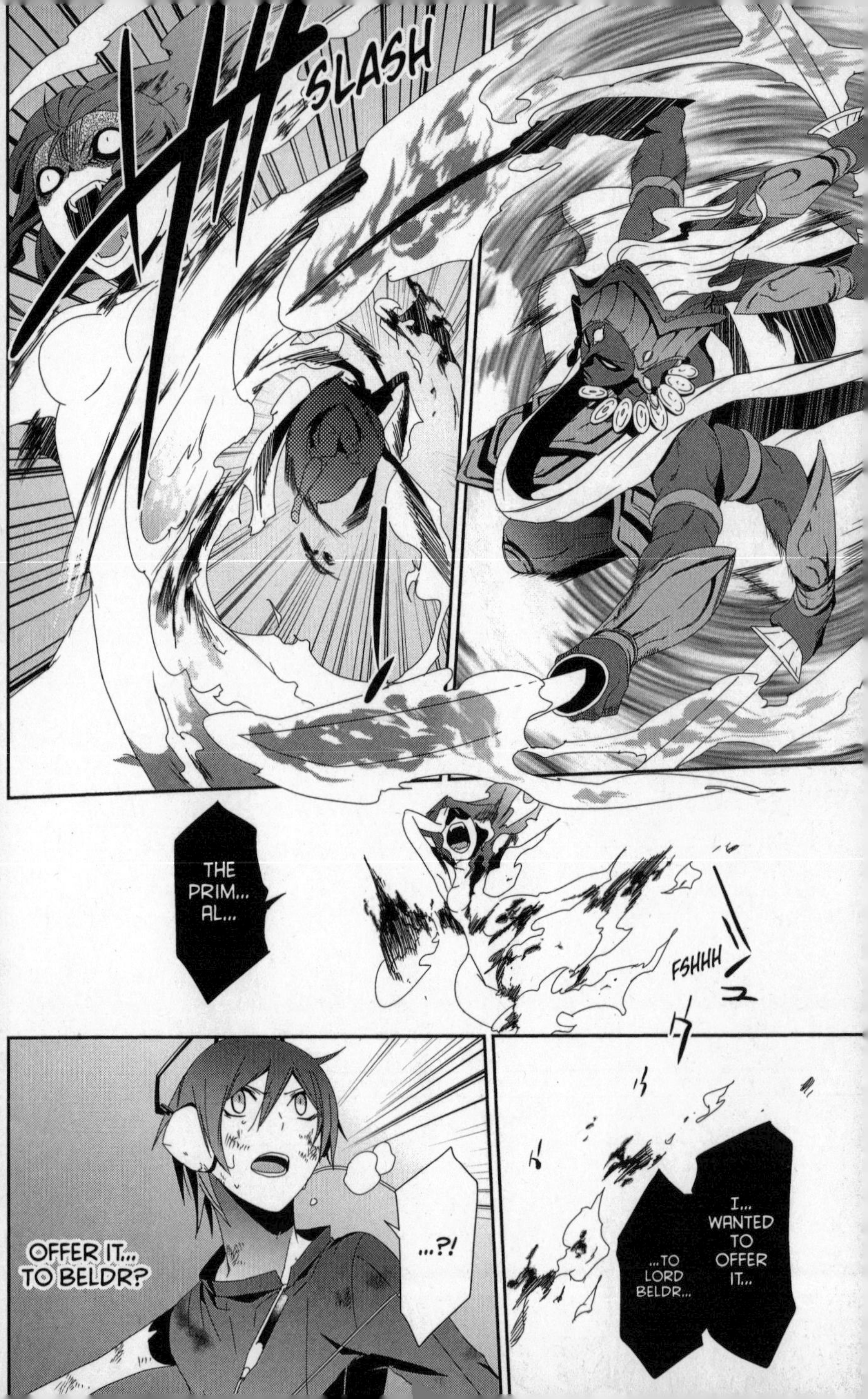
SLASH
FSHHH
THE PRIM... AL...
I... WANTED TO OFFER IT...
...TO LORD BELDR...
...?!
OFFER IT... TO BELDR?

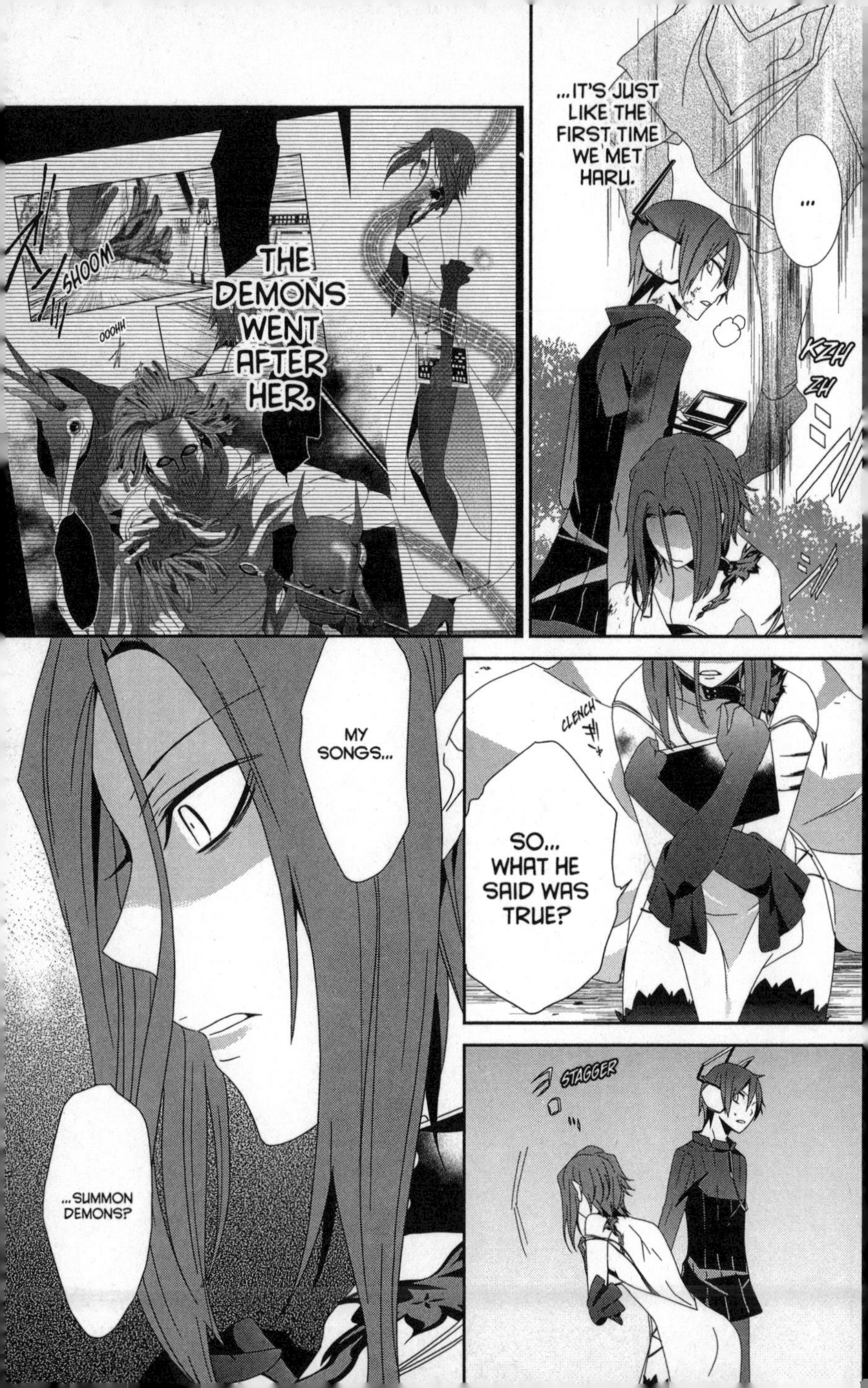
...IT'S JUST LIKE THE FIRST TIME WE MET HARU.
...
KZH
ZH
SHOOM
OOOHH
THE DEMONS WENT AFTER HER.
CLENCH
SO... WHAT HE SAID WAS TRUE?
STAGGER
MY SONGS...
...SUMMON DEMONS?

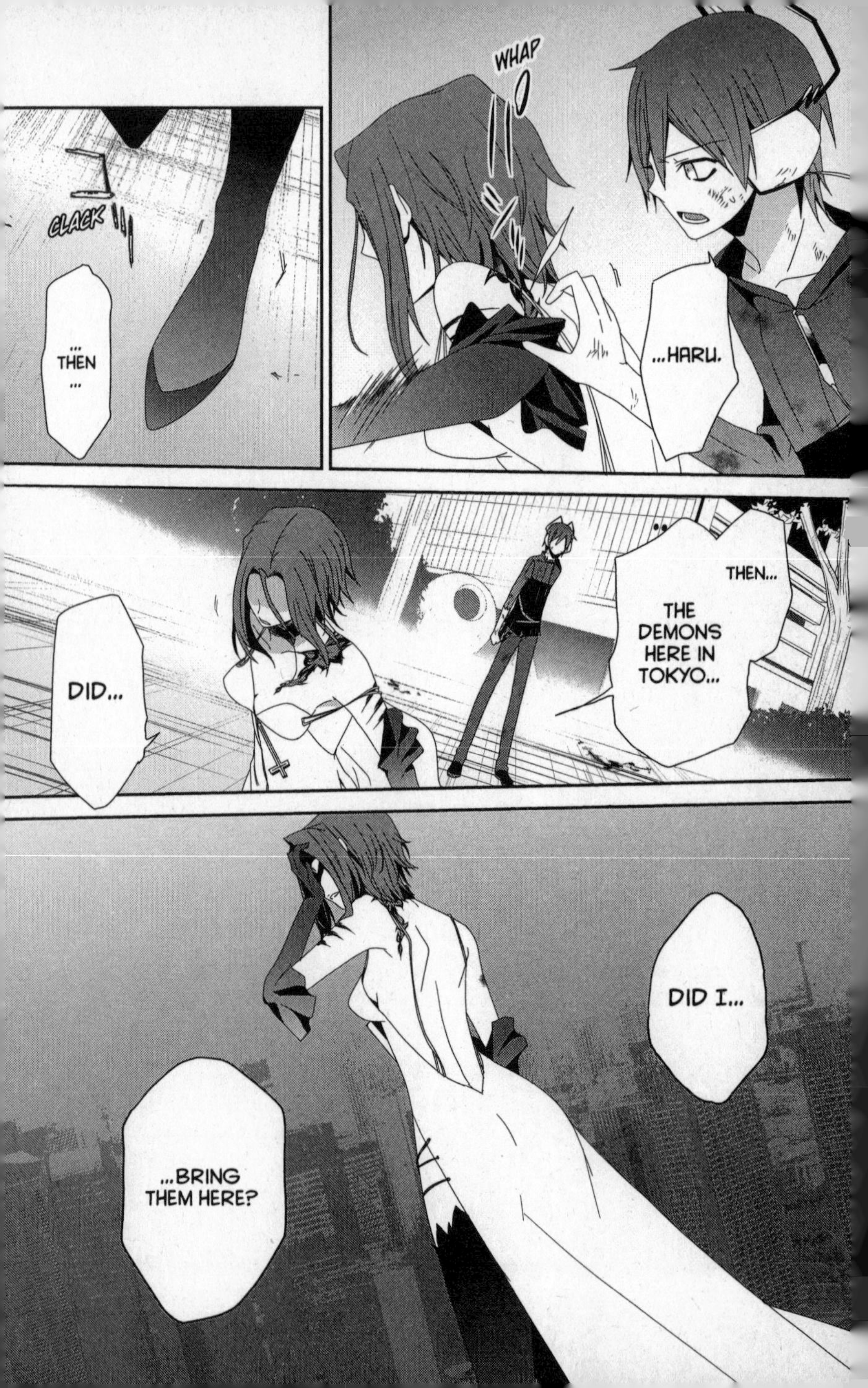
WHAP
...HARU.
CLACK
...THEN...
THEN...
THE DEMONS HERE IN TOKYO...
DID...
DID I...
...BRING THEM HERE?

PYRO JACK

HE IS KNOWN AROUND THE WORLD AS THE
PUMPKIN LANTERN SPIRIT, JACK-O'-LANTERN.
ORIGINALLY A GHOST LIGHT IN THE CORNWALL
REGION OF ENGLAND KNOWN AS WILL-O'-THE-
WISP, HE IS SAID TO BE A WANDERING DEAD
SOUL, SOMETHING SIMILAR TO WHAT THEY CALL
A HITODAMA IN JAPAN. HE APPEARS AT NIGHT TO
STARTLE TRAVELERS OR MAKE THEM LOSE THEIR
WAY BY LURING THEM AFTER HIM.

DEVIL SURVIVOR

デビルサバイバー

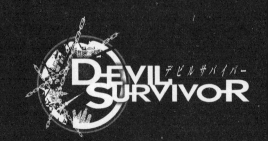

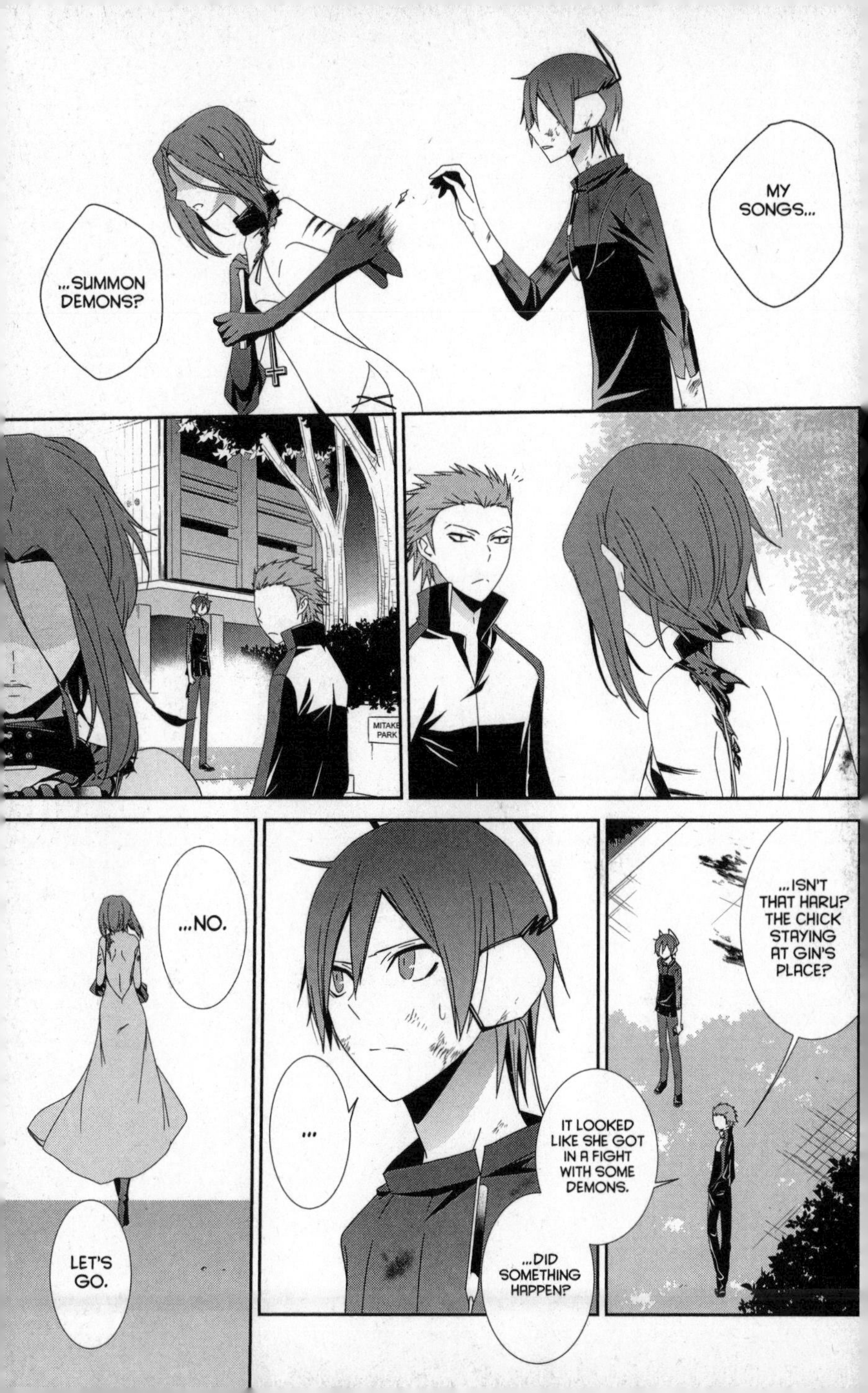
MY SONGS...
...SUMMON DEMONS?
MITAKE PARK
...ISN'T THAT HARU? THE CHICK STAYING AT GIN'S PLACE?
IT LOOKED LIKE SHE GOT IN A FIGHT WITH SOME DEMONS.
...DID SOMETHING HAPPEN?
...
...NO.
LET'S GO.

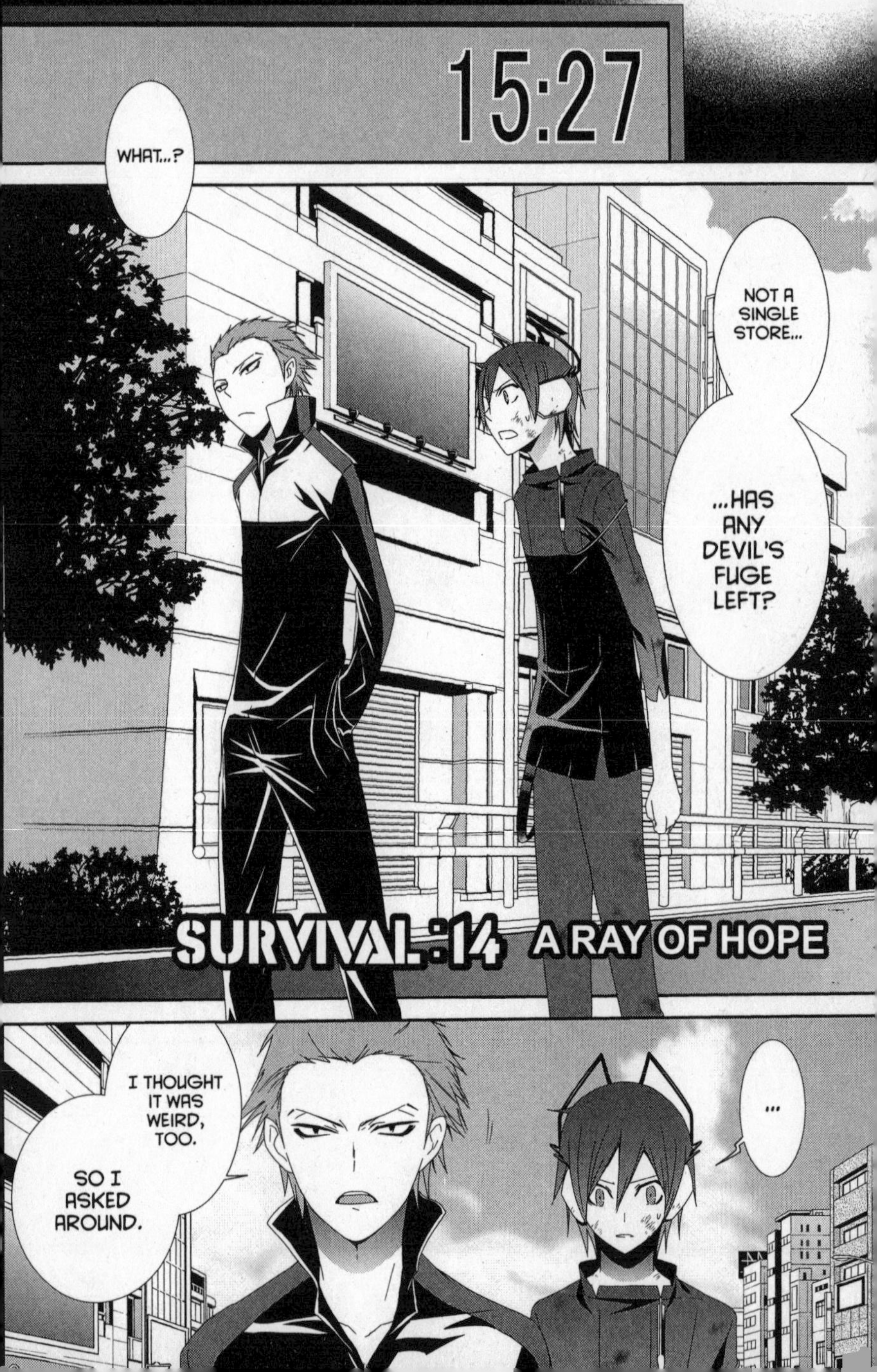
15:27
NOT A SINGLE STORE...
...HAS ANY DEVIL'S FUGE LEFT?
WHAT...?
SURVIVAL:14 A RAY OF HOPE
...
I THOUGHT IT WAS WEIRD, TOO.
SO I ASKED AROUND.

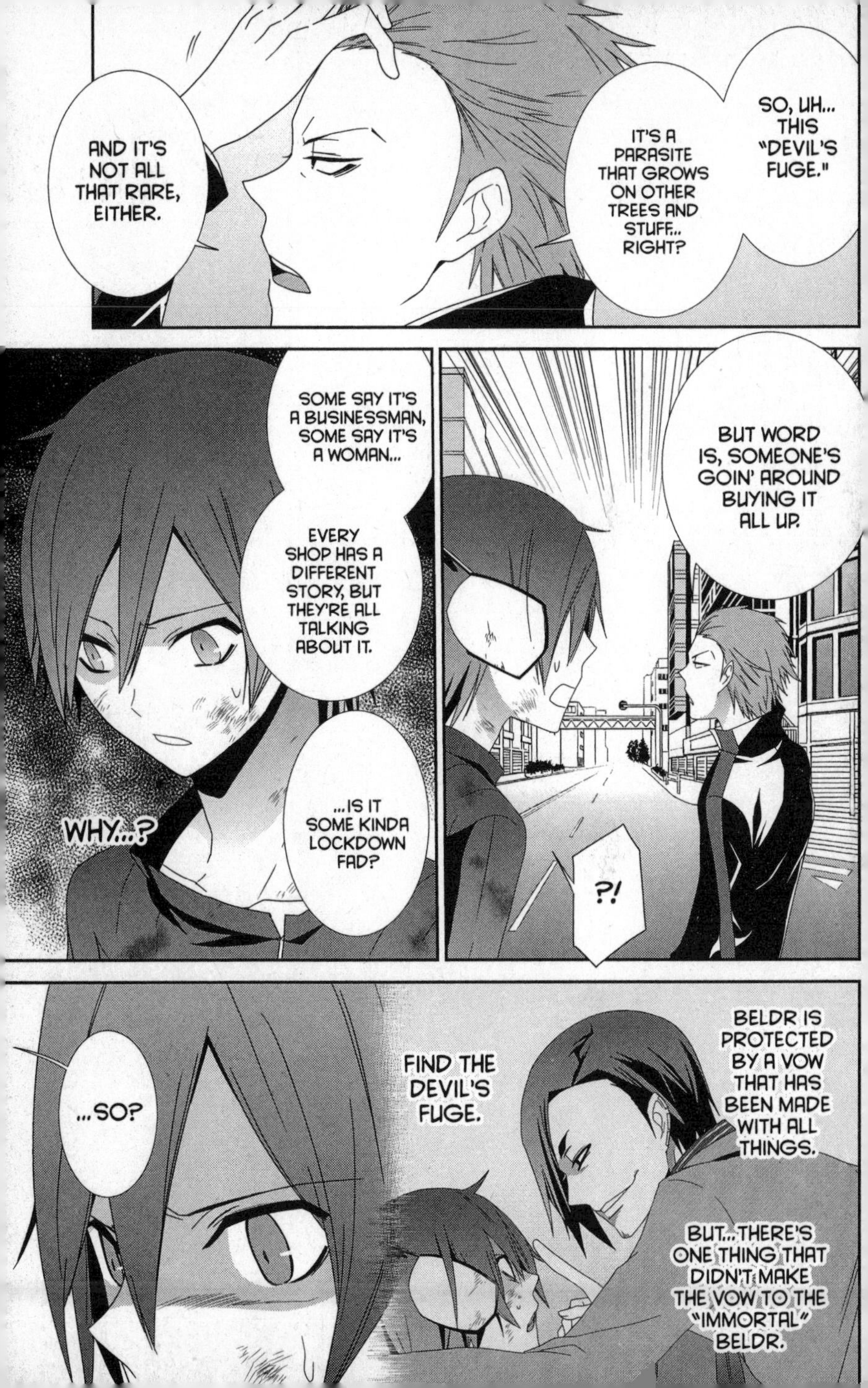
SO, UH... THIS "DEVIL'S FUGE."
IT'S A PARASITE THAT GROWS ON OTHER TREES AND STUFF... RIGHT?
AND IT'S NOT ALL THAT RARE, EITHER.
BUT WORD IS, SOMEONE'S GOIN' AROUND BUYING IT ALL UP.
?!
SOME SAY IT'S A BUSINESSMAN, SOME SAY IT'S A WOMAN...
EVERY SHOP HAS A DIFFERENT STORY, BUT THEY'RE ALL TALKING ABOUT IT.
...IS IT SOME KINDA LOCKDOWN FAD?
WHY...?
BELDR IS PROTECTED BY A VOW THAT HAS BEEN MADE WITH ALL THINGS.
BUT... THERE'S ONE THING THAT DIDN'T MAKE THE VOW TO THE "IMMORTAL" BELDR.
FIND THE DEVIL'S FUGE.
...SO?

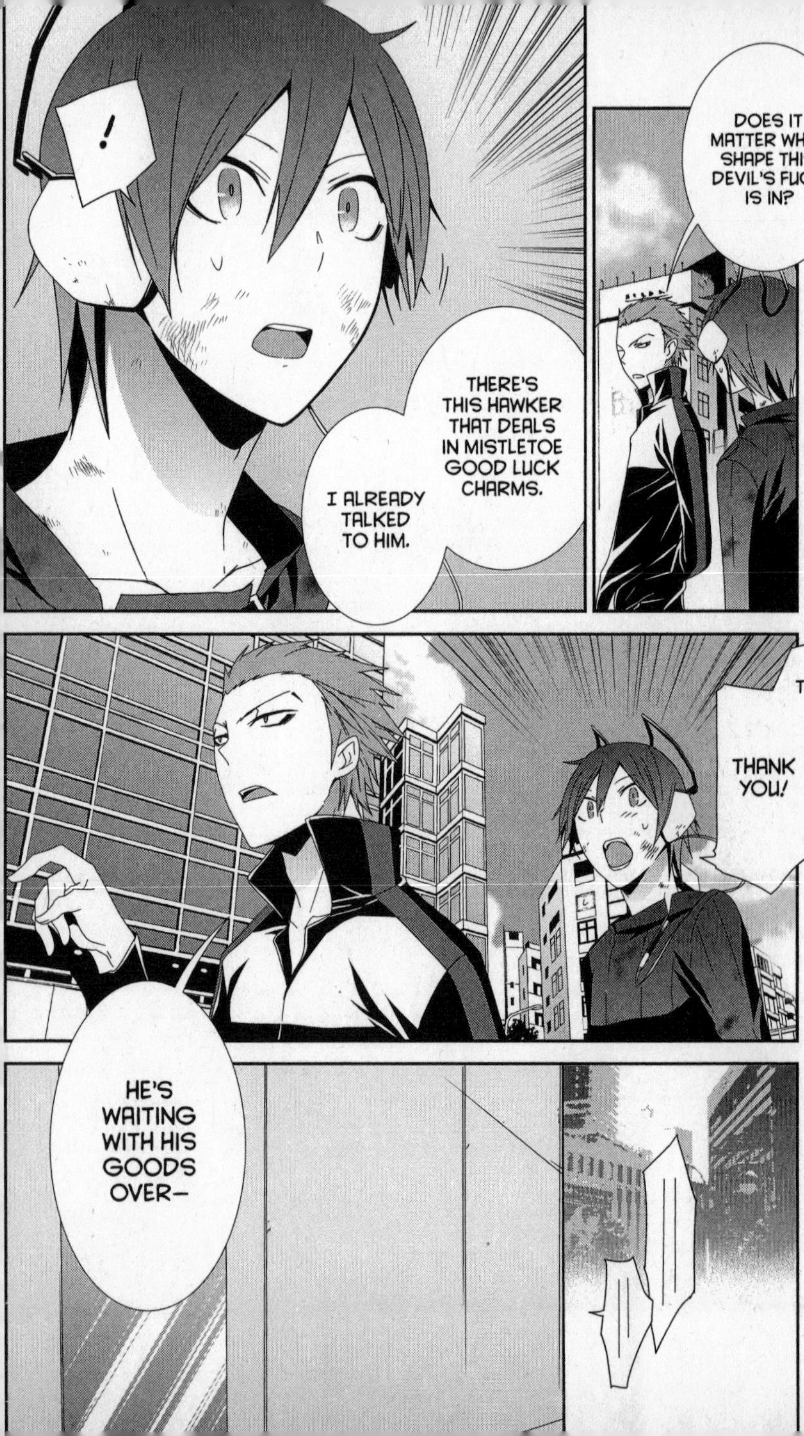
DOES IT MATTER WHAT SHAPE THIS DEVIL'S FUGE IS IN?
!
THERE'S THIS HAWKER THAT DEALS IN MISTLETOE GOOD LUCK CHARMS.
I ALREADY TALKED TO HIM.
TH—
THANK YOU!
HE'S WAITING WITH HIS GOODS OVER—

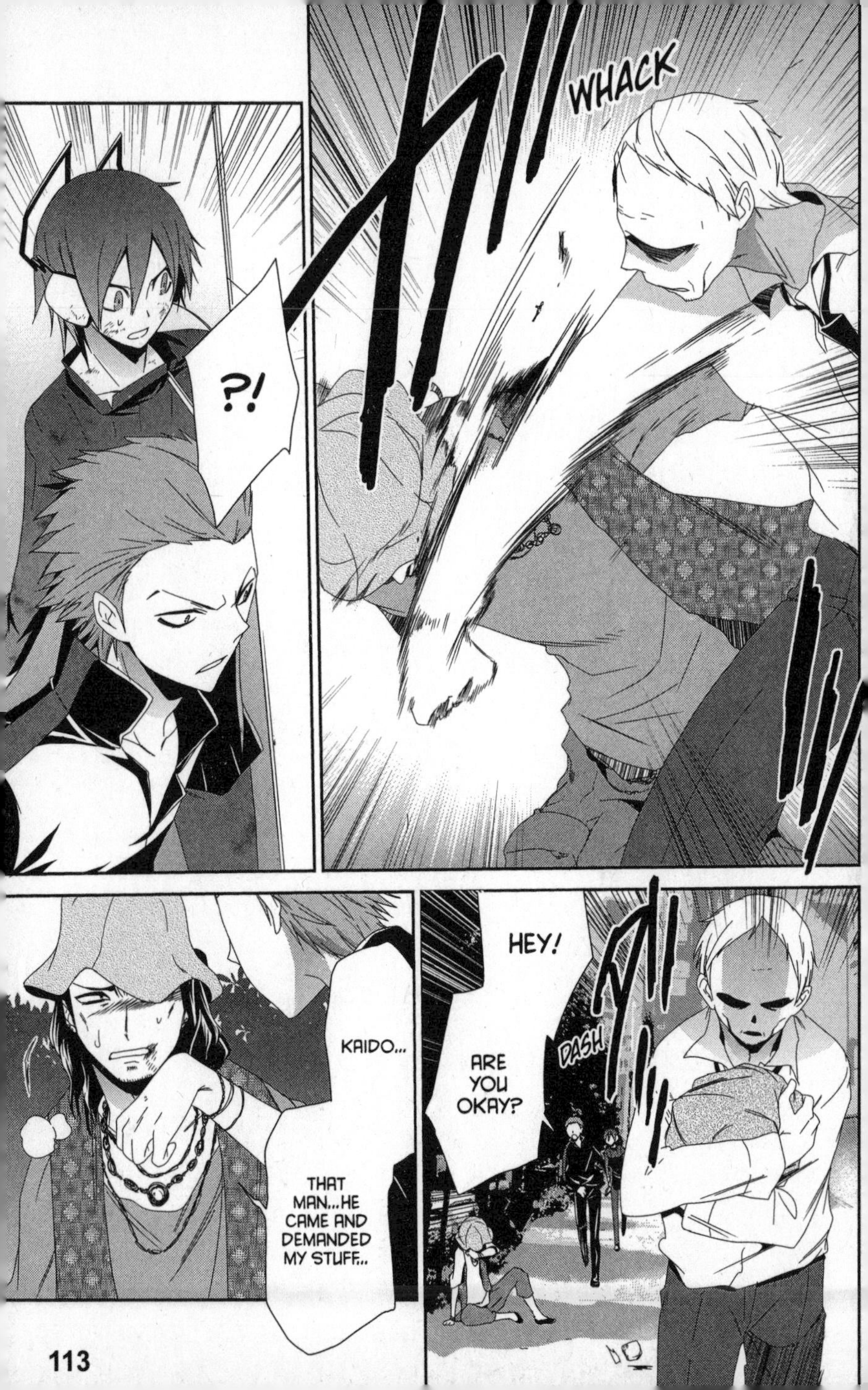
WHACK
?!
HEY!
DASH
ARE YOU OKAY?
KAIDO...
THAT MAN...HE CAME AND DEMANDED MY STUFF...

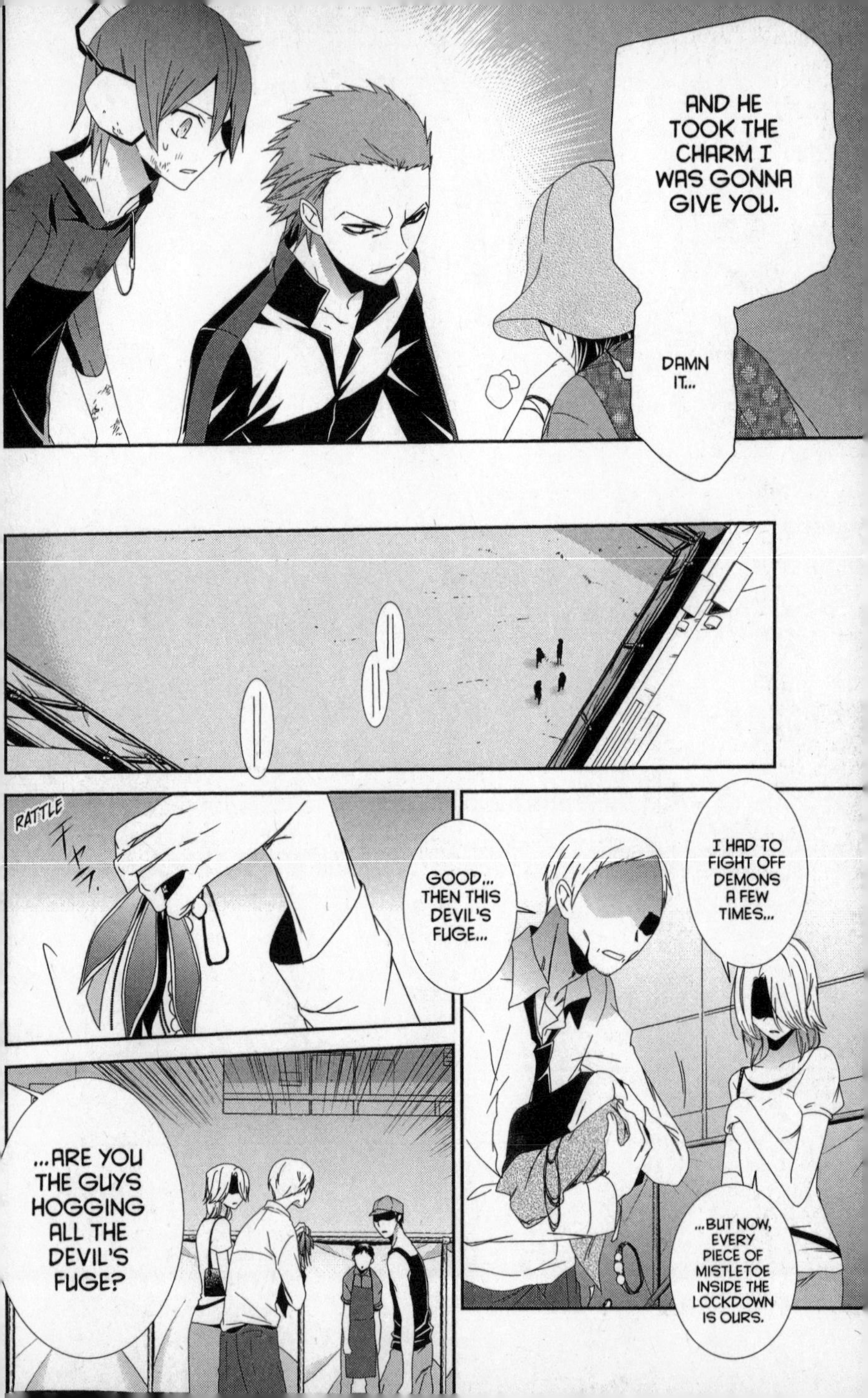
AND HE TOOK THE CHARM I WAS GONNA GIVE YOU.
DAMN IT...
I HAD TO FIGHT OFF DEMONS A FEW TIMES...
GOOD... THEN THIS DEVIL'S FUGE...
...BUT NOW, EVERY PIECE OF MISTLETOE INSIDE THE LOCKDOWN IS OURS.
RATTLE
...ARE YOU THE GUYS HOGGING ALL THE DEVIL'S FUGE?

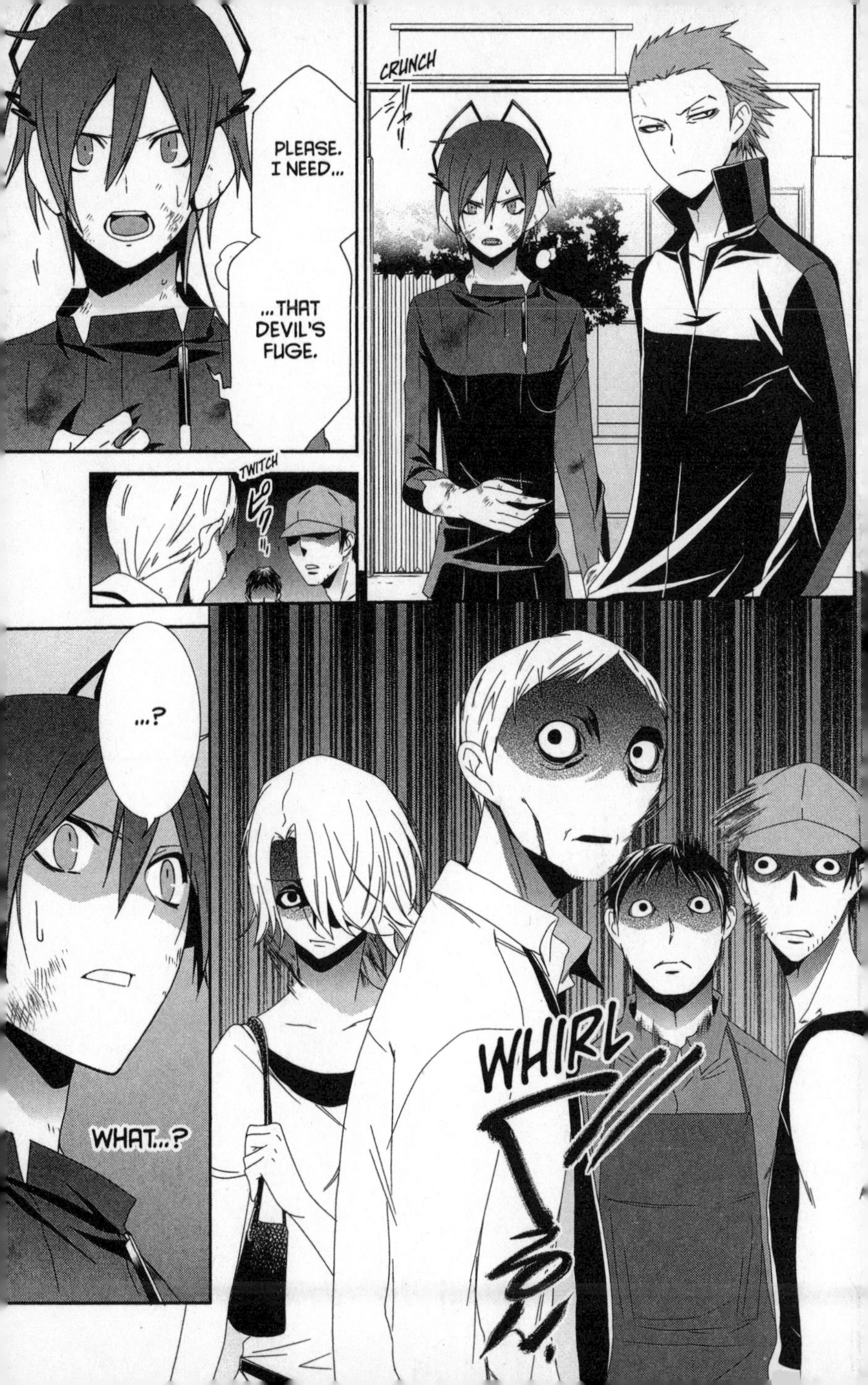
CRUNCH
PLEASE. I NEED...
...THAT DEVIL'S FUGE.
TWITCH
WHIRL
...?
WHAT...?

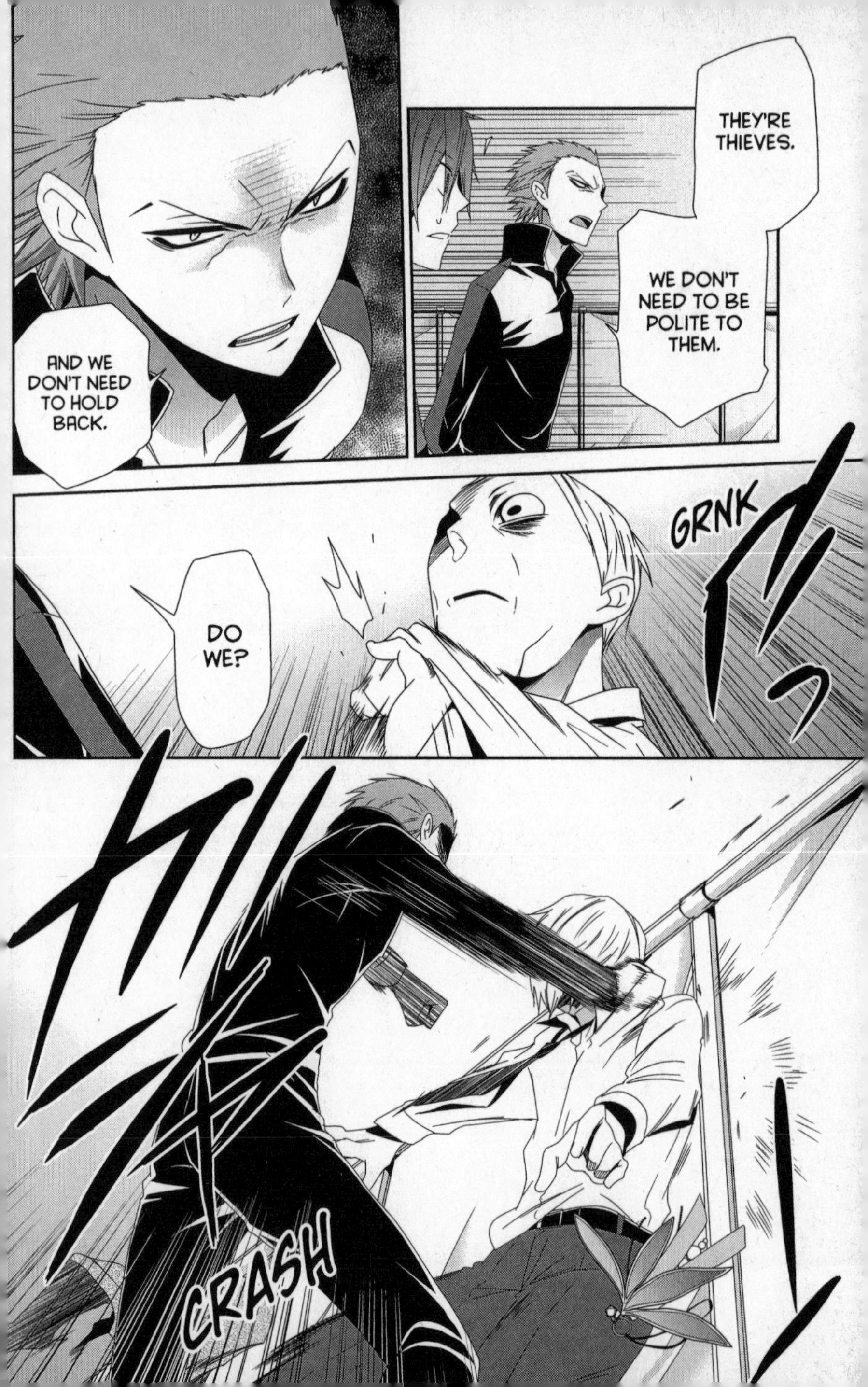
THEY'RE THIEVES.
WE DON'T NEED TO BE POLITE TO THEM.
AND WE DON'T NEED TO HOLD BACK.
GRNK
DO WE?
CRASH

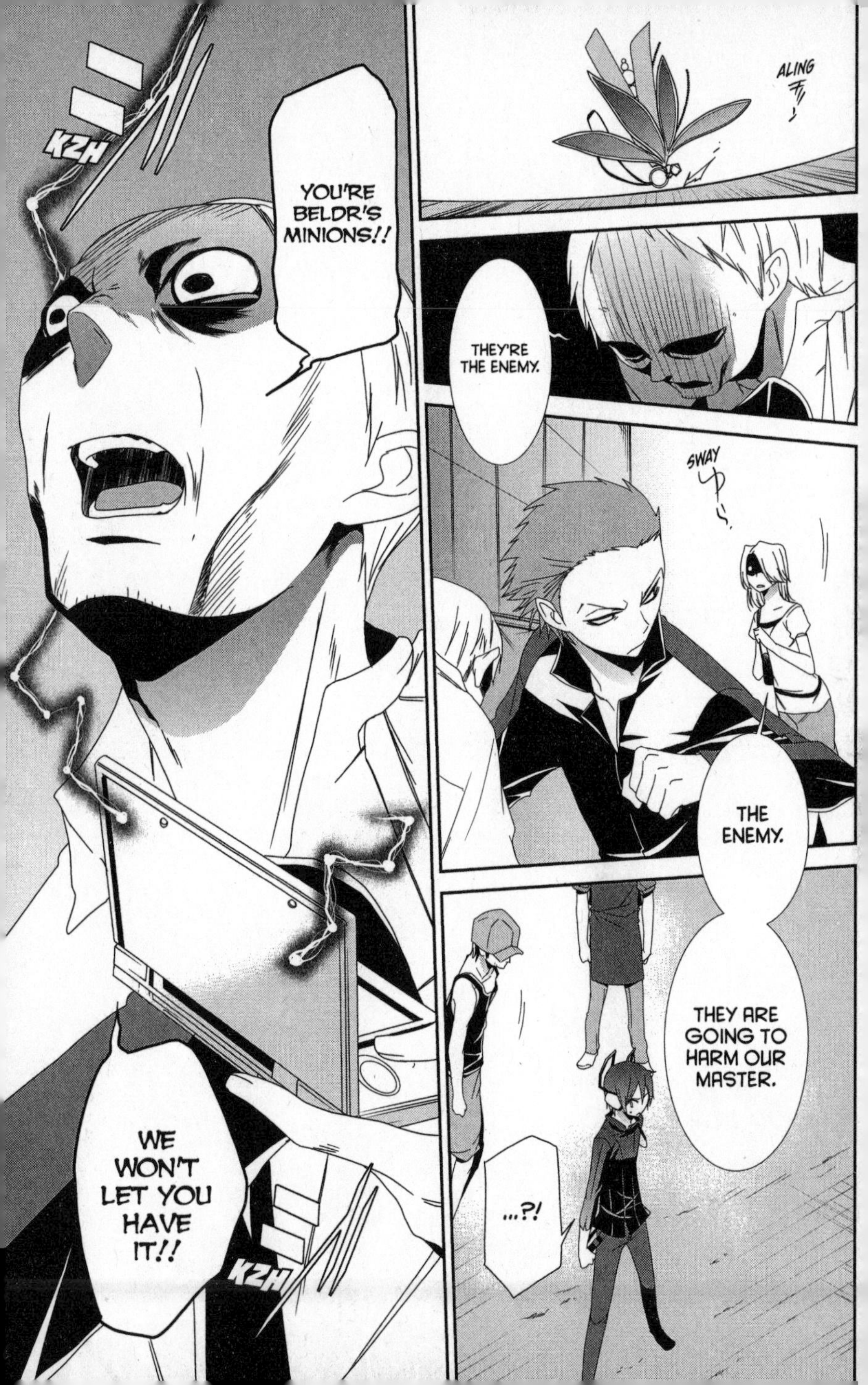
ALING
THEY'RE THE ENEMY.
SWAY
THE ENEMY.
THEY ARE GOING TO HARM OUR MASTER.
...?!
KZH
YOU'RE BELDR'S MINIONS!!
WE WON'T LET YOU HAVE IT!!
KZH

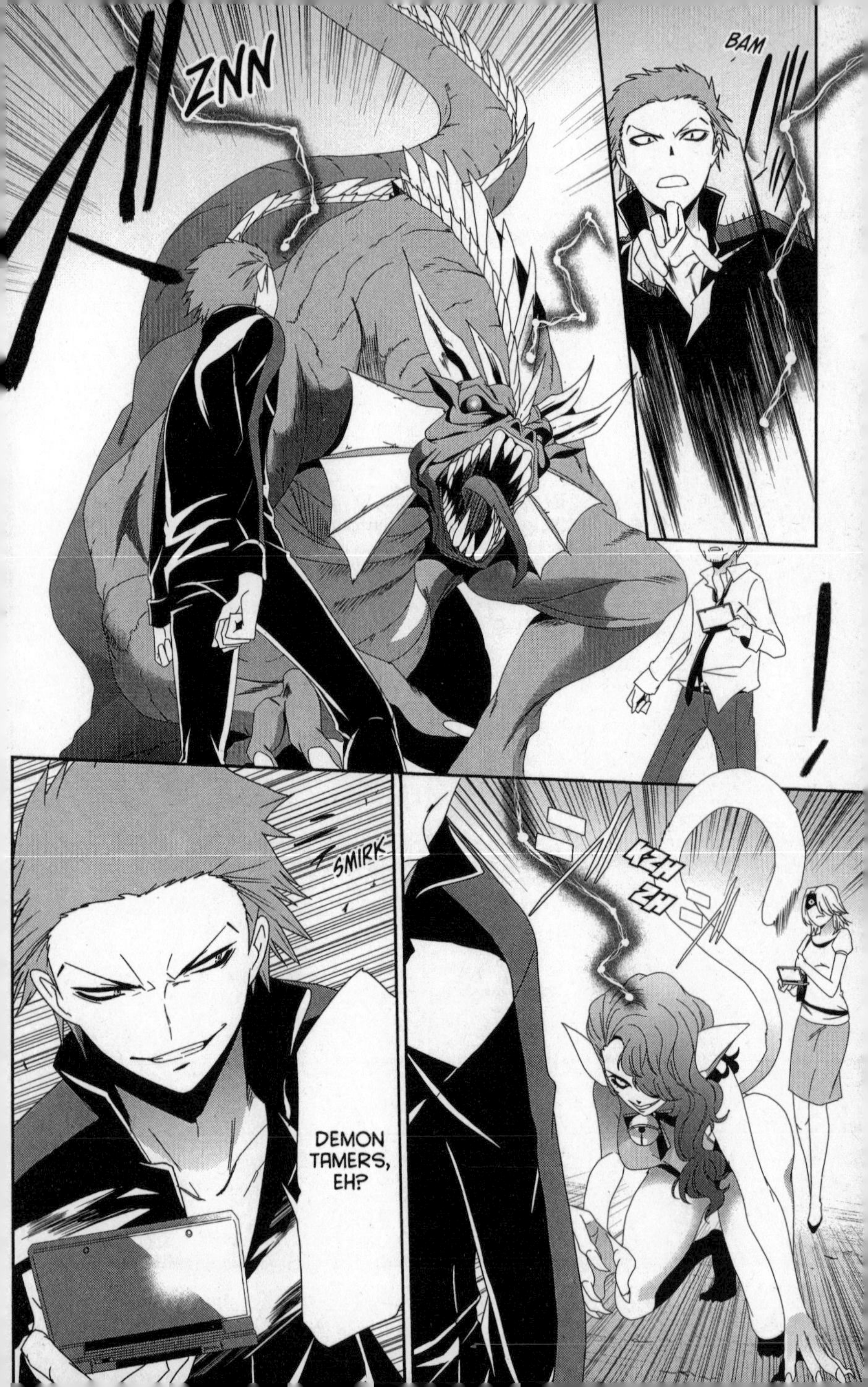
BAM
ZNN
KZH
ZH
SMIRK
DEMON TAMERS, EH?

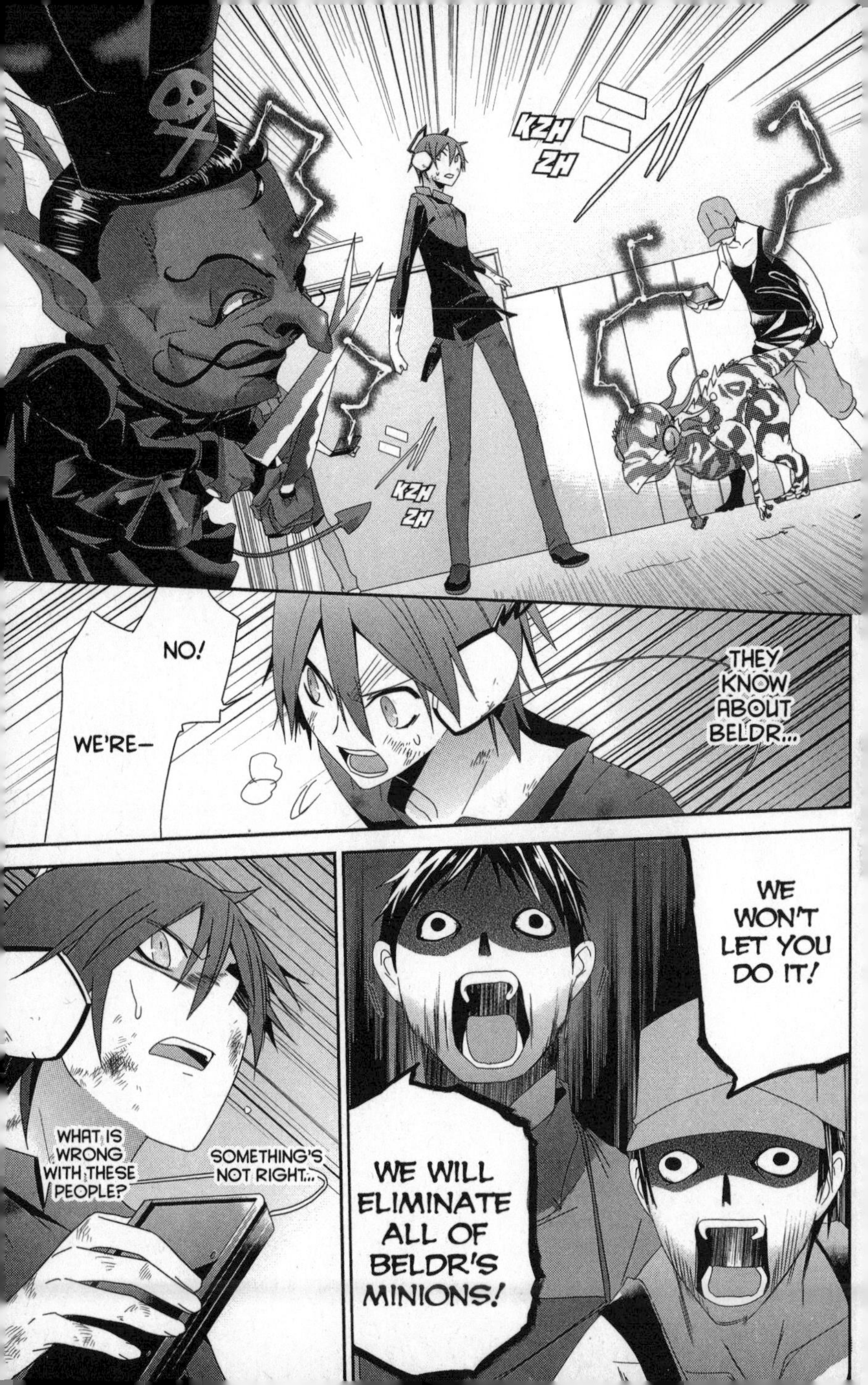
KZH ZH
KZH ZH
THEY KNOW ABOUT BELDR...
NO!
WE'RE–
WE WON'T LET YOU DO IT!
WE WILL ELIMINATE ALL OF BELDR'S MINIONS!
SOMETHING'S NOT RIGHT...
WHAT IS WRONG WITH THESE PEOPLE?

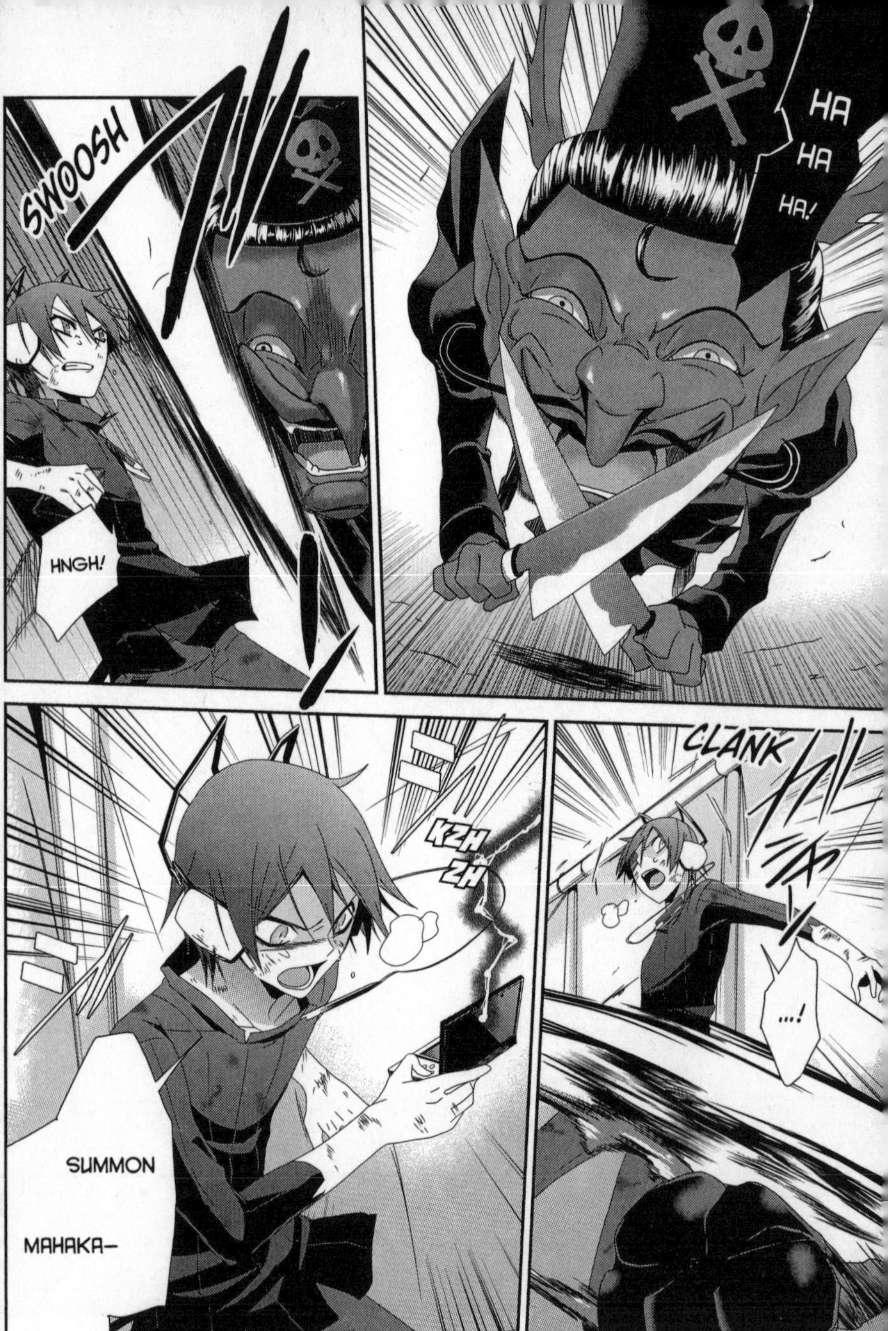
HA
HA
HA!
SWOOSH
HNGH!
CLANK
...!
KZH
ZH
SUMMON
MAHAKA-

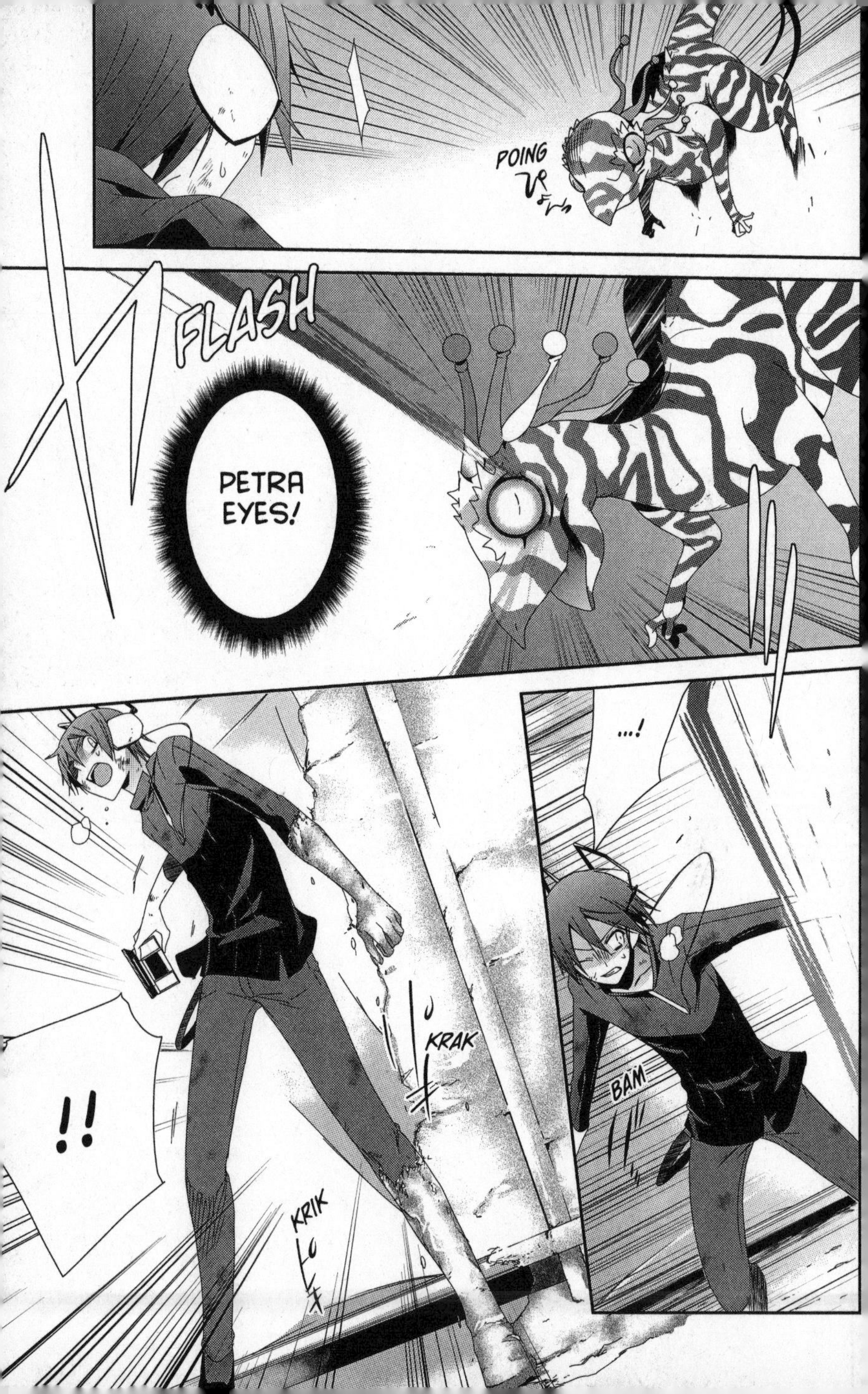
POING
FLASH
PETRA EYES!
...!
BAM
KRAK
KRIK
!!

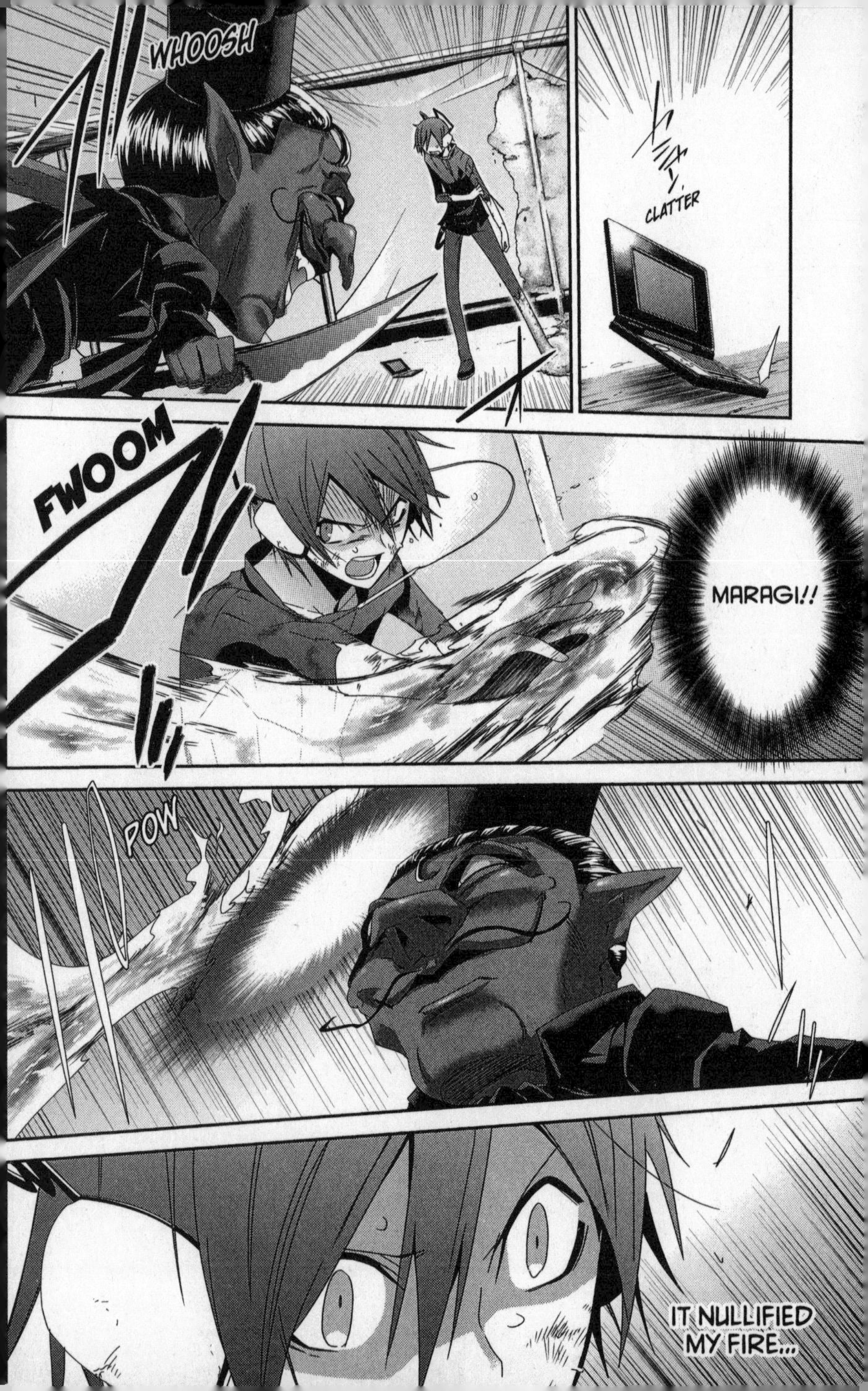
CLATTER
WHOOSH
MARAGI!!
FWOOM
POW
IT NULLIFIED MY FIRE...

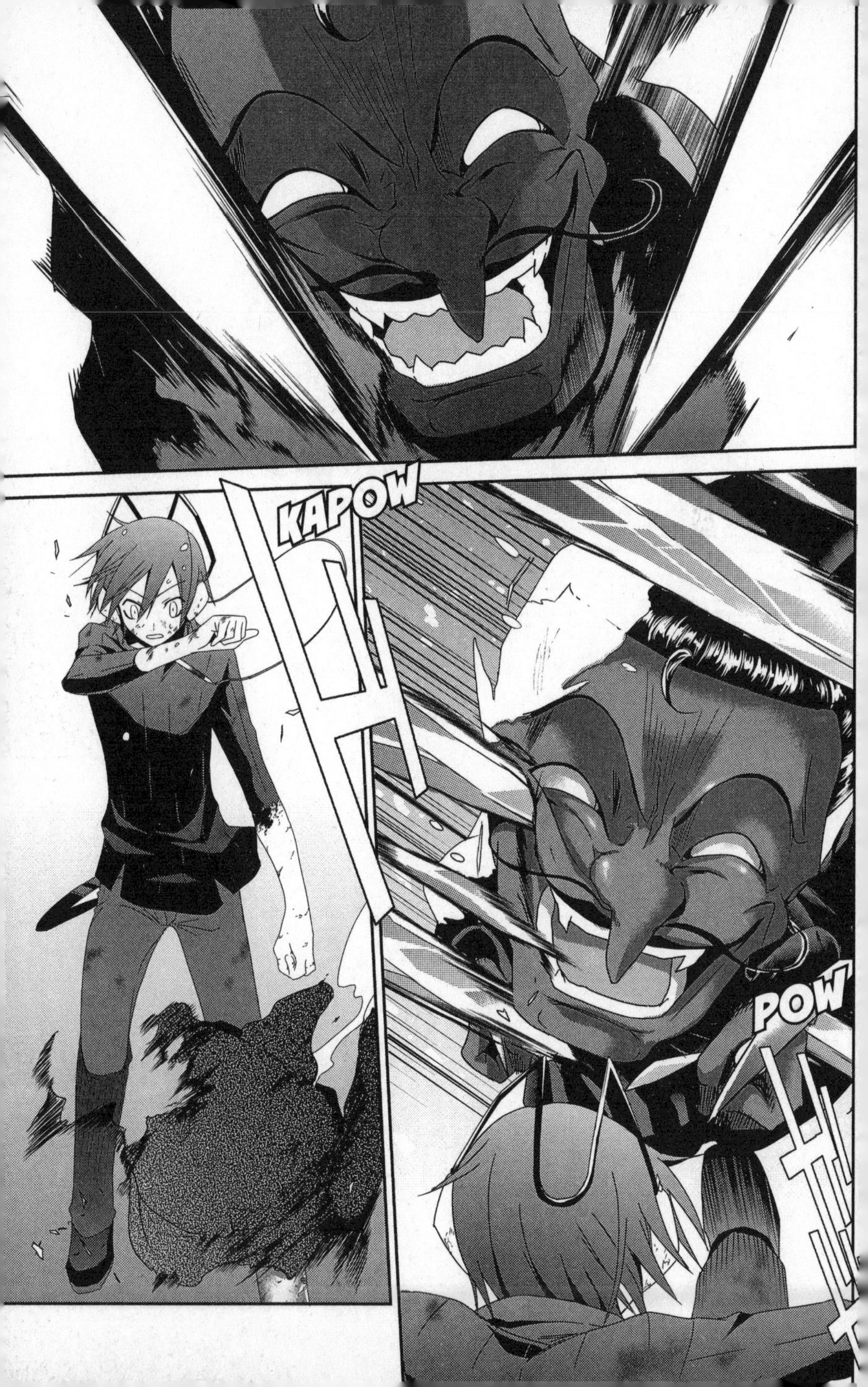
KAPOW
POW

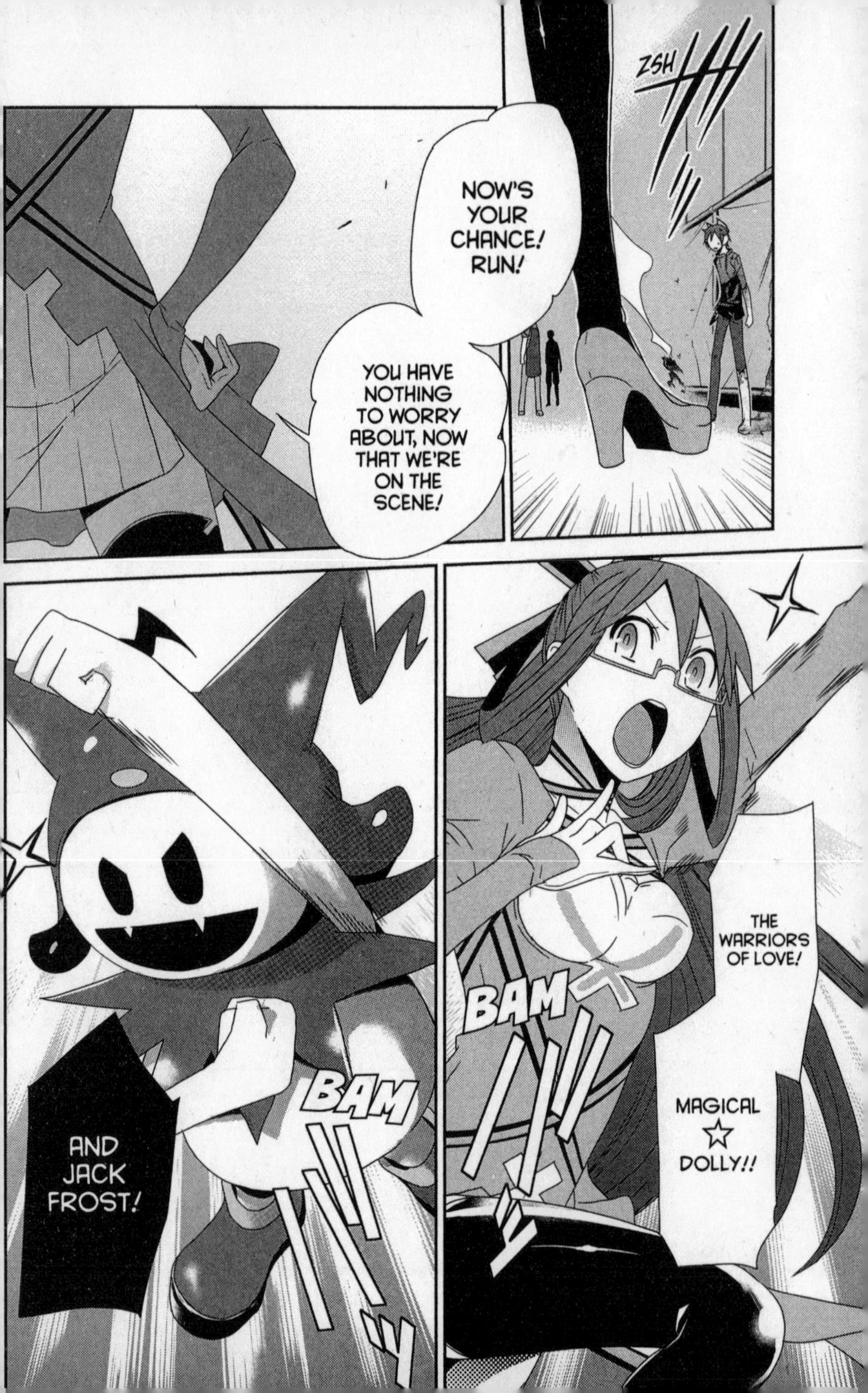
ZSH
NOW'S YOUR CHANCE! RUN!
YOU HAVE NOTHING TO WORRY ABOUT, NOW THAT WE'RE ON THE SCENE!
THE WARRIORS OF LOVE!
MAGICAL ☆ DOLLY!!
BAM
AND JACK FROST!
BAM

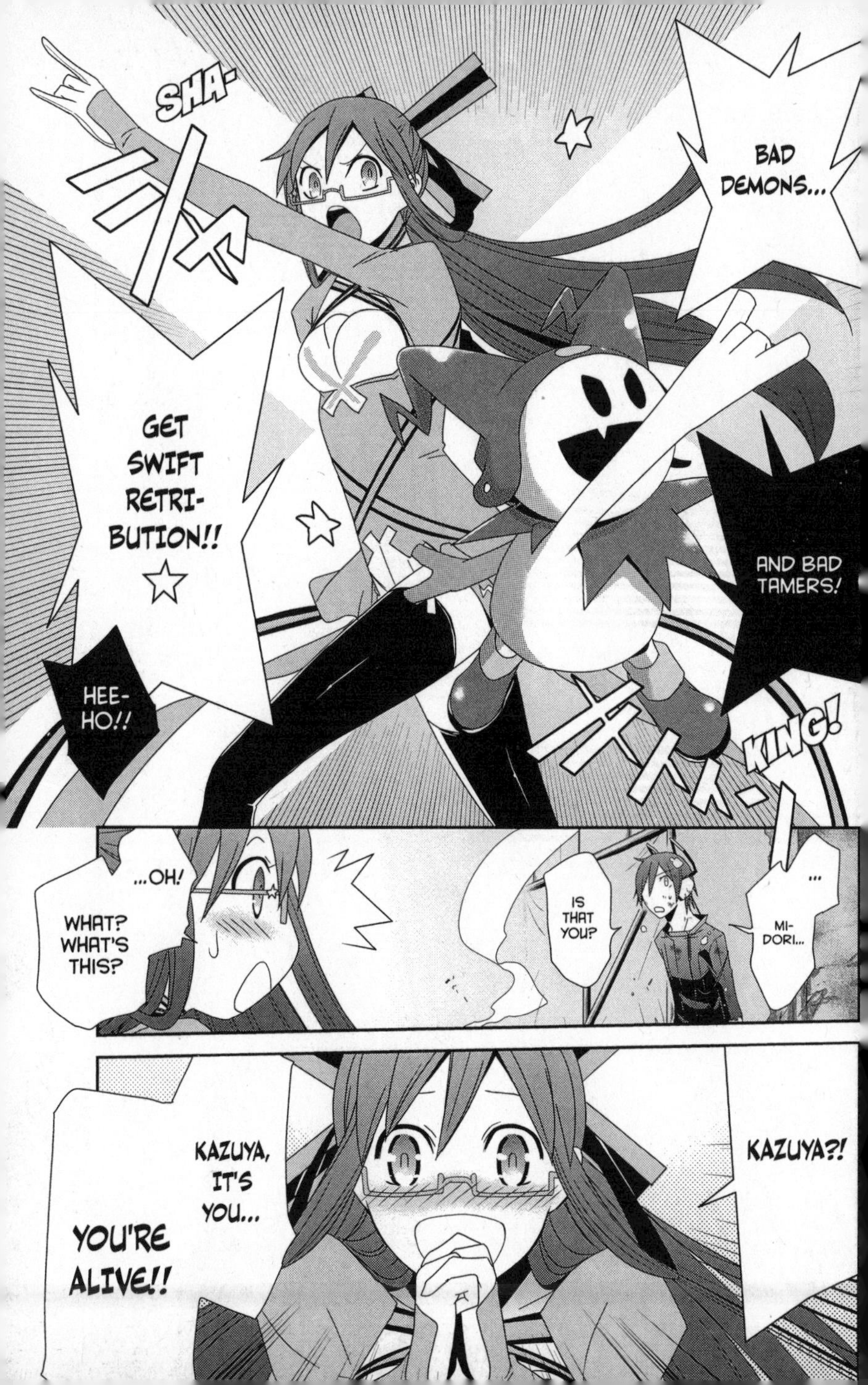
BAD DEMONS...
AND BAD TAMERS!
GET SWIFT RETRIBUTION!! ☆
SHA-
-KING!
HEE-HO!!
...
MI-DORI...
IS THAT YOU?
...OH!
WHAT? WHAT'S THIS?
KAZUYA?!
KAZUYA, IT'S YOU...
YOU'RE ALIVE!!

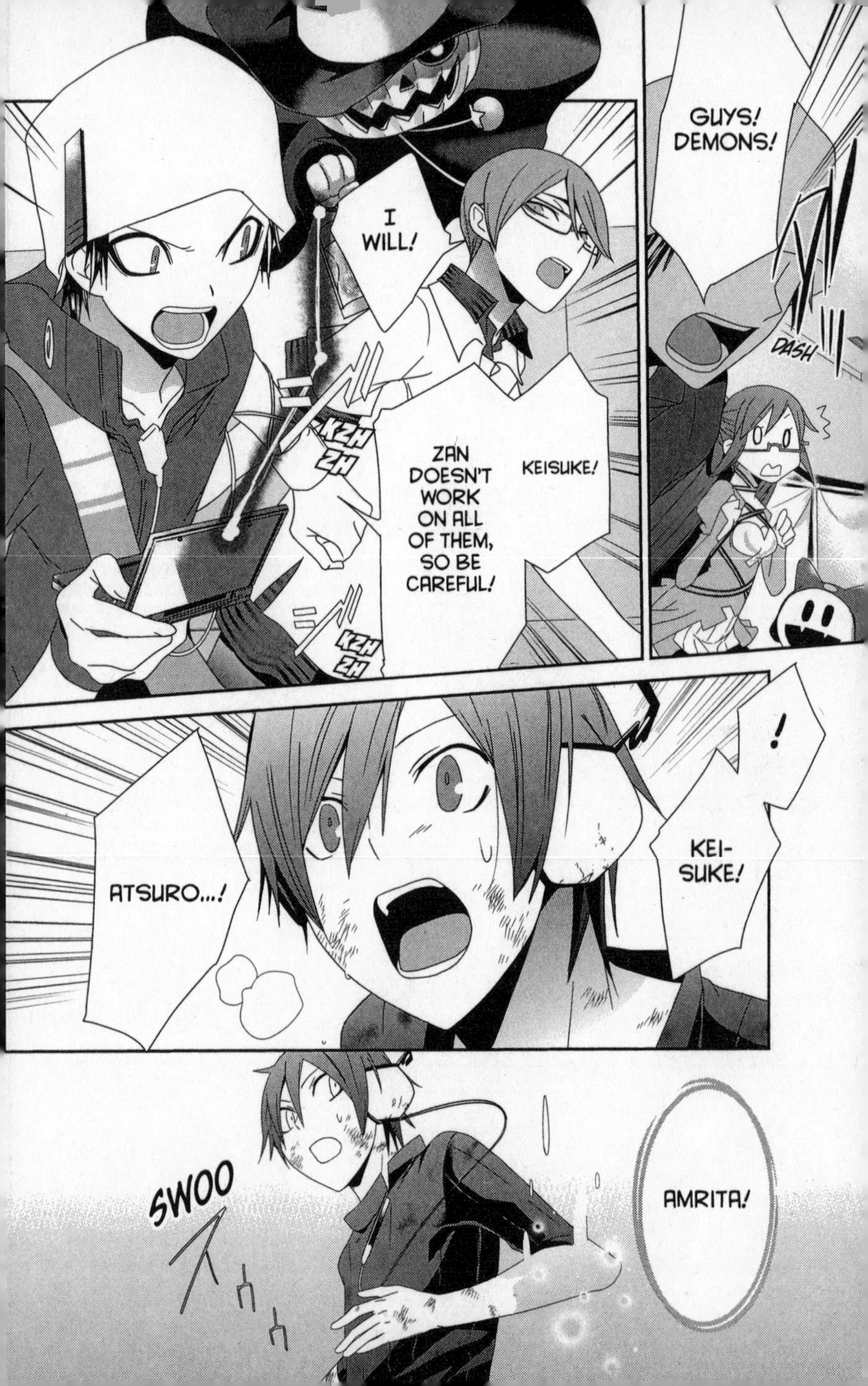
GUYS! DEMONS!
DASH
I WILL!
KEISUKE!
ZAN DOESN'T WORK ON ALL OF THEM, SO BE CAREFUL!
KZH ZH
KZH ZH
!
KEI-SUKE!
ATSURO...!
AMRITA!
SWOO

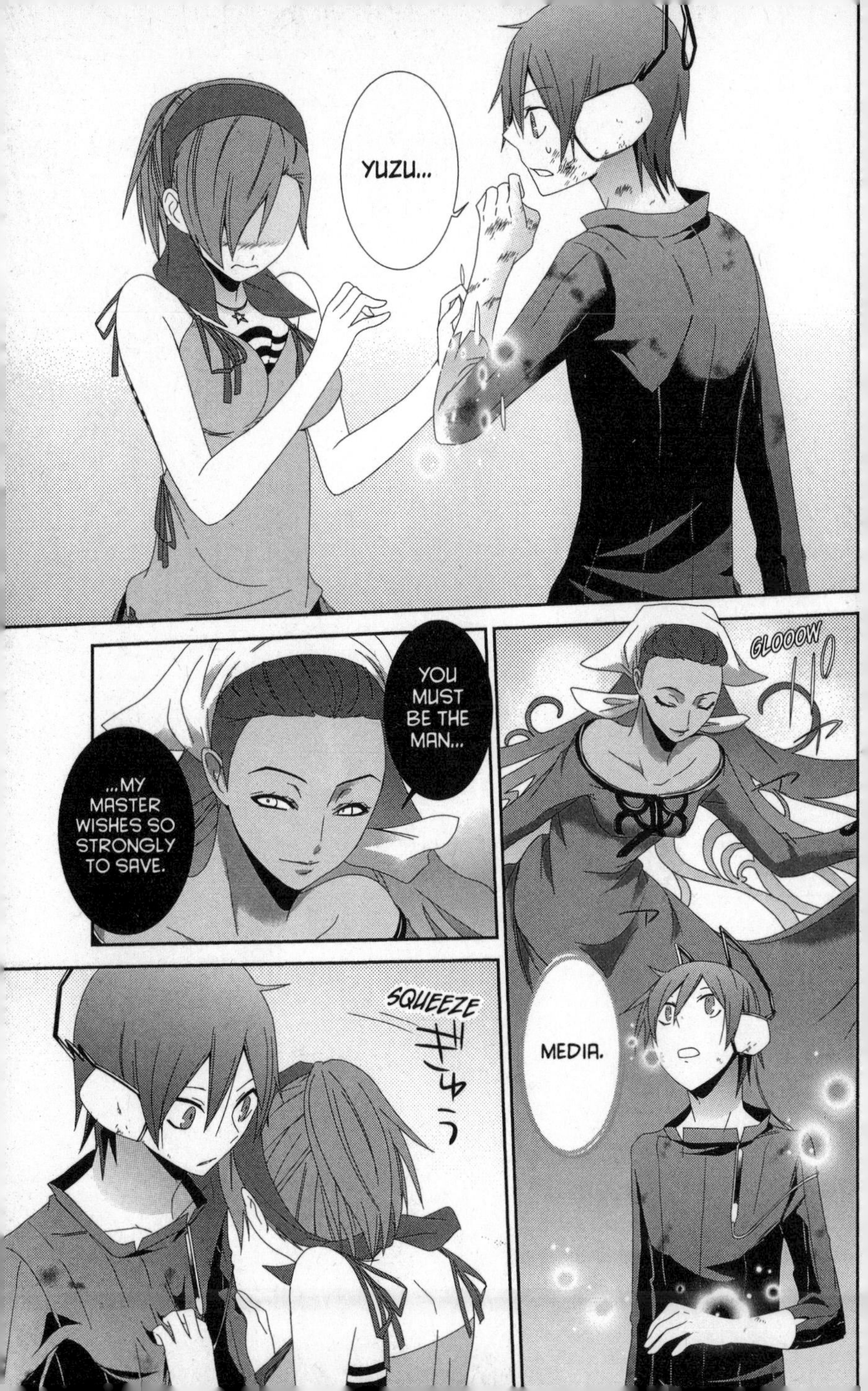
YUZU...
GLOOOW
MEDIA.
YOU MUST BE THE MAN...
...MY MASTER WISHES SO STRONGLY TO SAVE.
SQUEEZE
ぎゅう

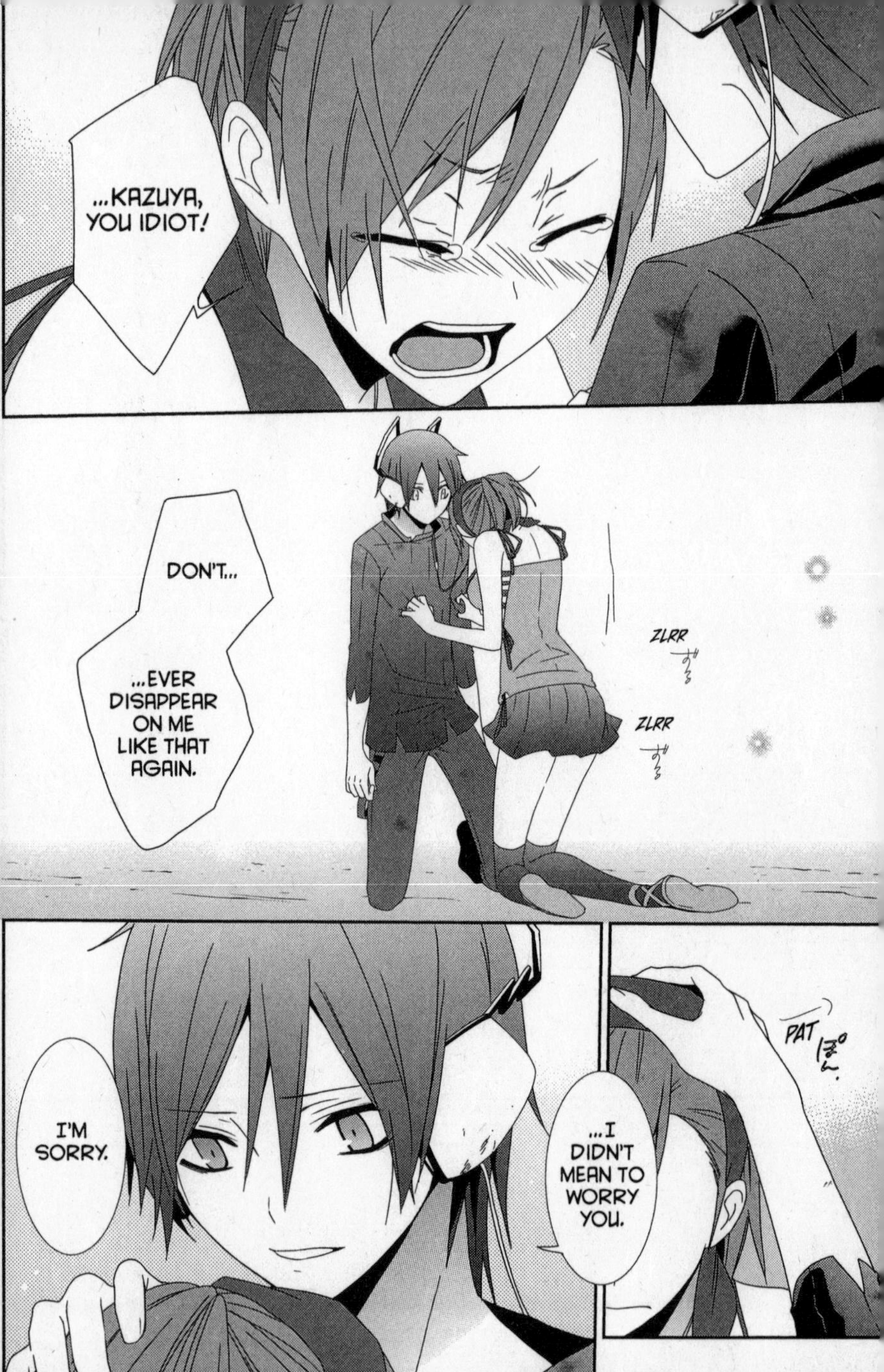
...KAZUYA, YOU IDIOT!
DON'T...
...EVER DISAPPEAR ON ME LIKE THAT AGAIN.
ZLRR
ずる
ZLRR
ずる
PAT
ぽん.
...I DIDN'T MEAN TO WORRY YOU.
I'M SORRY.

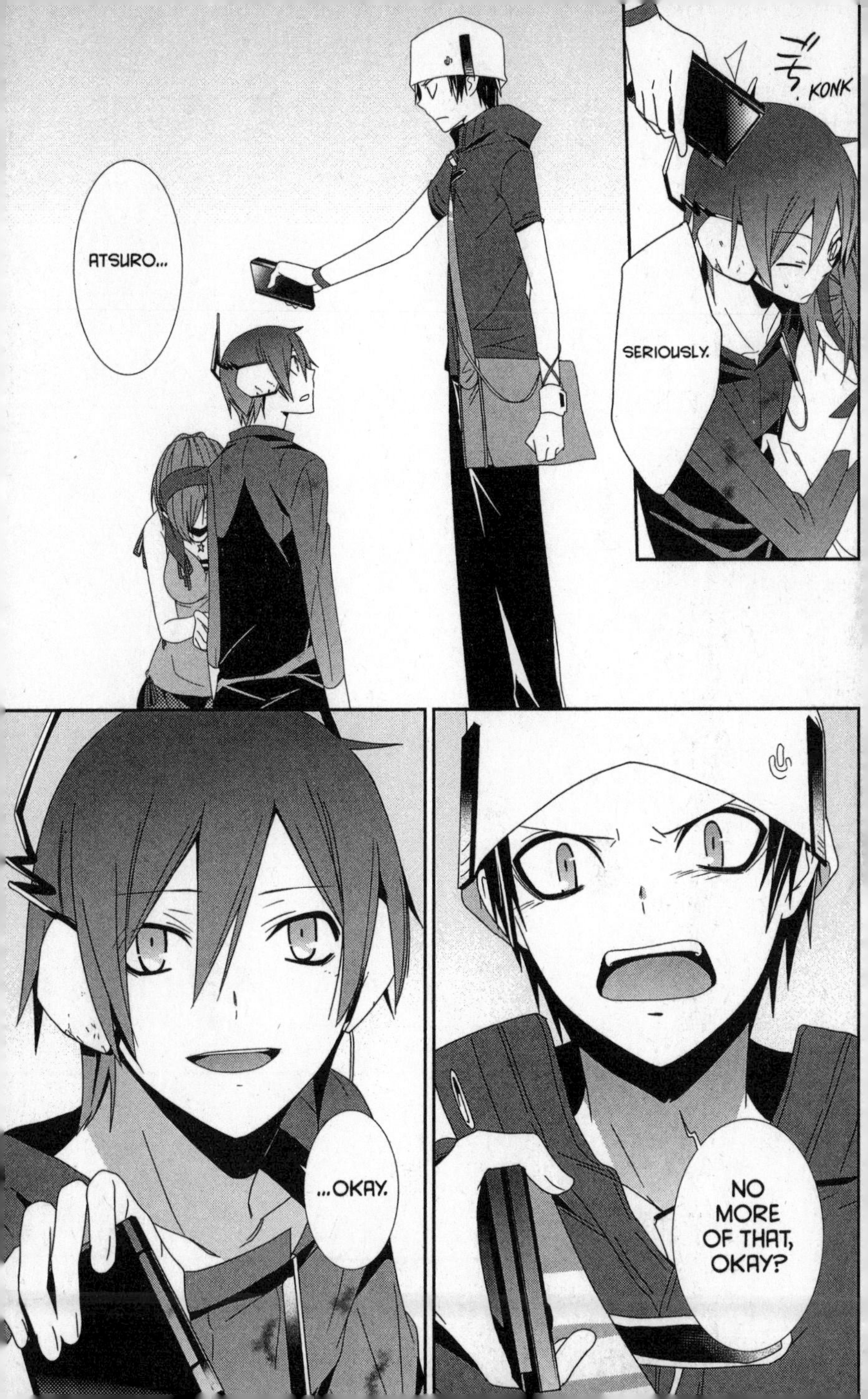
KONK
SERIOUSLY.
ATSURO...
NO MORE OF THAT, OKAY?
...OKAY.

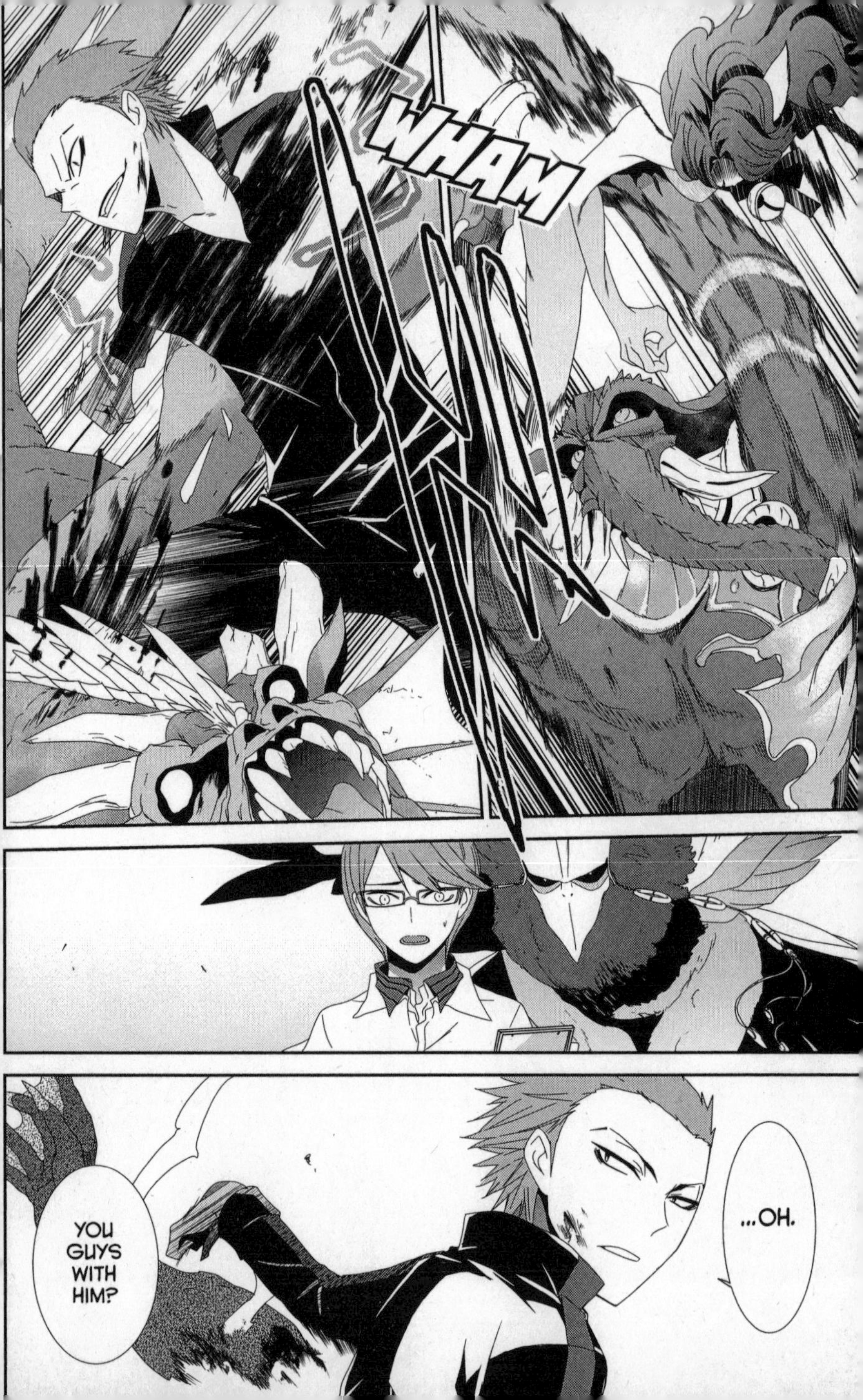
WHAM
...OH.
YOU GUYS WITH HIM?

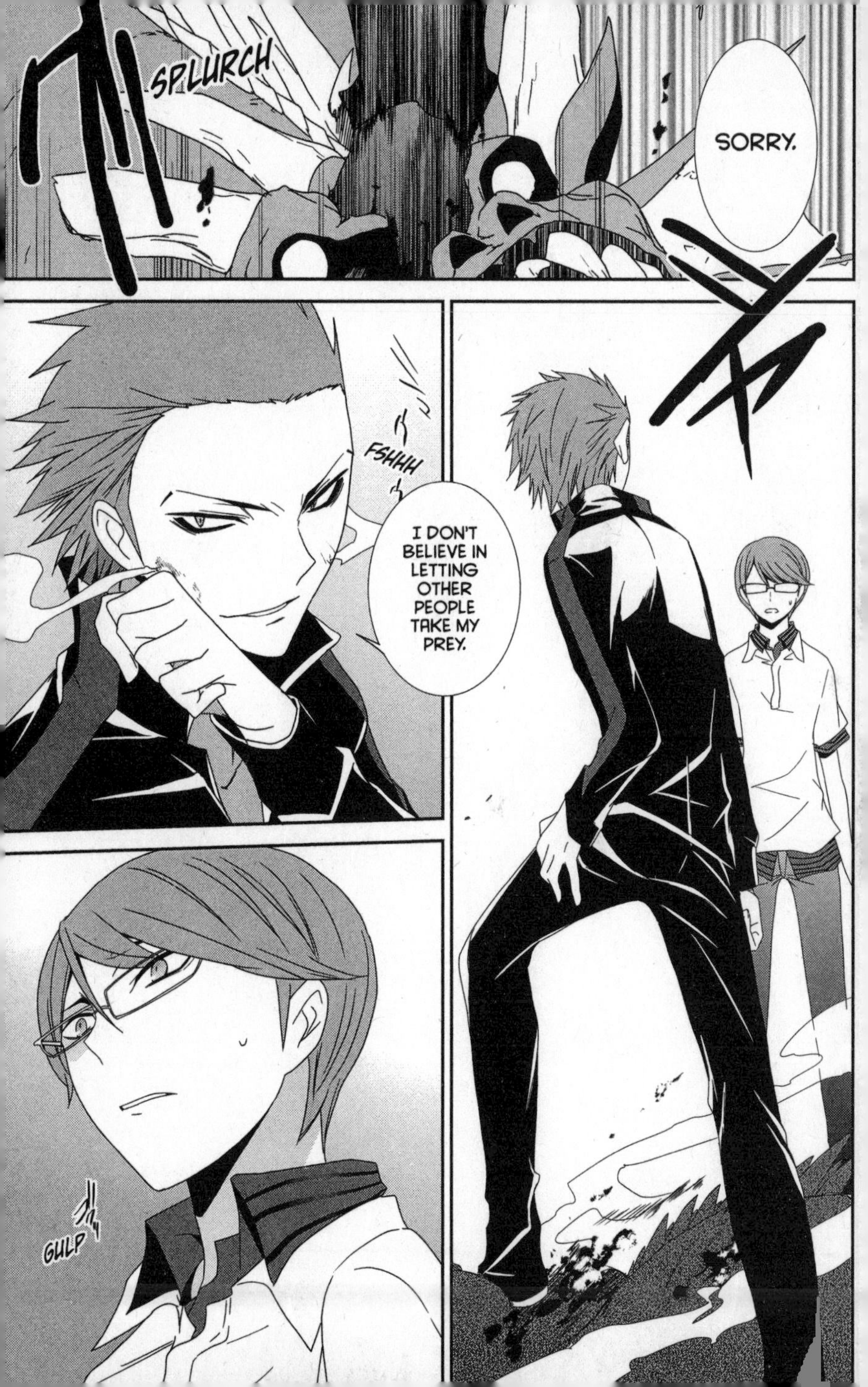
SORRY.
SPLURCH
FSHHH
I DON'T BELIEVE IN LETTING OTHER PEOPLE TAKE MY PREY.
GULP

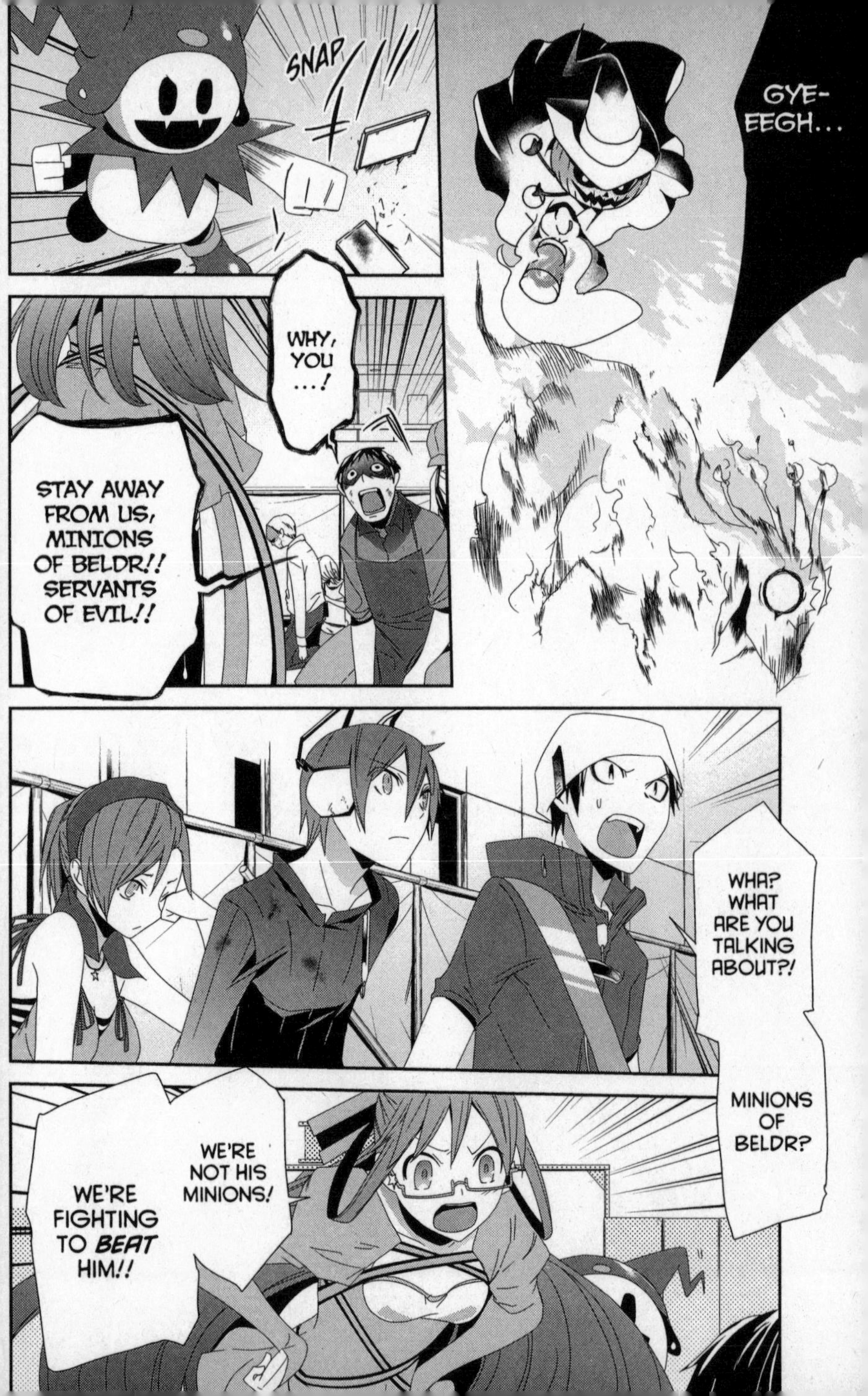
GYE-EEGH...
SNAP
WHY, YOU ...!
STAY AWAY FROM US, MINIONS OF BELDR!! SERVANTS OF EVIL!!
WHA? WHAT ARE YOU TALKING ABOUT?!
MINIONS OF BELDR?
WE'RE NOT HIS MINIONS!
WE'RE FIGHTING TO *BEAT* HIM!!

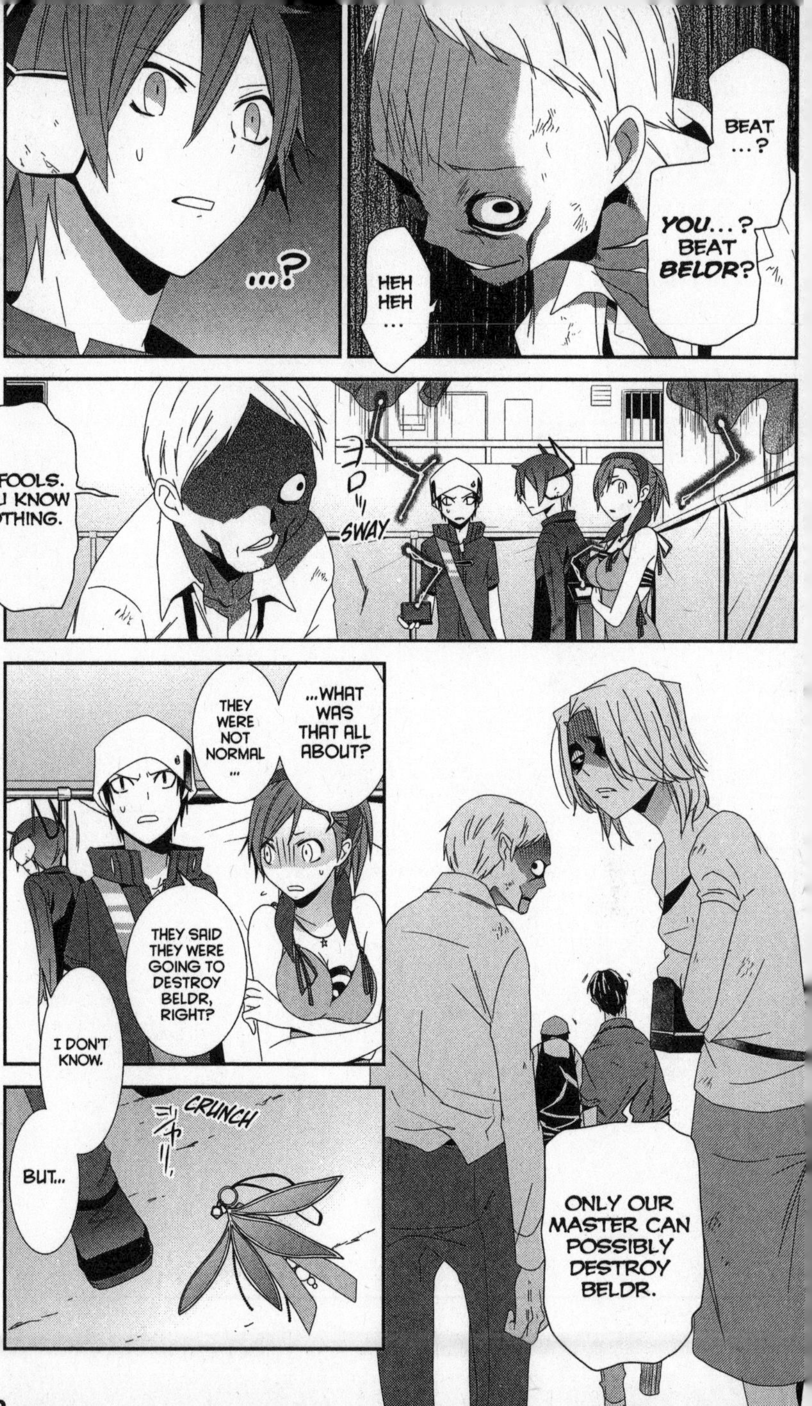
BEAT ...?
YOU...? BEAT BELDR?
HEH HEH ...
...?
...FOOLS. YOU KNOW NOTHING.
SWAY
ONLY OUR MASTER CAN POSSIBLY DESTROY BELDR.
...WHAT WAS THAT ALL ABOUT?
THEY WERE NOT NORMAL ...
THEY SAID THEY WERE GOING TO DESTROY BELDR, RIGHT?
I DON'T KNOW.
CRUNCH
BUT...

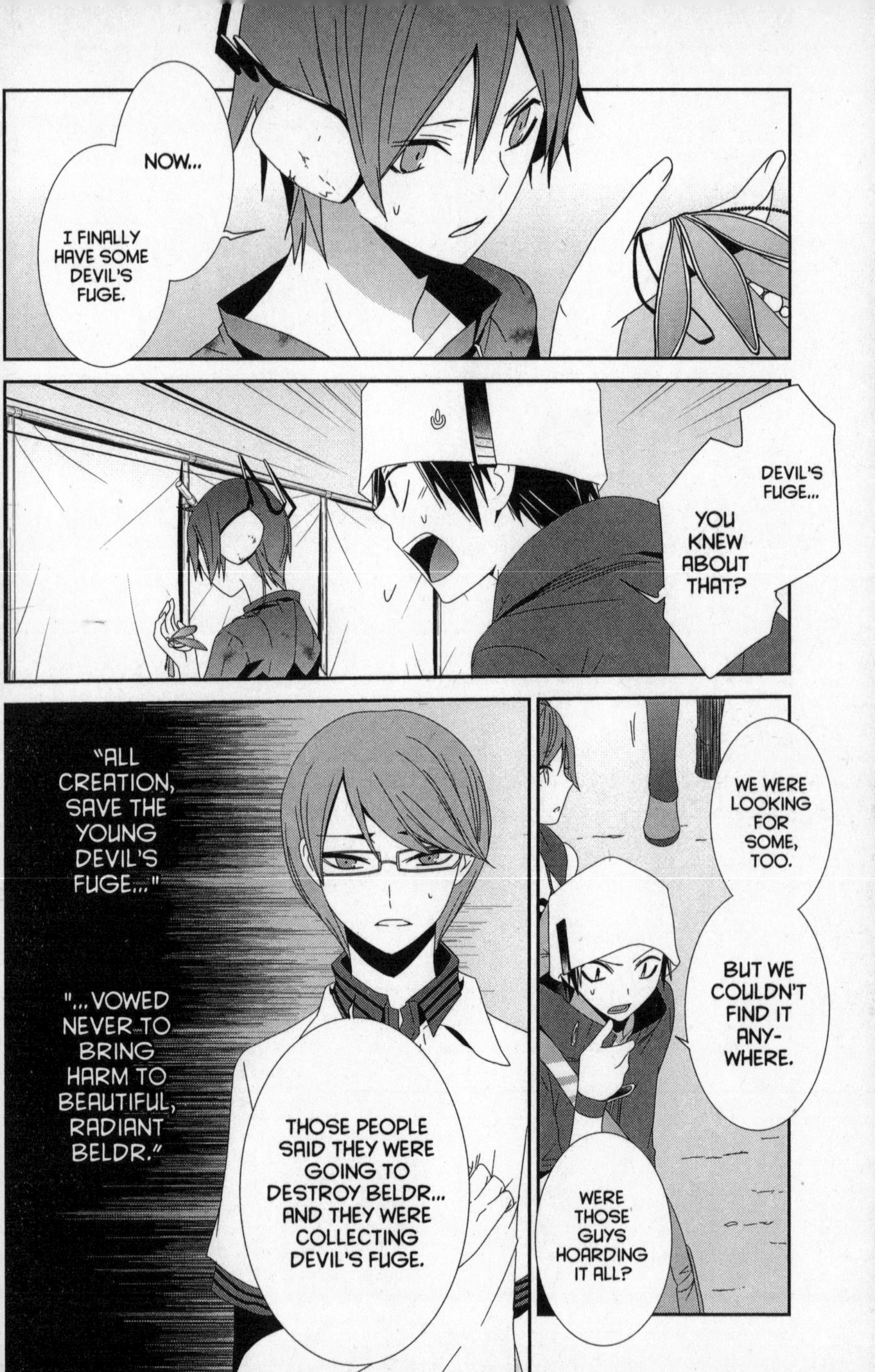
NOW...
I FINALLY HAVE SOME DEVIL'S FUGE.
DEVIL'S FUGE...
YOU KNEW ABOUT THAT?
WE WERE LOOKING FOR SOME, TOO.
BUT WE COULDN'T FIND IT ANY-WHERE.
WERE THOSE GUYS HOARDING IT ALL?
"ALL CREATION, SAVE THE YOUNG DEVIL'S FUGE..."
"...VOWED NEVER TO BRING HARM TO BEAUTIFUL, RADIANT BELDR."
THOSE PEOPLE SAID THEY WERE GOING TO DESTROY BELDR... AND THEY WERE COLLECTING DEVIL'S FUGE.

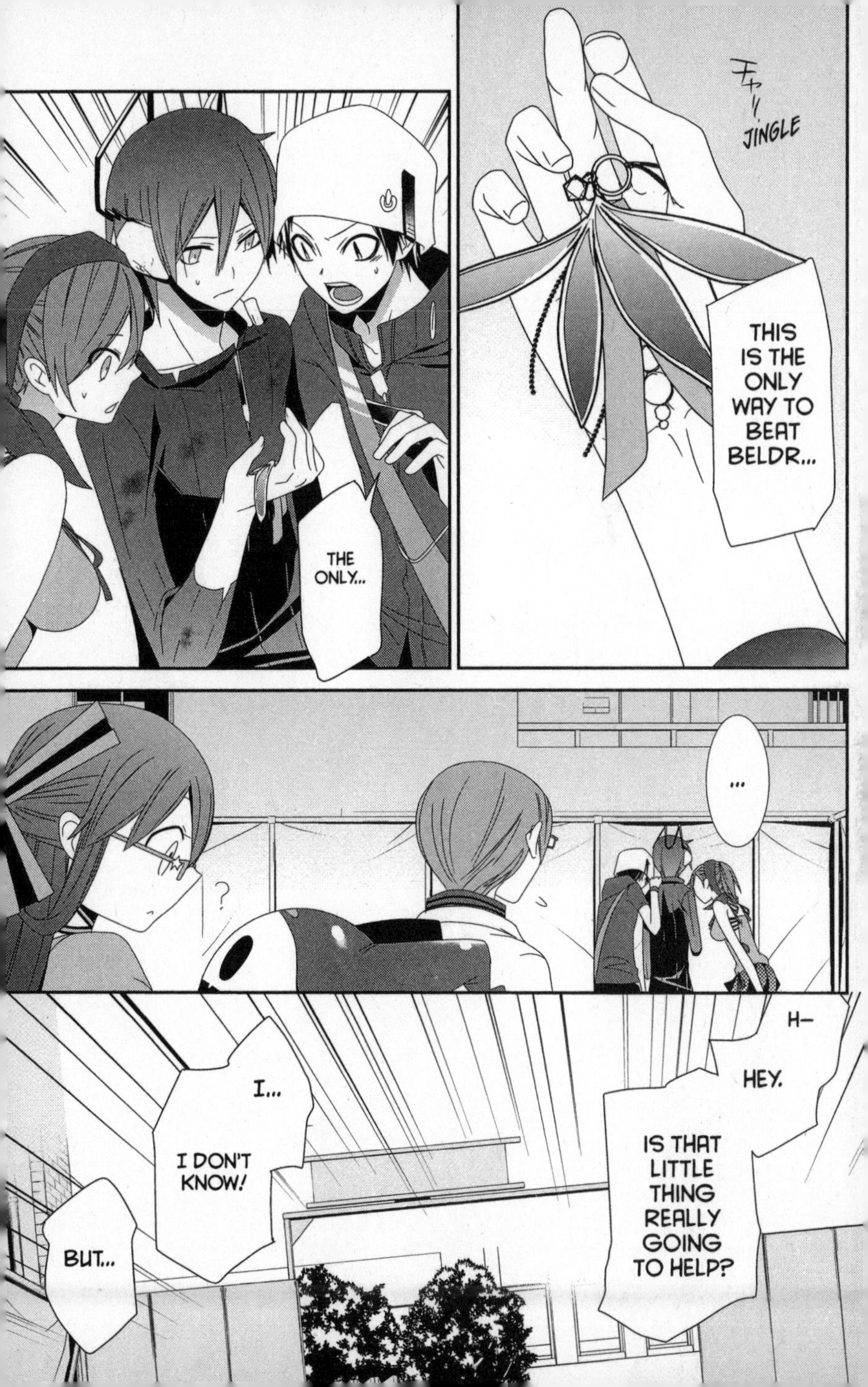
チャリ
JINGLE
THIS IS THE ONLY WAY TO BEAT BELDR...
THE ONLY...
...
?
H—
HEY.
IS THAT LITTLE THING REALLY GOING TO HELP?
I...
I DON'T KNOW!
BUT...

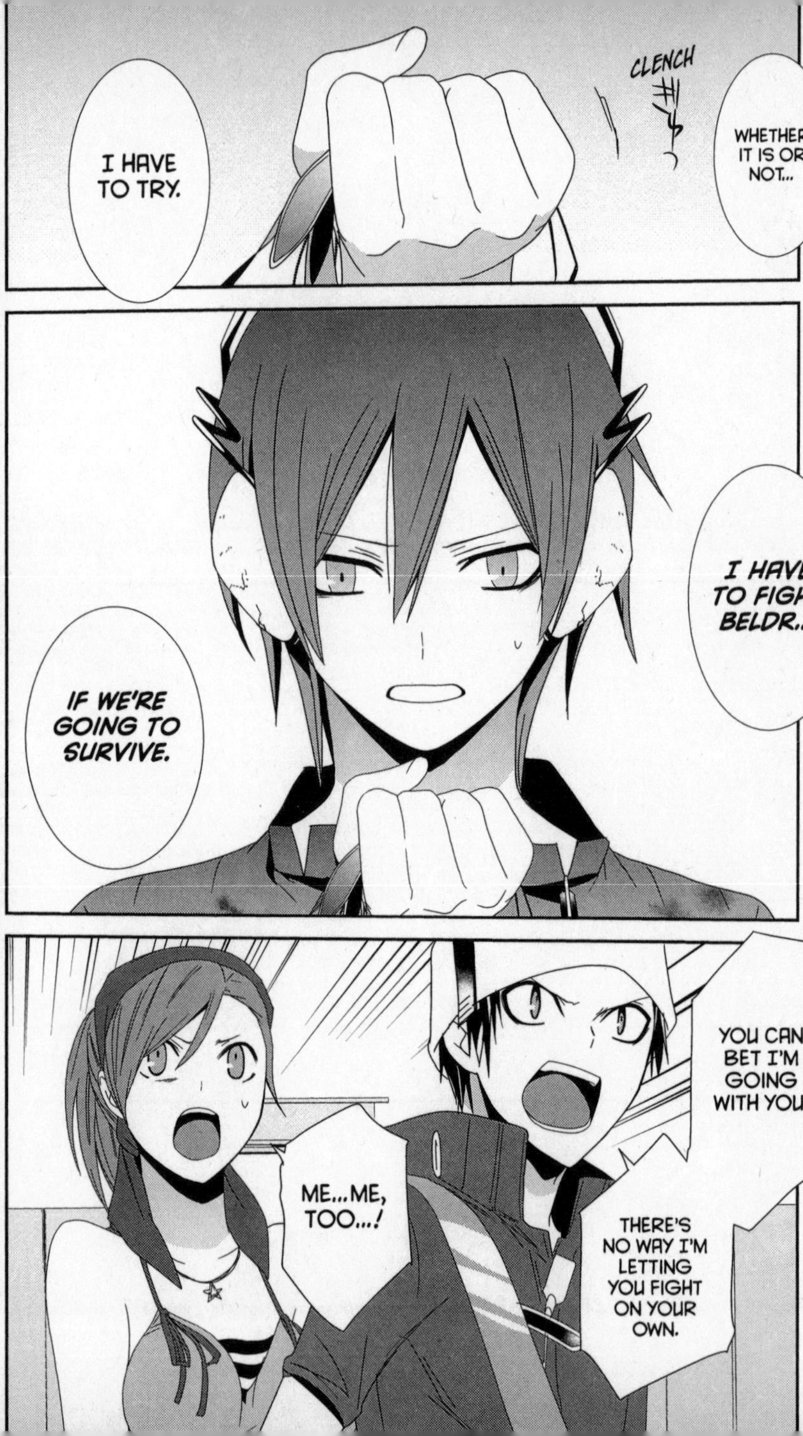
WHETHER IT IS OR NOT...
CLENCH
I HAVE TO TRY.
I HAVE TO FIGHT BELDR...
IF WE'RE GOING TO SURVIVE.
YOU CAN BET I'M GOING WITH YOU.
THERE'S NO WAY I'M LETTING YOU FIGHT ON YOUR OWN.
ME...ME, TOO...!

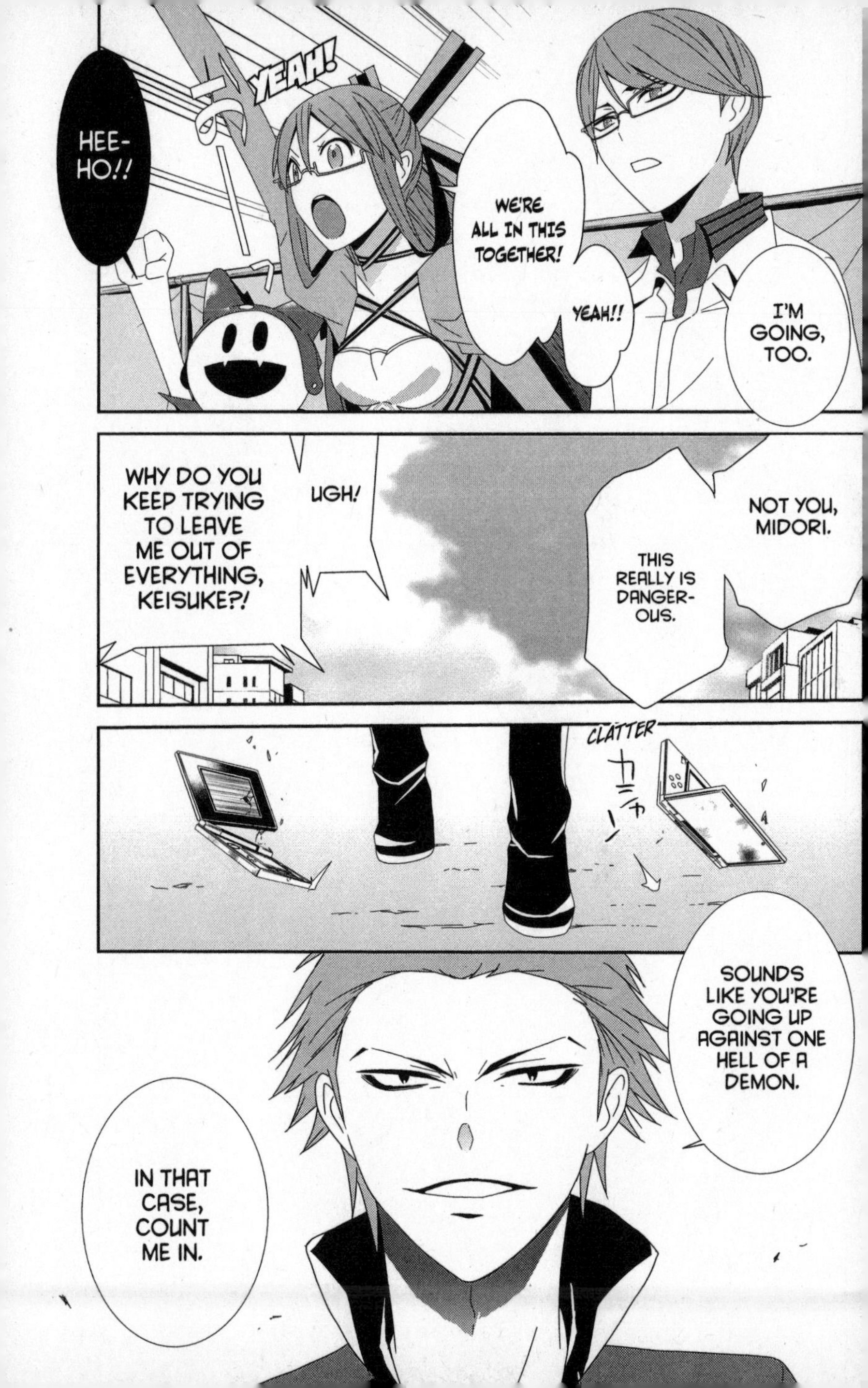
I'M GOING, TOO.
WE'RE ALL IN THIS TOGETHER!
YEAH!!
YEAH!
HEE-HO!!
NOT YOU, MIDORI.
THIS REALLY IS DANGER-OUS.
UGH!
WHY DO YOU KEEP TRYING TO LEAVE ME OUT OF EVERYTHING, KEISUKE?!
CLATTER
SOUNDS LIKE YOU'RE GOING UP AGAINST ONE HELL OF A DEMON.
IN THAT CASE, COUNT ME IN.

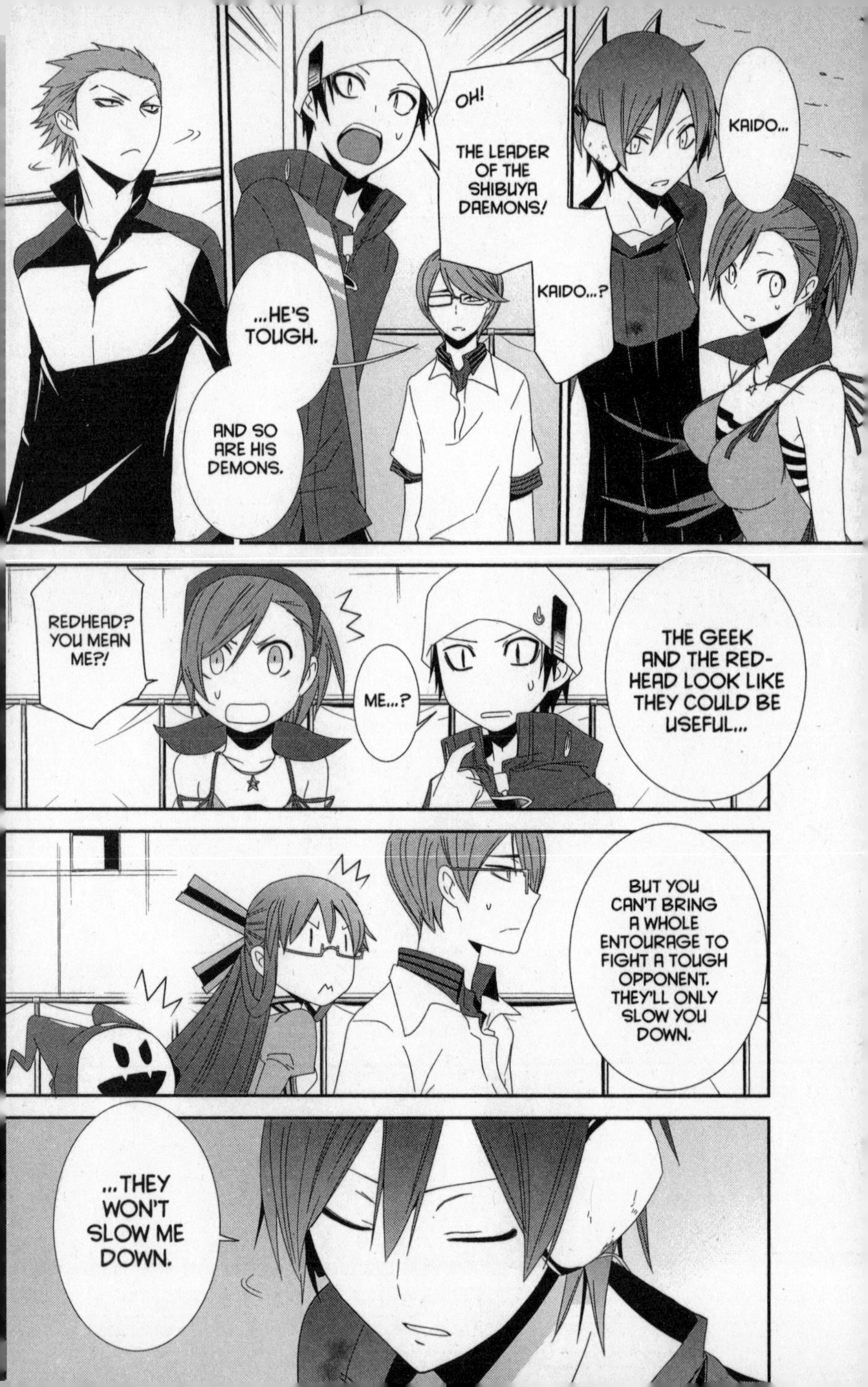
KAIDO...
KAIDO...?
OH! THE LEADER OF THE SHIBUYA DAEMONS!
...HE'S TOUGH.
AND SO ARE HIS DEMONS.
THE GEEK AND THE RED-HEAD LOOK LIKE THEY COULD BE USEFUL...
ME...?
REDHEAD? YOU MEAN ME?!
BUT YOU CAN'T BRING A WHOLE ENTOURAGE TO FIGHT A TOUGH OPPONENT. THEY'LL ONLY SLOW YOU DOWN.
...THEY WON'T SLOW ME DOWN.

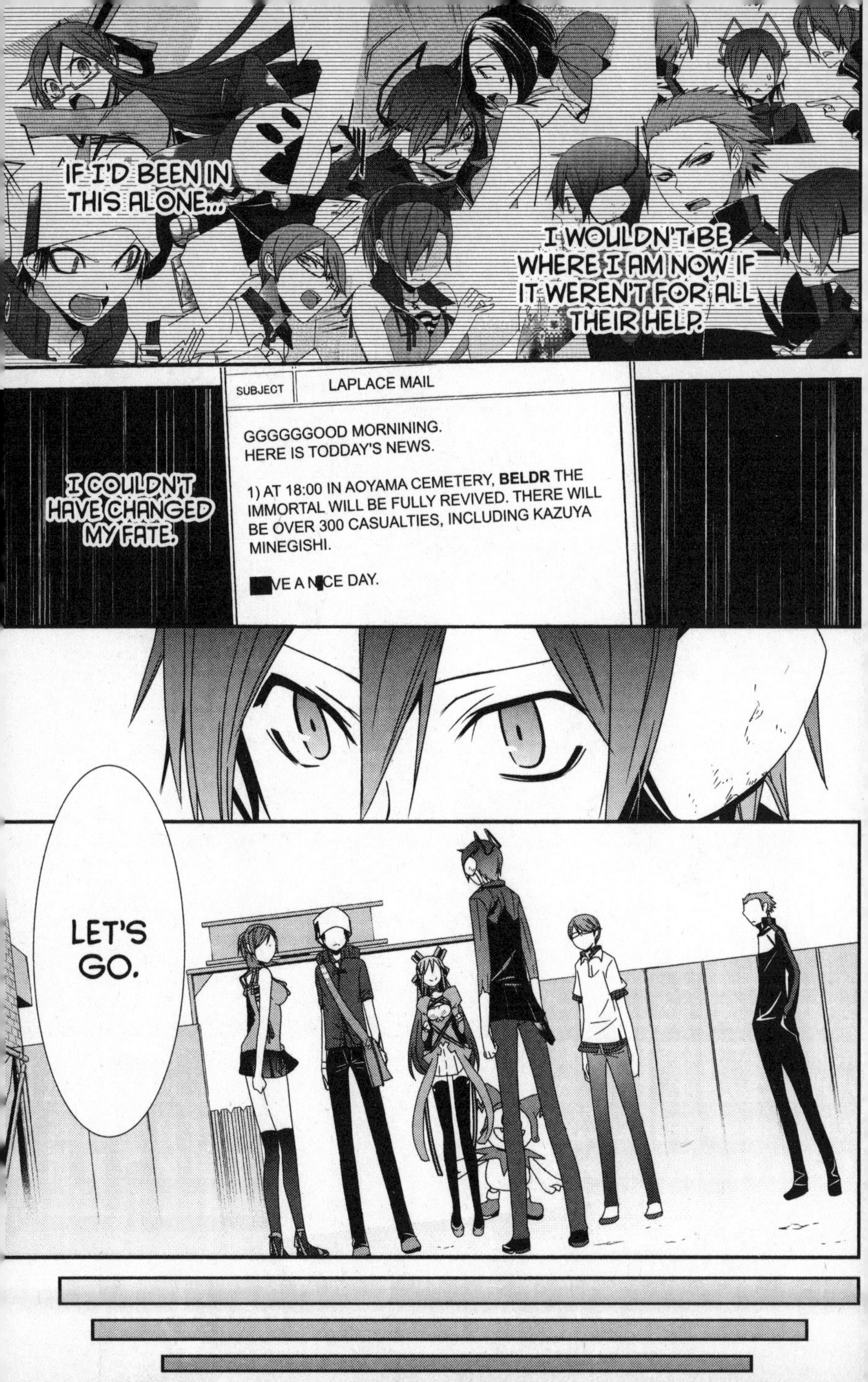
I WOULDN'T BE WHERE I AM NOW IF IT WEREN'T FOR ALL THEIR HELP.
IF I'D BEEN IN THIS ALONE...
SUBJECT
LAPLACE MAIL
GGGGGGOOD MORNINING.
HERE IS TODDAY'S NEWS.
1) AT 18:00 IN AOYAMA CEMETERY, **BELDR** THE IMMORTAL WILL BE FULLY REVIVED. THERE WILL BE OVER 300 CASUALTIES, INCLUDING KAZUYA MINEGISHI.
[redacted]VE A N[redacted]CE DAY.
I COULDN'T HAVE CHANGED MY FATE.
LET'S GO.

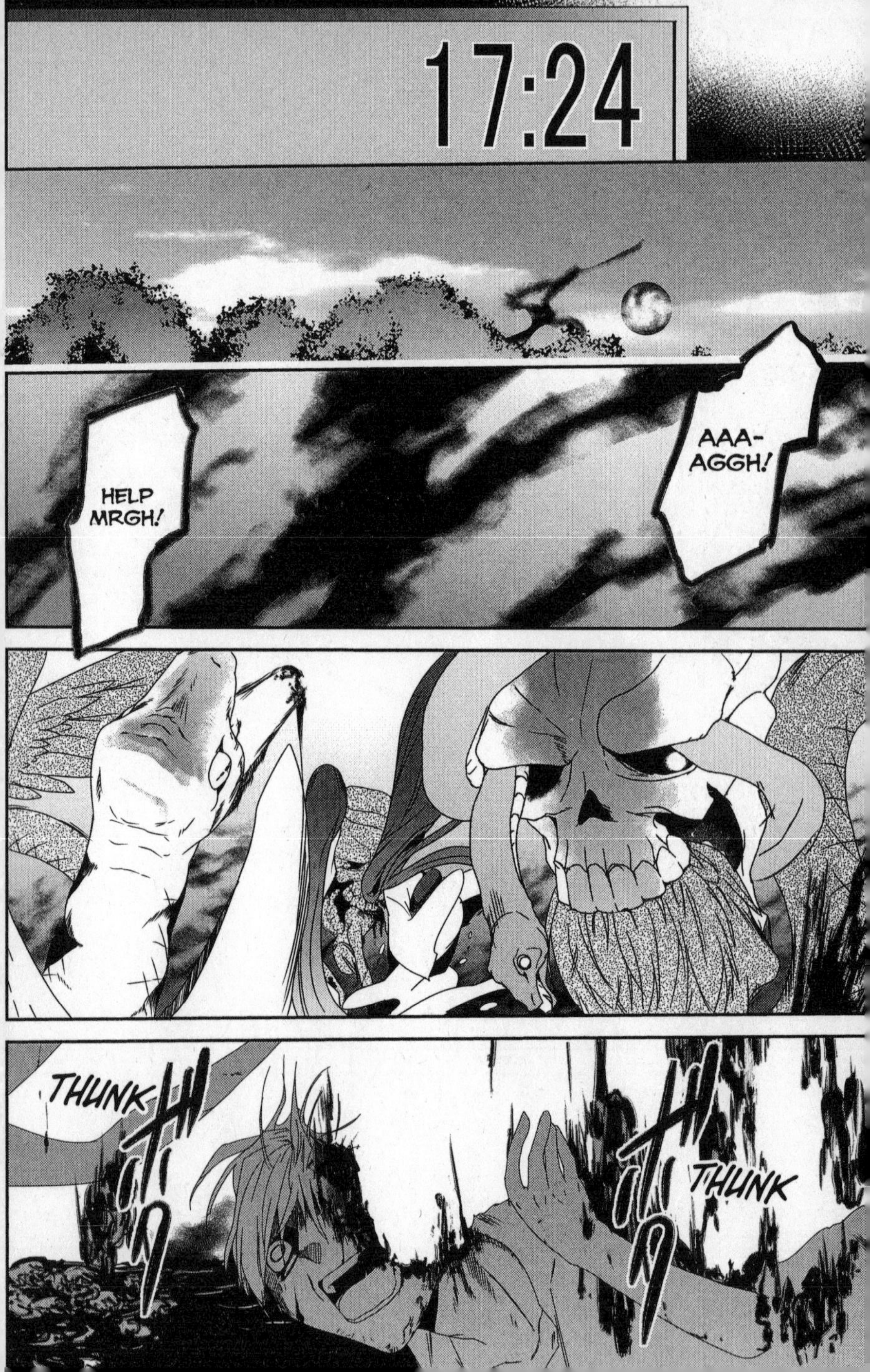
17:24
AAA-AGGH!
HELP MRGH!
THUNK
THUNK

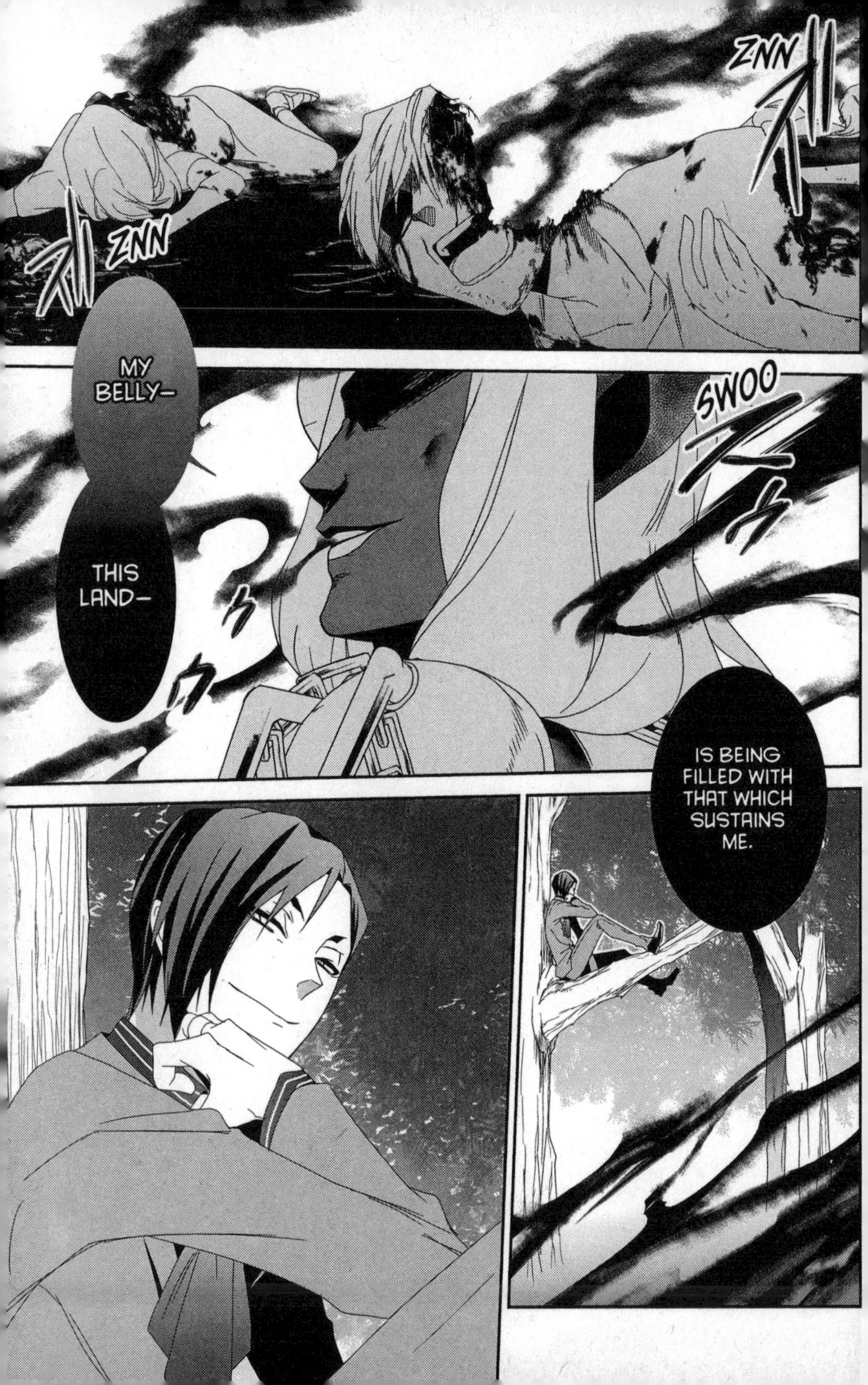
ZNN
ZNN
SWOO
MY BELLY—
THIS LAND—
IS BEING FILLED WITH THAT WHICH SUSTAINS ME.

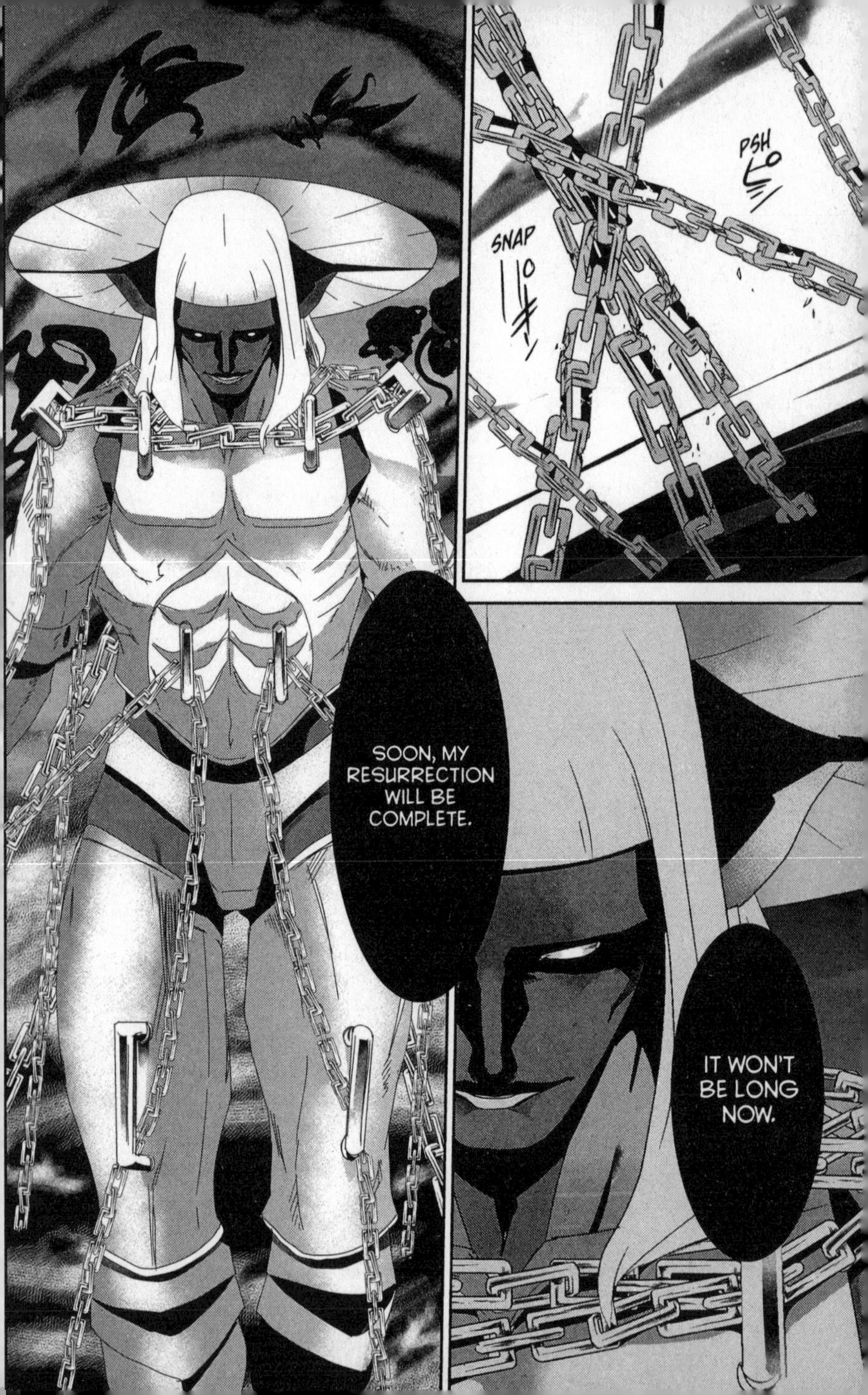
PSH
SNAP
SOON, MY RESURRECTION WILL BE COMPLETE.
IT WON'T BE LONG NOW.

JACK FROST

A FROST SPIRIT WITH A LOVABLE FORM
THAT APPEARS IN THE WINTER, AND MELTS
AWAY IN THE SPRING. HE IS MADE OF ICE
AND SNOW, BUT DON'T BE FOOLED BY
HIS LOVABLE FACE, OR YOU WILL MEET A
TERRIFYING FATE. JACK FROST FREEZES
PEOPLE WITH HIS COLD BREATH, SMILING
ALL THE WHILE. HE ORIGINALLY LOOKED
LIKE AN ABOMINABLE SNOWMAN, BUT
CHANGED HIS FORM, PERHAPS THE
BETTER TO FREEZE PEOPLE WITH

DEVIL SURVIVOR
デビルサバイバー

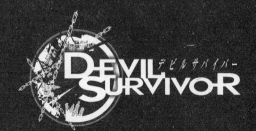

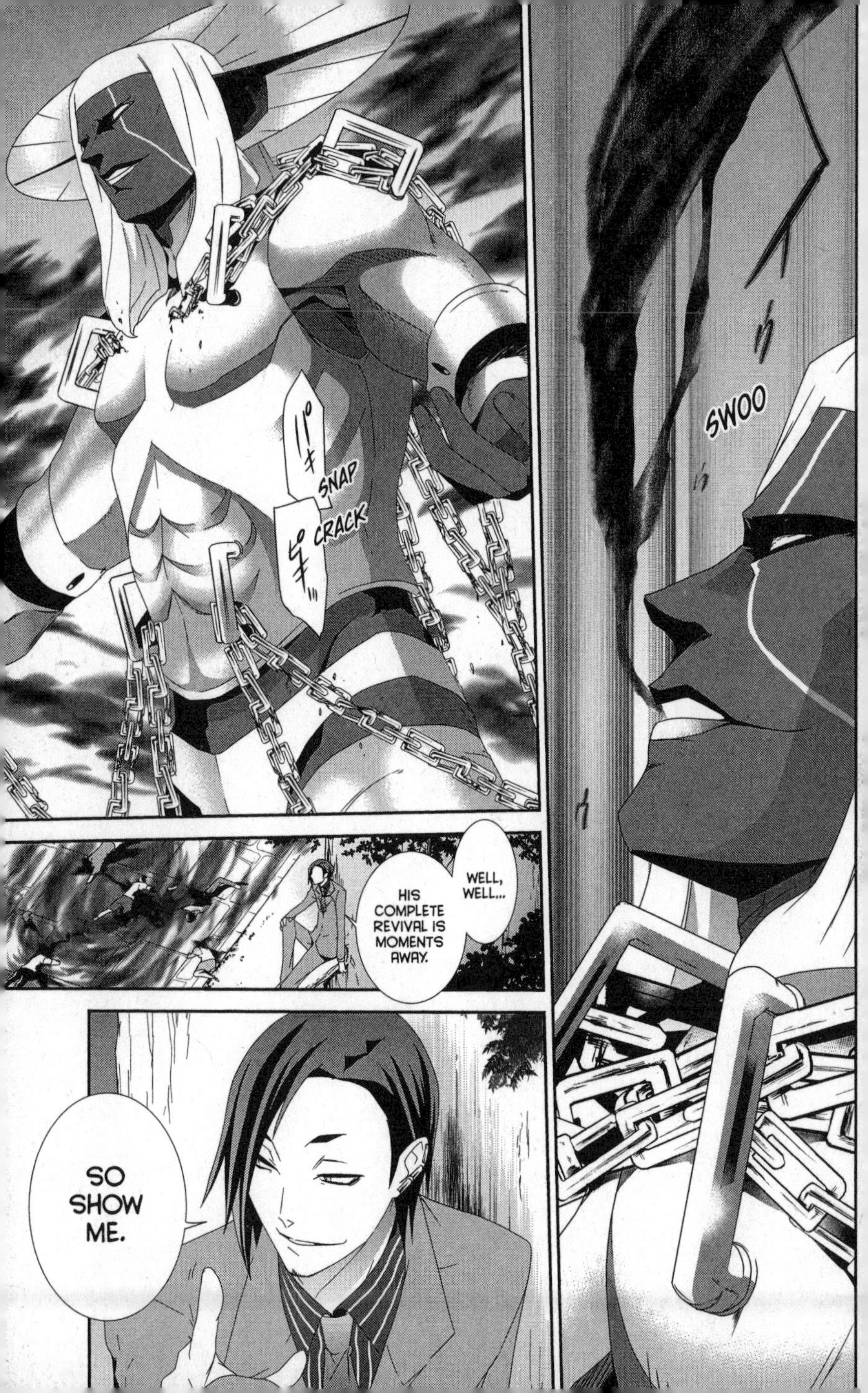
SWOO
パキ
SNAP
ピキ
CRACK
WELL, WELL...
HIS COMPLETE REVIVAL IS MOMENTS AWAY.
SO SHOW ME.

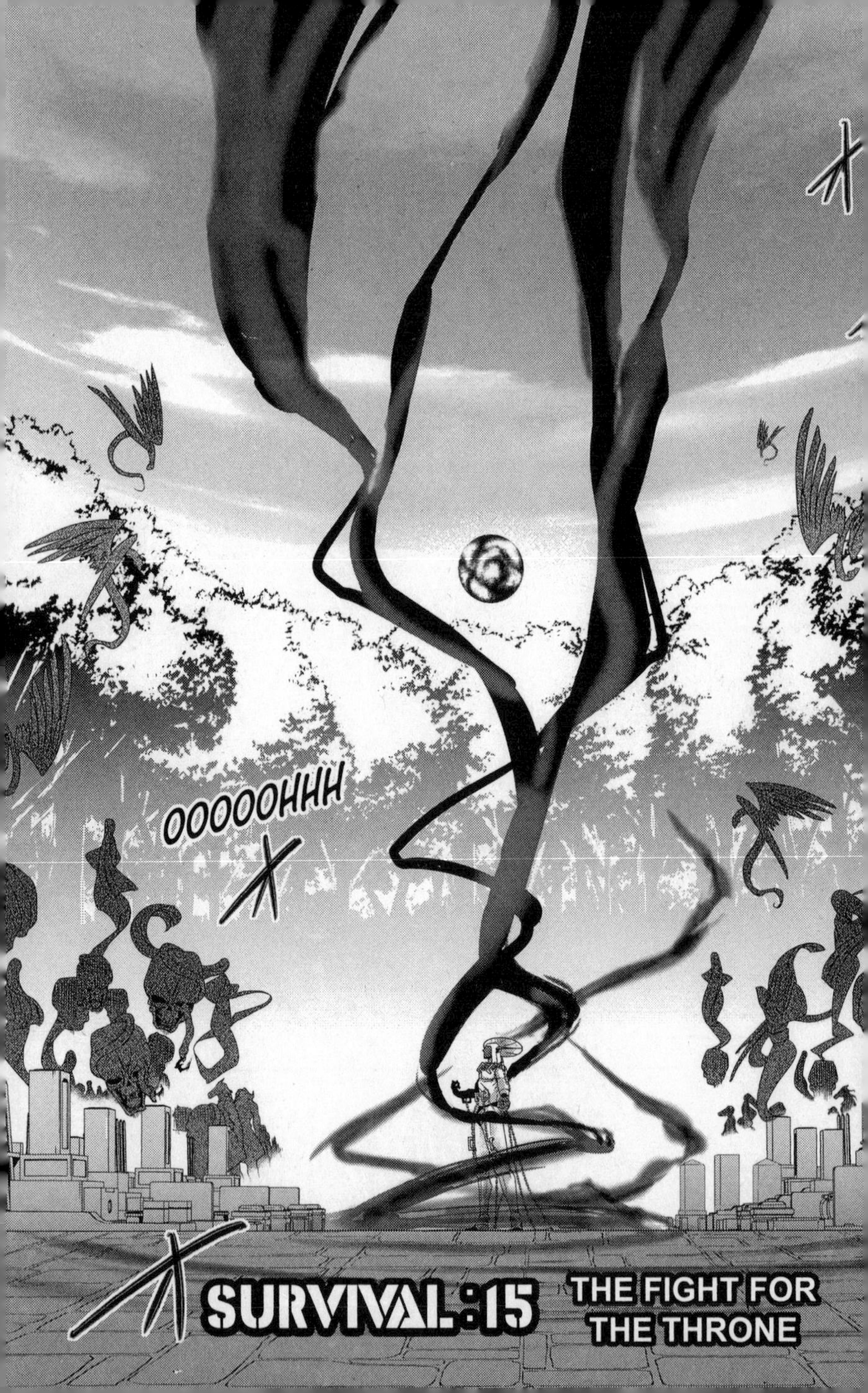
OOOOOHHH
SURVIVAL:15
THE FIGHT FOR THE THRONE

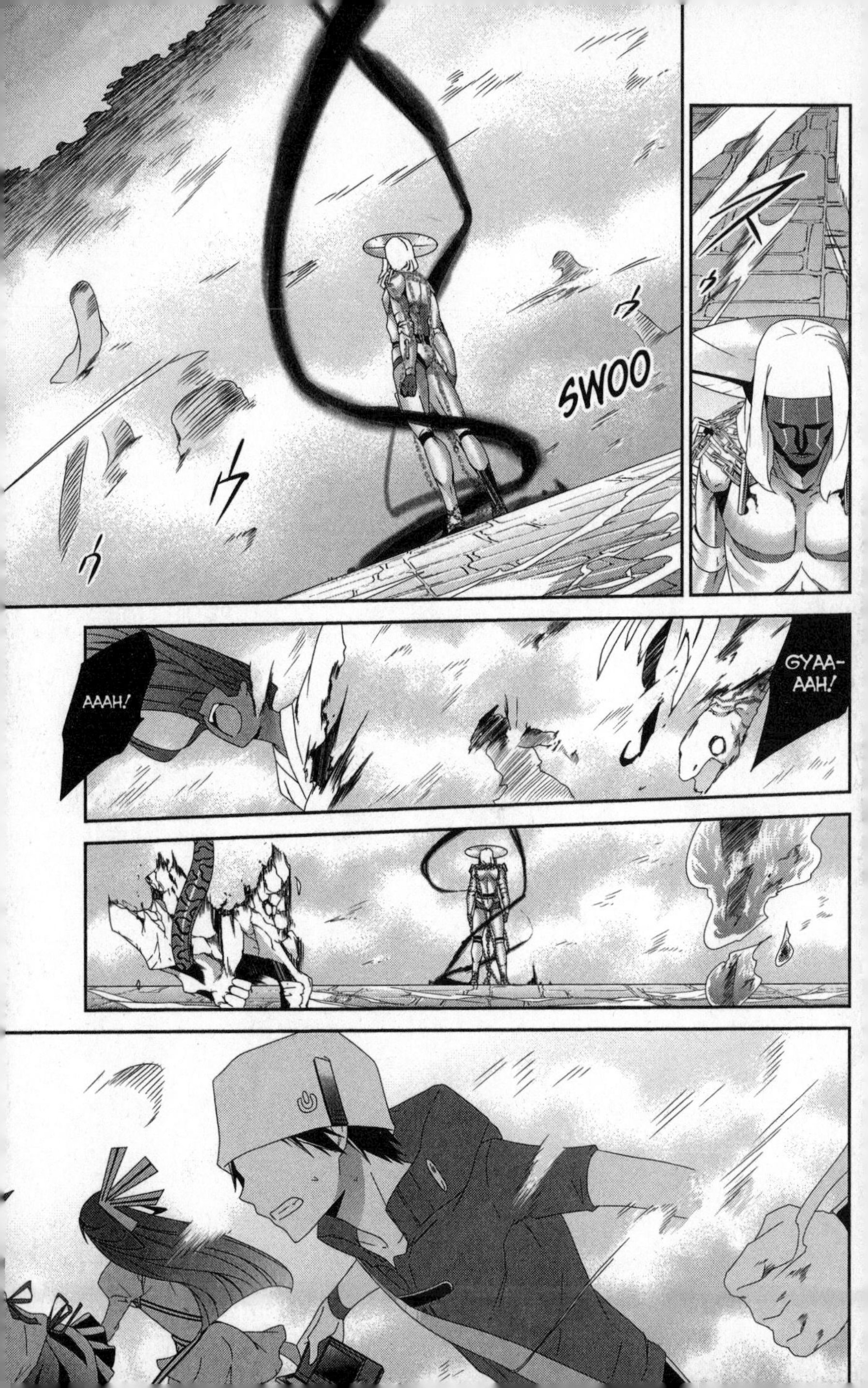
SWOO
GYAA-AAH!
AAAH!

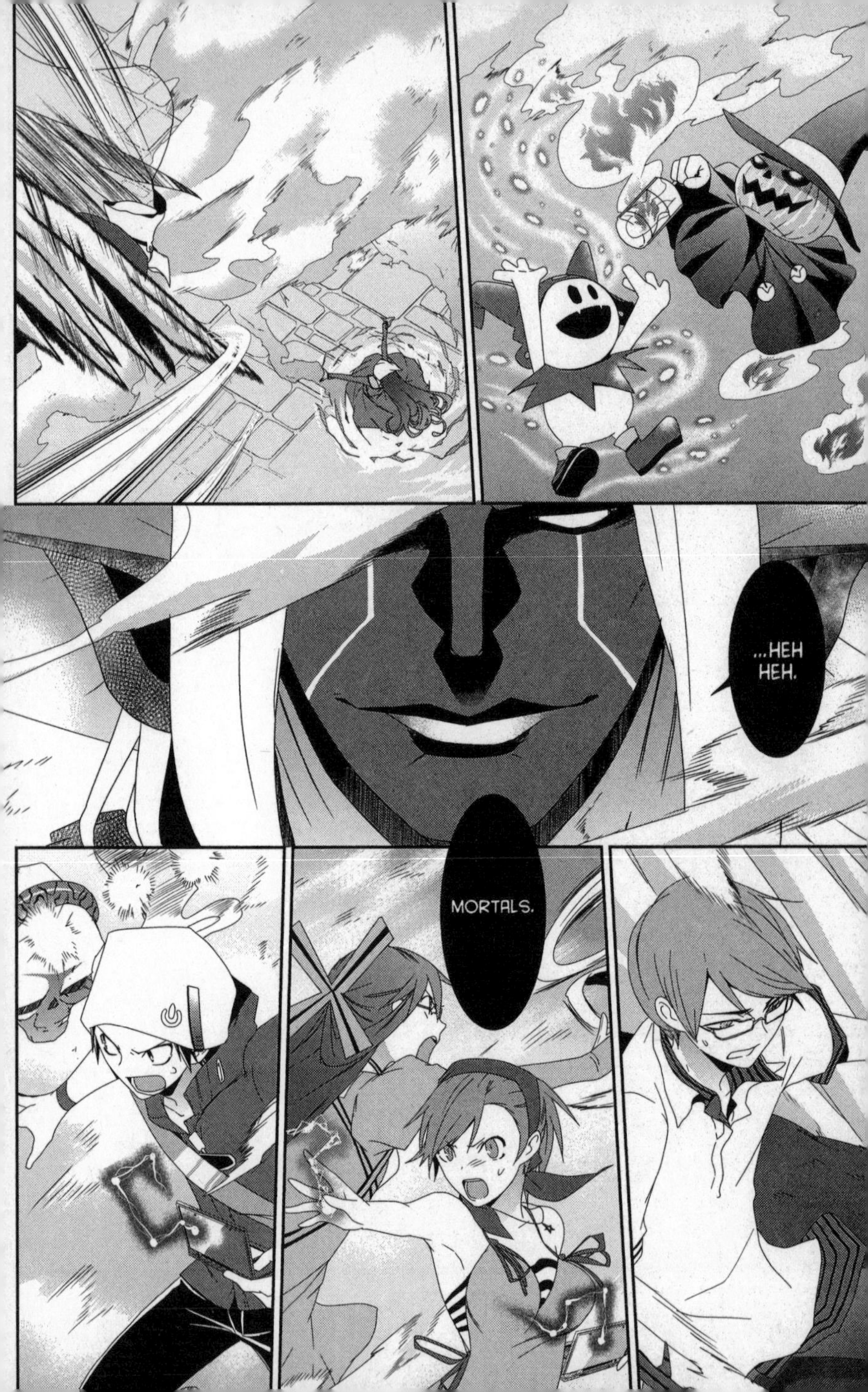
...HEH HEH.
MORTALS.

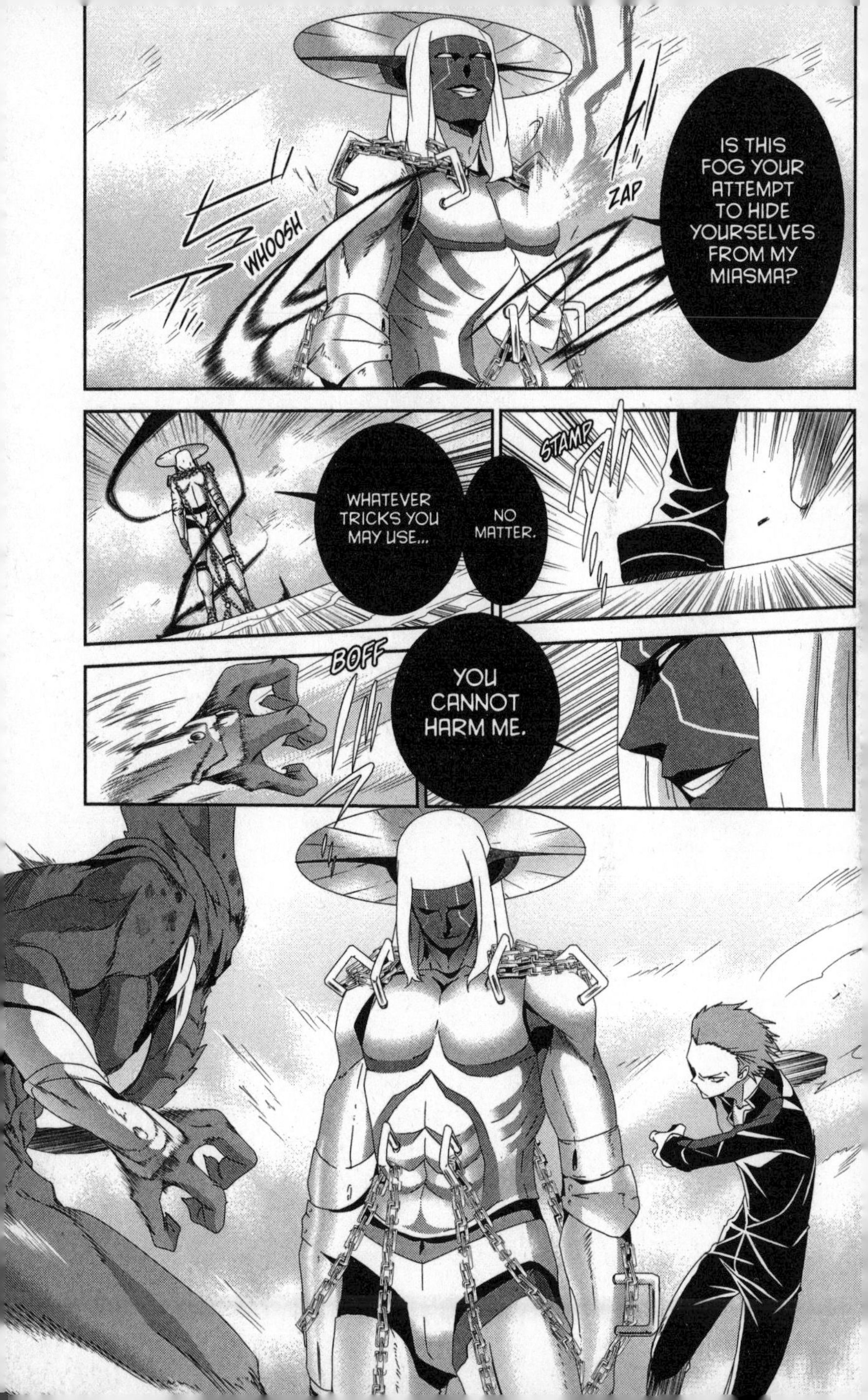
IS THIS FOG YOUR ATTEMPT TO HIDE YOURSELVES FROM MY MIASMA?
ZAP
WHOOSH
STAMP
NO MATTER.
WHATEVER TRICKS YOU MAY USE...
YOU CANNOT HARM ME.
BOFF

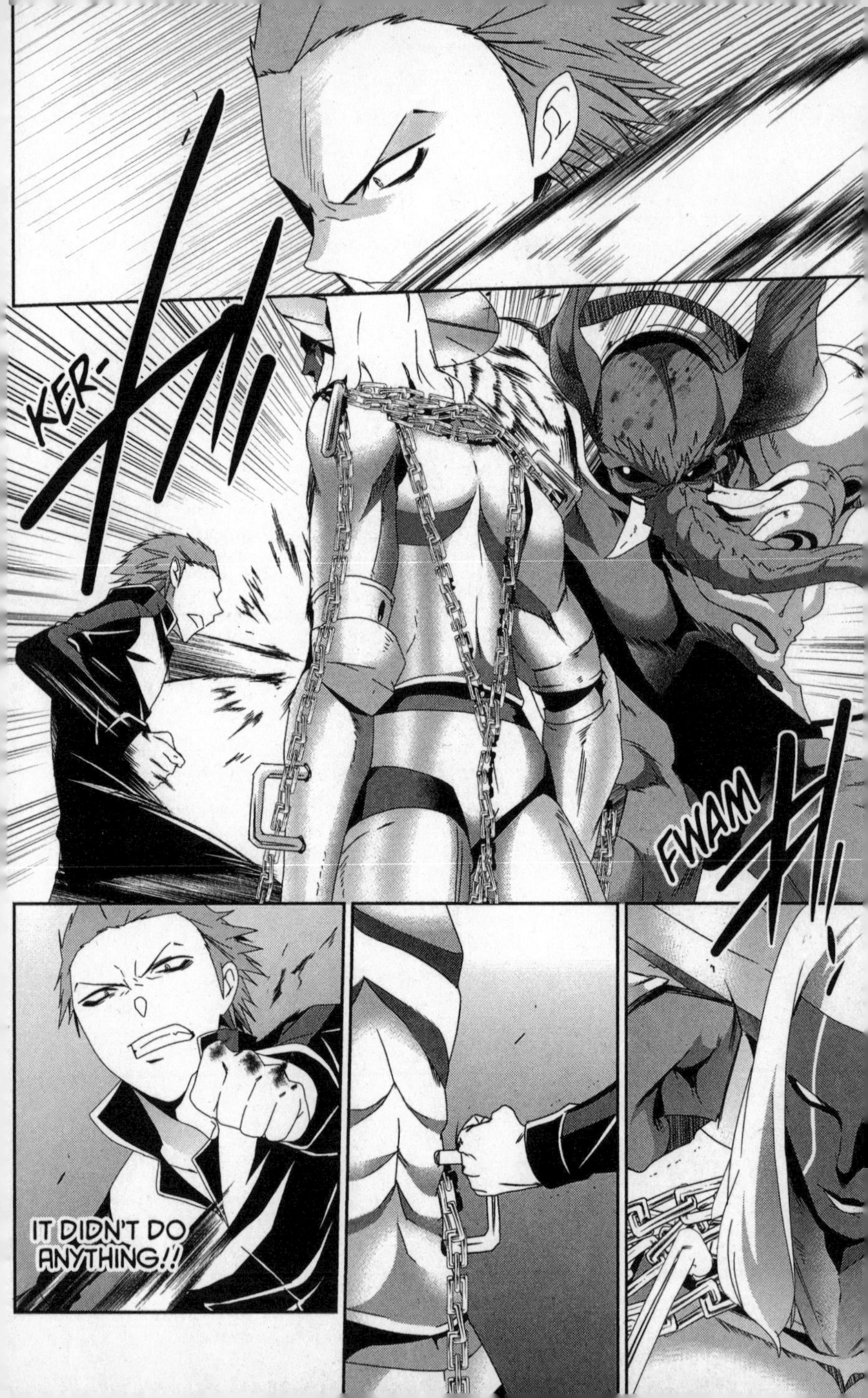
KER-
FWAM
IT DIDN'T DO ANYTHING!!

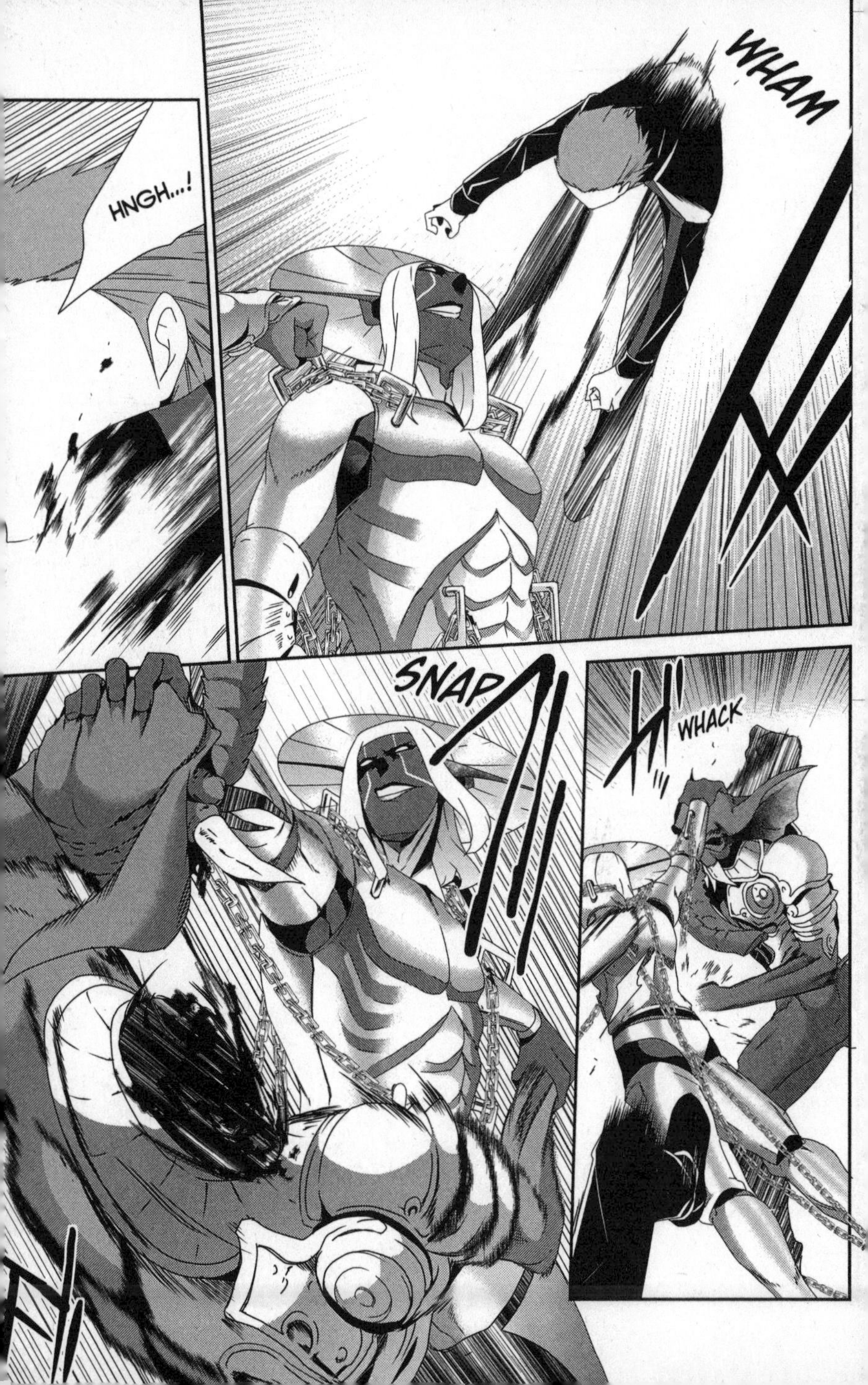
WHAM
HNGH...!
WHACK
SNAP

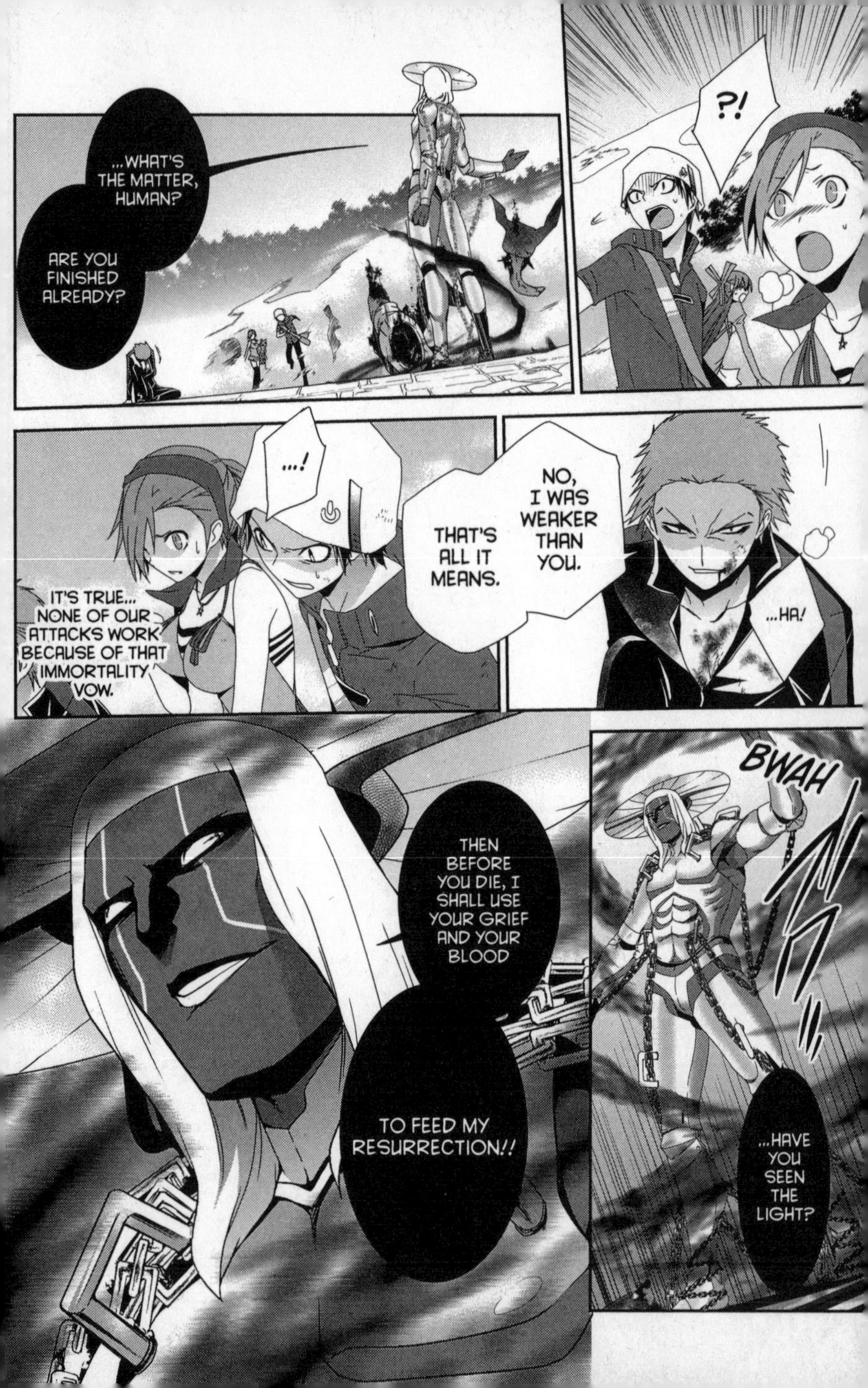
?!
...WHAT'S THE MATTER, HUMAN?
ARE YOU FINISHED ALREADY?
NO, I WAS WEAKER THAN YOU.
THAT'S ALL IT MEANS.
...HA!
...!
IT'S TRUE... NONE OF OUR ATTACKS WORK BECAUSE OF THAT IMMORTALITY VOW.
BWAH
...HAVE YOU SEEN THE LIGHT?
THEN BEFORE YOU DIE, I SHALL USE YOUR GRIEF AND YOUR BLOOD
TO FEED MY RESURRECTION!!

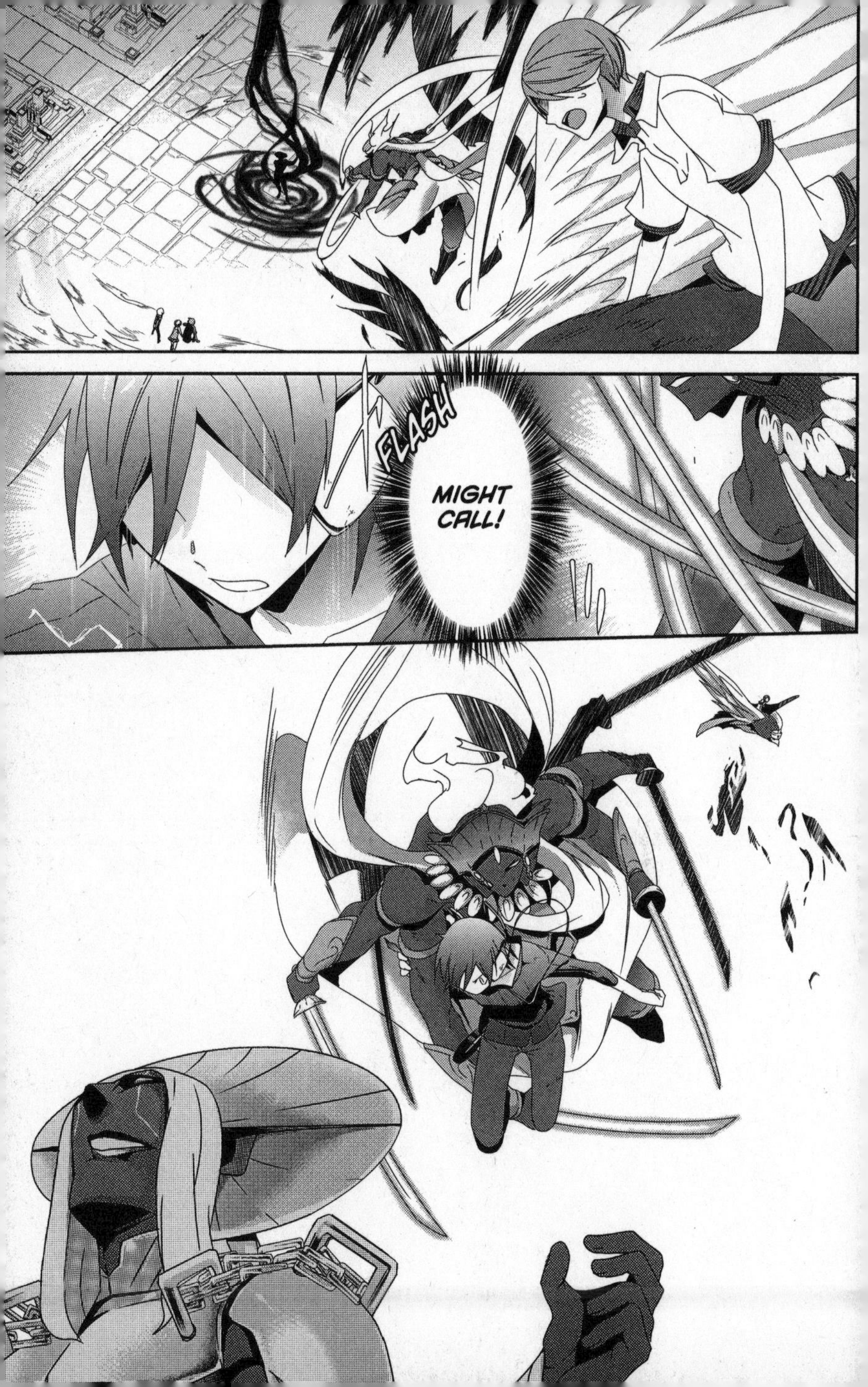
FLASH
MIGHT CALL!

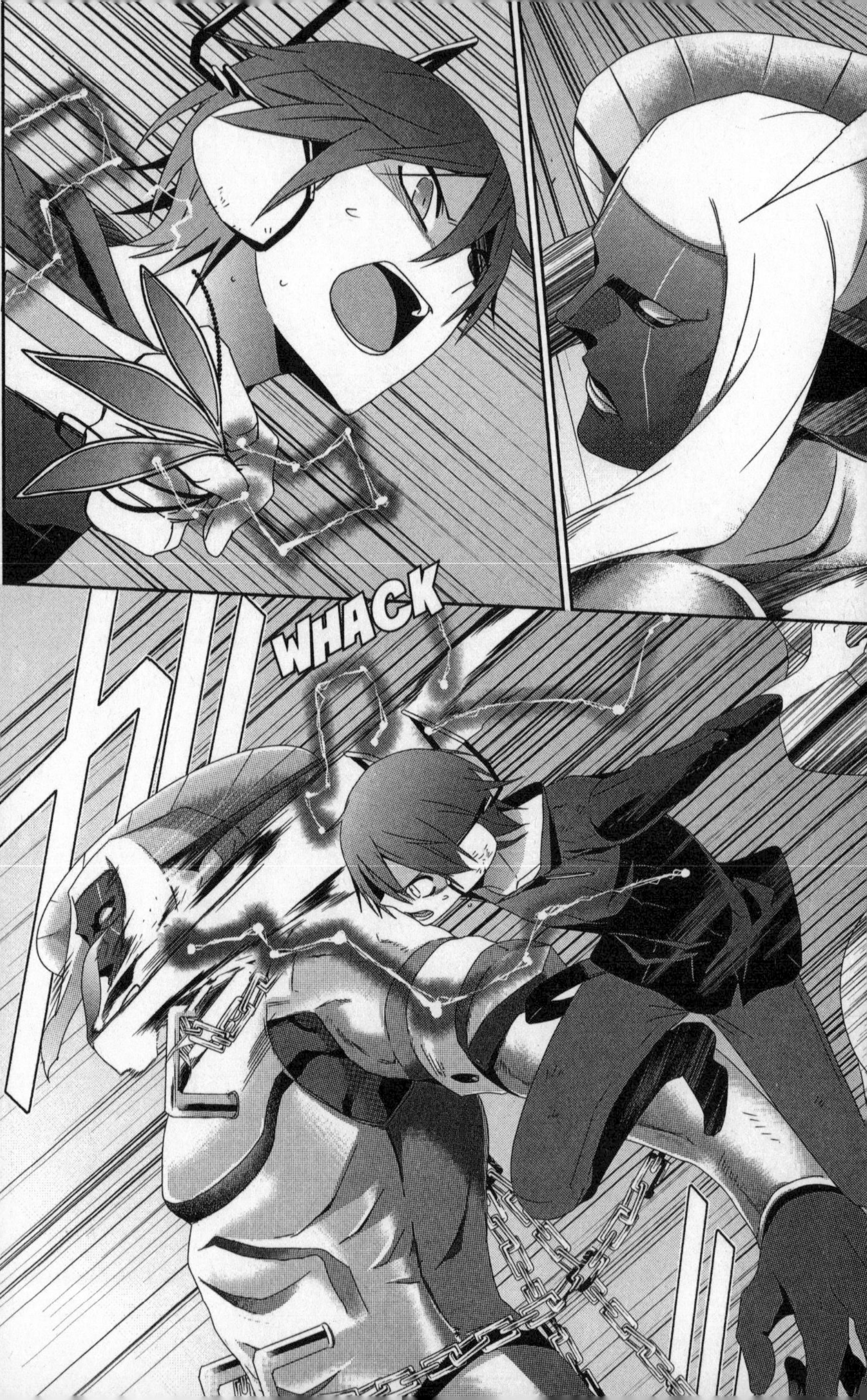
WHACK

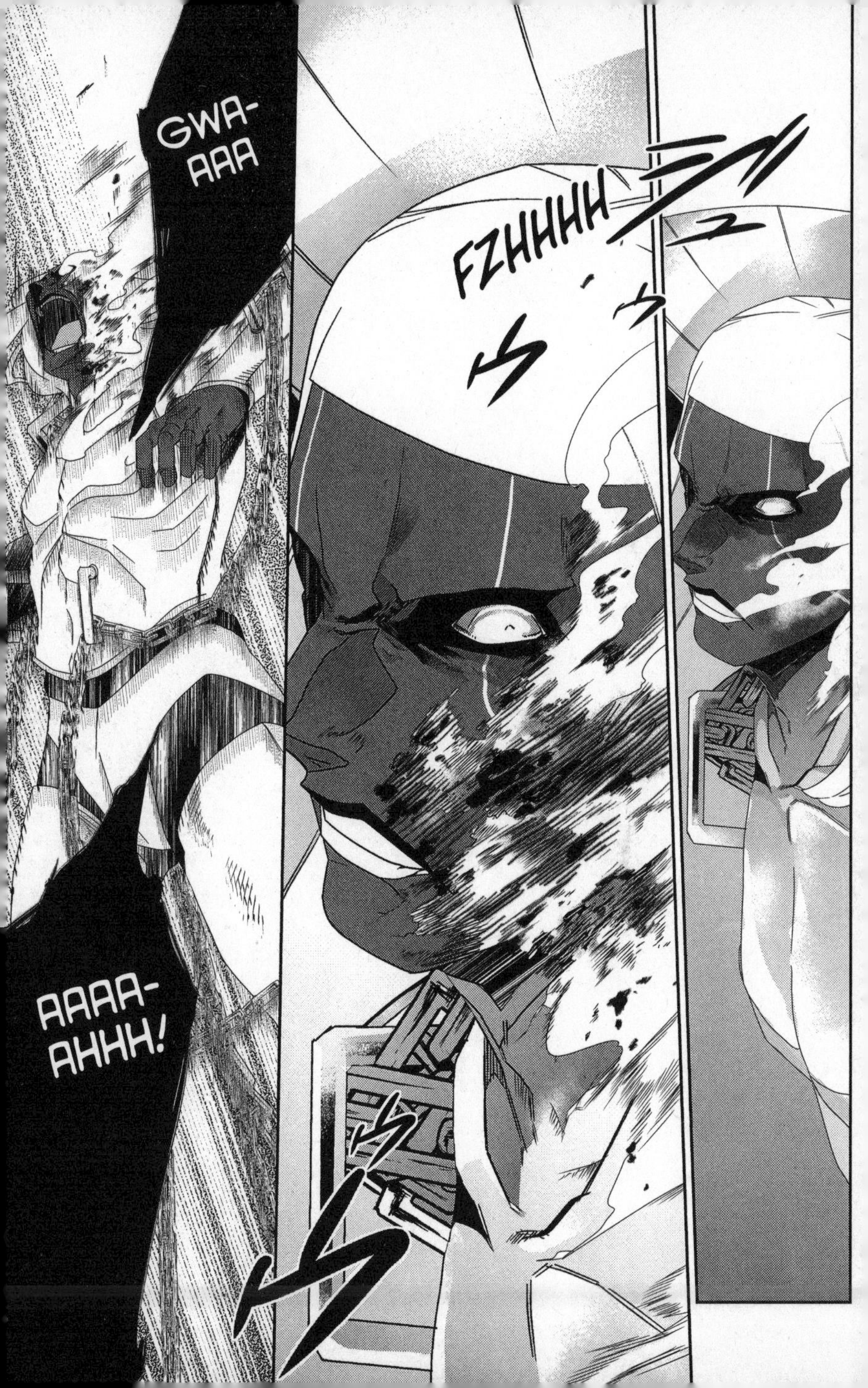
FZHHHH
GWA-
AAA
AAAA-
AHHH!

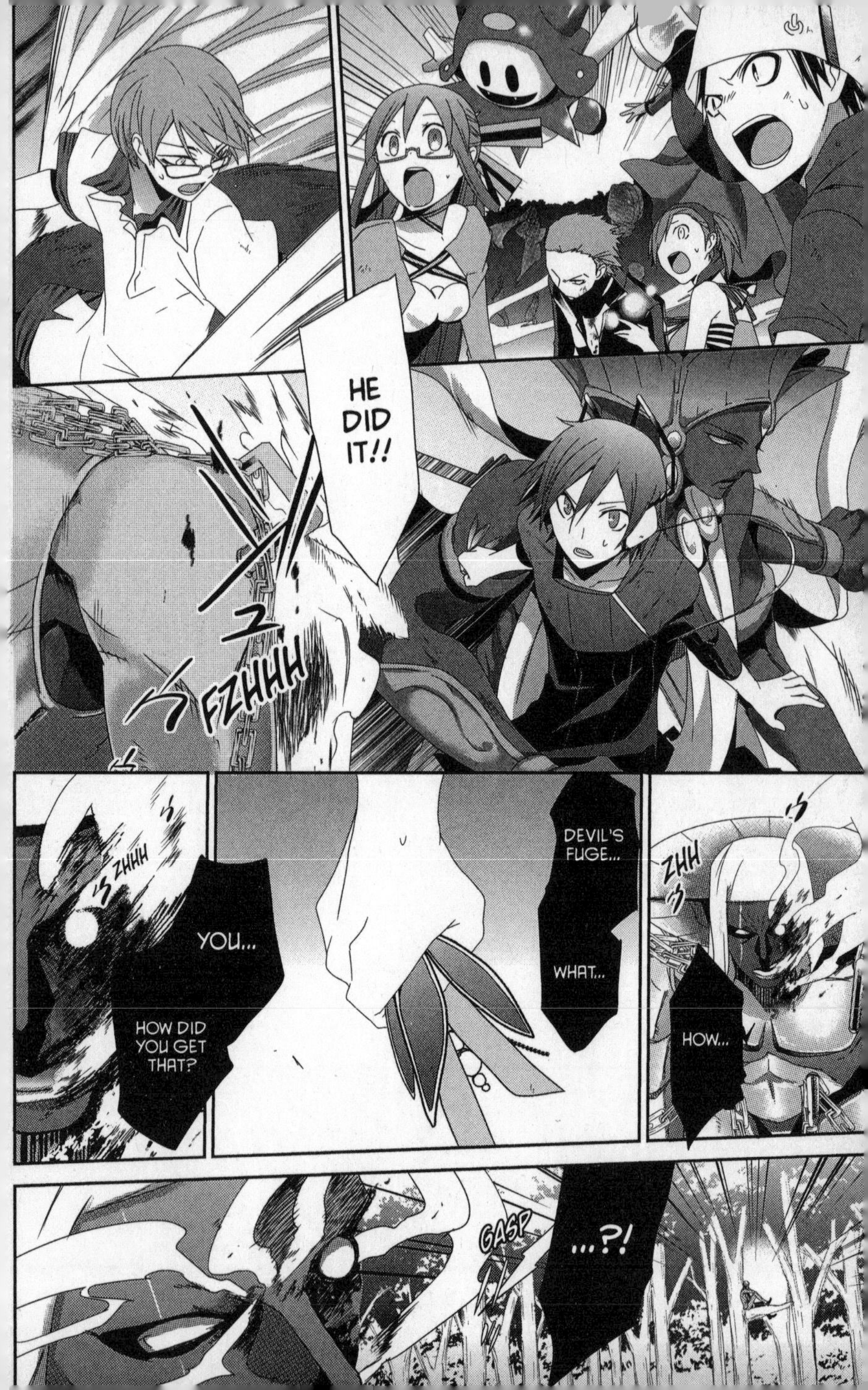
HE DID IT!!
FZHHH
ZHH
HOW...
DEVIL'S FUGE...
WHAT...
ZHHH
YOU...
HOW DID YOU GET THAT?
...?!
GASP

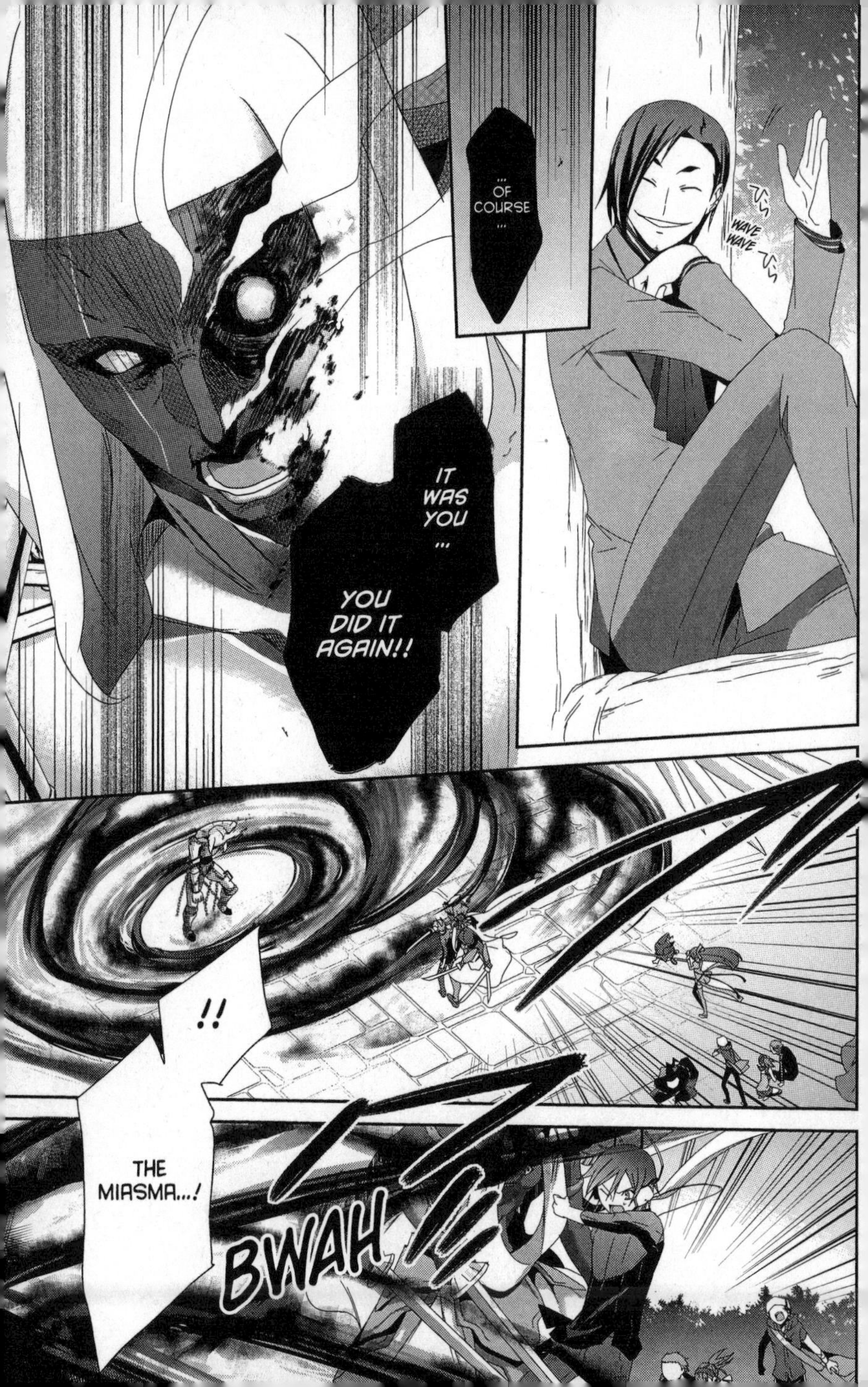
WAVE WAVE
...OF COURSE...
IT WAS YOU...
YOU DID IT AGAIN!!
!!
THE MIASMA...!
BWAH

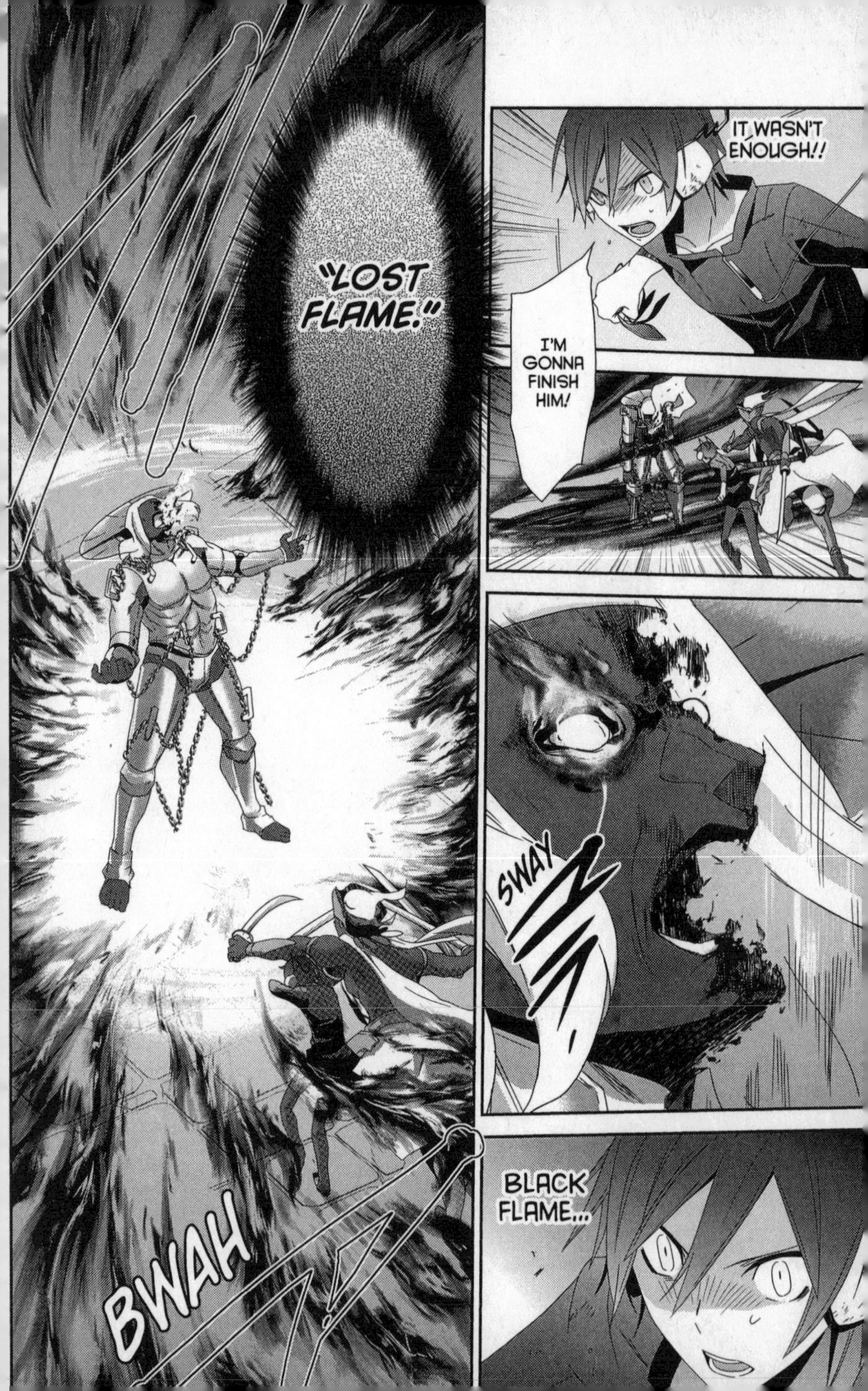
IT WASN'T ENOUGH!!
I'M GONNA FINISH HIM!
SWAY
BLACK FLAME...
"LOST FLAME."
BWAH

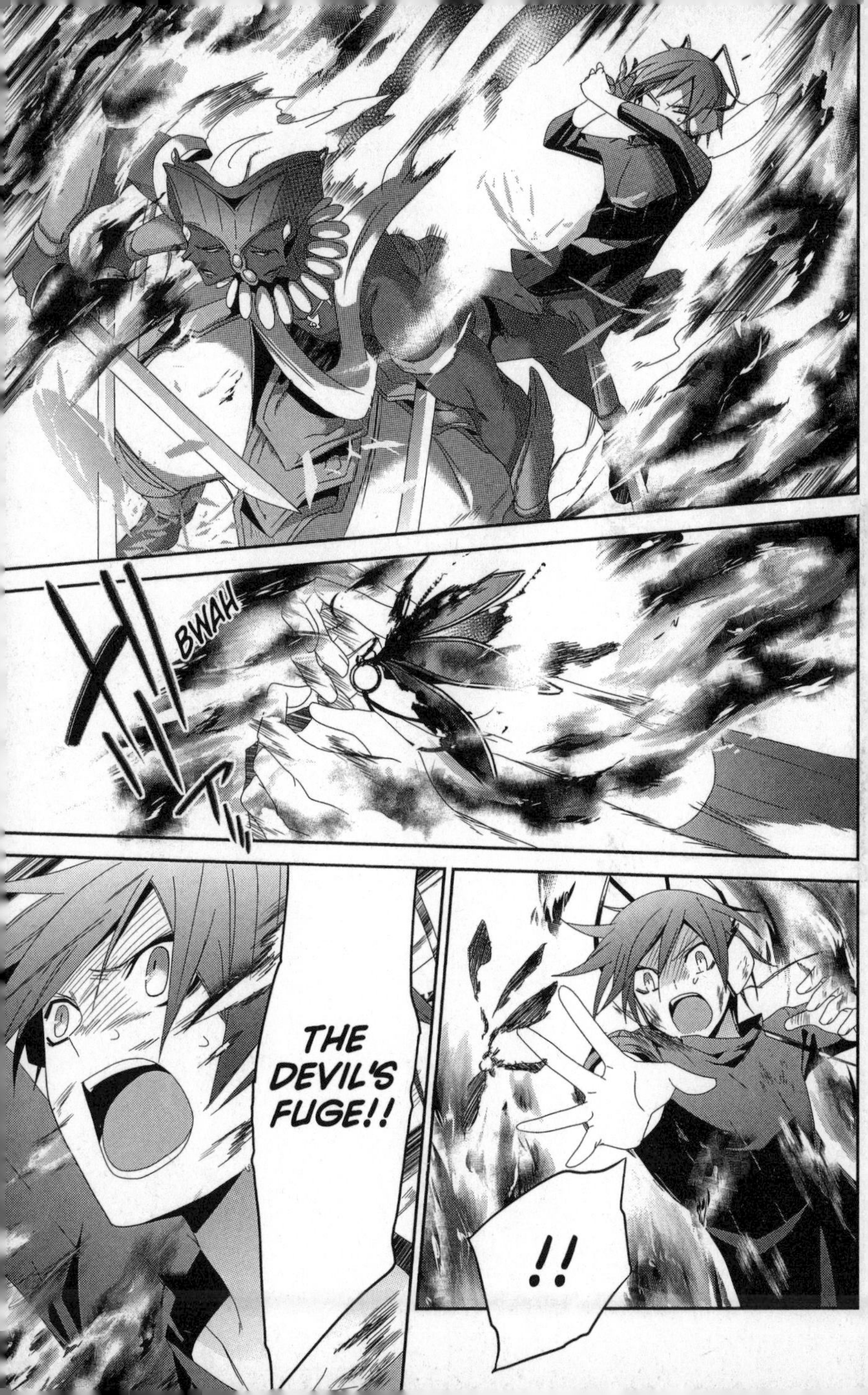
BWAH
!!
THE DEVIL'S FUGE!!

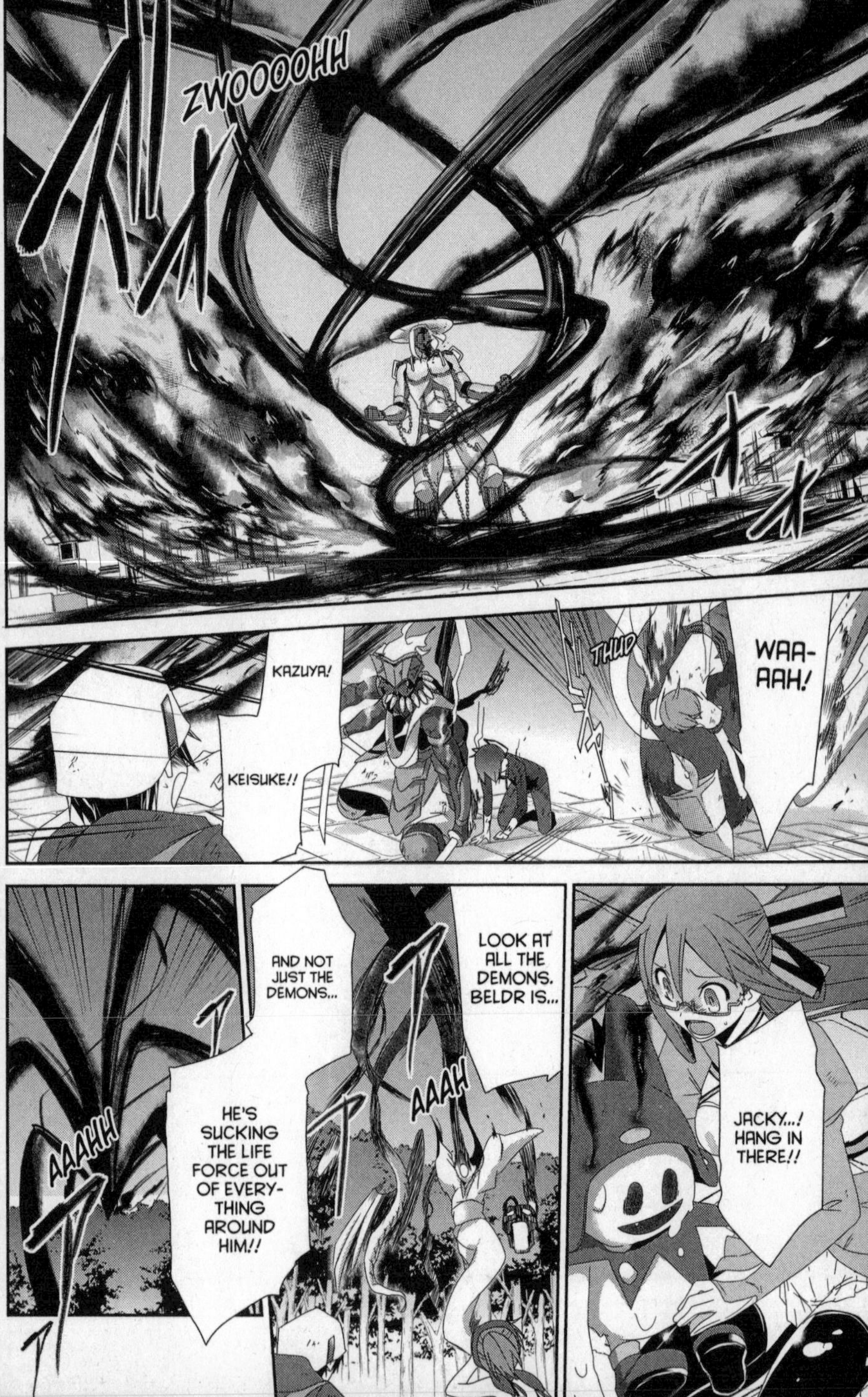
ZWOOOOHH
WAA-AAH!
THUD
KAZUYA!
KEISUKE!!
JACKY...! HANG IN THERE!!
LOOK AT ALL THE DEMONS. BELDR IS...
AND NOT JUST THE DEMONS...
AAAH
HE'S SUCKING THE LIFE FORCE OUT OF EVERYTHING AROUND HIM!!
AAAHH

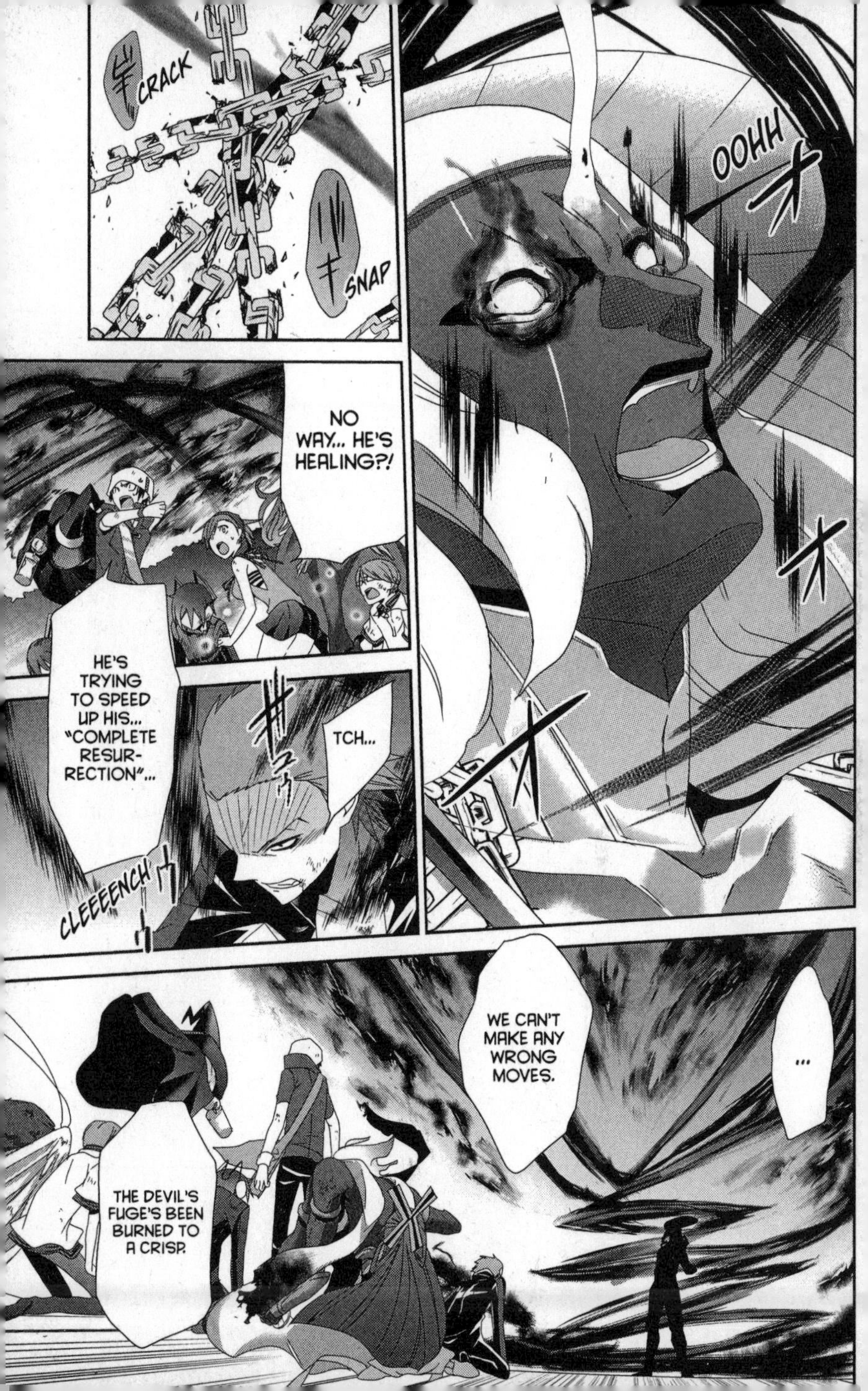
OOHH
CRACK
SNAP
NO WAY... HE'S HEALING?!
TCH...
HE'S TRYING TO SPEED UP HIS... "COMPLETE RESUR-RECTION"...
CLEEEENCH
...
WE CAN'T MAKE ANY WRONG MOVES.
THE DEVIL'S FUGE'S BEEN BURNED TO A CRISP.

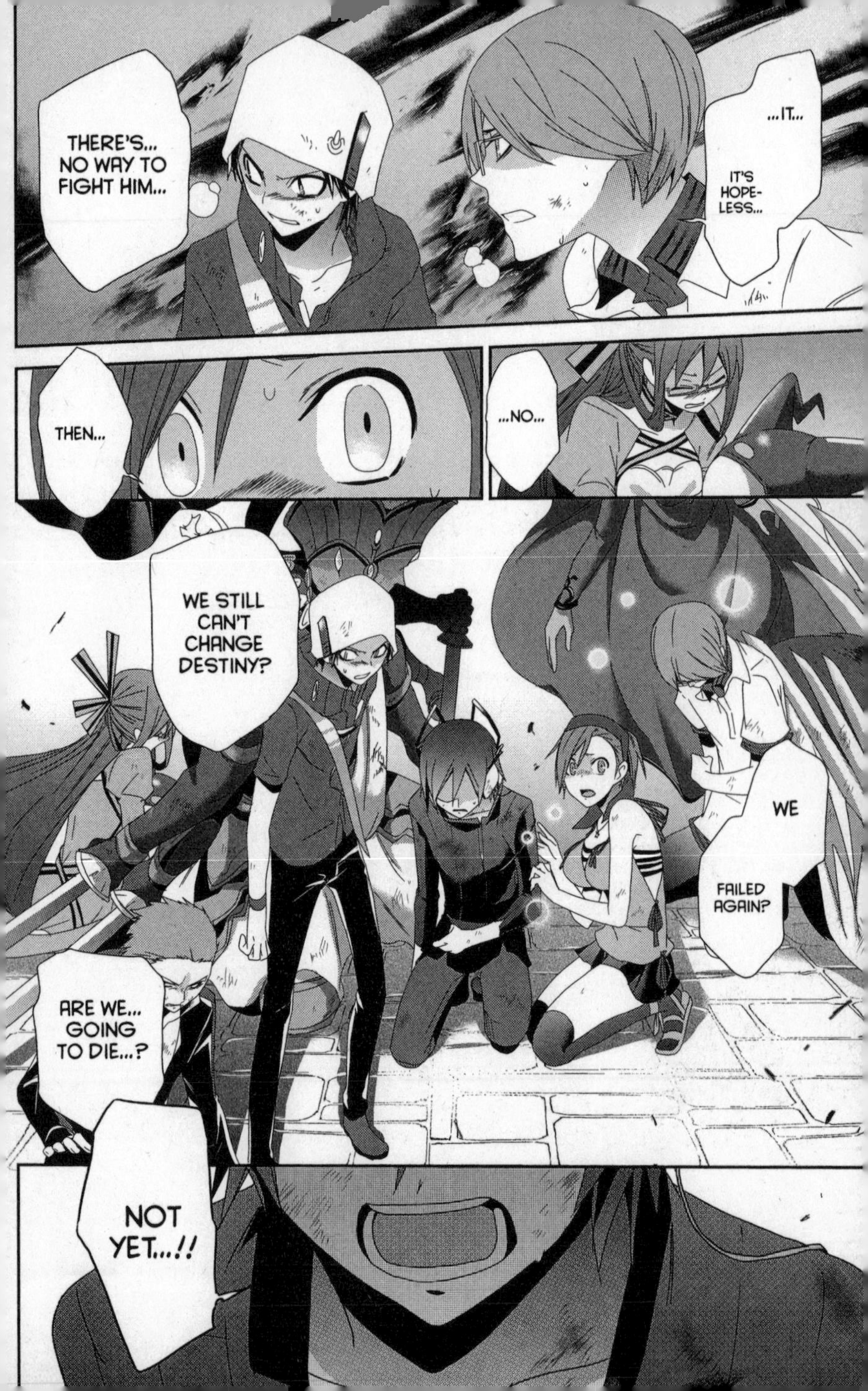
...IT...
IT'S HOPE-LESS...
THERE'S... NO WAY TO FIGHT HIM...
...NO...
THEN...
WE STILL CAN'T CHANGE DESTINY?
WE FAILED AGAIN?
ARE WE... GOING TO DIE...?
NOT YET...!!

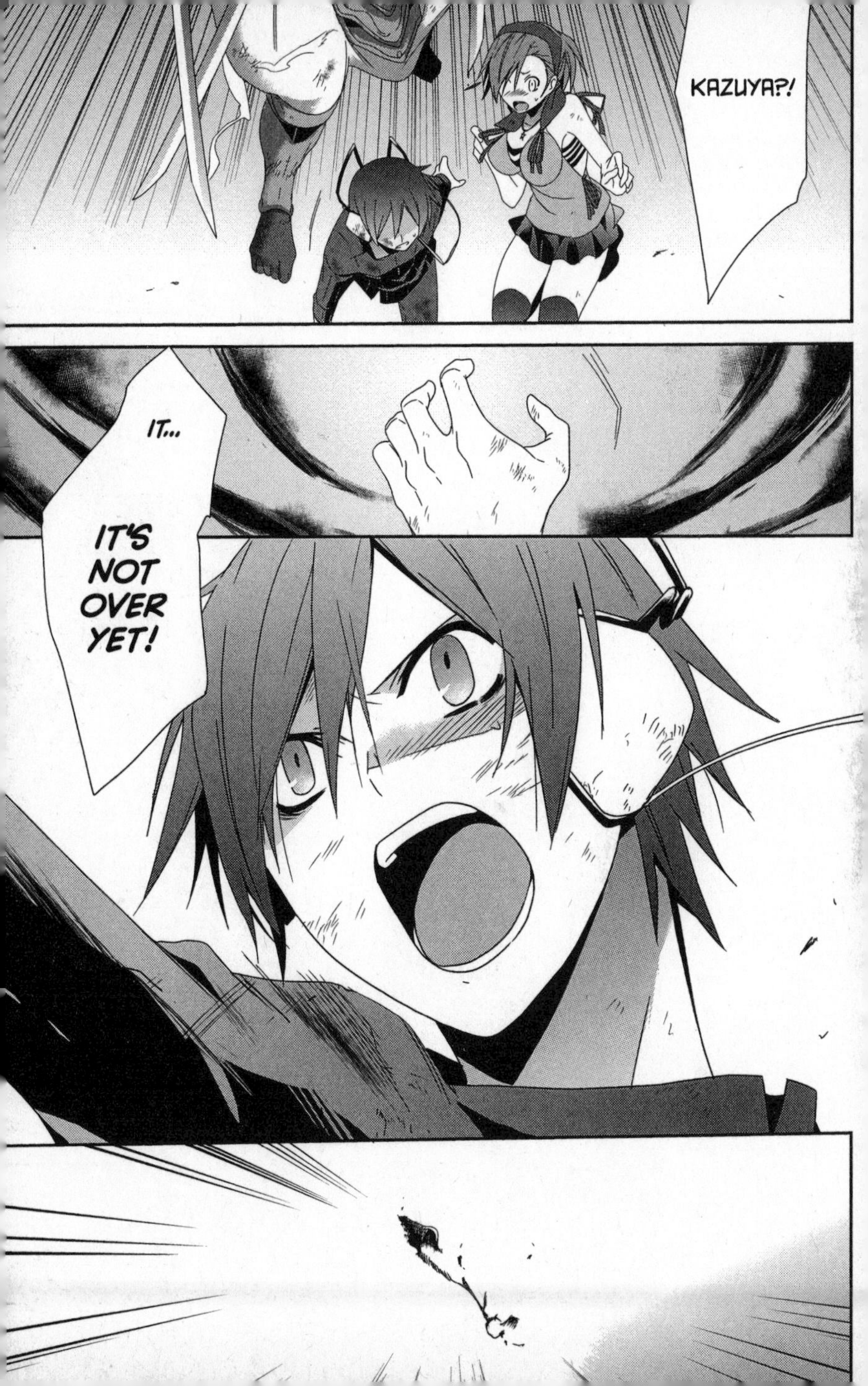
KAZUYA?!
IT...
IT'S NOT OVER YET!

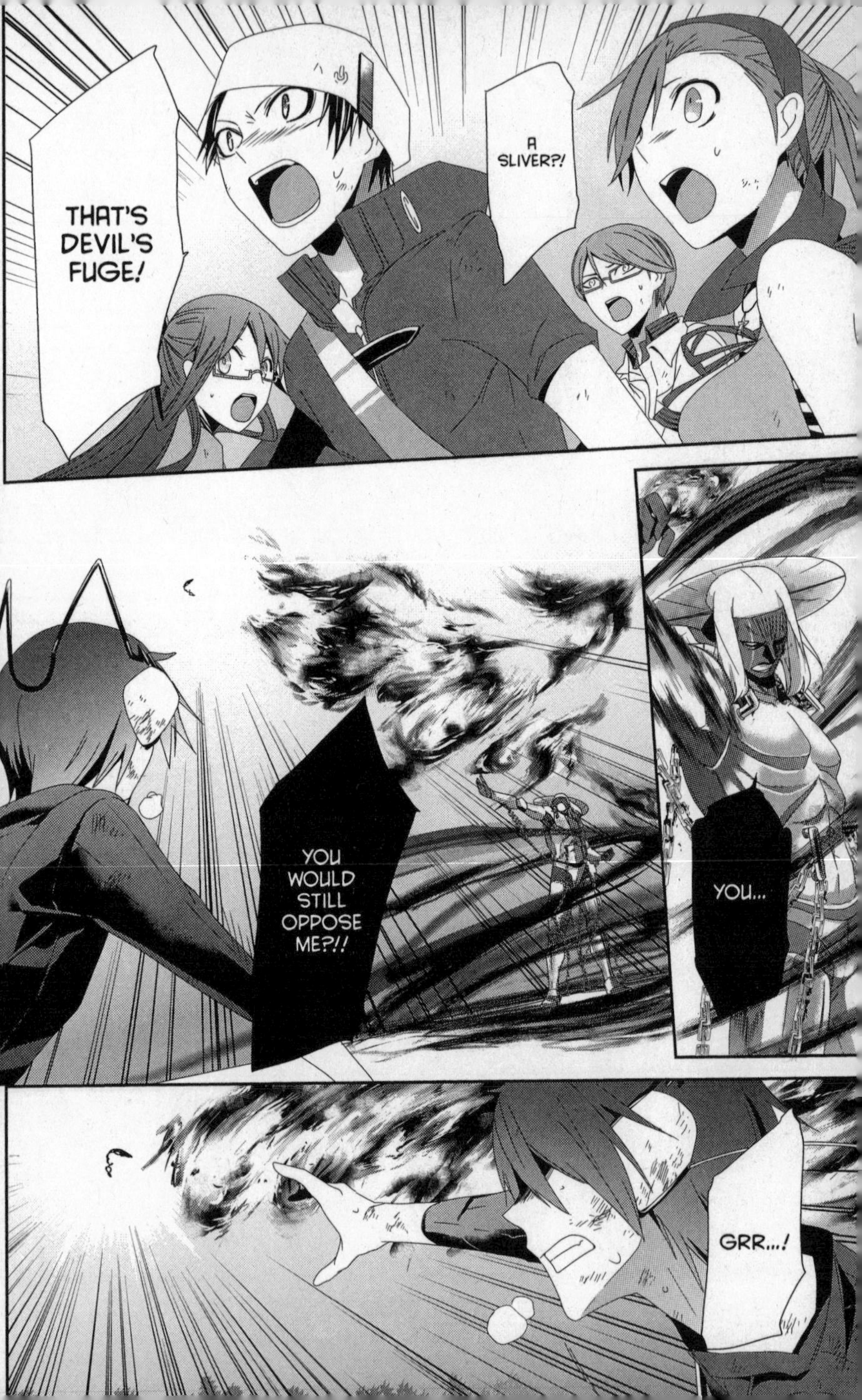
A SLIVER?!
THAT'S DEVIL'S FUGE!
YOU...
YOU WOULD STILL OPPOSE ME?!!
GRR...!

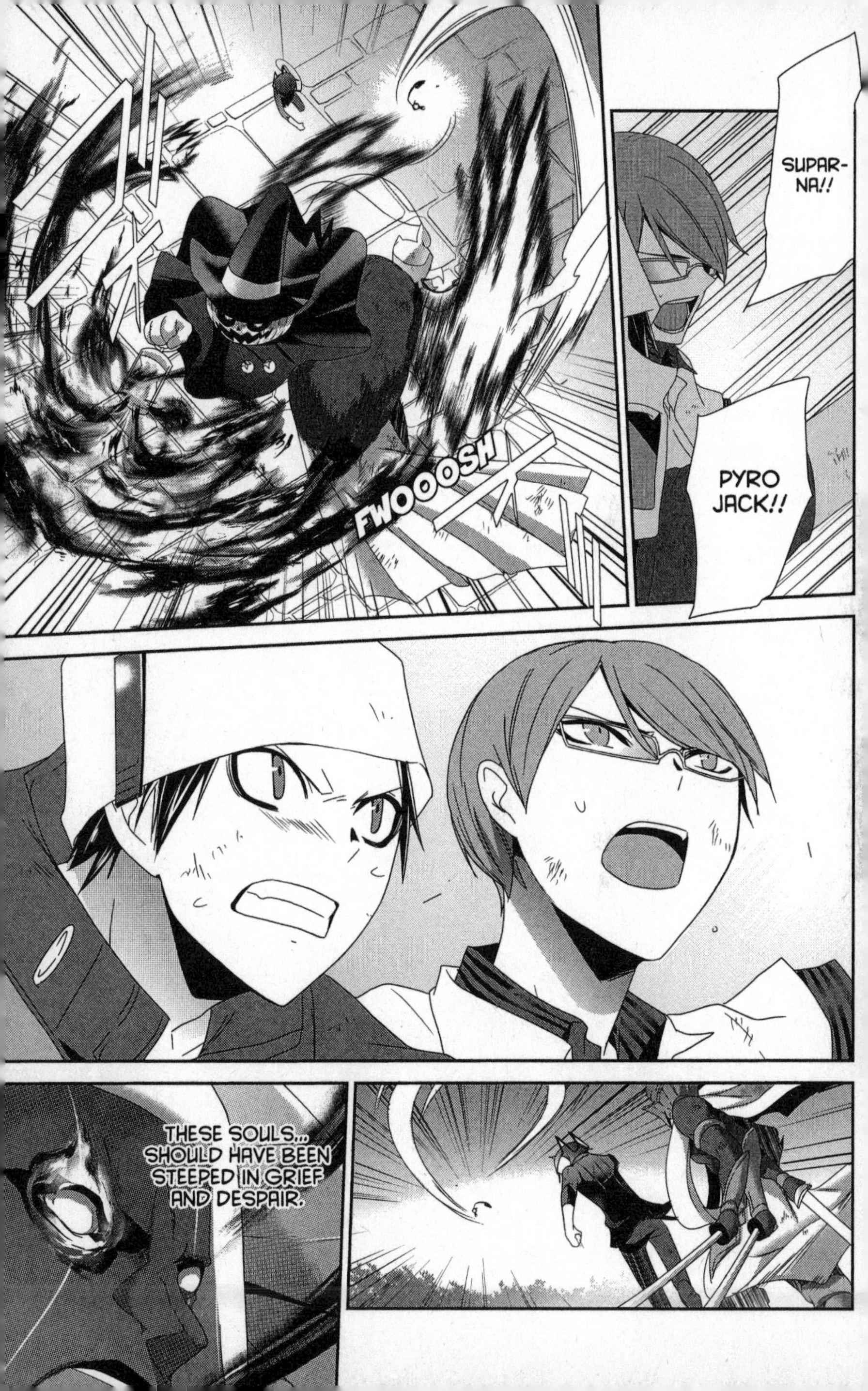
SUPAR-NA!!
PYRO JACK!!
FWOOOSH
THESE SOULS... SHOULD HAVE BEEN STEEPED IN GRIEF AND DESPAIR.

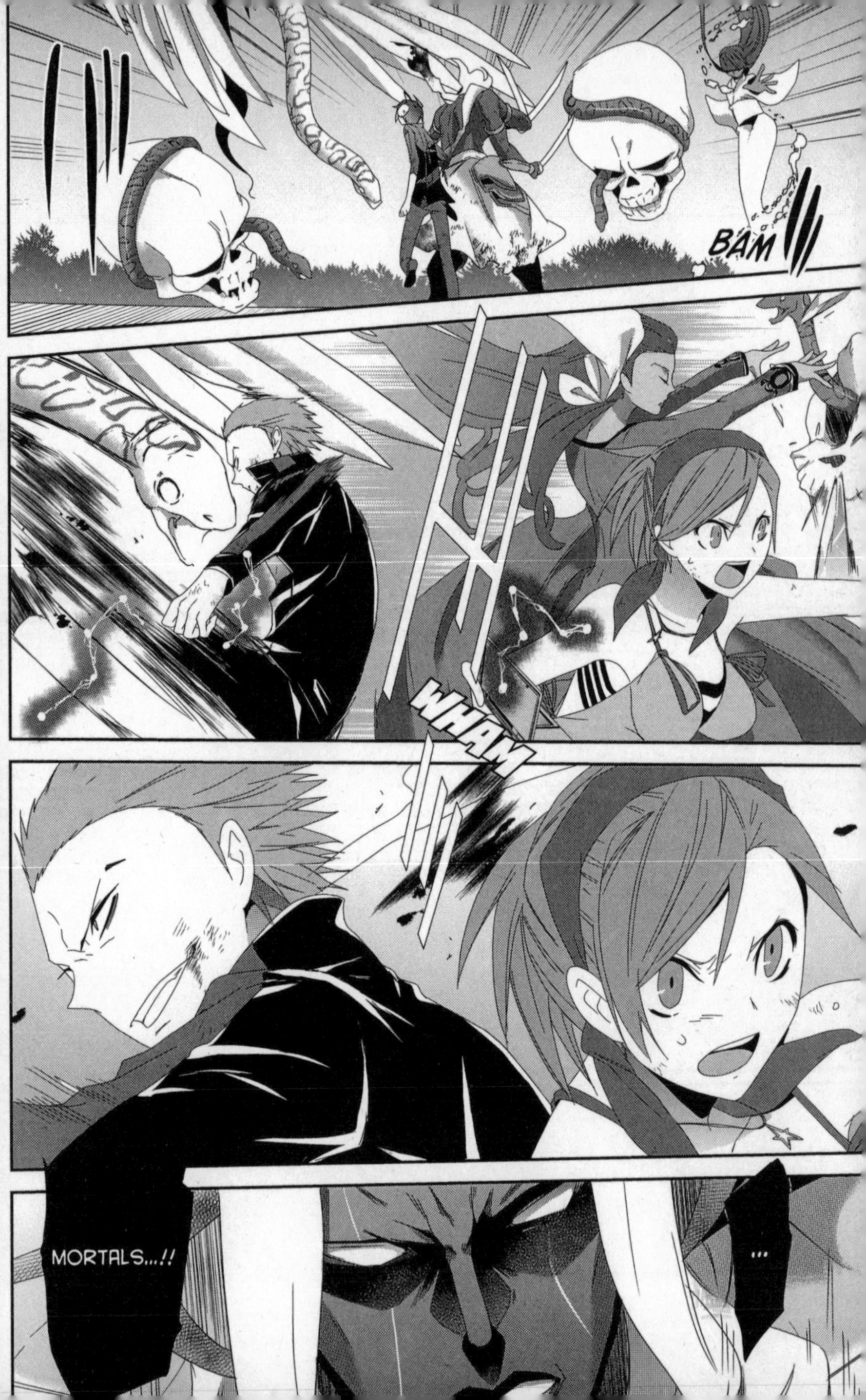
BAM
WHAM
...
MORTALS...!!

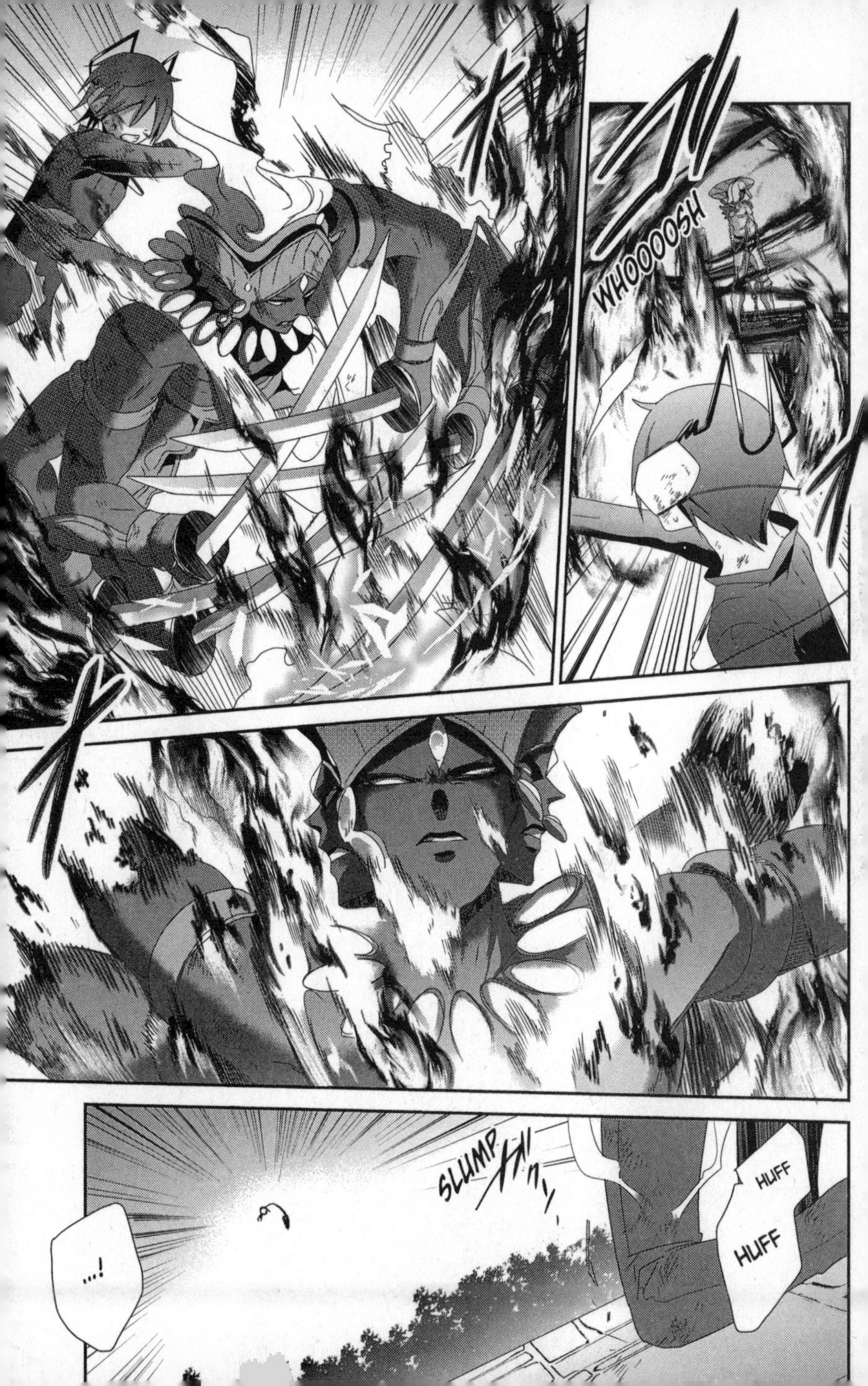
WHOOOOSH
SLUMP
HUFF
HUFF
...!

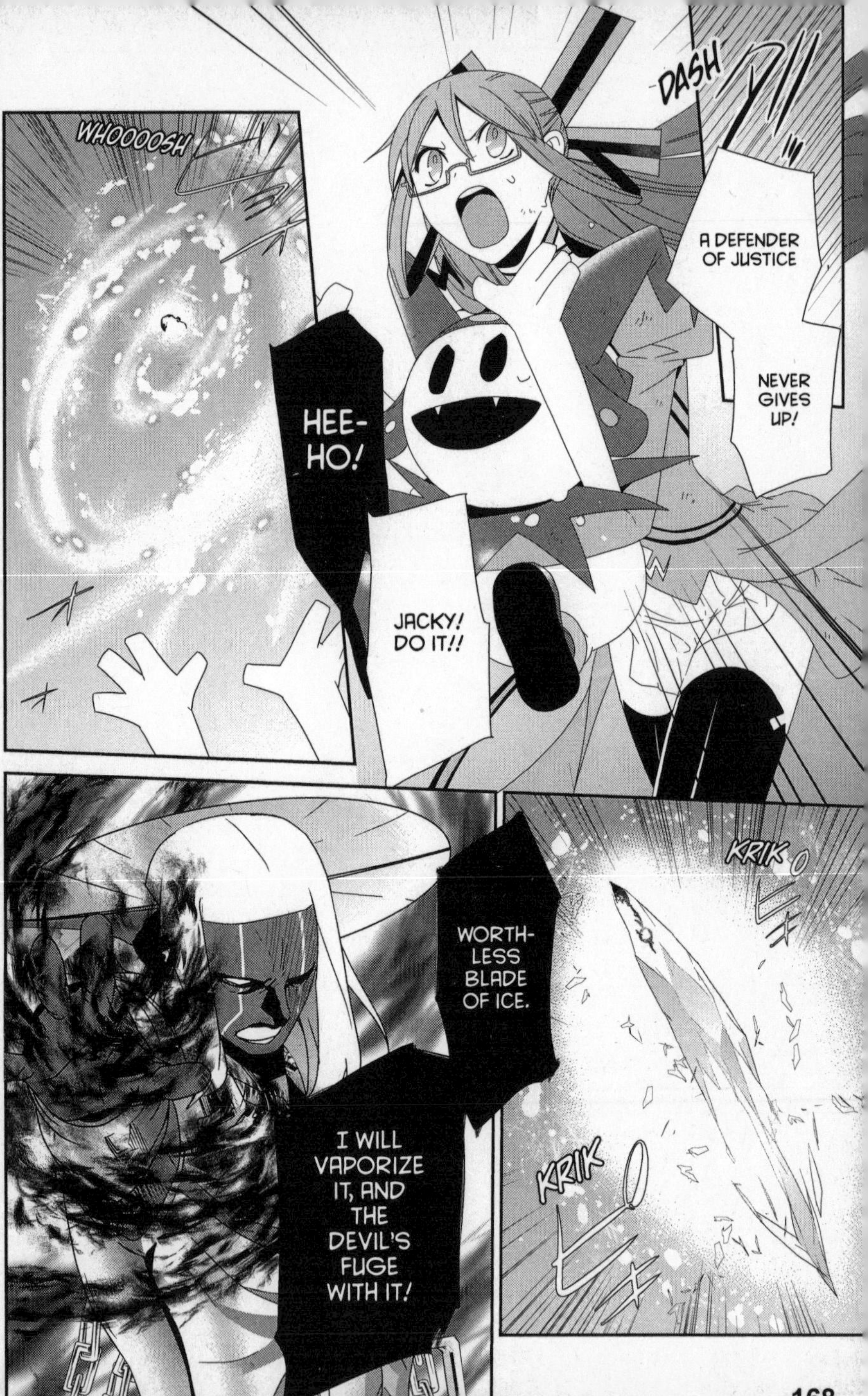
DASH
A DEFENDER OF JUSTICE
NEVER GIVES UP!
JACKY! DO IT!!
HEE-HO!
WHOOOOSH
KRIK
KRIK
WORTH-LESS BLADE OF ICE.
I WILL VAPORIZE IT, AND THE DEVIL'S FUGE WITH IT!

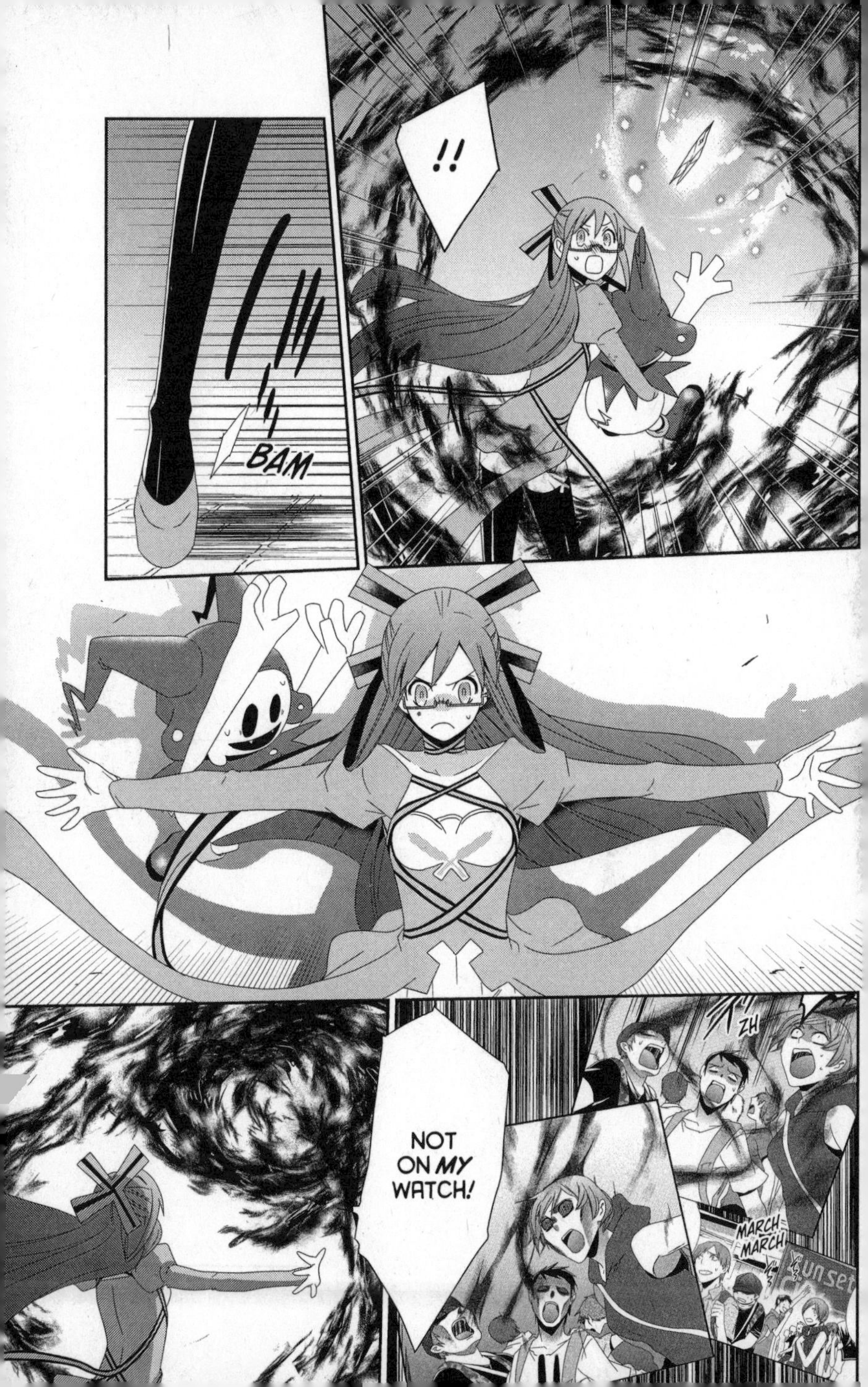
!!
BAM
ZH
MARCH MARCH
NOT ON MY WATCH!

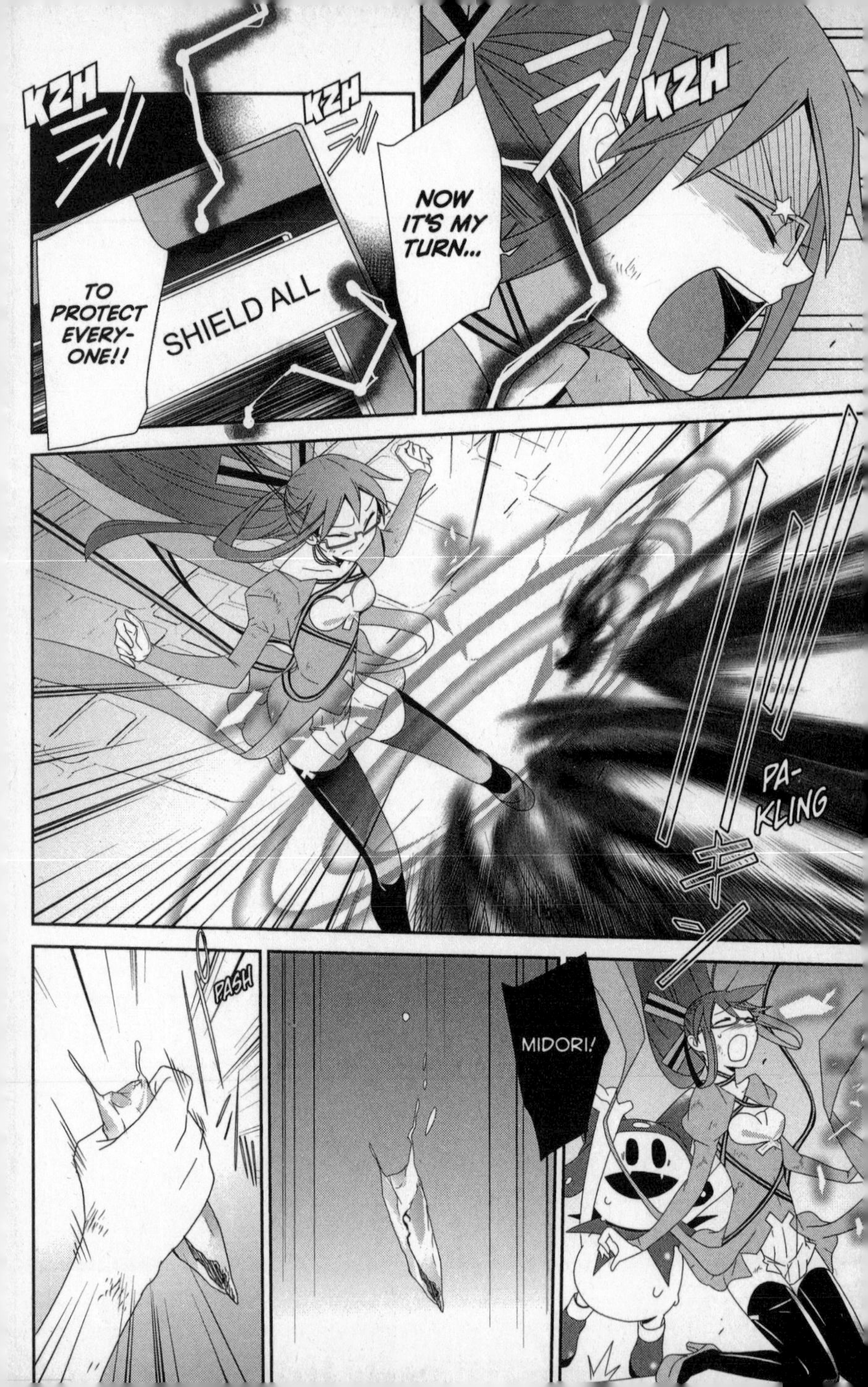
KZH
NOW IT'S MY TURN...
KZH
KZH
SHIELD ALL
TO PROTECT EVERY-ONE!!
PA-KLING
MIDORI!
PASH

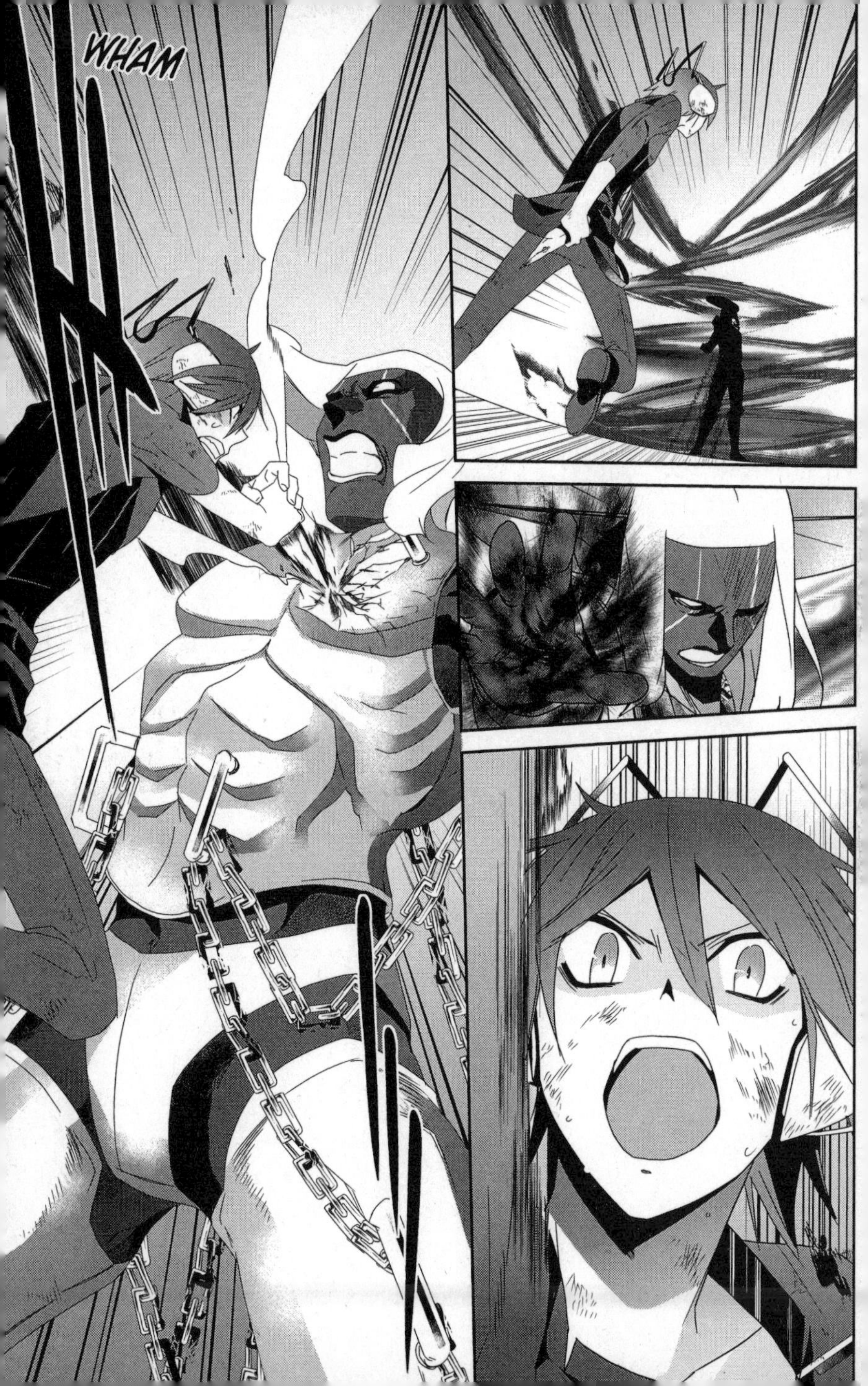
WHAM

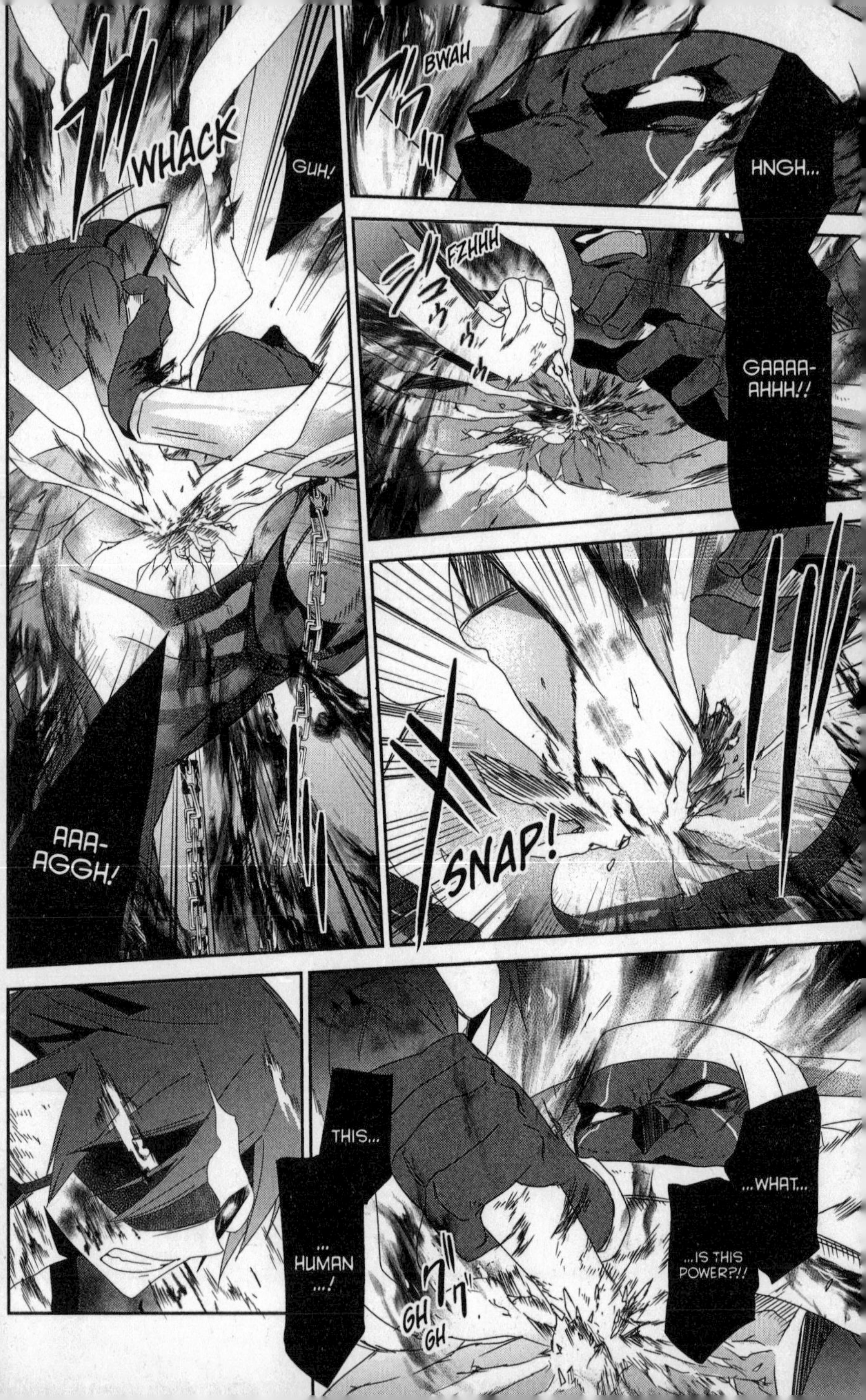
BWAH
HNGH...
FZHHH
GAAAA-AHHH!!
SNAP!
WHACK
GUH!
AAA-AGGH!
...WHAT...
...IS THIS POWER?!!
GH GH
THIS...
...HUMAN...!

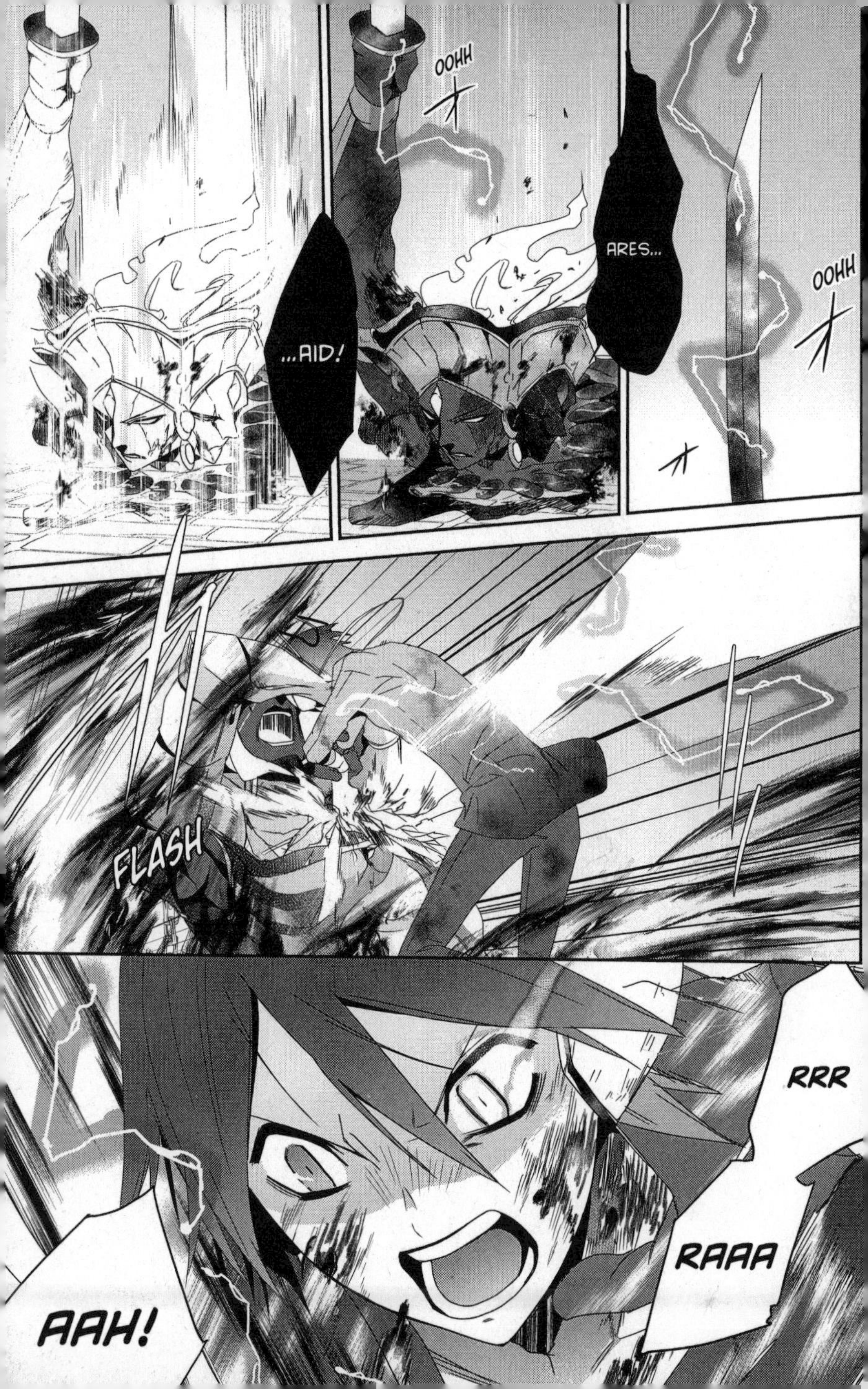
OOHH
OOHH
ARES...
...AID!
FLASH
RRR
RAAA
AAH!

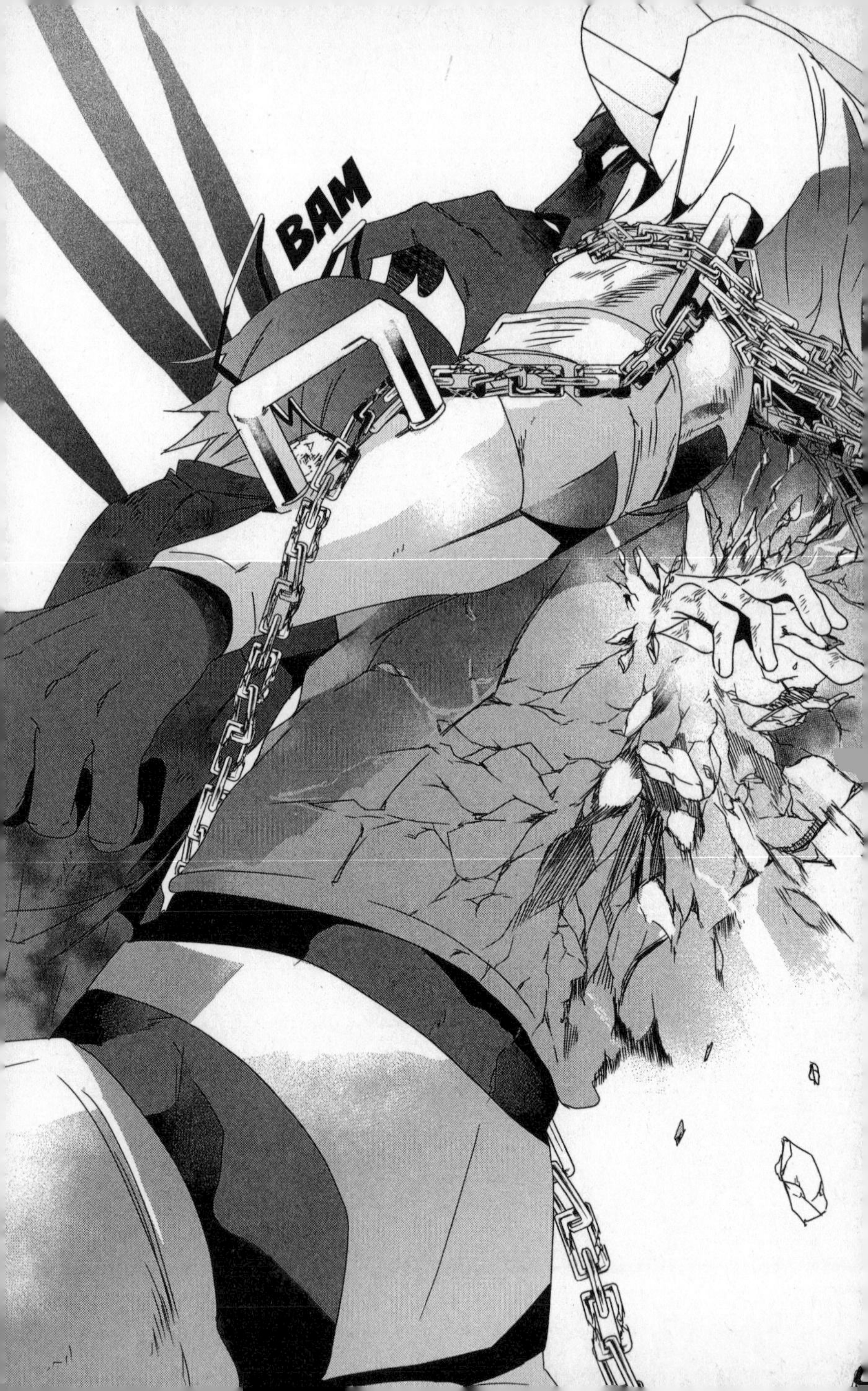
BAM

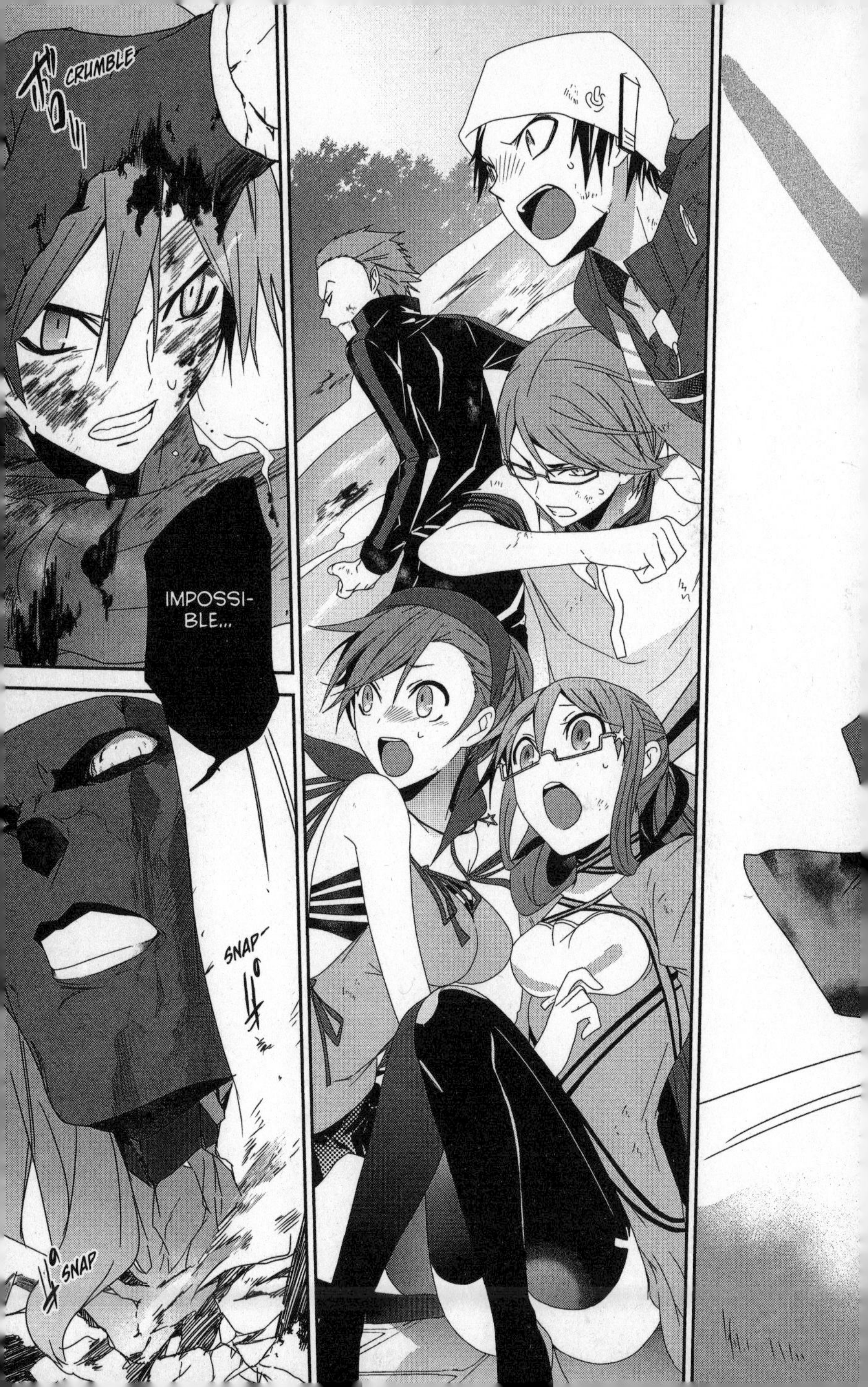
CRUMBLE
IMPOSSI-
BLE...
SNAP
SNAP

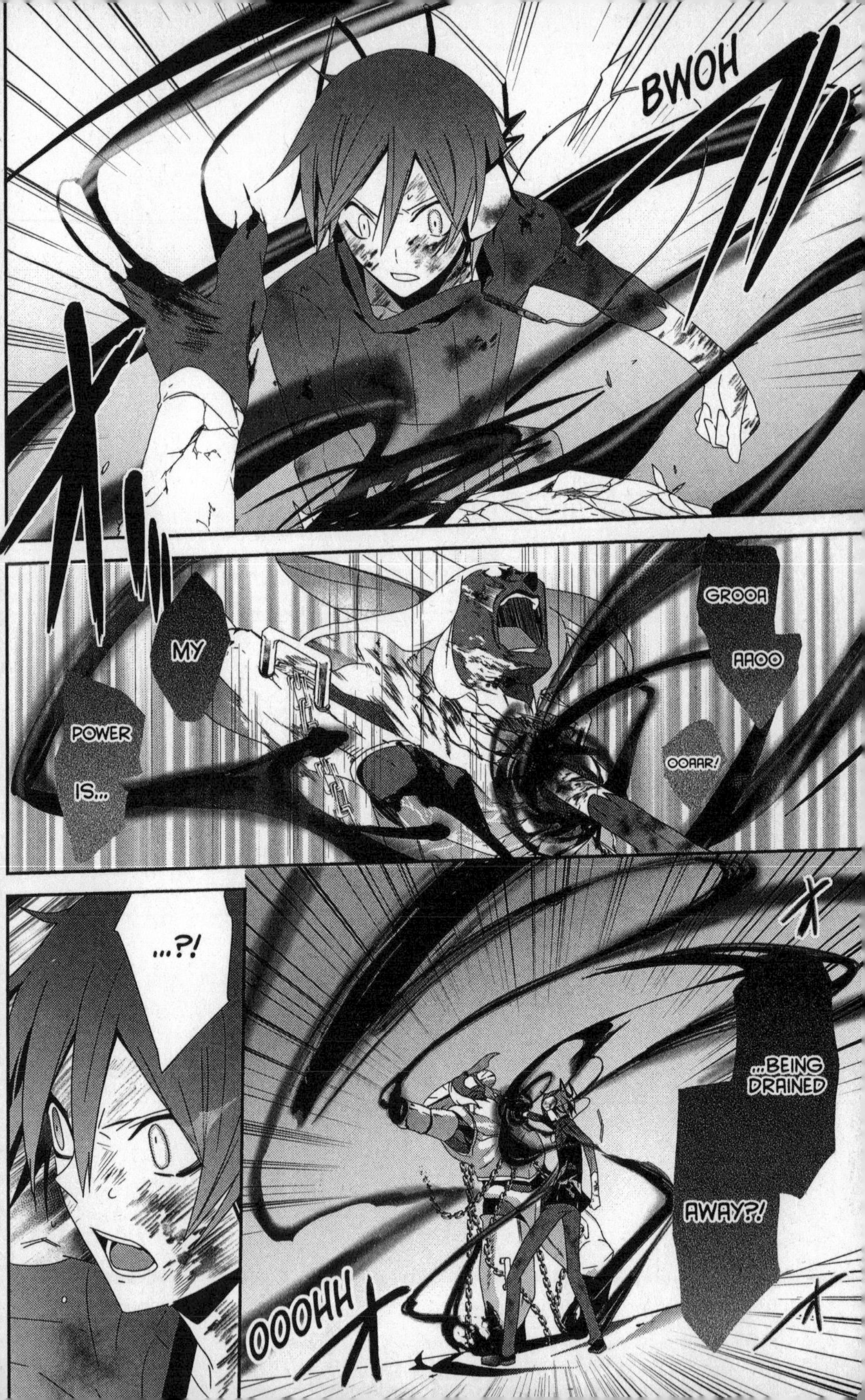
BWOH
GROOA
AAOO
OOAAR!
MY
POWER
IS...
...BEING DRAINED
AWAY?!
OOOHH
...?!

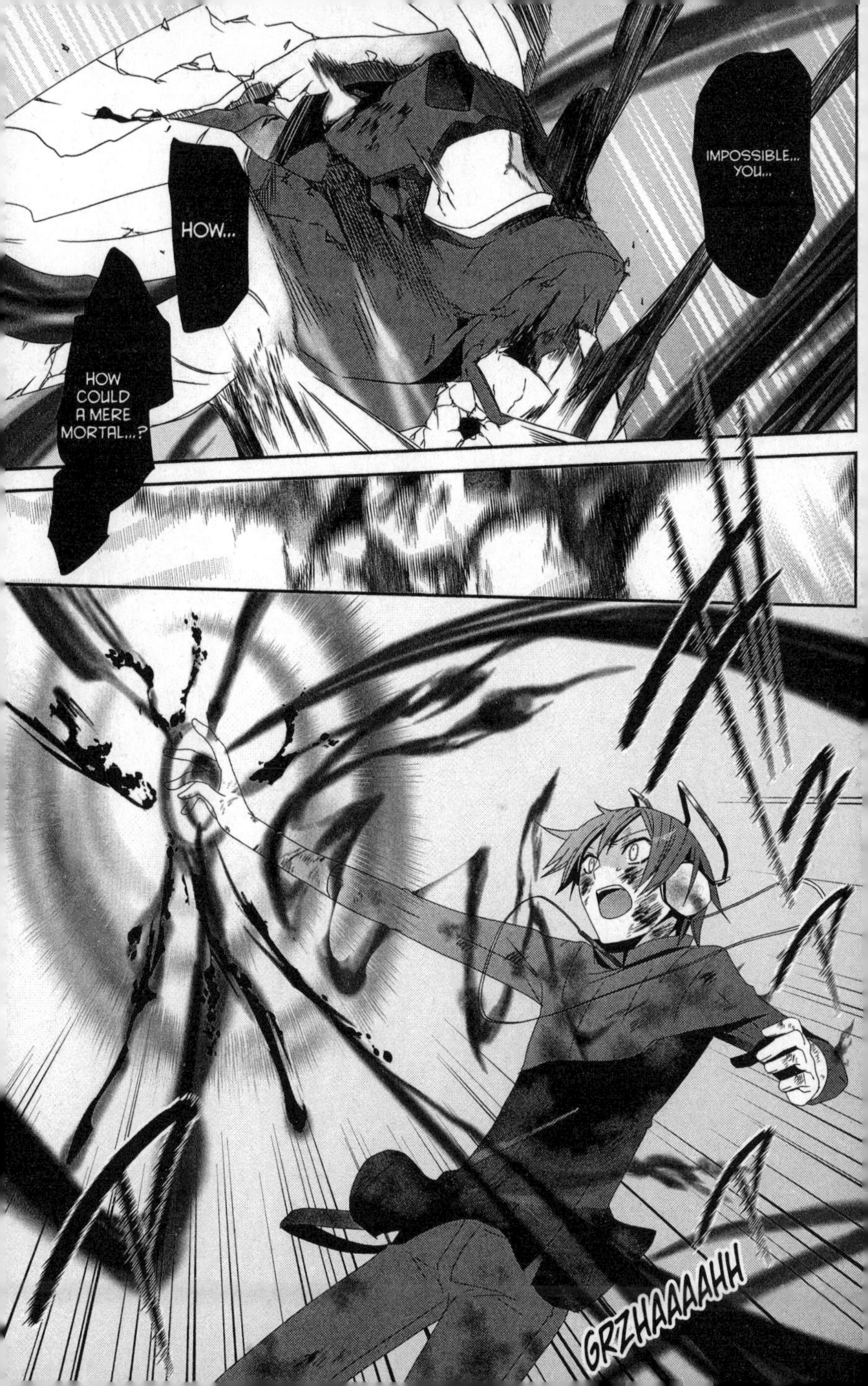
IMPOSSIBLE... YOU...
HOW...
HOW COULD A MERE MORTAL...?
GRZHAAAAAHH

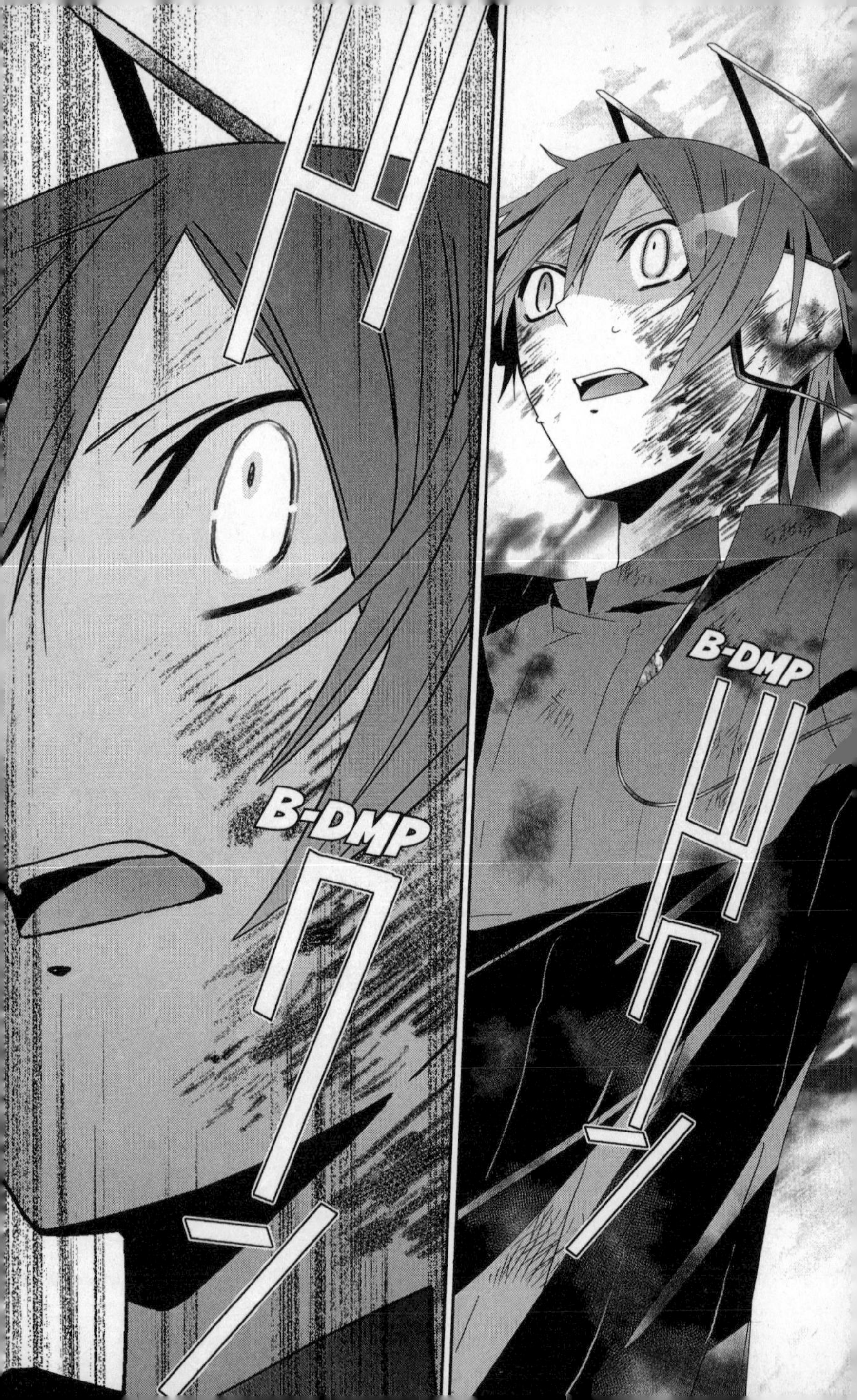
B-DMP
B-DMP

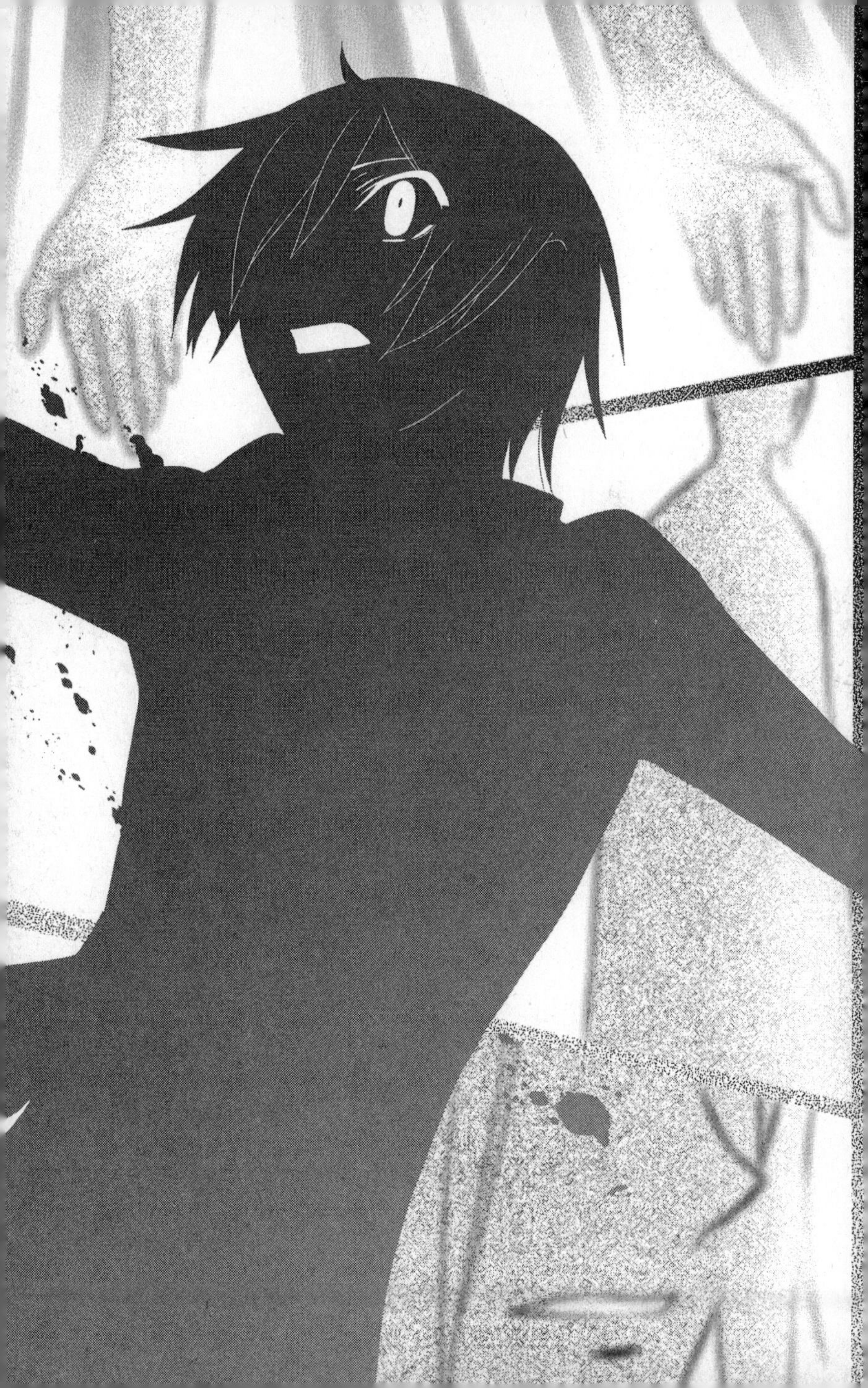

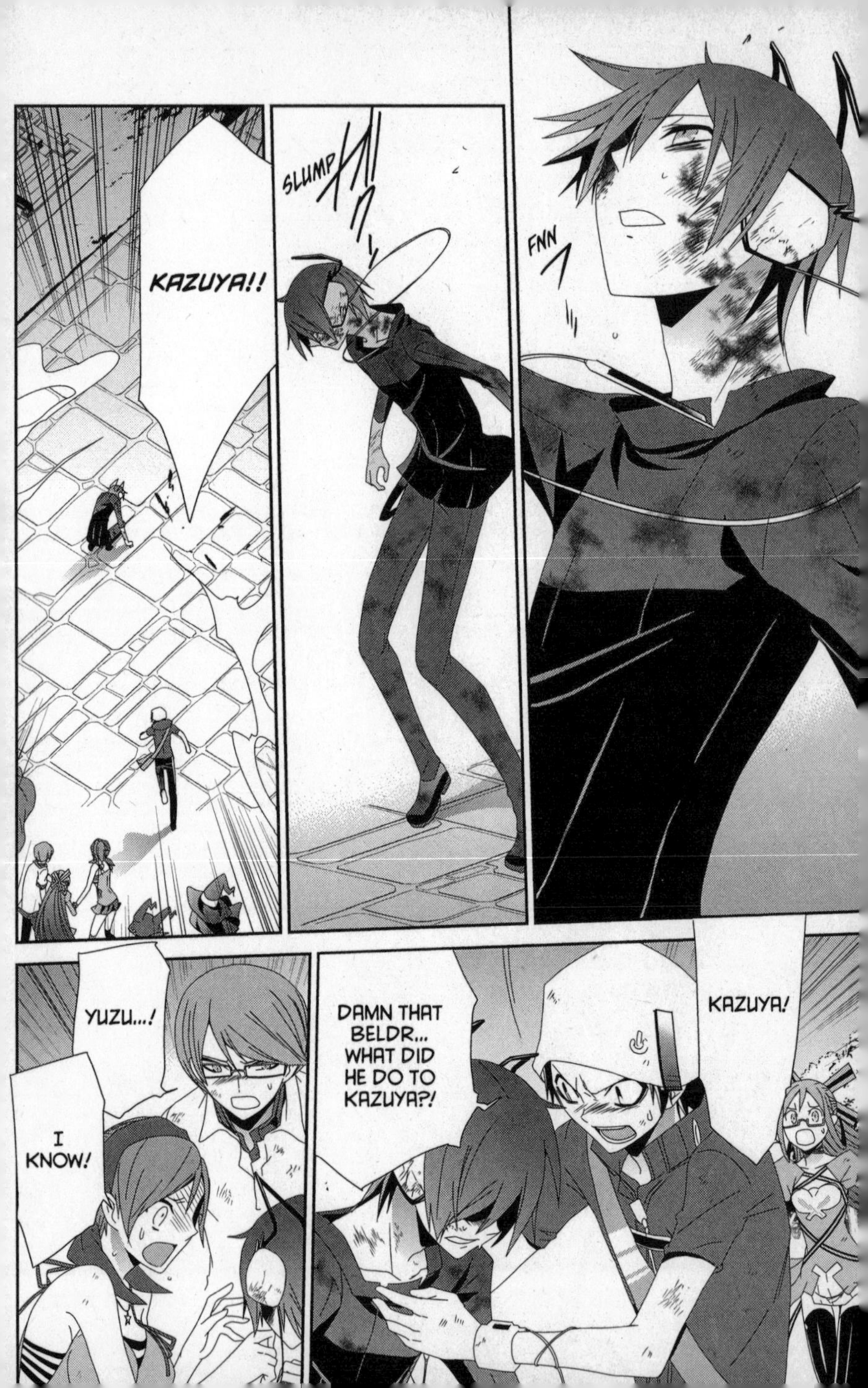
FNN
SLUMP
KAZUYA!!
KAZUYA!
DAMN THAT BELDR... WHAT DID HE DO TO KAZUYA?!
YUZU...!
I KNOW!

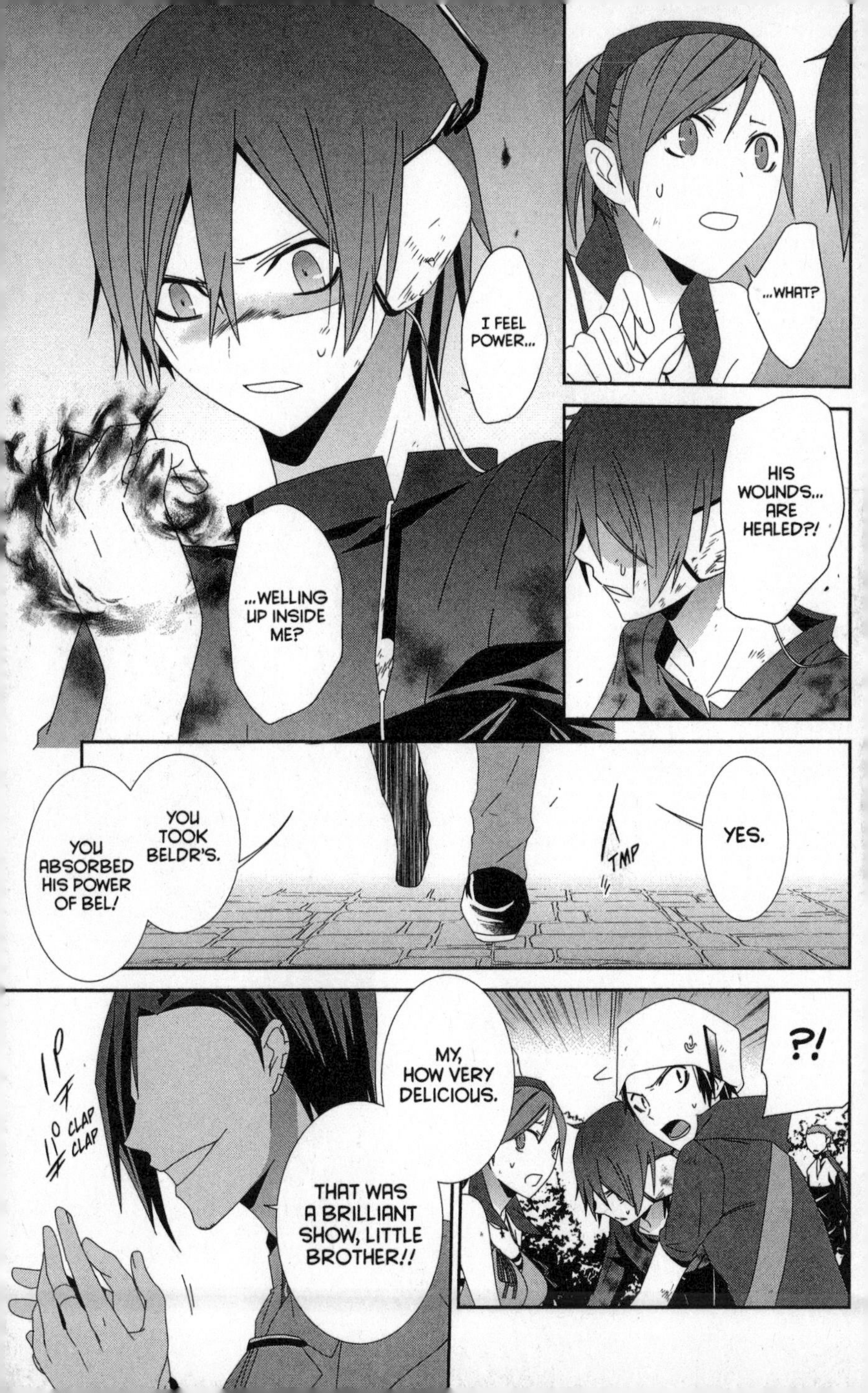
...WHAT?
HIS WOUNDS... ARE HEALED?!
I FEEL POWER...
...WELLING UP INSIDE ME?
YES.
TMP
YOU TOOK BELDR'S.
YOU ABSORBED HIS POWER OF BEL!
?!
MY, HOW VERY DELICIOUS.
THAT WAS A BRILLIANT SHOW, LITTLE BROTHER!!
CLAP CLAP

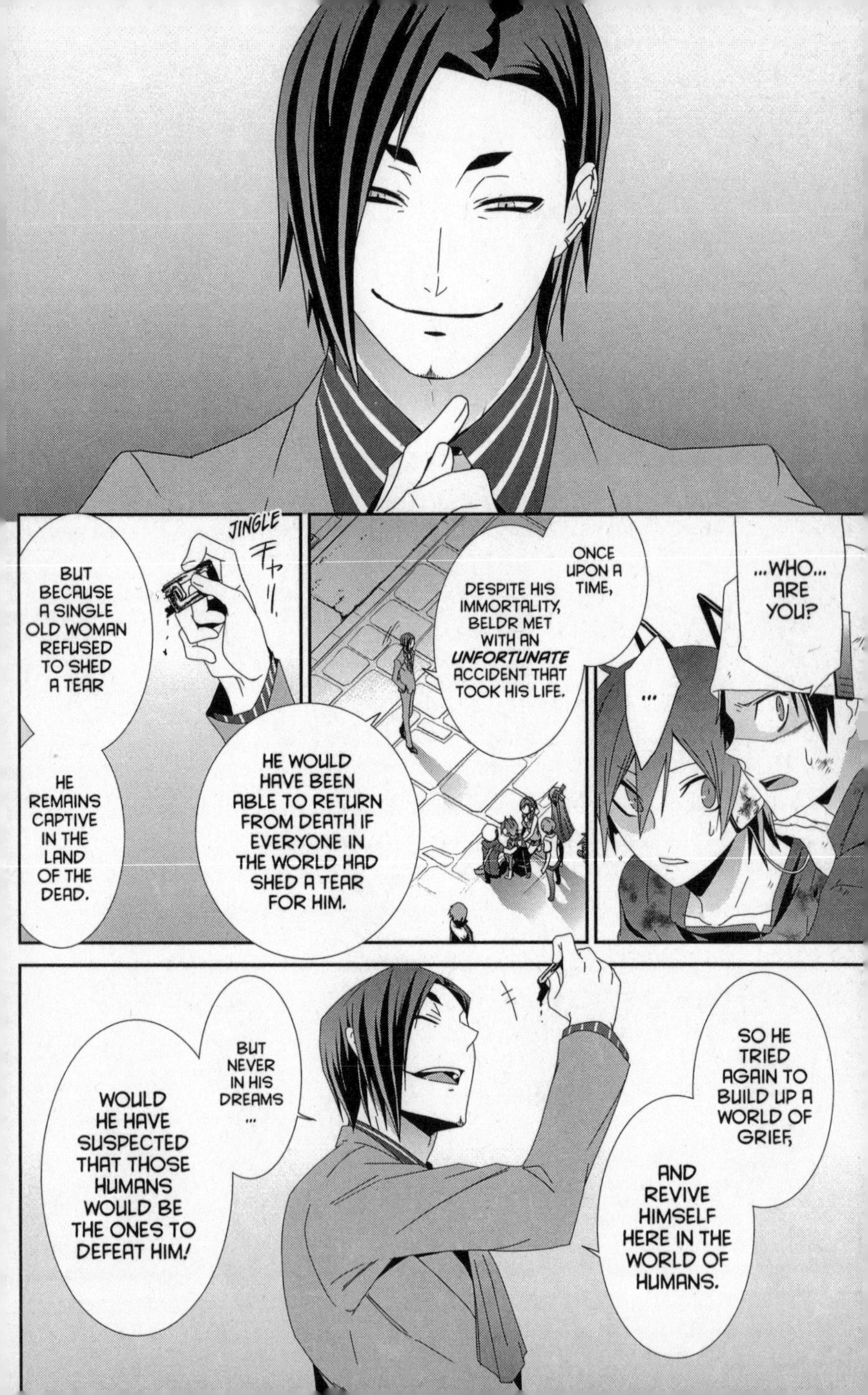
...WHO... ARE YOU?
...
ONCE UPON A TIME,
DESPITE HIS IMMORTALITY, BELDR MET WITH AN *UNFORTUNATE* ACCIDENT THAT TOOK HIS LIFE.
HE WOULD HAVE BEEN ABLE TO RETURN FROM DEATH IF EVERYONE IN THE WORLD HAD SHED A TEAR FOR HIM.
JINGLE
チャリ
BUT BECAUSE A SINGLE OLD WOMAN REFUSED TO SHED A TEAR
HE REMAINS CAPTIVE IN THE LAND OF THE DEAD.
SO HE TRIED AGAIN TO BUILD UP A WORLD OF GRIEF,
AND REVIVE HIMSELF HERE IN THE WORLD OF HUMANS.
BUT NEVER IN HIS DREAMS ...
WOULD HE HAVE SUSPECTED THAT THOSE HUMANS WOULD BE THE ONES TO DEFEAT HIM!

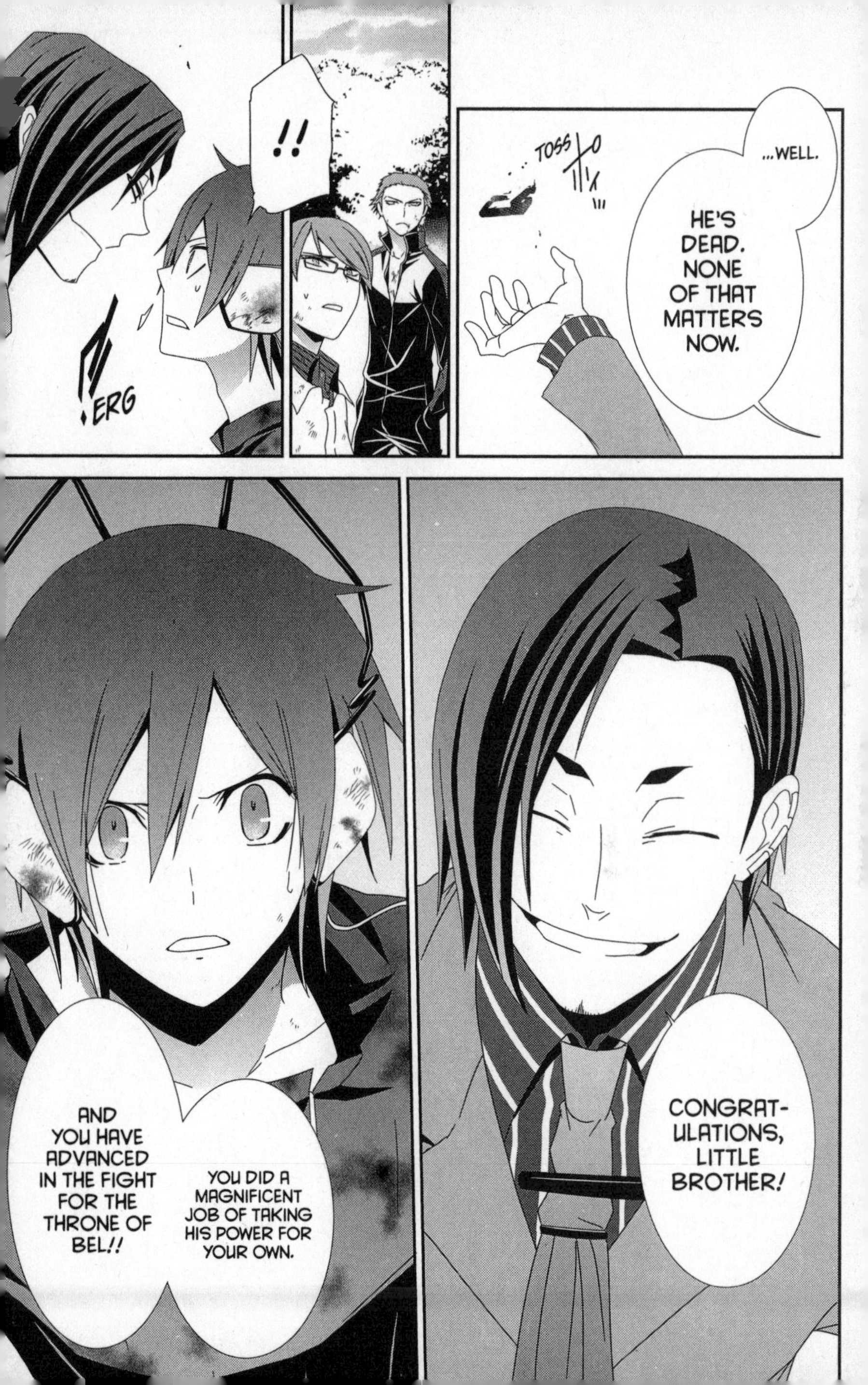
...WELL.
HE'S DEAD. NONE OF THAT MATTERS NOW.
TOSS
!!
ERG
CONGRATULATIONS, LITTLE BROTHER!
YOU DID A MAGNIFICENT JOB OF TAKING HIS POWER FOR YOUR OWN.
AND YOU HAVE ADVANCED IN THE FIGHT FOR THE THRONE OF BEL!!

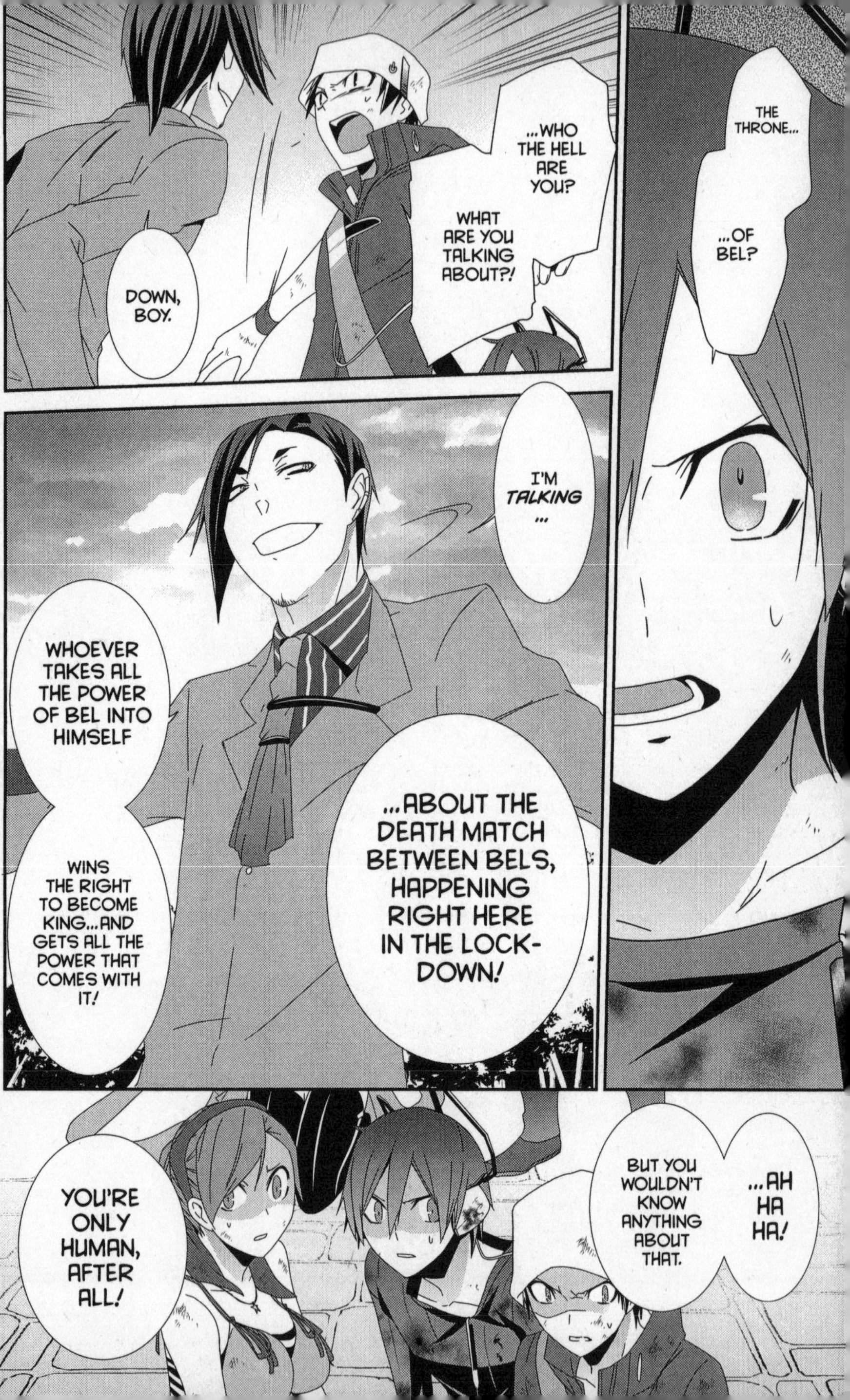
THE THRONE...
...OF BEL?
...WHO THE HELL ARE YOU?
WHAT ARE YOU TALKING ABOUT?!
DOWN, BOY.
I'M *TALKING* ...
...ABOUT THE DEATH MATCH BETWEEN BELS, HAPPENING RIGHT HERE IN THE LOCK-DOWN!
WHOEVER TAKES ALL THE POWER OF BEL INTO HIMSELF
WINS THE RIGHT TO BECOME KING...AND GETS ALL THE POWER THAT COMES WITH IT!
...AH HA HA!
BUT YOU WOULDN'T KNOW ANYTHING ABOUT THAT.
YOU'RE ONLY HUMAN, AFTER ALL!

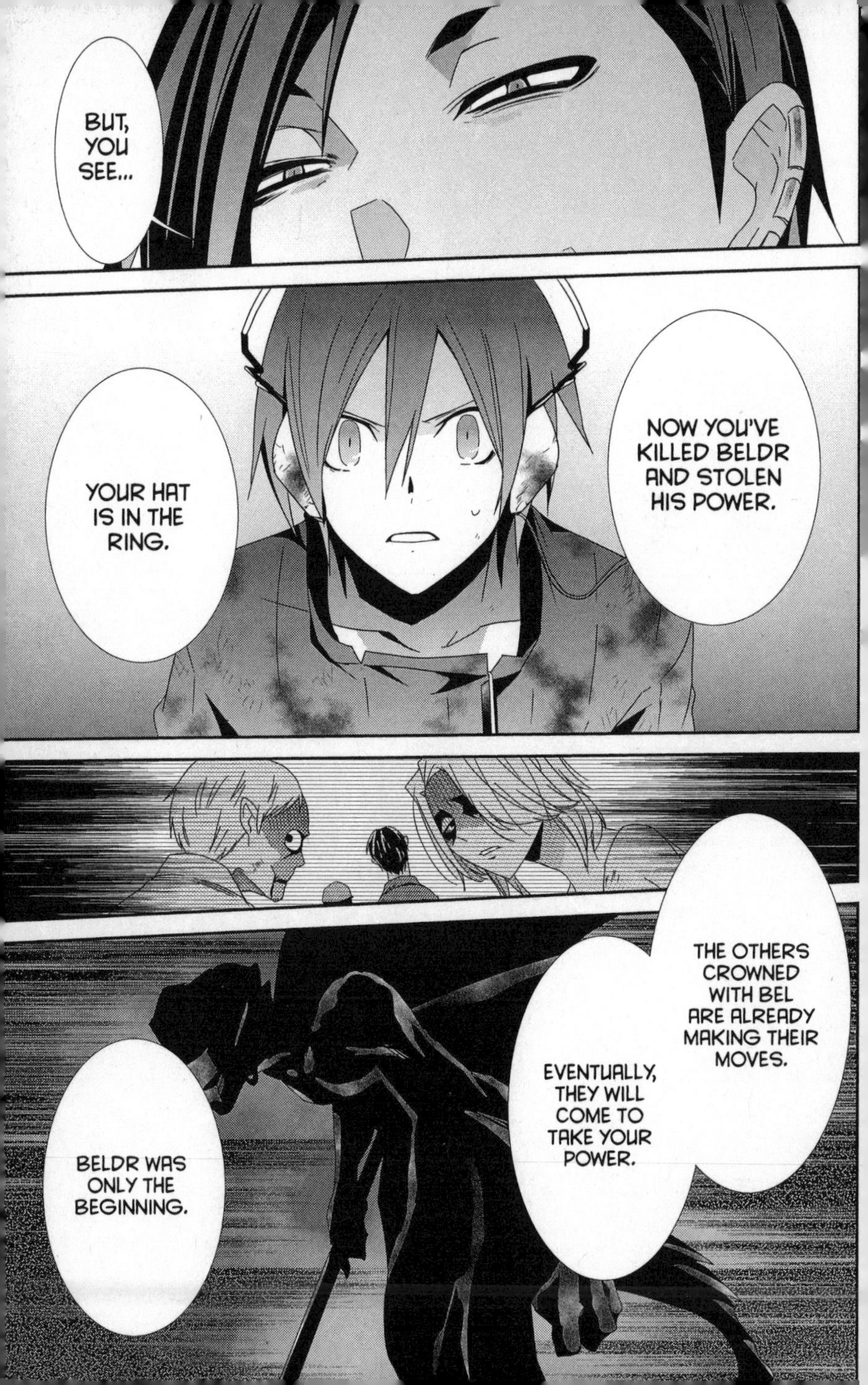
BUT, YOU SEE...
NOW YOU'VE KILLED BELDR AND STOLEN HIS POWER.
YOUR HAT IS IN THE RING.
THE OTHERS CROWNED WITH BEL ARE ALREADY MAKING THEIR MOVES.
EVENTUALLY, THEY WILL COME TO TAKE YOUR POWER.
BELDR WAS ONLY THE BEGINNING.

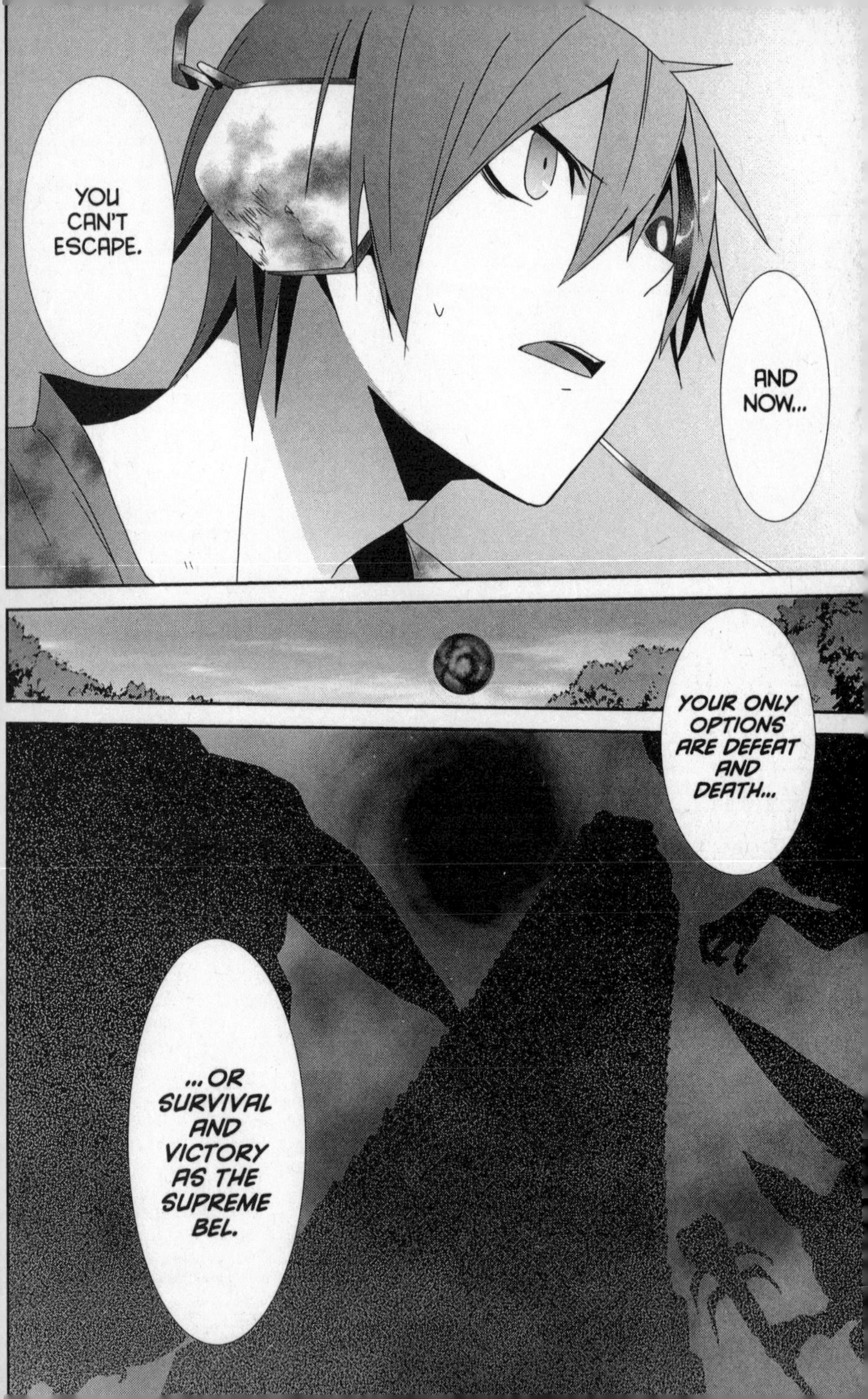
YOU CAN'T ESCAPE.
AND NOW...
YOUR ONLY OPTIONS ARE DEFEAT AND DEATH...
...OR SURVIVAL AND VICTORY AS THE SUPREME BEL.

BELDR

...OR. THE NORSE GOD OF LIGHT, SON OF ODIN AND FRIGG.
...ER OF FORSETI AND HUSBAND TO NANNA, HIS SIBLINGS
...UDE HOD AND HERMOD. HE WAS THE MOST BEAUTIFUL
... THE GODS, LOVED BY ALL, BUT WHEN HE STARTED
...NG NIGHTMARES, FRIGG GREW CONCERNED AND MADE
...RY LIVING AND NON-LIVING THING SWEAR NOT TO HARM
... ONLY THE MISTLETOE COULD NOT BE MADE TO SWEAR,
...EING TOO YOUNG. HEARING THIS, LOKI TRICKED HOD
...O PIERCING BALDR WITH THE MISTLETOE AND KILLING
...M. HEL, THE QUEEN OF THE UNDERWORLD, PROMISED
...T IF EVERYONE IN THE WORLD WOULD WEEP FOR HIM,
...E WOULD RESTORE BALDR TO LIFE, BUT THE GIANTESS
...OKK WOULD NOT CRY, AND HE DID NOT RETURN. WHEN
...WAS FOUND THAT THOKK WAS LOKI IN DISGUISE, THE
...OS PUNISHED HIM. HAVING LOST BALDR AND ALL LIGHT
...TH HIM, THE WORLD TOOK ITS FIRST STEPS TOWARD

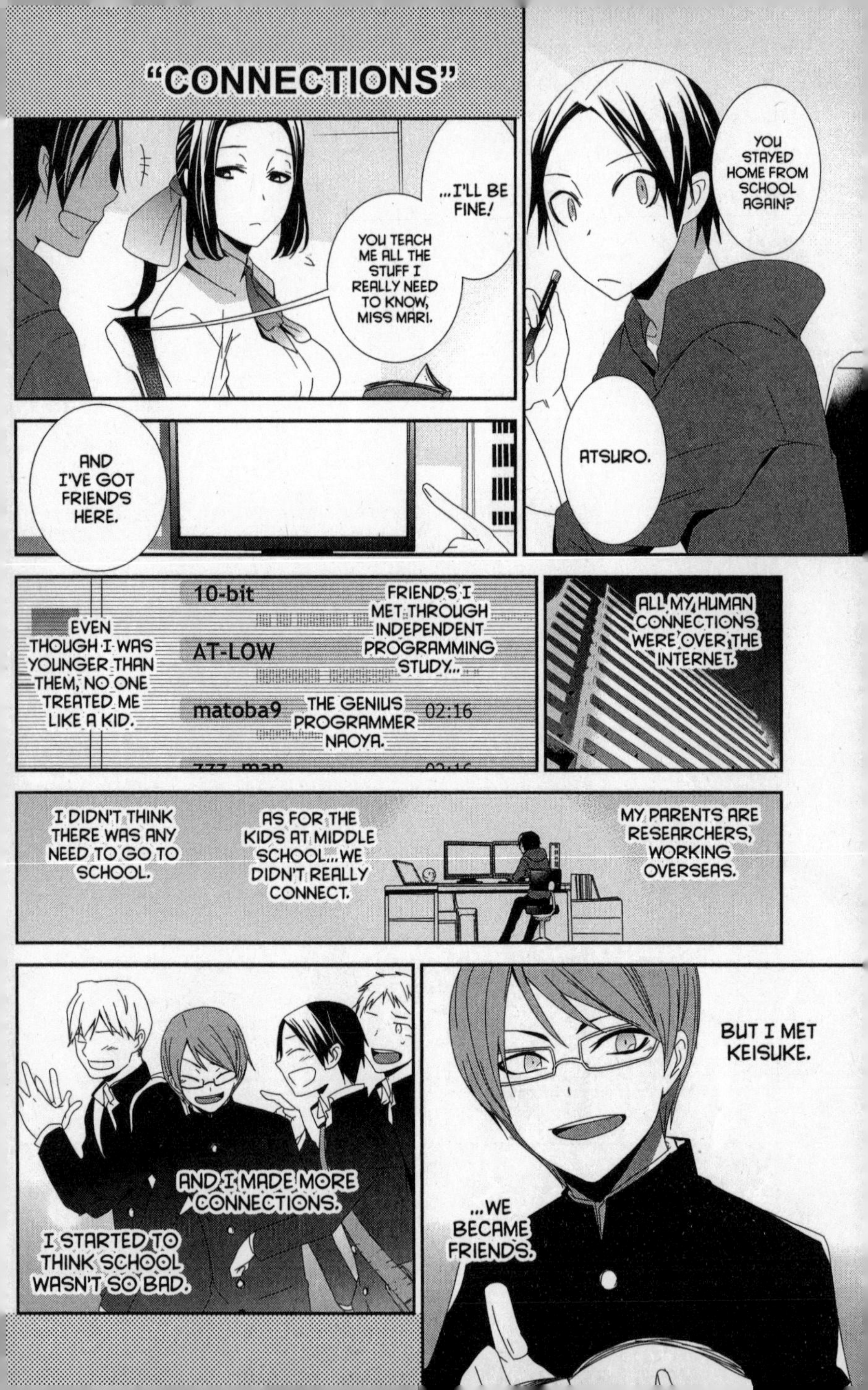

YOU STAYED HOME FROM SCHOOL AGAIN?
ATSURO.
"CONNECTIONS"
...I'LL BE FINE!
YOU TEACH ME ALL THE STUFF I REALLY NEED TO KNOW, MISS MARI.
AND I'VE GOT FRIENDS HERE.
ALL MY HUMAN CONNECTIONS WERE OVER THE INTERNET.
FRIENDS I MET THROUGH INDEPENDENT PROGRAMMING STUDY...
10-bit
AT-LOW
matoba9
02:16
THE GENIUS PROGRAMMER NAOYA.
EVEN THOUGH I WAS YOUNGER THAN THEM, NO ONE TREATED ME LIKE A KID.
MY PARENTS ARE RESEARCHERS, WORKING OVERSEAS.
AS FOR THE KIDS AT MIDDLE SCHOOL...WE DIDN'T REALLY CONNECT.
I DIDN'T THINK THERE WAS ANY NEED TO GO TO SCHOOL.
BUT I MET KEISUKE.
...WE BECAME FRIENDS.
AND I MADE MORE CONNECTIONS.
I STARTED TO THINK SCHOOL WASN'T SO BAD.

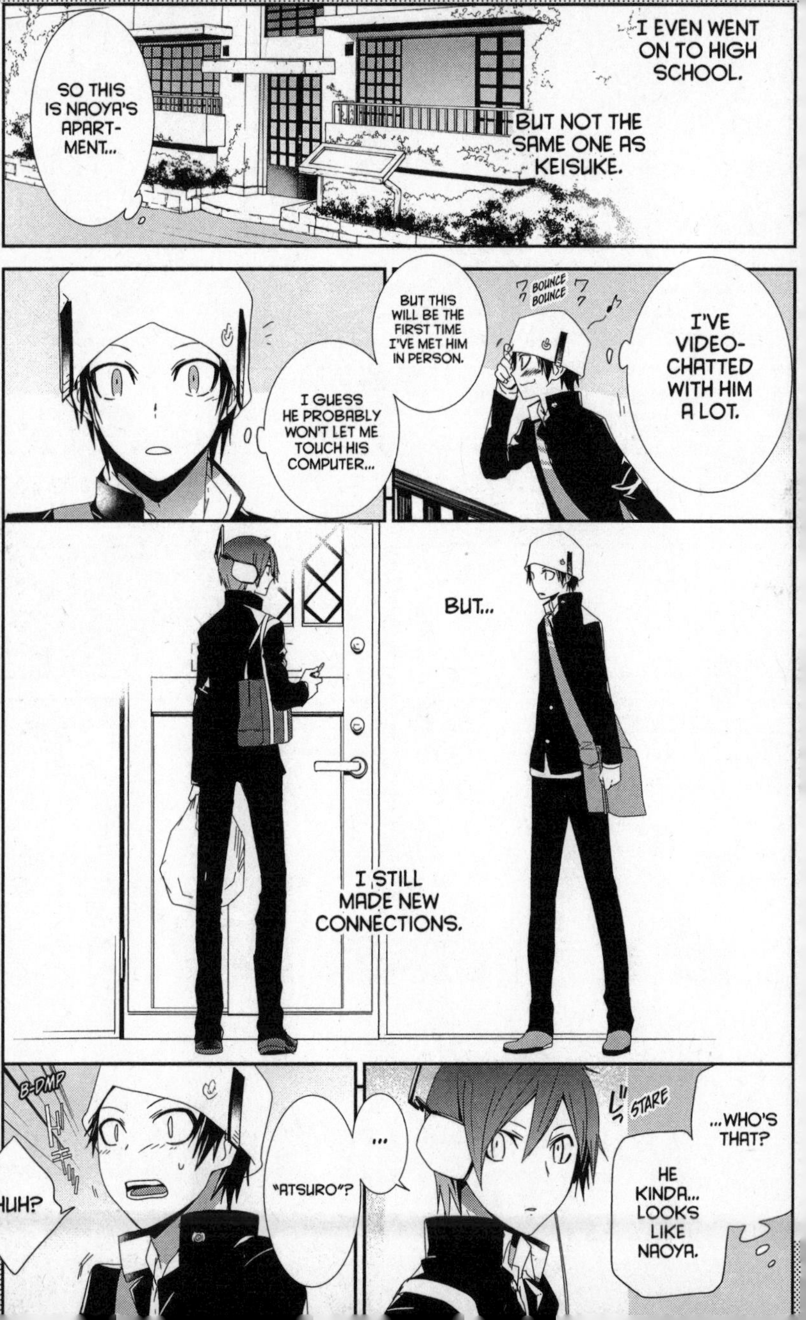
I EVEN WENT ON TO HIGH SCHOOL.
BUT NOT THE SAME ONE AS KEISUKE.
SO THIS IS NAOYA'S APARTMENT...
I'VE VIDEO-CHATTED WITH HIM A LOT.
BOUNCE BOUNCE
BUT THIS WILL BE THE FIRST TIME I'VE MET HIM IN PERSON.
I GUESS HE PROBABLY WON'T LET ME TOUCH HIS COMPUTER...
BUT...
I STILL MADE NEW CONNECTIONS.
STARE
...WHO'S THAT?
HE KINDA... LOOKS LIKE NAOYA.
...
"ATSURO"?
B-DMP
HUH?

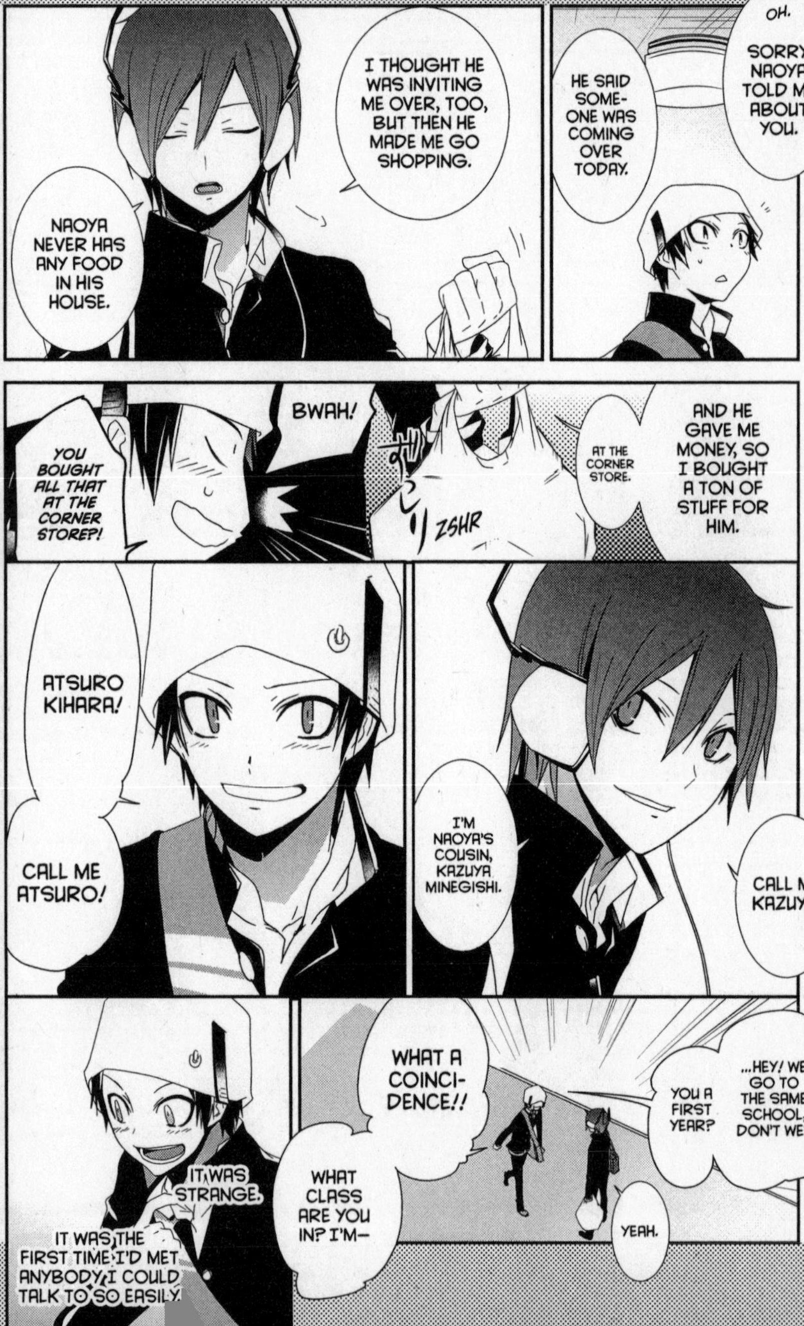
OH.
SORRY. NAOYA TOLD ME ABOUT YOU.
HE SAID SOME-ONE WAS COMING OVER TODAY.
I THOUGHT HE WAS INVITING ME OVER, TOO, BUT THEN HE MADE ME GO SHOPPING.
NAOYA NEVER HAS ANY FOOD IN HIS HOUSE.
AND HE GAVE ME MONEY, SO I BOUGHT A TON OF STUFF FOR HIM.
AT THE CORNER STORE.
ZSHR
BWAH!
YOU BOUGHT ALL THAT AT THE CORNER STORE?!
I'M NAOYA'S COUSIN, KAZUYA MINEGISHI.
CALL ME KAZUYA.
ATSURO KIHARA!
CALL ME ATSURO!
...HEY! WE GO TO THE SAME SCHOOL, DON'T WE?
YOU A FIRST YEAR?
YEAH.
WHAT A COINCI-DENCE!!
WHAT CLASS ARE YOU IN? I'M—
IT WAS STRANGE.
IT WAS THE FIRST TIME I'D MET ANYBODY I COULD TALK TO SO EASILY.

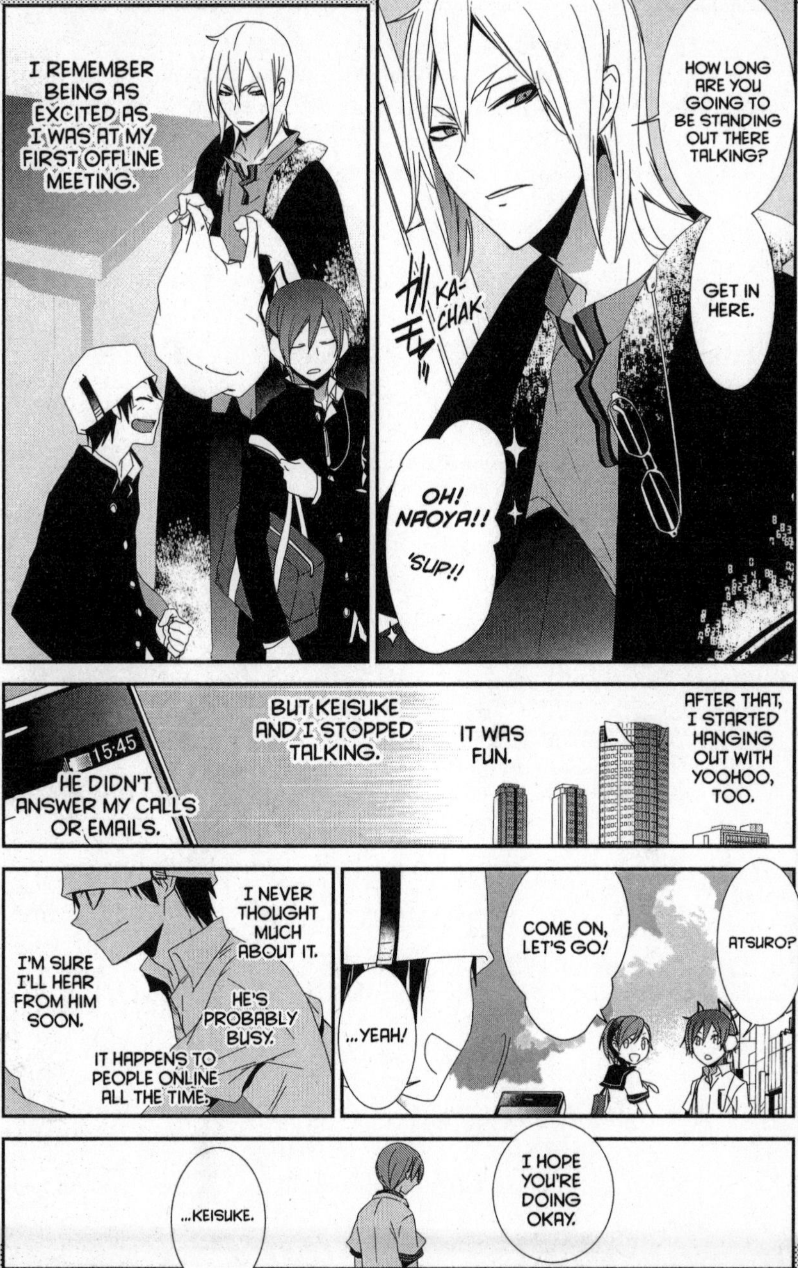
HOW LONG ARE YOU GOING TO BE STANDING OUT THERE TALKING?
GET IN HERE.
KA-CHAK
OH! NAOYA!!
'SUP!!
I REMEMBER BEING AS EXCITED AS I WAS AT MY FIRST OFFLINE MEETING.
AFTER THAT, I STARTED HANGING OUT WITH YOOHOO, TOO.
IT WAS FUN.
BUT KEISUKE AND I STOPPED TALKING.
15:45
HE DIDN'T ANSWER MY CALLS OR EMAILS.
ATSURO?
COME ON, LET'S GO!
...YEAH!
I NEVER THOUGHT MUCH ABOUT IT.
HE'S PROBABLY BUSY.
I'M SURE I'LL HEAR FROM HIM SOON.
IT HAPPENS TO PEOPLE ONLINE ALL THE TIME.
I HOPE YOU'RE DOING OKAY.
...KEISUKE.

A Kodansha Comics Trade Paperback Original.

Devil Survivor volume 3 copyright © 2013
©ATLUS ©SEGA All rights reserved.
©Satoru Matsuba

English translation copyright © 2016
©ATLUS ©SEGA All rights reserved.
©Satoru Matsuba

Published in the United States by Kodansha Comics,
an imprint of Kodansha USA Publishing, LLC, New York.

Publication rights for this English edition arranged through
Kodansha Ltd., Tokyo.

First published in Japan in 2013 by Kodansha Ltd., Tokyo.

ISBN 978-1-63236-261-2

Printed in the United States of America.

www.kodanshacomics.com

9 8 7 6 5 4 3 2 1

Translator: Alethea Nibley & Athena Nibley
Letterer: Paige Pumphrey
Editing: Lauren Scanlan